GOVERNMENTS OF THE WORLD

A Student Companion

OXFORD

GOVERNMENTS OF THE WORLD

A Student Companion

VOLUME 2: INDIA—SEYCHELLES

Richard M. Pious

Oxford University Press

New York Oxford

᠁am Delhi
Florence Hong Kong Istanbul Karachi
Kuala Lumpur Madras Madrid Melbourne
Mexico City Nairobi Paris Singapore
Taipei Tokyo Toronto Warsaw

and associated companies in
Berlin Ibadan

Published by Oxford University Press, Inc.
198 Madison Avenue, New York, New York 10016

Oxford is a registered trademark of Oxford University Press, Inc.

Design: Sandy Kaufman
Layout: Valerie Sauers
Picture research: Marty Baldessari, Wendy Wills

Library of Congress Cataloging-in-Publication Data
Pious, Richard M.
Governments of the world : a student companion / Richard M. Pious.
p. cm.
Includes bibliographic references and index.
1. Comparative government—Handbooks, manuals, etc. —Juvenile literature.
[1. Comparative government   Handbooks, manuals, etc.
2. World politics—Handbooks, manuals, etc.]
I. Title.
JF127.P56   1996
320.3—dc20   95-36684
                                                       CIP
                                                       AC
ISBN 0-19-508486-1 (3-vol. set)
ISBN 0-19-508484-5 (vol. 1)
ISBN 0-19-508485-3 (vol. 2)
ISBN 0-19-512296-8 (vol. 3)

1 3 5 7 9 8 6 4 2
Printed in the United States of America
on acid-free paper

On the cover: *(top left)Benito Mussolini; (top right) Nelson Mandela; (bottom) U.S. president Bill Clinton oversees the signing of the Middle East peace accords between PLO leader Yasir Arafat (right) and Israeli prime minister Yitzhak Rabin (left).*

Frontispiece: *A voter in Namibia casts a ballot in the 1989 elections.*

India

REPUBLIC OF INDIA (BHARAT)

• *Capital: New Delhi*

Political history Located in southern Asia on the Indian subcontinent, India was the site of the Indus River civilization, one of the world's oldest, established as early as 2500 B.C. by villages in Mohenjo-Daro (in what is now Pakistan). In 1750 B.C. Aryans, a people from what is now Iran, conquered much of the area in the Ganges Valley near Delhi. They introduced the Sanskrit alphabet and the Vedic religion, which involved belief in numerous gods associated with nature and was led by priests (Brahmans) who engaged in animal sacrifice. The Vedic religion eventually evolved into Hinduism. Buddhism was introduced by the Gupta dynasty (600 B.C.–A.D. 320) of northwestern India, whose rulers inaugurated a golden age of culture, introducing Sanskrit epic poetry, astronomy, and metalworking.

Arab invaders brought Islam to the area after A.D. 700. Between 1000 and 1400, Muslims in northern India ruled much of the subcontinent in separate principalities. The Islamic Moghul dynasty was established in 1526 and proceeded to unify most of India by force, though it could not convert the majority of the population from the Hindu religion.

Vasco da Gama discovered India for the Europeans in 1497, and Portuguese trading posts brought European influence to the area in the 16th century. Later in the 17th century British and French trading companies competed for influence. Through the British East India Company, Great Britain gained control of much of India in the 18th century. The first British governor-general was appointed in 1786, and the powers of the East India Company were ended by the India Act of 1858, which transferred its forces and colonial administrators to the British Crown. British colonial laws of 1919 and 1935 provided for limited self-government.

Nonviolent resistance to British rule, led by Mahatma Gandhi, mobilized millions of Indians to demand independence in the 1920s and 1930s. The Congress Party, a nationalist movement led by Jawaharlal Nehru, negotiated the terms of independence at the end of World War II. In 1947 British India was partitioned into two independent nation-states, India (whose population was mostly Hindu) and Pakistan (with a Muslim population). The partition was violent and bloody, with millions of refugees on both sides, leading to lasting enmity between the two nations. In 1950 India became a republic within the Commonwealth of Nations.

Government institutions India is the largest democracy in the world. Its president is the head of state for a five-year term and is elected by an electoral college composed of members of parliament and the state legislatures. Executive power is formally vested in the president, but he or she acts on the advice of the prime minister and members of the cabinet, who are accountable to the parliament. Legislative power is vested in the bicameral parliament, which consists of the 245-member Rajya Sabha (Council of States) and the 542-member Lok Sabha (House of the People). The majority of the members of the Rajya Sabha are chosen by the state legislatures; the remainder are selected by the president. The members of the Lok Sabha are directly elected and serve for five years.

India has an independent judiciary, which is headed by a supreme court.

Passengers clamor even for a spot on the roof of this overcrowded train leaving a regional fair in India, where overpopulation has long been a major problem.

India has a federal system, with 25 states and various territories. Each state is headed by a governor appointed by the president for a five-year term, but political power is exercised by a chief minister and council of ministers accountable to the state legislature.

Parties and movements India is a multiparty democracy, although the governing Congress Party has used corruption and intimidation to maintain its power. The Indian National Congress that led India to independence in 1947 was the largest party, governing in coalition with minor centrist parties in the early 1990s.

The Bharatiya Janata Party (Indian People's Party), made up of Hindu nationalists, became a formidable challenger for power in the 1990s. It won control over four northern state governments and in 1993 engaged in massive demonstrations in an attempt to topple the government. It suffered a crushing defeat in the 1993 parliamentary elections, however, and lost control of its state governments because of its extremist program. Minor parties representing poorer and lower caste

groups (caste refers to one's position in society) gained votes at the expense of the Congress Party.

In 1996 the Congress Party and its allies suffered a crushing electoral defeat, dropping from 271 to 135 seats, while the Janata Party and its allies made major gains, going from 115 to 185 seats and becoming the dominant force in a Hindu nationalist coalition government. A splintered parliament led to weak coalitions, and several cabinets fell from power because no stable majority could be formed.

Domestic issues Ethnic and religious violence has been a problem in many areas, including Sikh-Hindu conflict in the Punjab (northern India) and Sri Lankan-Tamil conflict in Tamil Nadu (southern India). Consequently, since the 1980s, the central government has assumed direct control of various states, particularly those in which the Congress Party has lost control in local elections.

Conflict between the dominant Hindus and minority Muslims often flares up in Indian cities, due to the instigation of ethnic hatred by some

Hindu nationalist politicians. In Bombay in 1993 fighting left hundreds dead and much of the city in ruins. Hindu nationalists have destroyed Muslim communities and many mosques, and they have called for a completely Hindu nation, fueling tensions between the 700 million Hindus and the 125 million Muslims.

Two Indian leaders have been assassinated because of ethnic violence. Indira Gandhi was killed by one of her Sikh bodyguards on October 31, 1984, in retaliation for the destruction of a Sikh holy shrine by the Indian army. Her son Rajiv Gandhi was killed by a bomb blast while campaigning in Madras on May 21, 1991. The government blamed Tamil extremists in southern India who were being prevented from aiding Tamil separatists in Sri Lanka.

India's weak central government has lacked the political support to impose unpopular economic measures, leading to economic stagnation and endemic corruption. India has the fifth largest industrial economy in the world, but it has lagged in obtaining foreign investment and technology. Since the mid-1980s it has begun to implement economic readjustment programs in cooperation with the International Monetary Fund and World Bank, which imposed these programs before lending money to India. As a result, India has privatized state enterprises, reduced inflation, and strengthened its currency. Private investment, particularly from Singapore and other Asian nations, has increased.

International issues India has fought several wars with Pakistan over disputed territory in Kashmir, and in the mid-1990s the two nations remained fully mobilized. Earlier, in the late 1980s, India and Pakistan had agreed not to attack each other's nuclear facilities. India fought a border war with China involving parts of Kashmir and Arunachal Pradesh, in northern India, in 1964; it was defeated by China. During the cold war India relied on the Soviet Union as a counterweight to these powers, though it was never formally allied with the Soviets and considered itself neutral and nonaligned.

In 1986 India improved relations with neighboring Bangladesh in matters involving water management and border controls. India has tense relations with Sri Lanka, due to past Indian military intervention on behalf of Sri Lankan Tamils.

India exploded a nuclear device in 1974 and it is probable that it has a number of nuclear bombs or missile warheads. India's relations with the United States became strained in 1993 when the United States persuaded Russia not to sell rocket engines to India for its space program, claiming that India was violating the terms of the Missile Technology Control Regime, an agreement to limit the spread of advanced missile technology.

In the 1990s Indian foreign policy was oriented toward economic coordination with the major world industrial powers, especially those along the Asian-Pacific Rim.

SEE ALSO
Bangladesh; Commonwealth of Nations; Kashmir; Pakistan; Sri Lanka

FURTHER READING
Collins, Larry, and Dominique Lapierre. *Freedom at Midnight*. New York: Simon & Schuster, 1975.
Kohli, Atul. *Democracy and Discontent: India's Growing Crisis of Governability*. New York: Cambridge University Press, 1990.
Mehta, Gita. *Snakes and Ladders: Glimpses of Modern India*. New York: Doubleday, 1997.
Wolpert, Stanley. *A New History of India*. 5th ed. New York: Oxford University Press, 1997.

Indochina

Indochina is the term for the colonies and protectorates united by France into the Indo-Chinese Union in 1893. These included Cambodia, which became a French colony in 1884; Laos, which became a protectorate in 1893; Annam and Tonkin (later North Vietnam), which became protectorates in 1894; and Cochin China (later South Vietnam), a colony after 1867.

The monarchs of these colonies and protectorates remained in power, subject to French authority exercised by a French governor-general based in Hanoi. Cochin China was administered separately by a French prefect, or colonial administrator, in Saigon. During World War II the Vichy government of occupied France granted military and commercial concessions to the Japanese, and the Japanese army and navy established port facilities in Indochina. In March 1945 the Japanese overthrew the Vichy administrators and established their own colonial rule. Nationalists revolted in Cambodia, Laos, and Vietnam and proclaimed themselves independent nations, beginning guerrilla wars against the Japanese.

British and French troops returned to Indochina in September 1945 after the Japanese surrendered to the Allies and, with the assistance of captured Japanese troops, retook Indochina for the French and forced it into the French Union. The nationalist leader Ho Chi Minh thereupon began a guerrilla war against the occupying French Army in Vietnam that lasted until the French were defeated on May 9, 1954, at the battle of Dien Bien Phu. The Geneva Accords of that year provided for two "military regroupment zones" in Vietnam and eventual unification under

whatever movement won all-Vietnam-ese elections. The United States helped establish a government in South Vietnam and placed it under the military protection of the Southeast Asia Treaty Organization (SEATO), a collective security organization consisting of the United States, Great Britain, France, Thailand, Pakistan, and Iran.

South Vietnam, with U.S. encouragement, refused to participate in the promised election, because it would have easily been won by the communist leader Ho Chi Minh. This decision precipitated a new round of guerrilla warfare in South Vietnam between government forces and the communist Viet Cong guerrilla movement. The Viet Cong were aided by the Viet Minh, armed communist forces from North Vietnam who smuggled supplies and equipment down south on the Ho Chi Minh Trail in Cambodia. To aid the South Vietnamese government, the United States committed 500,000 troops in the 1960s against the communist forces. In 1973 the Paris Peace Accords ended U.S. participation in the fighting. With the United States out of the area, the communists won control of Laos, Cambodia, and South Vietnam in 1975. North and South Vietnam were then unified into a single Vietnamese nation. The Khmer Rouge, a communist guerrilla movement in Cambodia, launched a campaign of autogenocide to eliminate political opposition, resulting in the deaths of millions of Cambodians and an invasion by Vietnam in 1979 to establish a more moderate communist regime. In 1989 Vietnam withdrew its forces.

By the mid-1990s the Indochinese countries had reestablished ties with Western nations, including the United States, and were opening their societies to Western investment, technology, and tourism.

SEE ALSO
Cambodia; French Union; Ho Chi Minh; Khmer Rouge; Laos; Southeast Asia Treaty Organization (SEATO); Vietnam; Vichy regime

FURTHER READING
Hammer, Ellen Joy. *The Struggle for Indochina*. Stanford, Calif.: Stanford University Press, 1954.
Moss, George. *Vietnam, An American Ordeal.* Englewood Cliffs, N.J.: Prentice Hall, 1990.
Moss, George, ed. *A Vietnam Reader: Sources and Essays*. Englewood Cliffs, N.J.: Prentice Hall, 1991.

Indonesia

REPUBLIC OF INDONESIA (REPUBLIK INDONESIA)

• *Capital: Djakarta*

Political history The 16,500 islands that comprise Indonesia were the site of Buddhist and Hindu civilizations dating back to A.D. 500, including a Buddhist kingdom on Sumatra (A.D. 600) and a Hindu kingdom on Java in the 1300s. In the 1500s traders from the Arabian Peninsula and India brought Islam to the islands, and it became the dominant religious and cultural influence. In the late 1500s, Portuguese traders were ejected by the British, who then lost the islands to the Dutch. After 1602 the Netherlands East India Company was granted administrative power over the islands by the Dutch government, and in 1816 they became a Dutch colony. The Japanese occupied Indonesia during World War II.

After 1945 a four-year war against Dutch rule ended with independence within a "union" of former Dutch colonies. Indonesia abrogated the

A fishing village on the north coast of Java, one of the five largest islands of the Indonesian archipelago.

agreement in 1956 and gained complete sovereignty. Irian Barat, consisting of the western half of New Guinea, was ceded by the Dutch to Indonesia in 1963. Since 1965, when the army crushed the Communist Party and removed civilian president Sukarno, Indonesia has been ruled by an authoritarian military regime, operating behind a facade of civilian governmental institutions.

Government institutions Indonesia has a presidential system. The president is elected by the 1,000-member People's Consultative Assembly, which includes the 500-member House of Representatives (400 of its members are directly elected and 100 are appointed by the president) and an additional 500 members from the armed forces and other social organizations. Legislative power is exercised by the House of Representatives. In reality, however, the president dominates the House of Representatives, which passes all government proposals. Provincial governors are appointed by the president, as are the justices of the Supreme Court of Justice and the lower court judges.

Different laws apply to Indonesians, Europeans, and other Asians. Indonesians are subject to Muslim law regarding civil matters; Europeans are subject to a civil code established in 1847; alien Asians are subject to special laws regarding guest laborers.

Parties and movements Since 1960 the president has had the power to dissolve any party whose membership is less than one-quarter of the electorate or whose policies oppose the state. The governing party is the Sekber Golkar (Governing Alliance). Two other parties are permitted, the United Development Party (Muslim) and the Indonesian Democratic Party (Christian social democrats). Since the late 1960s the government has suppressed leftist, socialist, and communist movements. President Suharto has been elected to five five-year terms, beginning in 1971, running unopposed every time. His main opponent in the late 1990s was Megawati Sukarnoputri, the daughter of former president Sukarno and the leader of a coalition of anti-Suharto political movements and parties, including the Indonesian Democratic Party.

Domestic issues There are more than 350 distinct ethnic groups living on the 13,000 inhabited Indonesian islands. The central government has been primarily concerned with preventing autonomy or secessionist movements in the outer islands. Indonesia invaded East Timor—a small island rich in natural resources in the southwest of the island chain inhabited primarily by Catholics who had been colonized by the Portuguese—in 1976, one year after the Portuguese departed. It has waged war against Timorese seeking independence, and more than 200,000 of the 700,000 inhabitants have been killed in the fighting and accompanying famines. The United Nations has sponsored talks between Indonesia and Portugal over the future status of East Timor.

The industrial development plans of the government, fueled in part by revenues from oil production, have been successful, and Indonesia has one of the fastest-growing economies in the world. It is home to aircraft, automobile, shipbuilding, space satellite, and telecommunications industries. Many business enterprises are controlled by army officers, as well as by the five sons of President Suharto.

Although the proportion of Indonesians living in poverty has dropped from 60 to 15 percent since 1975, the growing income inequality between business executives and financiers (many of them ethnic Chinese) benefiting from foreign investment and Muslim urban and rural workers has led to discontent, which the government has occasionally diverted away from itself and into anti-Chinese and anti-Western demonstrations.

International issues During the 1950s, under leftist President Sukarno, Indonesia was a leader of the Nonaligned Movement, a group of Third World nations that refused to take sides between the United States and the Soviet Union during the cold war. But Sukarno's foreign policy was often anti-Western and pro-Soviet; he opposed, for example, U.S. attempts to build anticommunist alliances of pro-Western nations in Asia. The U.S. Central Intelligence Agency sponsored a group of military officers on the outer islands who rebelled against the central government between 1957 and 1959. The insurrection failed and Sukarno then governed with the support of the Communist Party and pro-government army commanders. This uneasy alliance ended in 1965, when an attempted coup by a left-wing junior officer to establish a more radical regime led senior officers to launch a countercoup. The Communist Party was destroyed by the army, and hundreds of thousands of its members were killed or imprisoned. President Sukarno was allowed to remain in power for one year as a figurehead, then was eased out of office by the army in 1967.

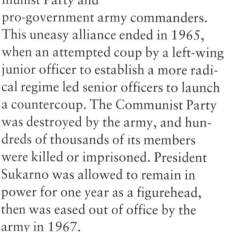

Under President Suharto, who succeeded Sukarno in 1967, Indonesia followed a genuine policy of nonalignment until the end of the cold war. In the 1990s it maintains close economic relations with Western nations and has gained a great deal of private investment from U.S. corporations, which are attracted by a low-wage work force that produces consumer goods, especially electronic products, in demand in U.S. and other Western markets.

Indonesia has signed an agreement with Australia allowing oil exploration

Balinese islanders perform a traditional dance called gambuh. *Indonesia is home to many distinct peoples, languages, and cultures.*

in the Timor Gap (offshore waters) and in 1990 resumed defense cooperation with that nation.

Human rights The Indonesian army killed several hundred thousand communists in 1965 in its coup against Sukarno's government and imprisoned 750,000 communists in prisons or relocation camps.

In the 1990s the government has acted without restraint against civilians on East Timor fighting for independence. More than 200 unarmed Timorese demonstrating for independence were gunned down at Dili in November 1991 by the Indonesian army.

SEE ALSO
Nonaligned Movement

FURTHER READING
Crouch, Harold. *The Army and Politics in Indonesia*. Rev. ed. Ithaca, N.Y.: Cornell University Press, 1988.
Liddle, William. *Politics and Cultures in Indonesia*. Ann Arbor: University of Michigan Press, 1988.

Inter-American Development Bank (IDB)

The IDB is a lending agency founded in 1959 to promote regional development in Central and South America. It includes all the Western Hemisphere nations (except for Cuba) as well as some countries in western Europe and Israel. Its powers are vested in a board of governors, and management is controlled by a board of executive directors. The United States contributes the most money to the fund, but a majority of voting rights is held by borrower nations.

In the 1960s, the IDB provided loans as part of the Alliance for Progress, a program of economic assistance developed by the Organization of American States. Through 1990 it had made $47 billion in low-interest loans for highways, ports, airports, and other facilities. For the first half of the 1990s the bank's lending capacity exceeded $25 billion.

SEE ALSO
Alliance for Progress; Organization of American States (OAS)

International Bank for Reconstruction and Development

SEE World Bank (International Bank for Reconstruction and Development)

International Court of Justice

SEE World Court (International Court of Justice)

International Labor Organization (ILO)

The ILO has been a specialized agency of the United Nations since 1946; before that it was a unit of the League of Nations. The ILO develops health, safety, and occupational standards for industrial workers, providing international benchmarks by which people can measure labor conditions in their countries. Its administration offices, known as the secretariat, provides technical assistance to labor ministries throughout the developing world. It also attempts to end sex discrimination in employment.

In the 1990s many industrial nations with highly paid work forces faced competition from countries whose workers received low wages and no benefits; what role the ILO should play in encouraging nations (and the corporations located within them) to provide fair compensation for workers became an important issue for the organization.

SEE ALSO

League of Nations; United Nations (UN)

FURTHER READING

Patterson, Charles. *The Oxford 50th Anniversary Book of the United Nations.* New York: Oxford University Press, 1995.

International law

International law consists of the customs, usages, and rules that govern relations among nation-states. International law enables sovereign states to engage in cooperative ventures and to settle disputes peacefully. *Positive* international law includes treaties, conventions, declarations, protocols, and executive agreements that nations have made and to which they consider themselves bound, as well as resolutions passed by international organizations such as the United Nations. *Customary* international law includes the customs and usages of diplomacy to which nations are expected to adhere, whether or not they have been embodied in formal agreements. *Case* law relies on the decisions of the World Court (International Court of Justice) and other international tribunals that establish principles that all nations are expected to follow.

International law is based on principles developed in western Europe at the time of the Roman Empire. The Romans

developed the law of nations *(jus gentium)* to regulate relations with the non-Roman tribes adjacent to their empire. In the Middle Ages international law defined the standards of behavior that rulers of different European states or principalities could expect from one another.

Modern international law was developed primarily by British and French legal commentators, beginning after the Peace of Westphalia in 1648, which ended the Thirty Years War between Catholics and Protestants in the German states, and extending through the 19th century. During these three centuries, they created conventions regarding acceptable conduct in war, methods of resolving disputes short of war, and principles of international commercial law and the law of the seas.

Since World War II the development of human rights law and prosecution of war criminals for crimes against humanity have expanded the role of international law in establishing standards of right conduct. After World War II the victorious Allies prosecuted Nazi war criminals in the Nuremberg trials, and in the 1990s the United Nations established tribunals to try those involved in war crimes in the Balkans and Rwanda.

In 1955, the World Court convened in The Hague, the Netherlands, to hear a territorial dispute between Portugal and India.

International law developed principles in new fields such as environmental and labor law in the 1970s and 1980s, and international organizations in the 1990s have established conventions involving technical and scientific matters, such as patents and copyrights, to protect producers of intellectual property (like computer software, video games, movies, and music) from "pirates" selling unlicensed copies.

World trade has been stimulated by international trade agreements such as the General Agreement on Tariffs and Trade (GATT) and the North American Free Trade Agreement (NAFTA), and the provisions of these agreements are also a part of international law.

SEE ALSO

General Agreement on Tariffs and Trade (GATT); Nuremberg trials (1945–46); United Nations (UN); War crimes; World Court (International Court of Justice)

FURTHER READING

Brownlie, Ian, ed. *Basic Documents in International Law.* 4th ed. New York: Oxford University Press, 1995.
Falk, Richard A. *The Status of Law in International Society.* Princeton, N.J.: Princeton University Press, 1970.
Friedmann, Wolfgang. *The Changing Structures of International Law.* New York: Columbia University Press, 1964.
Levi, Warner. *Contemporary International Law.* Boulder, Colo.: Westview, 1991.

International Monetary Fund (IMF)

The IMF was established in 1945 in the aftermath of the Bretton Woods Conference, a meeting of industrial nations that set up an international monetary system to replace the gold standard at the end of World War II. The IMF promotes coordination of monetary policies among Western industrial nations so that they will not increase or decrease the value of their currencies by their own devices (such as by printing too much money, in order to pay their bills) or raise or lower their interest rates in order to expand their own economies at the expense of other nations. The IMF facilitates adjustments in their balance of payments so that a nation that imports far more than it exports, and therefore runs a large trade deficit, is encouraged to take austerity measures in order to better live within its means. The IMF also attempts to stabilize the rate of exchange, and thus the value, of major currencies used in international trade. (Unlike the World Bank and the various regional banks, the IMF does not make loans for development projects.)

The IMF has 160 members. Each member nation sends a representative to the policy-making board of governors. A 22-member board of executive directors administers the IMF. The United States, United Kingdom, Germany, France, Japan, and Saudi Arabia all have permanent representation as executive directors. Each member nation makes a financial contribution to the fund; its subsequent voting power is based on the amount of its contribution. The United States has one-fifth of the votes. The IMF itself invites nations to become members and may refuse to admit a nation whose monetary policies are not up to its standards.

The IMF provides nations with hard currency, in the form of Special Drawing Rights (SDRs), which is the right to obtain certain currencies. SDRs are available to members for short-term loans (of U.S. dollars, Japanese yen, French and Swiss francs, British pounds, and German marks) to provide temporary assistance with the settlement of international accounts. The IMF's "conditionality" policy requires nations in serious economic difficulty to

Plantation workers in Dominica prepare bananas for export. In its development programs for emerging nations, the IMF encourages the cultivation of cash crops for exports.

develop economic programs that meet IMF priorities for their economic reform before being granted funds to assist in the adjustment of trade and currency imbalances. These requirements usually involve drastic cuts in government expenditures, an anti-inflation program, a willingness to honor prior debts incurred, and the selling of state enterprises to private investors. Nations must meet performance criteria and submit progress reports annually.

The IMF also makes loans through its Structural Adjustment Facility and Extended Structural Adjustment Facility. These loans are virtually non-interest-bearing and are made to the poorest nations for three-year programs (or longer) to develop new strategies for long-term economic growth.

In the early 1990s more than 60 nations were involved in IMF programs of structural adjustment and austerity, many of whom complained that these economic policies were causing great hardship. In 1995 the International Conference on the Rights of Women, held in Beijing, China,

took a hard line against IMF structural adjustment programs, claiming that they hurt women of developing nations because these nations were required to cut social welfare programs that had assisted poor women.

In the 1990s, the IMF was the major vehicle for Western assistance to the nations of the former Soviet Union and eastern Europe as they attempted to transform their socialist systems into free-market capitalism.

SEE ALSO

Bretton Woods Agreement; Gold standard; World Bank (International Bank for Reconstruction and Development)

FURTHER READING

Gwin, Catherine, et al. *Pulling Together: The International Monetary Fund in a Multipolar World.* New Brunswick, N.J.: Transaction Books, 1989.
James, Harold. *International Monetary Cooperation since Bretton Woods.* New York: Oxford University Press, 1996.
Killick, Tony, ed. *The Quest for Economic Stabilization: The IMF and the Third World.* New York: St. Martin's, 1984.

Intifada

The *intifada* (Arabic for "uprising") was a revolt in 1987 by Palestinians living in the West Bank and Gaza Strip against Israeli occupation and the military government that enforced it. The Israelis had taken control of the West Bank from Jordan and of the Gaza Strip from Egypt after the Six-Day War of 1967. Although Israelis regarded the Gaza Strip as occupied land, many Israelis viewed the West Bank as a part of Israel that had finally been recovered, basing their claims on the fact that Jews had settled in Judaea and Samaria (the Hebrew names for the West Bank) since biblical times. Israel annexed East Jerusalem, the major Arab city on the West Bank, but stopped short of annexing the remaining territory. Nevertheless, more than 100,000 Israelis settled in the West Bank with the encouragement and financial assistance of the Israeli government, leading the Palestinian Arabs to believe that the ultimate goal of the Israelis was the annexation of the entire territory.

The intifada began in December 1987 when Palestinians displayed the outlawed Palestinian flag, engaged in unauthorized marches and demonstrations, and organized resistance to the occupation, some of which involved throwing stones and bottles at Israeli forces. In the following four years more than 1,000 Palestinians were killed, thousands more were wounded, and 16,000 were arrested by Israeli occupation authorities.

Although these demonstrations failed to dislodge the Israeli military, the battle for world public opinion was won by the demonstrators. The focus of the Arab-Israeli conflict shifted back to Palestinian demands for a separate sovereign state and away from territorial and security issues involving Israel and other Arab states.

The intifada succeeded in reversing the trend toward economic integration of the territories into a greater Israeli economy, and it reduced the incentives for Israel to continue with its military occupation of the territories. The high monetary and human costs of attempting to contain the intifada led the Israeli government to begin peace negotiations with the Palestine Liberation Organization (PLO), the leading Palestinian nationalist organization, beginning in 1993. These negotiations were conducted by Israeli foreign minister Shimon Peres and a delegation of Palestinians who met in Oslo, Norway. Their work resulted in a "framework for peace" in 1994, signed in Washington, D.C., by PLO leader Yasir Arafat and Israeli prime minister Yitzhak Rabin, that committed Israel and the PLO to ending Israeli occupation of the West Bank.

Within a year, Jericho had been established as the administrative headquarters of the Palestinian Authority, and the Israelis had also evacuated the Gaza Strip. By late 1995, negotiations had been concluded on further Israeli withdrawals from West Bank towns, and a second Washington ceremony was held to sign more agreements. By 1997, however, an Israeli plan to turn over only 9 percent of the West Bank land to the Palestinians (as an interim step prior to a final peace agreement) was rejected by Palestinians as insufficient.

Two Islamic fundamentalist groups, the Hamas (Islamic Resistance Movement) and Islamic Holy War, were opposed to peace negotiations because they wanted to replace Israel with a Palestinian state. They began assassinating Palestinian collaborators and Israeli soldiers and police. They also detonated bombs in Israeli cities, killing many civilians. Israeli undercover agents arrested, and in some cases killed, Palestinians implicated in these activities.

SEE ALSO

Islamic fundamentalism; Israel; Palestine Liberation Organization (PLO)

FURTHER READING

Heacock, Roger, and Jamal Nassar, eds. *Intifada: Palestine at the Crossroads.* New York: Praeger, 1990.

Peretz, Don. *Intifada: The Palestinian Uprising.* Boulder, Colo.: Westview, 1990.

Schiff, Ze'ev, and Ehud Ya'ari. *Intifada: The Palestinian Uprising—Israel's Third Front.* Edited and translated by Ina Friedman. New York: Simon & Schuster, 1990.

Iran

ISLAMIC REPUBLIC OF IRAN (JOMHORI-E-ISLAMI-E-IRÂN)

• *Capital: Tehran*

Political history Located in southwest Asia, the area below the Caspian Sea was settled by the Parsa, an Indo-European group related to the Indian Aryans, who supplanted earlier settlers around 1000 B.C. and gave the name Persia to the area. In 549 B.C. Cyrus the Great created the Persian Empire, beginning the Achaemenian dynasty. The Persians, because of attempts to expand their empire, became enemies of the Greeks, and eventually Alexander the Great conquered the area for the Greeks in 333 B.C. Persia regained its independence under the native Parthians, a Greek-speaking group of Persians who ruled from 247 B.C. to A.D. 224 and who fought against the Romans and limited their westward expansion. The Sassanians, in power from 224 to 637, conquered the area and introduced the Zoroastrian religion. Their empire expanded into what is now Iraq, Georgia, and Arabia. Arabs from Medina, a city on the Arabian Peninsula, conquered the Sassanians and introduced Islam in the 7th century. Turks and Mongols ruled Persia from the 11th century to 1502, at which time it regained independence under the Safavid dynasty. The British and Russians vied for control after the 1780s, with each side currying favor with the ruling Qajar dynasty. In 1907 the British and Russians agreed to divide Persia into two spheres of influence. As part of the effort to westernize government institutions, the Qajar ruler agreed to create a national assembly (Majlis) and a written constitution limiting the powers of the monarch.

In 1925, a military officer, Reza Pahlavi, established the Pahlavi dynasty after deposing the last Qajar ruler and declared himself shah (king). In 1935 the shah replaced the name Persia with Iran as a symbol of his desire to transform and modernize the nation. In 1941 Reza Shah abdicated in favor of his son, Mohammad Reza Shah Pahlavi, at the insistence of the British and Americans, because the father had supported Hitler and the Nazi movement. During World War II and through 1946 British and Soviet troops occupied Iran in order to secure transit routes for supplies to the Soviet Red Army.

In 1953 a U.S.-supported coup d'état overthrew a nationalist regime headed by Prime Minister Mohammad Mosaddeq that had reduced the young shah to a figurehead, turned the country toward the Soviet Union, and nationalized the oil industry, a source of vast wealth for Western oil companies. The coup restored the shah's power, but in 1978 the regime of Mohammad Reza Shah Pahlavi fell after a broad-based popular revolt organized by Islamic clerics.

An Islamic republic was established in 1979 under the direction of Supreme Religious Leader Ayatollah Ruhollah Khomeini. To do so, he overturned a fundamental precept of the Shiite Muslim faith that discouraged clerical involvement in government. And he assumed power over the opposition of most of the other senior ayatollahs (religious leaders). Khomeini developed a political theory, the *velayat-e faqih* (rule by the clergy), that called for guardianship of the state by Islamic jurists, specialists in Islamic law. Most of them were drawn from the lower ranks of Islamic scholars, the *hojjat-ol-Eslams*, who ranked below the conservative ayatollahs.

Government institutions Iran is an Islamic theocracy, in which religious bodies are superior to civil institutions of government. Supreme authority is vested in the spiritual leader, the *wali faqih*. An 83-member Assembly of Experts, popularly elected for an eight-year term, interprets the constitution and selects the spiritual leader. A Council of Guardians, with 12 members, supervises elections and ensures that legislation is in accordance with Islamic law.

A president exercising executive power is popularly elected for a term of four years. Legislative power rests with the 270-member Islamic Consultative Assembly (Majlis), whose members are popularly elected. A 23-member cabinet of ministers consists mostly of secular officials appointed by the president. The Committee to Determine the Expediency of the Islamic Order rules on disputes between the Majlis and the Council of Guardians.

Parties and movements In 1987 the Islamic Republican Party, which had assumed control of the state after the 1979 revolution, was dissolved in an internal power struggle. Underground communist and Islamic parties are suppressed by the government, as are exiled groups loyal to the former shah or leaders of the secular government that initially replaced him. With all parties banned, only candidates chosen by a council of mullahs (religious leaders) can run for office. Elections are usually contested by several candidates running for each position, giving voters a range of views from which to choose.

Domestic issues The Iranian economy is weak in the aftermath of the decade-long war with Iraq in the 1980s, a struggle that left hundreds of thousands of Iranians disabled with war wounds. With more than 40 percent unemployment, many of the urban poor *(mostazafin)* who fought the war have lost their revolutionary zeal for an extremist Muslim regime in Iran. In addition, the depressed price of oil has sharply reduced government revenues in the 1990s.

One group of Iranians, primarily businessmen, wants close ties with the West for aid and development. Another group, primarily Islamic fundamentalist clerics, would bar contacts with most Western nations. Under the leadership of President Hashemi Rafsanjani in the 1990s, Iran sold some assets of the *bonyads,* holding companies for expropriated wealth of the shah and his allies, and a few of its state enterprises. But much of the economy is controlled by Islamic foundations, whose enterprises receive state subsidies and contracts. They are supported by Ayatollah Ali Khamenei, the successor to the Ayatollah Khomeini. Free-market innovations are supported by the *bazar* (merchants and financiers) but were rejected by a majority of the Majlis in 1993. Iran has had trouble paying interest on its $30 billion foreign debt.

International issues After the 1979 revolution, Iranian students seized the U.S. embassy in Tehran and took 62 Americans hostage to protest the granting of asylum to the ousted shah by the United States. Mobs shouted "Marg bar Amrika" ("Death to America"). After a failed rescue attempt in 1980 by the U.S. Army, the hostages were released in January 1981 following an accord in which the United States pledged noninterference in Iranian affairs. (The U.S. embassy then

Supporters of the Ayatollah Khomeini in Tehran hold aloft newspapers proclaiming the imminent trial of U.S. diplomats taken hostage in the American embassy in 1979.

became a training camp for the Revolutionary Guards, the most militant of the groups backing the new Islamic regime.) In 1985 and 1986 the United States sold thousands of antitank and antiaircraft missiles to Iran in order to secure the release of American hostages held by the pro-Iranian Party of God in Lebanon, then used the profits from the sale to arm the Nicaraguan contras, fighting to overthrow the leftist Sandinista government in Nicaragua.

In 1987 the United States began escorting Kuwaiti ships through the Persian Gulf, breaking a threatened Iranian blockade there against Iraq and resulting in several naval incidents. The Gulf Cooperation Council, a group of Arab states bordering the Persian Gulf, has condemned Iranian attempts to annex several islands in the Persian Gulf.

Iran and the United States remain adversaries in the region, and the United States considers Iran one of the world's major supporters of state-sponsored terrorism. The United States imposed an embargo on all U.S. trade with Iran in May 1993, but American products are still imported by distributors who violate it.

From 1980 to 1988 Iran fought a long war with Iraq to defend its borders, with the loss of hundreds of thousands of its soldiers, but finally agreed to a cease-fire in 1988. Iran remained neutral during the Persian Gulf War between the United States and Iraq in 1991.

Iran has supported Islamic regimes in the Sudan and has assisted Islamic fundamentalist groups in Egypt and Afghanistan. The religious leaders in Iran issued a *fatwa* (religious edict) imposing a death sentence on the British writer Salman Rushdie in 1988 for what it considered blasphemy against Islam in his novel *The Satanic Verses*—an action that has strained Iran's relations with the United Kingdom.

In 1994 Iran intervened in the selection of the supreme head of the world's 100 million Shiite Muslims, announcing that Ayatollah Ali Khamenei had been chosen as their leader, without waiting for his election by the dozen grand ayatollahs in Iran and Iraq.

Iran has received strategic weapons and assistance from Germany, China, and North Korea in its attempt to become a nuclear power.

Human rights Iran has executed and harassed members of the Baha'i religious faith, evangelical Christians, Sunni Muslims (the majority branch of Islam, but a minority group in Iran), and Jews. Conversion from Islam to another religion is punishable by death, after trial by religious courts. Iran's Islamic "moral police" require everyone to obey a strict interpretation of religious law, levying fines and prison sentences on citizens who publicly violate Islamic law.

SEE ALSO

Iraq; Islamic fundamentalism; Khomeini, Ayatollah Ruhollah Mussavi

FURTHER READING

Bakhash, Shaul. *The Reign of the Ayatollahs.* New York: Basic Books, 1984.
Chubin, Shahram. *Iran's National Security Policy.* Washington, D.C.: Brookings Institution, 1994.
Hashim, Ahmed. *The Crisis of the Iranian State.* New York: Oxford University Press, 1995.
Keddie, Nikki. *Roots of Revolution.* New Haven: Yale University Press, 1981.
Metz, Helen Chapin, ed. *Iran: A Country Study.* 4th ed. Washington, D.C.: Federal Research Division, Library of Congress, 1989.
Rahnema, Saeed, and Sohrab Behdad. *Iran After the Revolution.* New York: St. Martin's, 1994.
Shirley, Edward. "Not Fanatics, and Not Friends." *Atlantic Monthly,* December 1993, 105–12.

Iraq

REPUBLIC OF IRAQ (AL JUMHURIYAH AL IRAQIYAH)

• *Capital: Baghdad*

Political history Located on the Tigris-Euphrates plain, just north of the Arabian Peninsula in southwest Asia, Iraq is the site of one of the world's oldest civilizations. Sumerian city-states existed there more than 7,000 years ago and from them the Babylonian, Assyrian, and Akkadian empires were formed. Persia conquered the area in 500 B.C.; the Greeks under Alexander the Great briefly held sway after 333 B.C. and then gave way to the Seleucids, who ruled until 141 B.C., and the Sassanians, who were defeated by the Arabs, who converted the people to Islam in the 7th century A.D.

After the 16th century Iraq was part of the Ottoman Empire. The British occupied it during World War I and it became a kingdom in 1921 under a British mandate. In 1932 it gained independence under the Hashemite dynasty, a pro-British royal house from Saudi Arabia. After a military coup in 1958, the monarchy was abolished. The Ba'ath Party seized power in 1968, and Iraq has been a one-party authoritarian state ever since.

Government institutions All political power is exercised by the leader of the Ba'ath Party, Saddam Hussein, who is also president and commander in chief. According to the constitution, executive power is supposed to be shared by a president and an eight-member Revolutionary Command Council (RCC); legislative power is shared by the RCC and a 250-member National Assembly whose members are popularly elected to four-year terms. However, Saddam (as he prefers to be known) reigns supreme, and the RCC simply follows his lead. The administrative departments are supervised by an appointed council of ministers. There are civil, criminal, and religious *(sharī'a)* courts, but *sharī'a* law does not take precedence over civil law.

Parties and movements Iraq is dominated by the National Progressive Front of the Ba'ath Party and several

Even after their country's defeat in the Persian Gulf War, these Iraqis continue to demonstrate their support for Saddam Hussein.

smaller parties allied with it. In 1991 other parties were legalized, provided they were not based on religion, race, or ethnicity, but none is permitted to challenge the regime for power. Illegal opposition groups include an Islamic fundamentalist group and the Iraqi Communist Party.

Domestic issues The aftermath of the Persian Gulf War, fought against the United States and a coalition of Western allies in 1991 after Iraq's invasion of Kuwait, left Iraq's economy in ruins. Its overseas financial assets are frozen, trade with other nations in many strategic goods is embargoed, and under UN sanctions some of its proceeds from oil sales go to Kuwait for reparations.

Unemployment and inflation are high, and aside from the reconstruction of the country's infrastructure and arms industry, there is little economic growth. The United Nations was feeding more than 2 million Iraqis in the mid-1990s. Medicine is in short supply, and the infant mortality rate has quadrupled since the 1991 war. Meanwhile, Saddam Hussein and his supporters have built 50 palaces and luxury homes, at a cost of more than $1.5 billion. Hussein has protected himself against various coup at-

tempts and army mutinies (one fomented by units of his elite Republican Guard and another plotted by his chief of intelligence) by creating a new presidential guard, headed by his son Uday Hussein.

In the south, a Shiite Muslim rebellion flares occasionally but is contained by government troops. In northern Iraq a UN-mandated "safe haven" for Kurds, a primarily agricultural ethnic group whose members are Sunni Muslim, has created what amounts to a separate Kurdish administration, although Iraq has stalled on negotiations to form a Kurdish Autonomous Region.

International issues Iraq has committed several acts of aggression against other states in the region. In 1980 it invaded Iran to gain full control of the Shatt-al-Arab waterway that provides its only access to the Persian Gulf. The war was suspended in 1988 with minor territorial gains by Iraq at an enormous cost in lives. During and after that war, Iraq received large quantities of U.S. economic aid with which it purchased arms, and it was able to buy advanced weapons from several nations, including equipment to improve its own conventional weapons industries. It began development of chemical, biological, and nuclear weapons by purchasing equipment from West Germany, Switzerland, Italy, and France.

In August 1990 Iraq invaded oil-rich Kuwait, which it has historically viewed as part of its territory, overthrew its monarchy, and annexed it as the "19th province." A coalition of UN forces, led by the United States, defeated the Iraqi military early in 1991 and restored the Kuwaiti monarchy. Iraq accepted UN terms for peace, including "no-fly" zones in which it was prohibited from flying fixed-wing aircraft in the south against the Shiites and in the north against the Kurds. UN Resolutions 687, 707, and 715 provided for UN monitoring of the destruction of Iraq's chemical and biological weapons, its program for making nuclear weapons, and ballistic missiles with a range of more than 95 miles. Although the UN and the International Atomic Energy Agency inspectors have destroyed chemical weapons, SCUD missiles, and a nuclear weapons factory at Al-Atheer, Iraq is believed to be developing missiles, nuclear weapons, and poison gas. In 1994 the United Nations created a monitoring system to ensure that Iraq could not acquire long-range ballistic missiles, nuclear warheads, and chemical and biological weapons.

The United States has created a Fifth Fleet in the Persian Gulf, with 200 war-planes and 100 Tomahawk missiles ready to deter future Iraqi aggression. The U.S. Army has equipment in Kuwait and Qatar ready to supply two armored brigades that could be sent to protect these nations against Iraqi aggression. The United States has concluded defense agreements with the Gulf states and has sold advanced weaponry to states near Iraq. It enforced the UN resolutions by striking at Iraqi armament factories with missiles and destroying the Al-Nida in-telligence complex in Baghdad. In 1995 President Bill Clinton sent the military to Kuwait after Iraq held maneuvers near its borders, forcing the Iraqi military to pull its forces out of southern Iraq.

In 1995 King Hussein of Jordan encouraged the defection of one of Saddam's top lieutenants, General Husein Kamel, who had been in charge of Iraq's strategic weapons programs. Jordan and Saudi Arabia backed Kamel in his efforts to organize a resistance movement against Saddam Hussein, but it was ineffectual.

Human rights Iraq is a police state, and dissidents have been subjected to torture and murder. The regime has executed profiteering merchants as an "anti-inflation" measure. In the 1980s Kurds in the north were subjected to genocidal military attacks that included the use of poison gas. The Iraqi military engaged in numerous war crimes during its occupation of Kuwait in 1991.

In the 1990s the Iraqi army destroyed Shiite villages in the south and more than 50,000 Shiite marsh Arabs (those who lived in southern marshes along the Shatt-al-Arab) were killed in an offensive begun in 1992. More than 200,000 other residents have fled, many into Iran. Marshes have been drained in an attempt to drive out the Shiites, threatening a way of life that has existed in the south for thousands of years.

SEE ALSO

Ba'ath movement; Hussein, Saddam; Iran; United Nations (UN)

FURTHER READING

Al'Khalil, Samir. *Republic of Fear.* Berkeley: University of California Press, 1989.
Farouk-Sluglett, Marion, and Peter Sluglett. *Iraq Since 1958.* New York: St. Martin's, 1991.
Marr, Phoebe. *The Modern History of Iraq.* Boulder, Colo.: Westview, 1985.
Simons, Geoff. *Iraq: From Sumer to Saddam.* New York: St. Martin's, 1994.

Ireland

REPUBLIC OF IRELAND (EIRE)

• Capital: Dublin

Political history An island located to the west of England, Ireland was settled by Celtic tribes who had arrived from England and mainland Europe around 400 B.C. Saint Patrick brought Christianity to the region in A.D. 432. Norse tribes invaded and controlled much of Ireland after 795, until their defeat in 1014 by High King Brian Boru. It was then ruled by the Five Fifths (kingdoms) of Ulster, Meath, Leinster, Munster, and Connacht until it became a part of England in 1171, when King Henry II was acknowledged as its monarch. English rule was encouraged by Pope Adrian IV and his successor Alexander III, both of whom wanted the Irish church to be brought under English supervision. Ireland was then controlled by the lords of Kildare, Irish nobles who accepted the supremacy of the British Crown.

The Irish people remained loyal Catholics after Henry VIII severed connections with the Roman Catholic Church and created a separate English church, and they chafed under English rule even more after the 1691 Protestant Ascendancy ended the religious upheavals in England and established it firmly as a Protestant nation. After several attempted revolts, the British subjugated the Irish militarily. By the Act of Union of 1801, the United Kingdom of Great Britain and Ireland was established.

Irish nationalists fought for independence thereafter. During World War I their activities culminated in the Easter Rebellion in Dublin in April 1916, during which the Irish attacked British mili-

JUSTICE TO IRELAND.
"She gave them some Broth without any Bread, Then whipp'd them all Round, and sent them to Bed."

This 1846 cartoon reflected the prevailing British view of the Irish as unruly ragamuffins in need of the firm hand of English discipline. At the time, hundreds of thousands of Irish were dying as the result of a great famine.

tary forces and pro-British government offices, and issued a declaration establishing the Irish Provisional Government. After five years of revolutionary activity, led by Eamon De Valera and his Sinn Féin (We Alone) movement, the British agreed to independence. The Irish Free State was established as a self-governing dominion within the British Commonwealth in 1920. However, the six northern counties, which had Protestant majorities, remained within the United Kingdom. A civil war ensued in Ireland between those favoring and those opposing the Anglo-Irish Treaty of 1920, and the peace party, now led by De Valera, prevailed, leaving Northern Ireland in the hands of the British.

In 1937 the last sovereign powers of the British Crown were ended. Ireland assumed full sovereignty, though it remained a member of the British Commonwealth, and the name of the Irish nation was changed to Eire. In another name change, the Republic of Ireland was proclaimed in 1949, and the last links with the British Crown were severed, as Ireland withdrew from the Commonwealth of Nations.

Government institutions Ireland has a parliamentary system, with the president as head of state. Governing power rests with a prime minister and cabinet, which remain accountable to a majority of the legislature. Parliament consists of a 166-member House of Representatives and a 60-member Senate, whose members serve for a maximum of five years. The House is elected by the people through proportional representation of parties; the Senate is chosen in part by the prime minister and partly by panels representing different sectors of society, including universities. An independent judiciary is headed by a supreme court.

Parties and movements Ireland has a multiparty system. In the early 1990s the largest party was the Fine Gael (United Ireland Party), a centrist group. The conservative Fianna Fáil (Republican Party) is the major opposition party, though for much of Ireland's history it was in the majority. The Labour Party holds a balance of power and has formed coalitions with each of the major parties in the 1980s and 1990s. A coalition of centrist and leftist parties—the Fine Gael, the Labour Party, and the Democratic Left—controlled the government in 1995. The opposition was led by the Fianna Fáil, which remained the largest single party in parliament.

Domestic issues Unemployment was high in the 1980s, and many young people emigrated. Ireland promotes free trade and has industrialized in order to export finished goods as well as traditional crafts, such as linen and glassware. It has successfully attracted much foreign investment and its economy is becoming integrated into the European Union, which has provided it with subsidies for highways and other public works. With the economy growing (by more than 6 percent annually) and unemployment dropping (from 16 percent to below 10 percent) in the 1990s, and with the Irish enjoying higher per capita income than the British, economic issues seem less significant than social issues.

Until the 1990s, the Catholic Church determined Ireland's social policy. In 1995, however, the Irish government made abortion counseling legal, although the actual operation cannot be performed in Ireland. A referendum on the right to obtain a divorce was also passed in late 1995. In that year the president of the country, Mary Robinson, and 12 percent of its legislators were women. Controversial social issues (such as abortion and divorce laws) are now high on the nation's agenda for reform, with a young group of reformers challenging the moral authority of the Catholic clergy to influence social policies.

International issues The highest priority of Irish foreign policy is to participate in the settlement of the violence between Catholics and Protestants in Northern Ireland. Under the 1985 Anglo-Irish Agreement, the United Kingdom must consult Ireland about affairs in Northern Ireland, giving it a role in the final settlement.

Ireland is a member of the United Nations, the European Union, and the Conference on Security and Cooperation in Europe, and it plays a major role in humanitarian assistance efforts in other nations. It also contributes troops to UN peacekeeping operations around the world.

SEE ALSO
Commonwealth of Nations; De Valera, Eamon; Northern Ireland; United Kingdom

FURTHER READING
Bew, Paul, et al. *The Dynamics of Irish Politics.* London: Lawrence & Wishart, 1989.
Coakley, John, and Michael Gallagher, eds. *Politics in the Republic of Ireland.* Dublin: Folens, 1993.

Kearney, Richard, ed. *Across the Frontiers: Ireland in the 1990s.* Dublin: Wolfhound, 1988.

Keogh, Dermot. *Twentieth-Century Ireland.* New York: St. Martin's, 1995.

Morgan, Kenneth O., ed. *The Young Oxford History of Britain and Ireland.* New York: Oxford University Press, 1997.

Ireland, Northern

SEE Northern Ireland

Irish Republican Army (IRA)

The IRA is a revolutionary organization founded in 1916 as the military wing of the Sinn Féin movement for Irish independence. It fought against the British army in the Easter Rebellion of 1916 in Dublin, and its military resistance led the British to recognize the independence of the Irish Free State in 1920.

The IRA opposed the agreement that kept the six northern counties of Ulster part of the United Kingdom, and it split over how best to resist the British domination of the north; a group known as the "irregulars" launched a sabotage campaign against the Irish Free State between 1922 and 1923. The Irish government retaliated by banning the IRA in 1931 for alleged support of the "irregulars." During the 1930s and World War II, the government cracked down on the IRA for its anti-British sabotage activities, arresting and executing several of its leaders.

In the 1960s civil unrest began between Catholics in Northern Ireland demonstrating for their civil rights and

the Protestant majority, which often discriminated against the Catholic minority; an armed group of Protestants (called the Provisionals) attacked Catholic demonstrators. In 1969 the IRA split again between "official" and "provisional" wings, with the former calling for a socialist state and the latter engaging in a campaign of sabotage and guerrilla warfare against British soldiers who had been sent to the province to quell the unrest and seemed, to the IRA, to be taking the side of the Protestants.

The IRA has often attempted to assassinate political figures in Northern Ireland and in England. It killed Lord Mountbatten (a first cousin of the queen and a royal adviser) in 1979, and bombed department stores and other public buildings throughout the United Kingdom, including the financial district known as The City in London.

Northern Ireland's divisions persist even unto death: Members of the Royal Ulster Constabulary warily monitor the funeral of two IRA soldiers ambushed by British troops.

Between 1970 and 1992 the IRA killed 900 British security troops in Northern Ireland, while losing some 300 of its own members. It has received funds and explosives from the Libyan government, which often backs terrorist groups opposing British political influence. The IRA's violent activities have been disavowed by the Irish government, as well as by John Hume, the leader of the Catholic Social Democratic Labour Party, the largest party among Catholics in Northern Ireland.

In 1994 the IRA and British prime minister John Major announced a cease-fire in Northern Ireland. Gerry Adams, the president of Sinn Féin, the IRA's political arm, and his No. 2 man, Martin McGuinness, strengthened their control over the IRA and committed it to political negotiations. Under the agreement, the British withdrew 400 troops from Northern Ireland. President Bill Clinton permitted Adams and other IRA leaders to visit the United States and to raise money for their organization, putting a strain on Anglo-American relations. In 1995, talks were broken off after the British insisted that the IRA demilitarize as a prelude to further negotiations. The IRA insisted that it would disarm only after a final agreement had been reached. Talks resumed in 1997.

SEE ALSO
Ireland; Northern Ireland

FURTHER READING
Bell, J. Bowyer. *The Irish Troubles: A Generation of Violence, 1967–1992.* New York: St. Martin's, 1993.

Iron Curtain

SEE Cold war

Islamic Conference (Organization of the Islamic Conference)

The Islamic Conference is an organization created in 1971 by all nation-states in which the majority of the population is Islamic in order to promote Islamic solidarity. It includes 44 countries, as well as the Palestinian Authority, which is the institution administering domestic affairs for Palestinians in the West Bank and Gaza. The part of Cyprus controlled by Turkey has observer status.

The Islamic Conference promotes Islamic coordination in diplomacy, economic development, cultural activities, and activities regarding the holy places in Jerusalem and elsewhere in the Arab world. The conference supports the attempts of the Palestinian people to achieve a sovereign state. It has supported the territorial integrity of Bosnia, and some of its members have defied the United Nations embargo to provide Bosnia with arms.

The Islamic Solidarity Fund supports Islamic universities in several nations. The Conference of Ministers of Foreign Affairs of the Islamic Conference endorsed a boycott of Salman Rushdie's 1988 novel *The Satanic Verses* on grounds of blasphemy, although it did not endorse the Iranian *fatwa* (decree of the religious court) sentencing Rushdie to death.

The Islamic Conference also organizes funding for humanitarian assistance for communities affected by war and drought. It strongly opposed the Soviet invasion of Afghanistan in 1978 and coordinated financial assistance to the *Mujaheddin*, the Islamic resistance fighters there. It supported the 1980 boycott of the Moscow Olympic games by some Western and Muslim nations to protest the Afghanistan invasion. Since the breakup of the Soviet Union, it has assisted the Muslim republics of central Asia in their Islamic cultural and religious reawakening.

SEE ALSO

Afghanistan; Islamic fundamentalism; Islamic Group; Palestine Liberation Organization (PLO)

FURTHER READING

Ahsan, Abdullah. *The Organization of the Islamic Conference.* Herndon, Va.: International Institute of Islamic Thought, 1988.

Islamic fundamentalism

Islamic fundamentalism is a religious and political movement that calls for the renewal of Islamic civilization and the rejection of Western influences. Adherents call for the return to *sharī'a*, Islamic religious law. *Sharī'a* is based on the precepts of the Koran, the Muslim holy book, which fundamentalists interpret literally as the word of God. *Sharī'a* calls for, among other things, strict penalties for criminal behavior, as well as modest dress for women, the segregation of men and women in all public places, a ban on alcohol and pornography, and a rejection of Western-style parliamentary democracy with its separation of church and state. Governmental institutions, such as a parliament, would continue to exist in fundamentalist states, but they would be subordinated to the religious authorities.

Islamic fundamentalism developed as a reaction to Western secularism in Egypt, which adopted a constitutional

monarchy in its 1923 constitution. Because Coptic Christians (members of an Egyptian Christian sect) were granted legal equality with Muslims, a reaction among some devout Muslims (who believed that because they were the religious majority, they had the right to impose their religious views on the state) led the cleric Hasan al-Banna to form the Muslim Brotherhood. Its goal was to rid Egypt of British influence, and its street demonstrations were partly responsible for the fall of the corrupt, pro-Western ruler King Farouk in 1952. The military officers who took power offered the Muslim Brotherhood a place in the government, but its members soon split with the military rulers, and the Brotherhood was outlawed. In 1981 the offshoot fundamentalist group Jihad (which translates as "holy struggle") assassinated Egyptian president Anwar Sadat after he made peace with Israel. He was succeeded by army general Hosni Mubarak, who in the 1990s was engaged in putting down armed Muslim militants.

In 1982 the Ba'ath (secular Arab nationalist) rulers of Syria put down a fundamentalist revolt in the city of Hama, organized by the Islamic Liberation Party, by razing the city and killing thousands of its inhabitants. Fundamentalist plots against the government of Tunisia

Covered head to toe in traditional dress, as prescribed under a strict interpretation of Islamic law, Iraqi women take their children to fetch water in the dark days following their nation's defeat in the Persian Gulf War.

were uncovered in 1983 and 1985, although the Islamic party there, called the Islamic Tendency Movement, remains powerful. Muslim militants seized the Grand Mosque in Mecca, Saudi Arabia, in 1979, hoping to spark a revolution, but they were soon crushed by the military. Saudi Arabia banned fundamentalist movements in 1993 because they were gaining influence among junior officers in the military.

Islamic fundamentalists gained power in Afghanistan after the withdrawal of Soviet troops in 1989. In Iran, since the fall of the shah in 1978, a Guardianship Council ensures the government's fidelity to Shiite Muslim precepts (the Shiites are a minority sect within Islam but constitute the majority in Iran). A fundamentalist government influenced by the National Islamic Front assumed power in the Sudan in 1990 and reaffirmed the institution of Islamic law, which had been introduced in 1983 by a military government. The Jamiat-i-Islami movement of fundamentalists is influential in Pakistan. Fundamentalists have been engaged in a guerrilla war in Algeria and would have assumed power had the army not stopped them after they won free elections in 1992.

Islamic fundamentalists have been involved in many terrorist activities in the West, hoping to end Western backing for regimes they opposed. In Paris they were responsible for a series of bombings in the late 1980s and mid-1990s as a protest against French support for the Algerian military rulers. Extremists linked to Egyptian Sheikh Omar Abdel Rahman were responsible for the bombing of the World Trade Center in New York City in 1993. In 1996 the sheikh was given a life sentence by a U.S. court for his part in the conspiracy, prompting the Islamic Group to issue a statement that "the Americans have chosen war with Islam" and to threaten to strike at American "interests and people" in revenge. Islamic extremist groups have also provided safe havens and financial support to Western terrorist organizations.

SEE ALSO
Afghanistan; Algeria; Ba'ath movement; Egypt; Islamic Conference (Organization of the Islamic Conference); Islamic Group

FURTHER READING
Esposito, John L. *The Islamic Threat: Myth or Reality?* New York: Oxford University Press, 1995.
Hourani, Albert. *Arabic Thought in the Liberal Age.* New York: Cambridge University Press, 1983.
Sivan, Emmanuel. *Radical Islam: Medieval Theology and Modern Politics.* New Haven: Yale University Press, 1990.

Islamic Group

The Islamic Group was founded in 1973 as the student wing of the Muslim Brotherhood, an Islamic fundamentalist organization based in Egypt. In 1975 it split with the Brotherhood and began advocating a violent solution to the corruption of Egyptian politics. It joined with Islamic Holy War, a radical Islamic guerrilla group, in a coup attempt against President Anwar Sadat, and when Sadat was assassinated in 1978 it launched an uprising in the southern Nile town of Asyūt that was contained after two days of fighting.

The Islamic Group has support in southern Egypt and in the slums of Cairo because its attacks on corrupt government officials are popular with the poor. It is supported by the governments of Iran and the Sudan and by contributions from its members. Its religious leader is Sheikh Omar Abdel Rahman, a theologian who has called for a holy war against the West.

The most spectacular terrorist action of the Islamic Group was the bombing of the World Trade Center in New York City in 1993, an action that killed five people, injured hundreds, and disrupted financial activity in New York City for months. Members of the organization were soon arrested in the United States and Egypt. The Egyptian government then cracked down on the Islamic Group, conducting a series of raids throughout Egypt to capture and imprison its members.

SEE ALSO
Egypt; Islamic fundamentalism; Sadat, Anwar

FURTHER READING
Rubin, Barry. *Islamic Fundamentalism in Egyptian Politics.* New York: St. Martin's, 1990.

Isolationism

Isolationism is an approach to making foreign policy that keeps to a minimum one nation's relations to other nations. Isolationists believe that joining international organizations and making treaty commitments with other nations weakens sovereignty and is not in the national interest. Isolationists oppose participation in multilateral organizations, such as the United Nations, or in collective security arrangements, such as NATO. Japan, for example, completely closed itself off to foreign influences in the 16th century in order to maintain its cultural integrity, and it did not end its isolationist policy until a U.S. fleet forced it to admit Western powers in the 1850s.

In the 18th and 19th centuries Russia alternately opened itself to Western influence or closed itself off

completely, depending on who was in power. The British government, until the beginning of World War II, opted for a policy in which it shifted alliances with nations on the European continent in order to defuse possible political crises and maintain stability on the continent, but it had no permanent alliances or commitments.

The United States initially followed George Washington's warning in his farewell address to avoid "entangling alliances" with European powers. At the end of World War I, Senate rejection of the Treaty of Versailles, negotiated by President Woodrow Wilson—and with it any possibility that the United States would enter the League of Nations, established in the treaty—was a victory for American isolationists. The failure of the League of Nations to stop Axis aggression, and passage of the Neutrality Acts by the U.S. Congress, against the advice of President Franklin Roosevelt, did not appease Nazi Germany and its Axis allies. Instead, the war expanded and the United States was dragged directly into the fighting after Japan bombed Pearl Harbor in Hawaii on December 7, 1941.

The failure of isolationist policy to keep the United States out of World

Flanked by a portrait of Adolf Hitler, the American aviator Charles Lindbergh (left) meets with Nazi leader Hermann Göring (right). Lindbergh was perhaps the best-known advocate of American isolationism in the years leading to U.S. involvement in World War II.

War II discredited American isolationists. Instead, the notion of collective security, involving the efforts of an alliance of nations to deter or repel aggression, became the fundamental principle of U.S. diplomacy. At the end of the war, the isolationist Republicans in Congress almost uniformly switched to support the creation of the United Nations, the Truman Doctrine (which provided aid to Greek and Turkey), the NATO military alliance to provide security in Western Europe, the Organization of American States (OAS) to provide collective security in Latin America, foreign aid programs, the Korean War to repel the invasion of South Korea by North Korea, and other policies that brought the United States from isolationism to its position as leader of the free world during the cold war.

In the 1990s, a new isolationism in the United States manifested itself in Congress and involved opposition to the use of U.S. forces in peacekeeping operations (particularly if they were to serve under the command of foreign officers) as well as opposition to funding UN activities or the activities of many international development organizations. As a result, funding for the U.S. Department of State, for foreign assistance to developing nations, and for contributions to international organizations was severely cut by Congress.

SEE ALSO
League of Nations; North Atlantic Treaty Organization (NATO); Organization of American States (OAS); Roosevelt, Franklin D.; United Nations (UN); Wilson, Woodrow

FURTHER READING
Jonas, Manfred. *Isolationism in America, 1935–1941*. Ithaca, N.Y.: Cornell University Press, 1966.
Nordlinger, Eric. *Isolationism Reconfigured: American Foreign Policy for a New Century*. Princeton, N.J.: Princeton University Press, 1995.

Israel

STATE OF ISRAEL (MEDINAT ISRAEL)

• *Capital: Jerusalem*

Political history The area of southwest Asia bounded on the west by the Mediterranean Sea has been home to Jews since Moses led the Israelite tribes out of Egypt in biblical times. After absorption of the area into the Roman Empire, most of the Jewish population was dispersed throughout the empire and central Asia by the 3rd century A.D. In the 4th century, most of the area's inhabitants were converted to Christianity under the Romans. It was conquered by the Persians in 611, and then in 628 the Byzantine emperor Heraclius took it over by force. Muslims from Arabia defeated Heraclius and conquered the area between 636 and 640. Thereafter, numerous Muslim dynasties took control, including the Umayyads in the early 8th century, the Abbasids from Baghdad in 750, and the Fatimmids of North Africa in 980.

Christian Crusaders from Europe established control in 1100 and proclaimed the kingdom of Jerusalem. They fought continuously with Muslim rulers, including the sultan Saladin, who defeated them in 1187. The last of the Crusaders were driven out in 1291, and the area was controlled by the Mamluks, rulers of Egypt in the 14th century. In 1516 the Ottoman Empire gained control and, except for a brief period of Egyptian rule between 1831 and 1840, retained the territory until its defeat by the Allied powers in World War I.

Zionists—Jews calling for a Jewish homeland, known in the Bible as Zion—came from Europe to settle beginning in 1882. At the same time, Muslim Arabs

UNITED NATIONS
GENERAL ASSEMBLY
PARTITION PLAN, 1947

Jewish State

Arab State

Permanent
Trusteeship

LEBANON

SYRIA

Safad
Acre
Haifa
Sea of Galilee
Nazareth

Nablus

Tel Aviv
Jaffa
Jordan River

Jerusalem

*Mediterranean
Sea*

• Amman

Hebron

Dead Sea

Gaza

Rafah

Beersheba

TRANSJORDAN

EGYPT

ISRAELI BORDERS
AND ARMISTICE
LINES, 1949

Territory of Israel

Area under Jordanian
Control

Area under Egyptian
Control

Demilitarized Zone

LEBANON

GOLAN
HEIGHTS
SYRIA

Safad
Acre
Haifa
*Sea of
Galilee*
Nazareth

Nablus

Tel Aviv
Jaffa
Jordan River

WEST
BANK

Jerusalem

*Mediterranean
Sea*

• Amman

Hebron

Dead Sea

GAZA
STRIP
Gaza

Rafah

Beersheba

JORDAN

ISRAEL

EGYPT

'Aqaba

'Aqaba

ISRAEL AND
OCCUPIED
TERRITORIES, 1967

Israel before 1967

Occupied territory

LEBANON

SYRIA

Safad
Acre
Haifa
GOLAN
HEIGHTS
*Sea of
Galilee*

Nazareth

Nablus

Tel Aviv-
Jaffa
WEST
BANK
Jordan River

Jerusalem

*Mediterranean
Sea*

• Amman

GAZA
STRIP
Gaza
Hebron

Port
Said

Rafah

Dead Sea

JORDAN

Beersheba

Suez Canal

ISRAEL

Suez

SINAI

Gulf of Suez

'Aqaba

Gulf of Aqaba

EGYPT

SAUDI
ARABIA

Red Sea

ISRAEL AND OCCUPIED
TERRITORIES AFTER
ISRAELI-EGYPTIAN
PEACE TREATY,
MARCH 26, 1979

LEBANON

SYRIA

Safad
Acre
Haifa
GOLAN
HEIGHTS
*Sea of
Galilee*

Nazareth

Nablus

Tel Aviv-
Jaffa
WEST
BANK
Jordan River

Jerusalem

*Mediterranean
Sea*

• Amman

GAZA
STRIP
Gaza
Hebron

Port
Said

Rafah

Dead Sea

Beersheba

JORDAN

Suez Canal

ISRAEL

Suez

SINAI

Gulf of Suez

'Aqaba

Gulf of Aqaba

EGYPT

SAUDI
ARABIA

Red Sea

Jews congregate for prayer at the Wailing Wall, which they hold sacred as the wall of the Second Temple in Jerusalem. The wall borders a site holy to Muslims, the Al-Aksa Mosque.

from Syria and some Muslim Slavs from Bosnia moved to the area. In the Balfour Declaration of 1917, the British government, which had during World War I taken possession of Palestine (named after one of the Roman provinces in the area), committed itself to establishing a Jewish homeland in the area.

In 1923 the League of Nations gave the British government a mandate over Palestine, and the British allowed Jewish settlements. In the 1930s the influx of Jews sparked anti-Jewish riots instigated by Palestinian Arab nationalists and egged on by religious authorities such as the Mufti of Jerusalem, who feared the establishment of a Jewish state. In 1939 the British government restricted further Jewish immigration to no more than another 75,000, thus severely restricting the entry of Jews at the start of the Holocaust. Although hundreds of thousands of Jews attempted to escape the Nazi effort to exterminate them during World War II, they were forbidden by British colonial military and civilian officials from taking refuge in Palestine.

At the end of World War II, Jewish settlers launched a guerrilla war against the British to obtain their independence. Following a civil war between Palestin-

ian Jews and Arabs in 1947–48, a UN plan for independence partitioned the area into Jewish and Arab states. On May 14, 1948, Israel declared its independence under the leadership of its first prime minister, David Ben-Gurion.

Israel was immediately invaded by Arab armies from six nations. The Israelis defeated these armies and even gained additional territory, recognized in armistice agreements with Egypt, Jordan, Lebanon, and Syria signed in 1949. More than 700,000 Arabs fled Israel during and after the war, and close to 1 million Jews, many of them refugees from Arab nations, had entered Israel by the early 1950s, including large numbers from Yemen and Morocco. In 1950 Jordan annexed the Arab West Bank, which had been designated as an Arab state under the UN partition plan. That same year, Israel passed the Law of Return, granting every Jew in the world the automatic right to settle in Israel and become an Israeli citizen.

In June 1967, under the military leadership of General Moshe Dayan, Israel fought Egypt, Syria, and Jordan, after Egypt had closed off Israeli access to the Red Sea, in what became known as the Six-Day War. With its victory, Israel gained control of the West Bank and East Jerusalem (which had been under Jordanian control) as well as the Golan Heights (a part of Syria), the Gaza Strip (an area on the Egypt-Israel border that had been administered by Egypt and contained Palestinian refugees), and the Sinai Peninsula, a part of Egypt. Israel established military occupation of the West Bank and the Sinai Peninsula and annexed the Golan Heights and East Jerusalem. In 1973 Egypt and Syria launched a surprise attack against Israel on the holiest day of the year in the Jewish calendar—Yom Kippur, the day of atonement for sins. Under the leadership of prime minister Golda Meir, and with substantial diplomatic and military assistance from the United States, the Israelis repulsed the attacks and gained more territory in the Sinai and on the Golan Heights.

In 1978, under the leadership of prime minister Menachem Begin, Israel entered into peace negotiations with Egypt at Camp David in the United States, with President Jimmy Carter acting as mediator. Israel agreed to return the Sinai to Egypt, retaining the Gaza Strip for security purposes, in exchange for peace with Egypt. Israel was not able to conclude agreements with other neighboring Arab states because it refused to meet Arab demands that all territory it had occupied in the 1967 wars be returned. By 1997 there were 12,000 Israeli settlers on the Golan Heights, more than 125,000 on the West Bank (living among 1 million Arab residents), and 5,000 in the Gaza Strip, surrounded by 800,000 Palestinians living in towns and refugee camps.

In 1994 Israel concluded an agreement with the Palestine Liberation Organization (PLO) to turn over parts of the West Bank and certain governmental functions (such as administering the departments of health, education, and tourism) to a Palestinian Authority for a five-year period, during which time negotiations would take place concerning the future of Gaza, the West Bank, and Jerusalem and other issues. The Jericho District on the West Bank became the administrative seat of the Palestinian Authority, and the Gaza Strip was put under its jurisdiction in 1994.

In 1995 Israel concluded a second agreement with the PLO that returned most of the West Bank towns to the Palestinian Authority and provided for Palestinian elections. Negotiations were to continue over the next several years to resolve the final status of Jerusalem.

Government institutions Israel is a parliamentary democracy. A president, elected by the parliament, is the head of state. Until 1996 the president appointed as prime minister the leader of the largest party, who ran the government with a cabinet and was accountable to a majority in the parliament, called the Knesset. Beginning in 1996 Israeli voters directly elected the prime minister. The 120-member Knesset is chosen by proportional representation in direct elections, in which each party fills seats according to the proportion of the national vote it has obtained.

Israel does not have a written constitution, but its Knesset enacts fundamental laws to provide a framework of government and due process of law. An independent judiciary applies Ottoman law (from the centuries of Ottoman rule), British mandate law (instituted from 1921 through 1947), and statutes passed by the Knesset. Muslims, Jews, and Christians each have religious courts to deal with lawsuits involving social issues such as marriage and divorce.

Parties and movements Israel was governed by the Labor Alignment (a union of three social democratic parties) and its coalition of other parties until the 1970s, when the Likud bloc, a coalition of right-wing, conservative, and nationalist parties, assumed power under the leadership of Menachem Begin and his successor, Yitzhak Shamir. (The name Likud means "consolidation.") For a brief period there was a government of national unity consisting of both parties, but it soon collapsed.

In the early 1990s a Labor coalition under the leadership of Yitzhak Rabin governed with the support of an orthodox religious party and two small Arab parties. It was defeated by the Likud in elections in June 1996, when Benjamin Netanyahu won a direct election to be prime minister over Shimon Peres. Netanyahu won by only a 29,457-vote margin in an election in which 2,972,589 votes were cast. Like his Labor predecessor, Netanyahu put together a multiparty coalition. This Likud government then presided over peace negotiations with the PLO.

Israel's multiparty system gives disproportionate weight to orthodox religious parties that hold the balance of power between Likud and Labor; such parties can support either coalition to give it a majority in the Knesset and thereby dominate lawmaking. As a result, Netanyahu constantly had to juggle the conflicting demands of his coalition, which opposed concessions to the Palestinians, and Israeli public opinion, the majority of which favored concessions for peace.

Domestic issues Since becoming an independent state in 1948, Israel has been preoccupied with absorbing the hundreds of thousands of Jews who have entered the country from Arab lands, Latin America, Western Europe, and from the Soviet Union and Eastern Europe. The Israeli economy has moved from a highly socialistic one to one adopting a free-market approach since the beginning of Likud rule in the 1970s. Some of its 150 state enterprises are gradually being privatized, with shares sold to private investors. Welfare-state benefits have been trimmed. Unemployment remains high (more than 10 percent in the early 1990s), and many thousands of highly skilled scientists, engineers, and doctors cannot find work to match their skills, causing thousands to emigrate. Israel has a highly advanced economy, and its armaments, computer, and medical equipment industries rank with the best in the world. Its gross domestic product has grown at an impressive rate in the 1990s, and the government has kept inflation under control.

The Israeli population is composed of a diverse group of Jews, including religious and secular Jews, those with European backgrounds (the Ashkenazim) and those from Arab and African nations (the Sephardim), those favoring socialism and those favoring capitalism. The Arab minority—close to 20 percent of the population—calls for greater investment in health, education, and community development for its members and an end to their status as second-class citizens, who are unable, for example, to join the army or obtain important government jobs.

International issues Until 1994 Israel had gained recognition from only one Arab nation, Egypt, as part of a peace agreement to return the Sinai Peninsula to it. But Israel has at best a "cold peace" with Egypt, with few cultural or economic contacts. In 1994 Israel concluded a peace agreement with Jordan that included the establishment of diplomatic relations, the resolution of outstanding border disputes, and rights to water on the Jordan River. Since then, there has been considerable tourism and cultural exchange between the two nations.

Israel is also recognized by the PLO, with whom it has negotiated accords for Palestinian autonomy on the West Bank and Gaza. Israel has conducted negotiations with Syria about withdrawing from part or all of the Golan Heights in return for a "full peace," but these negotiations remained stalled as of 1997.

Israel has fought several wars with Arab states and has developed advanced weaponry to maintain an edge over Arab armies. Although Israel has stated that it will not be the first to introduce nuclear weapons in the Middle East, most observers believe that it is already a nuclear power.

Israel has become a close ally of the United States, which provides it with weapons and more than $3 billion in foreign aid annually but which has also pressured Israel to make territorial concessions to Arab states and negotiate with the Palestinians for a comprehensive peace settlement. At the request of the United States, Israel did not participate in the Persian Gulf War in 1991—even though missiles were fired on its cities by Iraq—thus enabling several Arab nations to remain in the Allied coalition (a group of nations led by the United States), something they would not have done had Israel entered the war against Iraq.

By the early 1990s Israel had gained diplomatic recognition from most of the nations of the world, including a number of non-Arab Muslim nations such as Turkey. It has joined several European regional organizations. The Arab boycott of companies that do business with Israel, instituted in 1949, was abandoned by the Arab League in 1995 but reinstated in 1997 as a result of an impasse in the peace process with the Palestinians. Israel has become a leading exporter of agricultural technology to some Muslim nations of the former Soviet Union in central Asia. It has established relations with the post-communist nations of eastern Europe and has pressed property and damage claims of Holocaust survivors with these nations.

Human rights The Israeli army suppressed a 1987 uprising of Palestinians, the *intifada*, in the West Bank and Gaza Strip, and the Israeli human rights group B'Tselem has documented that the army killed more than 1,000 civilians between 1987 and 1994. Palestinians in the occupied territories may not engage in political activity, and their expression of opinion is subject to government censorship. Israel has placed some Palestinian nationalists under administrative detention for long periods of time without trying them for crimes.

SEE ALSO

Ben-Gurion, David; Egypt; Holocaust; Intifada; Iraq; Jordan; League of Nations; Lebanon; Meir, Golda; Ottoman Empire; Palestine Liberation Organization (PLO); Rabin, Yitzhak; Syria; Zionism

FURTHER READING

Beilin, Yossi. *Israel: A Concise Political History*. London: Weidenfeld & Nicholson, 1992.
Gilbert, Martin. *Atlas of the Arab-Israeli Conflict*. 6th ed. New York: Oxford University Press, 1993.
Medding, Peter. *The Founding of Israeli Democracy*. New York: Oxford University Press, 1990.
Metz, Helen Chapin, ed. *Israel: A Country Study*. 3rd ed. Washington, D.C.: Federal Research Division, Library of Congress, 1990.
Sachar, Howard. *A History of Israel*. 2 vols. New York: Oxford University Press, 1987.

Italy

ITALIAN REPUBLIC (REPUBBLICA ITALIANA)

- *Capital: Rome*

Political history Located in southern Europe, the Italian peninsula consisted of small villages in ancient times. Between the 9th and 6th centuries B.C., much of the peninsula was controlled by the Etruscans, who inhabited the area between the Arno and Tiber rivers. The area was first unified by Rome in 264 B.C. as part of an empire that stretched from Britain in the northwest and Spain in the southwest to Germany in the northeast and the Euphrates River and Egypt in the southeast.

After the breakup of the Roman Empire in the 6th century A.D., various parts of the peninsula were invaded by barbarian tribes from northern Europe, including the Lombards, Franks, and Goths. Stable government was restored by Roman Catholic popes, who controlled the papal states, an area of several hundred square miles surrounding Rome in central Italy, and by the princes of northern city-states such as Florence, Genoa, Milan, and Venice—a system that lasted through medieval times and the Renaissance. Between the 15th and 18th centuries, these ministates were fought over by Spanish, French, and German ruling houses. The French emperor Napoléon briefly unified Italy and crowned himself king in 1805, but with his defeat in 1815

Austria became the leading power on the peninsula, which once again fragmented into separate city-states.

In the 1830s a nationalist movement, the Risorgimento, to end foreign influence and reunify Italy began under the leadership of Giuseppe Mazzini. Eventually, Victor Emmanuel II, king of Piedmont, became king of Italy in 1861. His House of Savoy retained the throne through World War II.

Until the 1920s Italy was ruled under a constitution that made the monarch head of state but gave governing power to parliament and a cabinet headed by a prime minister. After Benito Mussolini led the Fascist Party to power in 1922, he converted Italy's constitutional monarchy into a dictatorship with a figurehead king. Italy fought alongside other Axis powers in World War II, but after the overthrow of Mussolini by anti-fascist partisans in July 1943, it ended participation in the war. The German army then took full control of northern Italy until the end of the war. The monarch, King Victor Emmanuel III, retired in favor of his son Prince Umberto, who assumed the title of lieutenant general of the realm. Victor Emmanuel formally abdicated in May 1946. In June, Italian voters decided in a referendum to abolish the monarchy; Italy became a republic in 1946 and was quickly integrated into Western European institutions such as NATO and, later, the European Community.

Government institutions Italy is a parliamentary democracy. A president, elected by an electoral college consisting of members of parliament and additional electors from each region, holds office for seven years and is head of state. He appoints a prime minister who runs the government with a cabinet that is accountable to a majority in parliament. The parliament consists of the 315-member Senate and the 630-member Chamber of Deputies, both directly elected for five-year terms. One-quarter of each chamber's parliamentary seats are distributed proportionally, based on the percentage of votes won in the national election, to give minor parties some representation. The remainder are chosen by plurality or majority vote in the election districts.

There is an independent judiciary, and prosecutors function independently of the government. Italian magistrates, for example, may independently initiate investigations of major crimes and governmental corruption and may prosecute cases without clearance from the cabinet.

Parties and movements Italy is a multiparty democracy, and all of its cabinets are multiparty coalitions. Between the end of World War II and 1981, Italy was dominated by the Christian Democratic Party, which named all prime ministers. (It changed its name in 1994 to the Popular Party.) Since 1981 the Socialist Party, the second largest, has controlled the government several times. The Communist Party was once a major force in Italian politics, winning up to one-quarter of the votes in parliamentary elections until the 1980s, when its popularity diminished. It is now known as the Democratic Party of the Left and has renounced Marxist-Leninist ideology in favor of social democracy. In the 1990s the Northern League, a group calling for autonomy or secession for the northern industrial areas, gained strength, as did a neo-fascist party called the Italian Social Movement.

Corruption scandals have severely weakened the Christian Democrats, and a Socialist government was formed in 1992, followed by a nonpartisan government pledged to investigate scandals implicating Christian Democrats and Socialists. A 1993 referendum changed the system of representation in parliament in order to reduce the number of minor parties represented. The March 1994 elections resulted in a repudiation of the Christian Democrats and the wholesale elimination of almost all the deputies who had previously served in the Italian parliament. The winning coalition was the Freedom Alliance, consisting of the right-wing Forza Italia (a new party led by media mogul Silvio Berlusconi, who controlled many Italian television stations), the Northern League, and the National Alliance (a neo-fascist party). In opposition was the left-wing Democratic Alliance, consisting of the Democratic Party of the Left and the Communist Refounding (former communists), former socialists in the True Socialist Party, and some Greens (environmentalists). A small centrist coalition also formed, consisting of the Pact for Italy (a liberal party advocating free-market economics) and the Popular Party, a shrunken successor to the once-dominant Christian Democrats.

When Silvio Berlusconi became prime minister in 1994, he included five members of the neo-fascist party in his cabinet, the first time fascists had been in the Italian government for half a century. He was forced to resign, however, after being investigated by Italian magistrates for financial irregularities. He was succeeded by a caretaker cabinet of nonpolitical technocrats, as the Italian political crisis intensified in the mid-1990s.

The crisis of weak governments ended in the 1996 parliamentary elections, when the country moved closer to a two-party system, as voters chose either the liberal-left bloc Olive Tree (consisting of the Democratic Party of the Left, the Dini list [named for a local politician], the Greens, and the Popular Party) or the right-wing Freedom Alliance (consisting of Forza Italia, the National Alliance, and Christian Democrats). More than 500 of the 630 lower house seats were won by these two opposing blocs, with the Olive Tree bloc assuming power under the leadership of Romano Prodi. His coalition included communists, and he sometimes gained support from

the Northern League. The Olive Tree coalition also gained control of the Senate.

Domestic issues The rebuilding of the Italian economy after World War II made Italy one of the world's leading industrial powers. But endemic corruption, with links among party leaders, industrialists, and organized crime figures, became an integral part of the economy. Both the public payroll and state enterprises expanded, and such companies as ENI, the state petroleum company, provided employment, patronage, kickbacks, and slush funds for Socialist Party leaders in the industrial north. Meanwhile, the Christian Democrats controlled the poverty-stricken south of Italy by working with organized crime leaders in Naples, Sicily, and Calabria, an arrangement sanctioned by one of the leading members of the Christian Democrats, prime minister Giulio Andreotti.

In the 1990s, after taking testimony from 270 organized crime leaders awaiting trial, prosecutors began investigating more than 3,000 leading politicians (including one-quarter of the parliament, former prime ministers, many cabinet ministers, and hundreds of local officials) and corporate executives (including some from the state oil company and the car maker Fiat) for corruption and links with organized

Migrant workers demonstrate for work in the south of Italy in 1976. More recently, a burgeoning secessionist movement has advocated that the wealthier northern part of Italy separate itself from the more impoverished south.

crime, which precipitated a crisis in Italian politics.

The result of decades of corruption and political mismanagement is that Italy has a national debt of more than $1 trillion. Reforms begun in 1993 included selling off state enterprises and reforming laws governing the financing of political parties. These reforms have destroyed the power of the Christian Democrats and Socialists and have led to a complete overhaul of the party system, resulting in the formation of weak coalition governments that have, as of the mid-1990s, failed to gain the allegiance of the Italian people or the respect of other Western democracies.

Italy is plagued by organized crime families that control unions, small businesses, banks, hotels, and gambling casinos and engage in illegal operations such as extortion, loan sharking, and drug smuggling. They have engaged in torture and assassination of their gangland rivals as well as of politicians and police investigators. The most significant crime groups include the Camorra in Naples, N'Drangheta in Calabria, and the Cosa Nostra ("our thing" in English) in Palermo, organized as the "cupola" (named after a rounded roof built on top of an existing structure) to coordinate their activities. These groups control revenues of up to $70 billion annually, according to Italian prosecutors. Italy has sent thousands of soldiers to Sicily to protect magistrates and other officials against reprisals and terror bombings by organized crime figures. Organized crime groups arranged dozens of car bombings in Rome in the summer of 1993 to pressure the government to end a parliamentary investigation of its activities, but this terrorist campaign was unsuccessful.

International issues Italy has been a close ally of the United States through its participation in NATO. It played a major part in UN peacekeeping efforts in Lebanon in 1982. It plays a large role in humanitarian affairs, coordinating international relief efforts in Somalia, a former Italian colony, and in Albania.

In 1995 Italy called for its inclusion in the Contact Group, which consisted of five nations (Great Britain, France, Germany, Russia, and the United States) attempting to mediate in the war between Bosnian Muslims and Serbs, a demand rejected by other members of the group that wished to limit participation to more powerful nations. In response, Italy refused permission to the United States to deploy Stealth bombers on Italian bases, the first time Italy has rejected a military request by the United States since the creation of NATO in 1949.

SEE ALSO

Axis powers; Mussolini, Benito; North Atlantic Treaty Organization (NATO); United Nations (UN)

FURTHER READING

Hine, David. *Governing Italy*. New York: Oxford University Press, 1992.
LaPalombara, Joseph. *Democracy Italian Style*. New Haven: Yale University Press, 1987.
McCarthy, Patrick. *The Crisis of the Italian State: From the Origins of the Cold War to the Fall of Berlusconi and Beyond*. New York: St. Martin's, 1997.

Ivory Coast

REPUBLIC OF THE IVORY COAST (RÉPUBLIQUE DE LA CÔTE D'IVOIRE)

• *Capital: Yamoussoukro*

Political history The Ivory Coast is located on the west African coast. The Baulé, Bété, and Senoufou peoples had maintained independent kingdoms there until the French obtained territorial and trading privileges in 1842. It was declared a French protectorate in 1889 and was organized as a colony in 1893, then became a territory of French West Africa in 1894 and a republic in the French Union in 1948. It became an autonomous republic in the French Community in 1958, when it was the only one of the French African colonies that year to decline independence in favor of continued autonomy within the renamed French Union, a decision made by its pro-French leader Félix Houphouët-Boigny. It gained independence in 1960 when the new French government under President Charles de Gaulle decided to end France's colonial responsibilities in sub-Saharan Africa.

Government institutions The Ivory Coast has a presidential system, in which the president, elected every five years by popular vote, is the head of state and government. He appoints and chairs a council of ministers. In 1990 the constitution was amended to create the post of prime minister, who is appointed by the president. Legislative power is exercised by a 175-member elected National Assembly. There is an independent judiciary, headed by a supreme court.

Parties and movements The Ivorian one-party state transformed itself into a multiparty system when it legalized opposition parties and held the first contested presidential election in 1990, as part of the wave of democratization led by unions and university students. President Félix Houphouët-Boigny won 81 percent of the vote and his seventh consecutive term. His Democratic Party also won 163 of 175 seats in the legislature in 1990. The main opposition party is the Ivorian Popular Front, which won less than 20 percent of the vote in the 1990 presidential election.

Domestic issues The Ivory Coast has the largest per capita debt in Africa. It has been forced to reschedule its international debts because of falling prices for its coffee and cocoa exports. Austerity measures were introduced in 1990, contributing to governmental instability. The country is geographically divided between Christians and animists (who believe that spirits live in the woods and in animals) in the south and Muslims in the north, but there has been little religious conflict or other friction among the 60 different ethnic groups.

International issues
The Ivory Coast has taken a major role in attempting to mediate in the civil war in neighboring Liberia. French troops help to preserve the government from attempted coups d'état, either by its tiny military or other African governments. The Ivory Coast plays a major role in the Economic Community of West African States by economically supporting many of its activities.

Human rights The Ivory Coast League for Human Rights reported that 120 opposition members had been arrested during the 1990 elections. Internal security forces have used violence against students at the University of Abidjan protesting these arrests. Some 5,000 political prisoners were released by presidential decree in 1991. However, press censorship and the arrest of journalists critical of the president continue.

Made of wood, antelope horn, and plant fibers, this traditional mask from the Ivory Coast attests to the richness of the cultures that existed there long before European colonization.

SEE ALSO
France; French Community; French Union; French West Africa; Houphouët-Boigny, Félix

FURTHER READING
Handloff, Robert E., ed. *Côte d'Ivoire: A Country Study.* 3rd ed. Washington, D.C.: Federal Research Division, Library of Congress, 1991.
Zartman, I. William, and Christopher Delgado. *The Political Economy of the Ivory Coast.* New York: Praeger, 1984.
Zolberg, Aristide. *One-Party Government in the Ivory Coast.* Rev. ed. Princeton, N.J.: Princeton University Press, 1974.

Jamaica

• *Capital: Kingston*

Political history Located in the Caribbean Sea to the east of Cuba, Jamaica was settled around A.D. 1000 by Arawak Indians from the Antilles islands. They were decimated by disease and killed by Spanish colonialists after the discovery of the island by Christopher Columbus in 1492. The Spanish ruled the island from 1509 until 1655, when it was conquered by the English. African slaves were imported to work on sugar plantations by English settlers, who were able to defeat several slave revolts in the 17th and 18th centuries. Slavery was abolished in the 1830s, however, after public opinion turned against it in England. Afterward, the English settlers still dominated the island, using the former slaves as paid labor on the plantations.

Partial self-government was introduced in 1944 after demonstrations by Jamaican labor unions demanding it. Jamaica established its own legislature and cabinet to administer government departments. In 1958 it became a member of the West Indies Federation, an association of former British colonies in the Caribbean, and achieved complete internal self-government in 1959. Jamaica seceded from the federation in 1961, causing the federation to dissolve, and it became independent within the Commonwealth of Nations in 1962.

Government institutions Jamaica is a parliamentary democracy. The head of state is the monarch of the Commonwealth, who is represented in Jamaica by the governor-general. A prime minister, appointed by the governor-general, represents the majority party in parliament. A cabinet, appointed by the prime minister, is accountable to the parliament. In

the 21-member Senate, 13 members are appointed by the governor-general on the recommendation of the prime minister, and 8 are appointed on the recommendation of the leader of the opposition party. The 60 members of the directly elected House of Representatives serve for no more than five years before a new parliamentary election is held; members are eligible for reelection. An independent judiciary is headed by a supreme court.

Parties and movements Jamaica is a multiparty democracy. The two major parties are the People's National Party (PNP), a social democratic party, and the Jamaica Labour Party (JLP), which focuses on establishing a capitalist economy. After voting into office the JLP in 1980, Jamaicans then voted in 1989 for the return of Michael Manley to the post of prime minister; Manley was a member of the PNP who had pledged to do something about high unemployment. Though Manley resigned due to ill health, the PNP, under his successor, Percival Patterson, won a landslide victory with 52 seats in the 1993 parliamentary elections because of its populist appeals to the rural poor.

Domestic issues Jamaica suffers from a huge trade deficit and foreign debt. Attempts in the 1990s to deregulate the economy, sell off state enterprises, and introduce an austerity program have been unpopular and have

A typical British sugar plantation in Jamaica. The labor on such estates was performed by black slaves imported from Africa.

triggered urban unrest. A drop in sugar prices and declines in tourism due to increased crime have reduced island revenues. A flourishing drug trade, including the export of locally grown marijuana, has led to a rise in organized crime on the island and the corruption of some government officials.

International issues In the 1970s Jamaica had a formal policy of nonalignment but maintained close relations with Cuba when Manley was prime minister, because he was sympathetic to its socialist ideology. Since the early 1980s, it has reoriented its foreign policy and developed close ties with the United States and western Europe in order to obtain funds for investment. Jamaica has received foreign aid from the World Bank and has put into action an economic adjustment program developed with the International Monetary Fund in order to create a more stable economy.

SEE ALSO
Commonwealth of Nations

FURTHER READING
Payne, Anthony J. *Politics in Jamaica.* Rev. ed. New York: St. Martin's, 1995.

Japan

NIPPON

• *Capital: Tokyo*

Political history Located in the western Pacific Ocean just off the Asian continent, Japan has been ruled by emperors since 660 B.C. The House of Yamato, a line of imperial rulers, established a single kingdom on the islands in the 5th century A.D. The Japanese converted from pagan religions to Buddhism in the 6th century, and between the 6th and 11th centuries the islands were heavily influenced by the Chinese language, literature, and religion brought to the Japanese imperial court, which needed a written language and borrowed the Chinese calligraphy. From 1192 until 1867 governmental power was exercised by the shogun, a military warlord who relied on the samurai, or warriors, to maintain control of the population. The shogun ruled on behalf of the emperor, who had become a figurehead, isolated in the Imperial Palace.

Shogun Tokugawa Ieyasu expelled almost all European traders and Christian missionaries (except for a handful at Nagasaki) at the beginning of the 17th century, closing off Japan to the influence of the West for the next two centuries. In the 1850s U.S. commodore Matthew Perry took a naval squadron to Japan and forced the shogun to open Japan for trade. As Japan learned about the modern world and the superior military power of Western nations, and as the nobles realized that the shogun could not protect them from the West, the authority of the shogun as a military ruler became weakened.

Emperor Mutsuhito, who instituted the Meiji reign, took control of the country in 1868 in a violent revolution called the Meiji Restoration, ending the shogunate. The emperor delegated power to a group of young reformers, known as the *genro*, who directed Japan's economic and political modernization during the Meiji period. In 1871 feudal privileges of the *daimyo* (feudal lords)—such as their right to tax peasants, enforce laws, and raise a military

These badly burned survivors were about one mile from the center of the atomic bomb blast that leveled the city of Nagasaki in August 1945. They hold rice balls distributed by emergency relief workers.

force—and of the samurai were abolished in favor of a unified state dominated by a scientifically trained, Western-oriented bureaucracy. The government and industrial leaders soon made Japan into a world industrial power.

Japan then embarked on a period of territorial expansion. It fought wars with China in 1894–95 to obtain trading concessions on a par with Western nations. It fought a war with Russia in 1904–5 and defeated the Russian navy to obtain a protectorate over Korea, which it later annexed in 1909. In 1931 it invaded Manchuria, a province of China, and established the puppet state of Manchukuo.

In the 1930s Emperor Hirohito lost control of the government to a military regime headed by prime minister Tojo Hideki, who allied Japan with the other Axis powers (Nazi Germany and fascist Italy) during World War II. Japanese forces bombed the U.S. naval base at Pearl Harbor in Hawaii to prevent the United States from trying to stop their expansionist aims. They invaded a number of nations in Southeast Asia in December 1941.

Japan surrendered unconditionally to the United States in 1945 after the United States had dropped atomic bombs on Hiroshima and Nagasaki. Its defeat ended Japan's attempts at territorial expansion, and it was forced to surrender all of its South Asian possessions. Hirohito renounced his claim to divinity on August 15, 1945, as part of the peace imposed by the United States. Henceforth, the Japanese people would embody their sovereign governing power not in the emperor but in their government institutions, under a postwar constitution modeled on Western parliamentary principles.

Japan established a parliamentary democracy under the 1947 constitution, as required by its surrender terms, and the emperor was permitted by the Allies to remain on the throne as a figurehead. Japan was occupied by U.S. forces as a conquered territory but regained its sovereignty by negotiating a peace treaty with the Allied nations in 1952.

Japan rebuilt its industrial plants, which had been destroyed in the war. With government guidance and financial help, Japanese industrialists developed world-class products, especially automobiles, pharmaceuticals, consumer electronics, and computers.

By the 1990s, Japan had the second-largest industrial economy in the world, surpassed only by that of the United States in its output of technologically advanced products and gross national product.

Government institutions The emperor is the head of state but has no governing power. The prime minister runs the government and is appointed by the emperor after being designated by parliament. The prime minister appoints the other ministers of the cabinet. Legislative power is vested in the bicameral parliament, called the Diet, consisting of the 500-member House of Representatives, directly elected for a four-year term, and the 252-member House of Councillors. The members of the House of Councillors serve terms that last six years, with half elected every three years. Rules governing the economy are developed by the bureaucrats in the ministries, the unelected career officials who, by virtue of their expertise and influence, are often considered more powerful than the elected politicians.

The independent judiciary consists of a chief justice and 14 other judges of the Supreme Court. The chief justice is appointed by the emperor, who follows the recommendation of the prime minister; other judges are appointed by the cabinet. Every 10 years, Supreme Court justices must be reelected.

Parties and movements Japan has a multiparty system. The Liberal Demo-

More than a half-century after U.S. atomic bombs werer dropped on Japan, Tokyo is thriving. This business district in the city is encroaching on residential areas.

cratic Party—which is actually a conservative, business-oriented party—governed Japan from 1947 through 1993, while the Social Democratic Party was the second-largest party. In 1989, as a result of a sex scandal in the Liberal Democratic Party, the Social Democratic Party won a majority in the House of Councillors for the first time. In 1993, as a result of high-level corruption scandals within the Liberal Democratic Party, it fragmented, and many of its younger members broke away into smaller factions and parties. In June of that year the government fell after a vote of no confidence. In the legislative elections that followed, the Liberal Democratic Party lost control of the parliament by 33 seats, and a weak government consisting of a coalition of reform parties was formed. The Social Democratic Party, also hit by scandals, lost half its parliamentary seats to minor parties.

Japanese politics remains dominated by conservative parties, but they are splintering. The Japan Renewal Party, an offshoot of the Liberals, became a major third party in Japanese politics in the early 1990s. Other new conservative parties include the Japan New Party, the Harbinger Party, and the Clean Govern-

ment Party. In 1994 the Liberal Democratic Party, Social Democratic Party, and Harbinger Party formed a coalition government, headed by Tomichi Murayama, the first Social Democratic prime minister in Japan; most of the cabinet ministers were Liberal Democrats. In opposition was the Innovation Party. In 1994 Japan approved structural reforms to limit corporate financing of political parties.

Although the 1994 coalition of Social Democrats and Liberals was able to form a parliamentary majority, it soon fell and a new reform cabinet excluding the Social Democrats formed. It, too, was unable to maintain support in the parliament.

In January 1996 the Liberal Democratic leader, Kyutaro Hashimoto, was elected prime minister by parliament to head a coalition government. In September 1996 Hashimoto and the Liberal Democrats won a large victory in parliamentary elections. It was a triumph for his party and signaled the end of the reformist period that had, for three years, fragmented the existing parties. The main opposition party after 1996 was the New Frontier Party, a reformist coalition in which Social Democrats and

Communists were becoming insignificant, as the leftist parties were virtually wiped out.

Domestic issues The extensive corruption in Japanese politics, which involves links among organized crime, political leaders, and corporate executives, caused a crisis of confidence in Japan in the 1990s. Although Japan is a racially homogeneous society, there is a cultural split between those who lived through World War II and then participated in Japanese reconstruction (by saving money and working hard in order to make Japan's factories and businesses productive again) and the younger postwar generation, which is more interested in participating in a consumer society and in spending money to achieve a higher standard of living.

By the mid-1990s the Japanese economy was stalled, with growth rates for businesses lower than at any time since World War II. The result was widespread dissatisfaction with traditional politicians, resulting in major upheavals in the party system, the election of several unaffiliated candidates to run Japanese cities, and the beginning of a period (1993–96) of weak coalition governments and revolving-door prime ministers, who served for short periods of time with little public support.

International issues In 1947, as part of the post–World War II peace settlement, Japan renounced militarism. Article 9 of its "peace constitution" forbade the establishment of armed forces. Nevertheless, while technically adhering to the agreement, Japan has one of the largest military forces in the world, known as the Self-Defense Forces, though it does not have aircraft carriers, ballistic missiles, or nuclear weapons. Because of constitutional prohibitions, Japan has not sent troops on military or peacekeeping missions outside Japan. In 1992, it did send troops to Cambodia to help monitor UN-supervised elections. UN secretary-general Boutros Boutros-Ghali later called on Japan to amend its constitution to allow its forces to be used in peacekeeping missions, especially if it expects to gain a seat on the UN Security Council.

Japan served as a staging area for U.S. forces during the Korean War, and since 1955 it has had a defense treaty with the United States that has made it one of the major allies of the United States against the Soviet Union and China during the cold war. Japan provided billions of dollars to the U.S.-led coalition during the 1991 Persian Gulf War.

Japan, since the 1950s, has restricted imports in order to maintain a strong balance of trade. This policy is implemented through rules developed by the bureaucracy, such as prohibitions or restrictions on rice imports, and through the practices of Japanese corporations, such as the policy of favoring domestic over foreign producers when buying parts to produce automobile or consumer electronics, for example. Japan's huge favorable balance of trade with other industrial nations has caused friction with the United States and western Europe, because those countries are eager to export their goods into the Japanese markets. The Japanese and U.S. governments have agreed on the principle of opening up Japanese markets, but they often disagree on the precise measures to achieve this, and the Japanese have refused to set import goals favored by the United States.

Japan still relies on the United States to provide for its military security, especially given North Korea's efforts in the mid-1990s to develop atomic weapons. The United States agreed in 1995 to return some military bases on the island of Okinawa to Japan, bowing to the wishes of local inhabitants. Issues involving

Okinawa are resolved between the United States and Japan by the Special Action Committee on Okinawa, consisting of diplomats and military officers from both nations. The governor of Okinawa, Masahide Ota, called in 1996 for the removal of all U.S. forces on the island by 2015.

Japan is a major investor in China, though a territorial dispute involving five islands in the East China Sea remains an irritant. Japan has insisted that Russia return part of an island chain off the eastern coast of the island of Hokkaido (which Russia occupied in 1945 at the end of World War II). Japan has held up foreign aid to Russia until its territorial dispute is resolved.

Japan has apologized to South Korea for war crimes committed by Japanese occupation troops during World War II, but it has declared that its annexation of Korea in 1910 was legal and not forced on Koreans, a position that South Korea rejects. In 1995 Prime Minister Tomichi Murayama grudgingly apologized to Southeast Asian nations for aggression in World War II, in which up to 10 million people were killed by Japanese atrocities. The apologies were not acceptable to many of these nations, yet even these mild sentiments were protested by right-wing nationalists in Japan who believed that Japan had been justified in its harsh military actions and denied that the military had committed atrocities. China has insisted that Japan compensate it for injuries suffered during World War II, but Japan has responded that all claims were deemed settled in 1972 when China and Japan exchanged diplomatic recognition.

Japan's conduct during World War II has remained an obstacle for it in developing close relations with its neighbors.

Human rights The ethnic Korean minority in Japan suffers discrimination in employment and housing and is not integrated into Japanese society.

SEE ALSO

Axis powers; China; Cold war; Hirohito; Russia; Tojo Hideki

FURTHER READING

Buckley, Roger. *Japan Today*. 2nd ed. New York: Cambridge University Press, 1990.

Dolan, Ronald E., and Robert L. Worden, eds. *Japan: A Country Study*. 5th ed. Washington, D.C.: Federal Research Division, Library of Congress, 1992.

McNeil, Frank. *Democracy in Japan: The Emerging Global Concern*. New York: Crown, 1994.

Reischauer, Edwin O. *Japan: The Story of a Nation*. 4th ed. New York: McGraw-Hill, 1990.

Reischauer, Edwin O., and Marius B. Jansen. *The Japanese Today*. Enlarged ed. Cambridge: Harvard University Press, 1995.

Jihad

Jihad is the term for any struggle, peaceful or violent, to defend or expand the Islamic religion. Jihad is an individual religious duty for every male Muslim, because Muslims consider Islam to be a universal religion that will eventually be adopted by all peoples of the world. Peace with non-Muslim states is considered temporary, until they submit to what Muslims define as the will of God, so jihad is also the duty of the Islamic states. However, Christians, Jews, and followers of other monotheistic religions who have submitted to the sovereignty of Islamic states are not subject to jihad. Moreover, jihad is not required in cases in which an infidel (non-Muslim) power is militarily superior; in such cases Muslims may temporarily suspend hostilities and even pay tribute for their survival, as Muslim peoples in Caucasia and in the Middle East did in the 19th century to the Russian and British empires.

In modern times the term *jihad* has been used by Muslims and non-Muslims alike to refer to nationalist movements struggling against colonial powers, as in the struggles for independence in the Sudan and Egypt from the 1880s to the 1950s. It is also used to refer to a "holy war"—that is, one based on religious differences—by one state against another. The term is often used to refer to conflicts between Arab states and Israel, although strictly speaking these have been secular conflicts over territory and not religious conflicts over the truth of beliefs.

Resistance fighters in Afghanistan after the 1979 Soviet invasion called their struggle jihad; the Ayatollah Khomeini said he was waging jihad after he assumed control of Iran in 1979; and Islamic fundamentalists struggling against Israeli occupation of the West Bank in the 1990s claimed to be engaged in jihad. Jihad cannot be waged between Muslim states because, according to Islam, armed conflict between Muslims is unlawful (though it does occur).

SEE ALSO

Afghanistan; Iran; Islamic fundamentalism; Israel; Khomeini, Ayatollah Ruhollah Mussavi

FURTHER READING

Armstrong, Karen. *Holy War.* London: Macmillan, 1988.

John Paul II

- *Born: May 18, 1920, Wadowice, Poland*

As pope of the Roman Catholic Church and head of the Vatican city-state, John Paul II played a major role in the undermining of communist authoritarian states in Eastern Europe during the 1980s and in the defeat of the Soviet Union in the cold war. Born Karol Wojtyla, he was ordained as a priest in 1946 after working as a factory laborer. He was then educated in philosophy at the Jagiellonian University in Cracow and at the Angelicum Academy in Rome, and he served as a professor of ethics and moral theology at Lublin and Cracow Universities between 1953 and 1958. He became archbishop of Cracow in 1963 and was elevated to cardinal by Pope Paul VI in 1967. The College of Cardinals elected Karol Wojtyla pope on October 16, 1978, on the eighth ballot. He was the first non-Italian pope to be elected since 1523 and the first from Poland.

Pope John Paul II has traveled all over the world, preaching respect for the natural rights of people to exercise political liberty and live in conditions of decency. In accordance with the precepts of Christian Democracy, he has called for a greater commitment to alleviating the poverty and misery of the poor, especially in Third World nations. In the 1990s he condemned what he saw as excesses of market capitalism in Western Europe and the United States, especially their materialism and failure to provide adequately for the poor. During the cold war he was a strong opponent of communist rule, especially in Eastern Europe, where the Roman Catholic Church was instrumental in efforts to subvert and then overthrow communist governments. The pope, for example, appointed clerics to the churches in Eastern European nations who spoke out against communist abuses of power and helped organize cultural and educational groups—some of which were required to meet in secret—to undermine the legitimacy of the communist regimes. The pope has encouraged an interfaith dialogue between Jews and Catholics in order to reduce friction and misunderstandings, and he has apologized for the conduct of the Catholic clergy in the past in promoting or tolerating anti-Semitism.

Pope John Paul II has been one of the most influential leaders of the Catholic Church in modern times. His influence has been especially great in eastern Europe, particularly in his homeland of Poland.

On social issues, Pope John Paul II is a strong opponent of abortion and sexual permissiveness, following the ideas of the conservative wing of the church on these and other issues, such as maintaining the requirement of celibacy for priests. His efforts in Italy were repudiated in 1981 . when two-thirds of the Italian electorate voted to keep abortion rights.

In the 1990s the pope traveled extensively in many parts of the world, attempting to interest young people in the Christian message by holding huge rallies. His 1995 tour of sub-Saharan Africa was designed to reorient the African Catholic churches toward African traditions and away from European rites.

John Paul II was the target of an assassination attempt in 1981. He was wounded by Mehmet Ali Agca, a Turk whom Italian authorities believed was working for the Bulgarian secret service in an attempt to end the pope's activities in encouraging resistance to communist rule in Eastern Europe.

SEE ALSO
Vatican City

FURTHER READING

John Paul II. *Be Not Afraid*. New York: St. Martin's, 1984.
Szulc, Tad. *Pope John Paul II: The Biography*. New York: Scribner, 1995.
Wynn, Wilton. *Keepers of the Keys: John XXIII, Paul VI, and John Paul II, Three Who Changed the Church*. New York: Random House, 1988.

Johnson, Lyndon Baines

- *Born: Aug. 27, 1908, near Stonewall, Texas*
- *Died: Jan. 22, 1973, Johnson City, Texas*

Lyndon Johnson, the 36th president of the United States, took office in 1963 upon the assassination of John Kennedy. He expanded the role of the federal government in social welfare programs through the War on Poverty and other Great Society programs. He escalated the U.S. military commitment in Vietnam, and his failure to explain the need for such a commitment to the American people destroyed his credibility and, with it, his presidency.

Johnson grew up in Johnson City, Texas, which was named for his grandfather. He was educated at Southwest Texas State Teachers College, graduating in 1930. He served in the U.S. House of Representatives from 1938 to 1949, then in the U.S. Senate from 1949 to 1961. He was Kennedy's vice president from 1961 until Kennedy's assassination on November 22, 1963. Johnson then won the presidency in his own right in 1964 in a landslide victory over Republican opponent Barry Goldwater.

Between 1964 and 1966 Johnson won passage of many of his domestic programs in Congress. These included a civil rights act and voting rights act to end legal discrimination against African Americans, a federal aid to education act, health-care reimbursement for the aged and poor, new urban programs (including the establishment of the Department of Urban Affairs), a tax cut that sparked economic growth, and the establishment of the Department of Transportation.

Johnson was a consummate politician: he played poker with legislative leaders, constantly cajoled them, wheeled and dealed into the early morning hours, and lobbied personally with recalcitrant members. Nevertheless, Johnson never felt accepted by the eastern liberal Democrats who had supported his predecessor: "What do they want, what do they really want?"

President Lyndon B. Johnson greets U.S. troops in Vietnam. The U.S. involvement in Vietnam undermined Johnson's social programs at home, which were the most ambitious since Franklin Roosevelt's New Deal.

he once asked an aide. "I am giving them more liberal legislation than any president since Franklin Roosevelt, and all they can do is complain."

In foreign affairs, Johnson was an interventionist who was willing to use force against leftist and communist regimes. In August 1964, after reports of attacks on U.S. naval vessels in the Gulf of Tonkin, off the coast of Vietnam, he asked Congress for a resolution authorizing him to take all necessary measures to protect U.S. armed forces. Soon thereafter, in spite of his promise that "we seek no wider war," he escalated U.S. involvement in the area, first by ordering the bombing of North Vietnam in the winter of 1965. He then ordered U.S. troops into combat in the spring, then increased the troops to 100,000 by the fall, and finally placed more than half a million troops in the country by the end of 1966.

Johnson ordered officials in his administration to make no announcements about the escalations and denied that additional troops represented any change in policy. His deception led critics to charge his administration with a "credibility gap," and support for his policies dropped. His own party was deeply divided about his conduct of the war. Johnson railed

against critics of his own party, telling his aides about one such opponent that "the next time Senator Church wants a dam for Idaho, he can go ask [Vietnamese communist leader] Ho Chi Minh."

In February 1968 the North Vietnamese launched the Tet Offensive in Saigon and other cities. Americans watched television images of the U.S. embassy under siege, and public support for the war dropped sharply. In March, Johnson barely defeated an antiwar Democratic challenger in the New Hampshire presidential primary, and he withdrew from the race on March 31. He also announced a temporary halt in the bombing of North Vietnam in an attempt to seek peace. But the war continued with no letup on the ground, and U.S. casualties passed the 40,000 mark. "I can't get out, I can't finish it with what I have got. So what the hell do I do?" Johnson asked his wife, Lady Bird.

Johnson retired in 1969 to his ranch near Johnson City, Texas. He died of a heart attack on January 22, 1973, just one day before the signing of the Paris Peace Accords by Richard Nixon's administration that ended U.S. involvement in the Vietnam War.

SEE ALSO

Kennedy, John F.; Nixon, Richard Milhous; Vietnam

FURTHER READING

Dallek, Robert. *Flawed Giant: Lyndon Johnson and His Times, 1961–1973.* New York: Oxford University Press, 1998.

Dallek, Robert. *Lone Star Rising: Lyndon Johnson and His Times, 1908–1960.* New York: Oxford University Press, 1991.

Johnson, Lyndon. *The Vantage Point: Perspectives of the Presidency, 1963–1969.* New York: Holt, Rinehart & Winston, 1971.

Kearns, Doris. *Lyndon Johnson and the American Dream.* New York: Harper & Row, 1976.

Jordan

HASHEMITE KINGDOM OF JORDAN (AL MAMLAKA AL URDUNIYAH AL HASHIMIYAH)

- *Capital: Amman*

Political history Located just north of the Arabian Peninsula and to the east of the Jordan River, Jordan is a landlocked nation. The area was part of the Roman province of Palestine at the time of Christ, and in the 6th century it was part of the Byzantine Empire. It was conquered by the Arabs in the 7th century A.D., when the people converted from paganism or Christianity to Islam. A succession of Muslim rulers based in what is now Iraq, Iran, and Egypt controlled the territory at various times for the next 1,000 years. It became part of the Ottoman Empire in the 16th century.

In 1921 Abdullah, the son of Husayn ibn ʻAlī, the ruler of the Hejaz (kingdom) of Saudi Arabia, became the emir, or king, of the territory called the Emirate of Transjordan, on the eastern side of the Jordan River. He was installed as emir by the British as a reward for Arab assistance against the Ottoman Empire during World War I.

In 1946 Transjordan became the independent Hashemite Kingdom of Jordan, named after its Hashemite ruling house. Four years later, after the first Arab-Israeli war of 1948, Jordan annexed the West Bank territories in Palestine, which the United Nations had originally assigned to a Palestinian Arab state. (That state had never come into existence.) The following year, King Abdullah was assassinated by a Palestinian refugee to protest Hashemite rule over the West Bank. He was succeeded for a year by his eldest son Talal, who abdicated in 1952 in favor of his son Hussein, who became king.

Jordan joined in the Arab Federation with Iraq in 1958, but after the overthrow of the Iraqi monarchy that year, the federation ended. Jordan lost the West Bank territories in 1967 after its defeat by Israel in the Six-Day War. Israel annexed East Jerusalem and kept the other territories of the West Bank under military occupation. Jordan in 1969 gave up all claims to these territories in favor of the Palestine Liberation Organization, though its financial and commercial enterprises are active in the West Bank. More than 1 million Palestinian refugees from Israel and the West Bank territories live in Jordan. Combined with Palestinians already in Jordan, they have given the kingdom a Palestinian majority.

Government institutions Until the 1990s Jordan was ruled in an authoritarian fashion by King Hussein, who did not allow the parliament to meet between 1974 and 1984. Since then, the cabinet of ministers has become accountable both to the monarch and to parliament and cannot remain if parliament votes it out of office.

Executive power is held by the king, who governs with the assistance of an appointed council of ministers. Legislative power is vested in a bicameral National Assembly. The 30 members of the Senate are appointed by the king for four-year terms. The 80-member House of Representatives is directly elected for four-year terms.

The independent judiciary is headed by the Court of Cassation, consisting of seven judges. It reviews cases decided by the Court of Appeals, which has three judges. Cases are tried by civil and criminal Courts of First Instance. Magistrate's courts for the Muslim, Eastern Orthodox, Catholic, and Prot-

Palestinian refugee children attend classes at a camp inside Jordan in 1957. Today, a large majority of Jordan's population is Palestinian.

estant communities deal with family law. Disputes between religious courts, or between civil and religious courts, are resolved by a special tribunal appointed by the president of the highest court, the Court of Cassation.

Parties and movements King Hussein banned political parties in 1963. In 1971 Jordan became a one-party state, with the Arab National Union, a group supporting the monarchy and its pro-Western orientation, the only party permitted. The king and the main political movements signed a charter in June 1991 that legalized parties in return for their acceptance of the constitution and monarchy. However, movements linked to or financed by other Arab nations are banned.

After the 1992 elections, the Muslim Brotherhood, an Islamic fundamentalist group, controlled more seats in the Jordanian parliament than any other party. In the 1994 elections the Islamic Action Front, another fundamentalist party, lost almost half of its seats, however, in a vote widely interpreted to endorse the king's peace policies toward Israel.

Domestic issues More than 1.7 million Palestinians have immigrated

to the East Bank of Jordan in three waves of immigration (1948, 1967–70, 1973–75), and these constitute between one-third and one-half of the population of the nation. Along with Palestinians already on the East Bank, they make up the majority of Jordan's population. In 1970 the Jordanian army put down a revolt by the Palestine Liberation Organization that attempted to topple the monarchy and convert Jordan into a Palestinian state.

The loss of the West Bank to Israel after the Six-Day War of 1967 was a staggering blow to the Jordanian economy, but in the 1970s and 1980s the high price of oil and the lucrative transshipping of goods to Iraq helped fuel a boom. As the price of its support for Iraq during the 1991 Persian Gulf War, Jordan has lost much foreign aid and trade, while it has taken in hundreds of thousands of Palestinian refugees from the Gulf nations. Inflation and economic depression have caused several cabinets to fall. The monarchy has responded with political liberalization policies—including free elections and the encouragement of party formation—designed to defuse discontent. In the 1994 elections voters shunned Islamic and leftist parties, leaving parliament in the hands of a centrist bloc strongly supportive of the king's reforms.

International issues Since the 1950s Jordan has been allied with the United States and Great Britain. These nations protected the monarchy in the aftermath of the overthrow of the Iraqi monarchy, also descended from the Saudi Hashemites, in 1957. In the 1980s Jordan sided with its fellow Arab state Iraq in the war against non-Arab Iran, and it refused to join the allied coalition against Iraq in the Persian Gulf War, because King Hussein feared that if he did, Iraq might try to end his rule by inciting pro-Iraqi street demonstrations or an assassination plot.

Jordan resumed close relations with the United States in 1993, as it began participating in Middle East peace talks with Israel. In 1995 Jordan and Israel signed a treaty that ended the state of war that had existed between the two nations since 1948. The pact confirmed the Jordanian role as guardian of sacred Islamic shrines in Jerusalem, in particular the Dome of the Rock and the Al Aksa Mosque, which together constitute the third holiest site in the Muslim religion—it is said that from there Allah ascended to heaven. In 1995 Jordan ended its close ties with Iraq when it gave refuge to several high-ranking opponents of Saddam Hussein's regime. In 1996 Jordan restored close relations with Saudi Arabia and the Gulf states as a result of its hard line against Iraq.

SEE ALSO

Iraq; Islamic fundamentalism; Palestine Liberation Organization (PLO)

FURTHER READING

Metz, Helen Chapin, ed. *Jordan: A Country Study*. 4th ed. Washington, D.C.: Federal Research Division, Library of Congress, 1991.

Satloff, Robert B. *From Abdullah to Hussein: Jordan in Transition*. New York: Oxford University Press, 1994.

Wilson, Rodney. *Politics and the Economy in Jordan*. London: Routledge, 1991.

Junta

A junta is a group of military officers who take power through a coup d'état.

A junta proclaims martial law or a state of emergency and organizes itself under a name such as "Supreme Governing Council" or "Emergency Council of State." It dissolves the parliament and may substitute military courts for civilian courts of law while the state of emergency exists. The junta usually appoints a civilian council of ministers or a cabinet to implement its policies, which the junta or council then enacts by decree.

Juntas are inherently unstable. Their members struggle for power, other officers plot new coups, and banned political parties begin resistance movements. Most juntas, such as those in Argentina and Brazil in the 1970s, find it impossible to run the economy successfully because they have no experience in managing a modern economy, resulting in a loss of foreign investment due to the unsettled political climate and the restiveness of industrial workers and peasants. Eventually, a junta gives way to a dictator or reluctantly restores civilian rule, usually under pressure from foreign governments, international organizations, and development agencies.

Between the 1970s and 1990s juntas and military regimes have given way to democracies throughout Latin America, as well as in Greece. In the Soviet Union, a junta attempted to seize power in 1991 but failed when the Russian people rallied behind Russian president Boris Yeltsin and insisted on the restoration of the existing civilian leadership.

SEE ALSO

Coup d'état; Military regime

FURTHER READING

Finer, Samuel E. *The Man on Horseback: The Role of the Military in Politics*. 2nd ed. Boulder, Colo.: Westview, 1988.

Kashmir

Kashmir is a predominantly Muslim area in the northwestern part of the Indian subcontinent. When India and Pakistan achieved independence from the United Kingdom in 1947, Kashmir became a battleground between them. After the armistice lines were drawn, each nation occupied about two-fifths of the territory, with the last fifth, in the northeast, held by China. Ongoing disputes between India and Pakistan over the area have led to wars between these two nations, and tensions remained high in the 1990s.

Since 1990 the Hezbul *Mujaheddin* guerrillas, a fundamentalist Islamic group, have fought a war for Pakistan's annexation of Kashmir, using as their base the Pakistani-controlled area called Azad Kashmir. The guerrillas have been joined by several hundred Afghans from the Hezb-i-Islami party, a group of *Mujaheddin* that fought against occupying troops from the Soviet Union in the 1980s. The Jammu and Kashmir Liberation Front, another Islamic group, calls for complete independence but does not favor imposition of Islamic law. More than 20,000 civilians were killed in the conflict between 1990 and 1995.

India instituted direct central government rule over its sector, known as Jammu and Kashmir, between 1990 and 1996. After the pro-Indian National Conference Party won 54 of 81 parliamentary seats in the state elections in October 1996, the Indian government restored local rule.

The 300,000 members of the Indian Border Security Force in Kashmir have systematically destroyed villages believed to harbor guerrillas, fired on unarmed demonstrators, and tortured Muslim militants. Several human rights activists who have protested these actions have been mur-

dered by death squads. Asia Watch, a human rights group, has condemned the behavior of the Indian forces, as well as the guerrilla assassinations of civil servants, police, educators, and journalists. The destruction by Indian security forces in 1995 of the mausoleum of Kashmir's patron saint, Sheikh Nooruddin Wali, along with an adjacent mosque built in 1460 and much of the town of Charar-e-Sharief, further inflamed nationalist passions.

In retaliation for Pakistani support of Kashmir guerrillas, India has given support to its own rebels in the Pakistan city of Karachi, known in India as the "K for K" policy.

SEE ALSO

India; Islamic fundamentalism; Pakistan

FURTHER READING

Gargan, Edward. "Where Violence Has Silenced Verse." *New York Times Magazine,* November 22, 1992, 46–50.
Schofield, Victoria. *Kashmir in the Crossfire.* New York: St. Martin's, 1996.
Wirsing, Robert. *India, Pakistan, and the Kashmir Dispute.* New York: St. Martin's, 1994.

The state of Jammu and Kashmir, at India's northern tip, is the site of ongoing disputes between India and Pakistan.

Kazakhstan

*REPUBLIC OF KAZAKHSTAN
(KAZAK RESPUBLIKASY)*

- *Capital: Almaty (will move to Akmola in 2000)*

Political history Located in central Asia south of Russia, Kazakhstan was in ancient times successively conquered by Persians, Mongols, and Turkic tribes. The Kazakhs, a Muslim group from the Mongol Golden Horde (a set of tribes that swept westward from Mongolia to conquer much of central Asia and southeastern Europe) took control in the 16th century. In the 18th century Russia dominated the Kazakhs, and in 1731 it incorporated the area into the Russian Empire. In the 19th century, Russian colonists populated the area and began farming. In 1916 the Kazakhs were defeated in an uprising against Russian colonization and rule. After the Russian Revolution of 1917, Kazakhstan was incorporated into the Russian Republic. It became independent as a separate Soviet republic within the Soviet Union in 1936. Russian rule and domination had brought the end of the nomadic tribal society, and as many as 2 million Kazakhs were killed when they resisted the policy of the Soviet government to collectivize the land—that is, to have it farmed by large groups who held the land in common.

In 1991, upon the breakup of the Soviet Union, Kazakhstan declared its sovereignty and became a founding member of the Commonwealth of Independent States.

Government institutions Until 1991 Kazakhstan was governed by a Supreme Soviet, the legislature whose local Communist Party members took orders from the party leaders in Moscow. In 1991 a presidential system was adopted. The president, elected by popular vote, must be a fluent Kazakh speaker. The prime minister is elected by the parliament, which consists of a 47-member Senate (with 2 deputies from each region and 7 appointed by the president) and the Assembly (Majlis), which has 67 popularly elected deputies from single-member districts. The prime minister presides over a council of ministers, which runs the government.

The judiciary is supervised by the government. It consists of district courts and a supreme court whose members are chosen by the president and confirmed by the parliament. A constitutional council, consisting of seven members (three appointed by the president and four by the parliament), ensures that laws passed by parliament conform to the constitution.

Parties and movements Following the August 1991 attempted military coup in the Soviet Union, the Communist Party in Kazakhstan broke with the Communist Party of the Soviet Union, and it was suspended by the Soviet government from participation in Kazakh politics. It was reinstated in 1994 but has become a minority party in Kazakhstan. The People's Unity Party,

A young sheepherder rides the range in Kazakhstan. Like several other Central Asian countries that were once part of the Soviet Union, Kazakhstan has recently become a center of great international interest because of the vast potential wealth it contains in the form of oil deposits.

a nationalist movement composed largely of former Communists, is the largest, having won the March 1994 legislative elections. Kazakhstan is still dominated by former Communists, led by President Nursultan Nazarbayev, head of the People's Unity Party, and there has yet to be a transformation to a multiparty system, though there is a nationalist opposition Republican Party. Nazarbayev ran unopposed in 1991, and in 1995 he won a referendum extending his rule until the year 2000.

Domestic issues There are growing ethnic tensions between Kazakhs and the Russians, each constituting about 40 percent of the population (the remainder consists of various central Asian groups). The Russians are located in the north, in the large cities and in Almaty, while the Kazakhs live in rural areas and the south. The government is firmly under the control of the Kazakhs, and Russians are gradually emigrating.

Economic policy involves granting concessions for oil and gas exploration to Russia and Western companies in the Tengiz fields, which may hold 15 billion to 50 billion barrels of oil, and capitalizing and privatizing state enterprises (many of them previously dominated by Russians) involved in mining chrome, silver, coal, tungsten, lead, zinc, and bauxite.

Popular demonstrations against nuclear testing have led to the closing of nuclear test facilities formerly used by the Soviet Union.

International issues Kazakhstan maintains close economic ties with Russia, which relies on Kazakh grain, cotton, coal and metals, though Kazakhstan has refused to consider ceding land to Russia. The two nations are cooperating in the exploitation of the Tengiz oil fields.

Kazakhstan has established close economic ties with nations of western Europe and the United States as well as with South Korea and Japan in an effort to attract foreign investment. Close cultural relations exist with Turkey, because Turkish is linguistically similar to the Kazakh language.

Kazakhstan accepted $85 million from the United States to dismantle its nuclear weapons, in accordance with disarmament agreements between the United States and the Commonwealth of Independent States. The United States has also provided the Kazakhs with economic assistance since their independence, in an effort to create a favorable investment climate for U.S. oil companies.

To ensure against possible Russian territorial claims in the north, President Nazarbayev in 1995 made plans to move the capital from Almaty to the northern industrial city of Akmola by 2000.

SEE ALSO
Commonwealth of Independent States (CIS); Russia; Russian Revolution; Soviet Union (Union of Soviet Socialist Republics); Turkey

FURTHER READING
Mandelbaum, Michael. *The Rise of Nations in the Soviet Union.* New York: Council on Foreign Relations, 1991.
Motyl, Alexander. *The Post Soviet Nations.* New York: Columbia University Press, 1992.
Olcott, Martha B. *The Kazakhs.* Stanford, Calif.: Hoover Institution Press, 1987.
"Quiet Protest." *Economist,* Nov. 30, 1996.

Kennedy, John F.

- *Born: May 29, 1917, Brookline, Massachusetts*
- *Died: Nov. 22, 1963, Dallas, Texas*

John F. Kennedy, the 35th president of the United States (1961–63), alternately confronted the Soviet Union and negotiated with it in order to moderate superpower rivalry in the cold war; in domestic affairs he promised a New Frontier that would institute liberal social policies in education, welfare, and civil rights.

Kennedy came from a family active in Democratic politics; his father was a financier and former chairman of the U.S. Securities and Exchange Commission during Franklin Roosevelt's administration. Kennedy graduated from Harvard in 1940 and enlisted in the navy in 1941. On August 2, 1943, his patrol boat, *PT 109*, was sunk by the Japanese destroyer *Amigari*. Kennedy helped to rescue his 10 crew members and was awarded the U.S. Navy and Marine Corps Medal and a Purple Heart for his injuries. Because he was considered a war hero, Kennedy won election to the House of Representatives in 1946, was reelected twice, and was elected to the Senate from Massachusetts in 1952.

In 1960 Kennedy won the presidency. "Ask not what your country can do for you," Kennedy said in his inaugural address, "ask what you can do for your country." He challenged America's youthful idealists to join the Peace Corps, an organization of volunteers providing technical assistance to developing nations, which he created by executive order a few weeks later. He got Congress to create the Alliance for Progress in Latin America to provide foreign aid to developing nations there. He created an arms-control agency to pursue arms limitations talks with the Soviet Union. At Kennedy's urging, Congress passed a trade expansion act that significantly increased U.S. exports and opened up foreign markets. He pledged that an American would land on the moon by the end of the decade and greatly expanded the space program.

Kennedy's foreign policy emphasized militant anticommunism. In his inaugural address he laid down the gauntlet to communists: "Let every nation

John F. Kennedy brought a sense of youthful vibrancy and national purpose to American political life.

know, whether it wishes us well or ill, that we shall pay any price, bear any burden, meet any hardship, support any friend, oppose any foe to assure the survival and the success of liberty."

Kennedy approved a covert Central Intelligence Agency plan to topple Fidel Castro, the communist leader of Cuba. On April 17, 1961, some 1,500 Cuban exiles landed at the Bay of Pigs in Cuba, hoping to spark an uprising. They were surrounded and defeated by the Cuban army. At the last minute, Kennedy refused to provide them with air cover for their operation in order to avoid overt U.S. involvement. He later accepted full responsibility for the fiasco, noting that "victory has a hundred fathers, but defeat is an orphan." The 1,100 prisoners held by Castro were ransomed back to the United States for $53 million in food and medical supplies.

After East Germany constructed the Berlin Wall to seal off the communist side of the city from the West in August 1961, Kennedy traveled to Berlin to show solidarity with its citizens, proclaiming in German, "Ich bin ein Berliner," meaning to say "I am a Berliner" but actually saying "I am a pastry" (a Berliner was a popular piece of cake in the city). Nevertheless, the citizens of Berlin were cheered by his presence.

In October 1962 Kennedy found out that the Soviet Union had shipped offensive missiles and bombers to Cuba; after quarantining the island with U.S. naval forces, he insisted that the Soviets remove their offensive forces. Following a tense standoff they did so, after Kennedy secretly agreed to remove U.S. missiles based in Turkey as a reciprocal gesture. In August 1963 Kennedy and Soviet leader Nikita Khrushchev agreed to defuse some cold war tensions by signing a treaty banning atmospheric tests of nuclear weapons. This test ban significantly reduced levels of radioactive fallout, which had presented a health hazard around the world, especially to young children.

In 1961 Kennedy ordered U.S. military advisers and trainers—18,000 in all—to South Vietnam in order to prop up its pro-American government against attempts by communist guerrillas to undermine and overthrow it. He hoped to avoid sending in U.S. combat troops against the communists. The U.S. military advisers were unable to stabilize the South Vietnamese regime, and U.S. intelligence officials encouraged South Vietnamese military units to overthrow President Ngo Dinh Diem and install a new military leader. Although Kennedy hoped the new regime would improve the situation, the November 1, 1963, coup began a prolonged period of instability in South Vietnam that all but ensured that U.S. troops would be needed for the war.

Kennedy's New Frontier domestic program was designed to spur economic growth through tax credits for new investment by businesses. He called for federal funds for education, mass transit, public housing, job training, and a pro-

gram of regional development for Appalachia, an impoverished rural area of the South. Much of this legislation was stalled in Congress by a coalition of conservative Democrats and Republicans, though Congress did pass an increase in the minimum wage, higher Social Security benefits, and a public housing bill.

Kennedy sent troops to the University of Mississippi and University of Alabama in 1961 to ensure that African-American students could enroll (under federal court order) in spite of opposition from the governors of these states. Kennedy introduced civil rights legislation in late spring 1963 to guarantee blacks the right to use public accommodations such as restaurants and hotels, and the bill was eventually passed by Congress the following year.

On November 22, 1963, while visiting Dallas, Texas, to help unify the feuding state Democrats, John Kennedy was shot and killed by two bullets while riding in a motorcade through the center of town. He was succeeded by his vice president, Lyndon Baines Johnson.

Generally regarded as Kennedy's major achievement is the fact that his presidency began the transition from an era of confrontation to an era of negotiation in the cold war. Kennedy was the first president born in the 20th century; his youth, his vigor, his wit, and above all his style (defined by some as grace under pressure) created a "Camelot on the Potomac."

SEE ALSO

Alliance for Progress; Cold war; Castro, Fidel; Cuba; Johnson, Lyndon Baines; Khrushchev, Nikita Sergeyevich; Peace Corps; Soviet Union (Union of Soviet Socialist Republics); Vietnam

FURTHER READING

Mills, Judie. *John F. Kennedy*. New York: Franklin Watts, 1988.
Parmet, Herbert. *J.F.K.: The Presidency of John F. Kennedy*. New York: Dial, 1983.
Randall, Marta. *John F. Kennedy*. New York: Chelsea House, 1988.

Reeves, Richard. *President Kennedy: Profile of Power.* New York: Simon & Schuster, 1993.

Schlesinger, Arthur M., Jr. *A Thousand Days: John F. Kennedy in the White House.* Boston: Houghton Mifflin, 1965.

Kenya

REPUBLIC OF KENYA (JANHURI YA KENYA)

• *Capital: Nairobi*

Political history Located in east Africa, the area now known as Kenya may have been the location of the first human settlements. In the 8th century A.D. Arab traders exported spices and slaves from the Kenyan coast, and the area was visited by Chinese and Indian ships after the year 1000. By the 1800s the Masai and Kikuyu were grazing herds when Europeans explored the area.

In 1895 the territory became the East African Protectorate of Great Britain, then a Crown Colony in 1920. Between 1952 and 1956 the Kikuyu tribe led the Mau Mau rebellion (*mau mau* is a derisive term for British farmers) against British rule. The rebellion was a success; Britain granted Kenya internal self-government early in 1963, and the nation achieved full independence at the end of the year. After decolonization, Kenya became a republic within the Commonwealth of Nations in 1964 under the leadership of its first president, Jomo Kenyatta. Since Kenyatta's death in 1978, it has become an authoritarian regime with a facade of democratic institutions under President Daniel arap Moi.

Government institutions The president, who is directly elected for five years, serves as head of state; he must amass at least 25 percent of the vote in five of the eight provinces to avoid a runoff election. The president appoints a vice president and chooses his cabinet ministers from among members of the legislature. Legislative authority is vested in the unicameral 202-member National Assembly, 185 of whose members are elected for five-year terms. Fifteen members are chosen by the president, the Speaker is elected by other members, and the attorney general serves ex officio. The president appoints a court of appeal, a high court, and district courts. The Kadhi (a district Islamic court) handles cases involving Islamic law.

Parties and movements Between 1969 and 1991 Kenya was a one-party state, with the Kenya African National Union (KANU) the sole party. In December 1991 the constitution was amended

Kenyans gather to buy and sell produce in the Nakulima market in the capital city of Nairobi.

Nairobi is one of the most cosmopolitan cities in Africa. The United Nations Environment Program—the first such program to be located in Africa—has its headquarters there.

to allow for a multiparty system. Other parties include the Forum for the Restoration of Democracy, the Kenya National Democratic Alliance Party, and the Democratic Party. In the December 1992 elections these parties won 88 of the 202 seats in parliament. Moreover, 15 of the 21 members of the president's cabinet were defeated for reelection. These electoral setbacks have led President Moi to institute authoritarian rule and harass the political opposition. In 1991 Daniel arap Moi was proclaimed by his ministers to be President for Life; in 1992, however, under pressure from Western aid donors, he ran for reelection against other candidates to demonstrate that Kenya was a democracy.

Domestic issues Kenya is split into several feuding ethnic groups fighting over territory, particularly fertile farmland. The largest group is the Kikuyu, followed by the Lubiya, Luo, Kalenjin, Kamba, Masai, and Pokot. In western Kenya, President Moi's Kalenjin tribesmen, backed by the military, have

driven more than 200,000 Kikuyu out of their villages in the fertile Rift Valley.

In the 1990s the economy performed poorly, with a severe recession, high inflation, and commodity shortages, aggravated by a severe drought. Kenyan exports, especially coffee and tea, have suffered from low prices. A pattern of extensive corruption links state enterprises and party officials, and money-laundering scandals have forced the shutdown of many banks.

Kenya agreed to an austerity program developed by the World Bank and International Monetary Fund in 1991, then scrapped the plan early in 1993 over a dispute about the pace of privatization and cuts in the bureaucracy. Tourism and foreign investments, both major contributors to the economy, have dropped sharply because of political instability. Donor aid from Western nations was suspended in 1991 to force the Moi regime to hold free democratic elections. This cost Kenya nearly $360 million in the first two years of the boycott.

International issues The United States has maintained large naval bases in Kenya, which serve as a staging area for U.S. operations in the Persian Gulf and Indian Ocean, and it has been a major foreign aid donor. U.S. ambassadors in the past exerted strong pressure on the Moi regime to hold elections.

Kenya settled a border dispute with Tanzania, to the south, and reestablished full relations in 1993. Relations with Sudan and Ethiopia have been tense due to smuggling and cattle rustling by people on both sides of the borders. Kenya has played a mediating role in attempting to help rival warlords make peace in Somalia.

Human rights The government was implicated in atrocities against Kikuyu farmers forced from their lands in the Rift Valley in 1992 and 1994 by rival tribes that supported the governing party.

In the 1992 parliamentary elections, opposition candidates complained that they could not gain access to government-controlled radio and television and that there had been fraud against them at the ballot boxes.

SEE ALSO

Commonwealth of Nations; Kenyatta, Jomo; Mau Mau

FURTHER READING

Berg-Schlosser, Dirk. *Political Stability and Development: A Comparative Analysis of Kenya, Tanzania, and Uganda.* Boulder, Colo.: Rienner, 1990.
Haugerud, Angelique. *The Culture of Politics in Modern Kenya.* New York: Cambridge University Press, 1995.

Kenyatta, Jomo

- *Born: Oct. 20, 1890, Ichawerri, Kenya*
- *Died: Aug. 22, 1978, Nairobi, Kenya*

The father of Kenyan independence and the first president of Kenya (1964–78), Jomo Kenyatta was also one of the most influential thinkers in the development of African nationalism.

Born Kamau Ngengi, Jomo Kenyatta as a young man took his last name from the Kikuyu term for "fancy belt," an item that he liked to wear. The son of a farmer from the Kikuyu tribe, he was educated at a Church of Scotland mission school. He then became a clerk for Nairobi's city government. He joined the Kikuyu Central Association, an organization of Kikuyu tribesmen, and pressed for the return of tribal lands that the British administration had seized and leased to British settlers. In 1928 he was named the association's general secre-

tary and in 1929 began editing its newspaper. Kenyatta left for England in 1931 to do postgraduate study in anthropology at the London School of Economics. In 1938 he published his dissertation as a book, *Facing Mount Kenya,* one of the first books calling for an African national movement, in which he contrasted traditional Kikuyu culture favorably with European colonial practices.

In 1946 Kenyatta returned to Kenya, and the following year he founded the Kenya African Union, which united many tribes into an independence movement. He became principal of the Teacher Training College in Nairobi in 1947, where the teachers fanned the independence movement at his urging. In 1952 he was arrested by the British colonial authorities during the Mau Mau insurrections against colonial rule, on charges that he had helped organize the rebel movement. He was sentenced to seven years at hard labor in 1953, imprisoned in 1954, and freed in 1961. Kenyatta then became president of the party called the Kenya African National Union in 1961 and led it to parliamentary victory in Kenya's first elections, which were held in 1963, the year that Britain granted internal self-government.

Kenyatta became the first president of Kenya in 1964 after its independence. In office, he was pro-Western, welcoming foreign investment, and presided over the sale of white-owned farmlands to members of the Kikuyu tribe. To consolidate his power, he converted Kenya into a one-

In November 1976, Kenyatta met with U.S. Secretary of State Henry Kissinger in Nairobi. By that time, Kenyatta was regarded as one of Africa's senior statesmen.

party authoritarian state. One opposition party was dissolved in 1964, and a second one in 1968. Because of his heritage, Kenyatta favored the Kikuyu over other ethnic groups, although he was able to contain ethnic tensions and maintain peace and prosperity in Kenya until his death because of his authority as the leader of the independence movement.

SEE ALSO

Kenya; Mau Mau

FURTHER READING

Aseka, Eric. *Jomo Kenyatta.* Nairobi: East African Educational Publishers, 1992.
Kenyatta, Jomo. *Facing Mount Kenya.* London: Heinemann, 1979.
Murray-Brown, Jeremy. *Kenyatta.* 2d ed. Boston: Allen & Unwin, 1979.
Wepman, Dennis. *Jomo Kenyatta.* New York: Chelsea House, 1985.

Kerensky, Aleksandr

- *Born: Apr. 22, 1881, Simbirsk, Russia*
- *Died: June 11, 1970, New York, New York*

Aleksandr Kerensky was the leader of the Social Revolutionary Party from 1913 to 1917 and a transitional figure between czarist rule and the communist revolution in Russia. He became prime minister of the Russian provisional government in 1917 after the czar was overthrown by the communists, but he was unable to prevent the radical faction of communists, the Bolsheviks, from overthrowing him and seizing power.

The son of a teacher, Kerensky studied law and history at the University of St. Petersburg and received a law degree in 1899. He then became a criminal lawyer and defended revolutionaries accused of political crimes by the government. In 1912 he was elected to the Duma (parliament) from the Labor Party. Two years later, he was jailed by the czar for sedition when he opposed Russian entry into World War I. After the Russian Revolution of 1917, he became minister of justice, then minister of war and the navy. In July 1917, he became prime minister after Germany defeated a Russian military offensive. A pragmatic moderate and an eloquent speaker, Kerensky tried to gain support from all the revolutionary factions, but he was too moderate to win the support of the far left.

Because Kerensky had put down a military coup against the government (the Kornilov Uprising) in early September 1917, when Vladimir Lenin and the Bolsheviks launched a coup in November, Kerensky and his followers could not find any army units willing to support them. They were quickly ousted by the Bolsheviks. Kerensky went into exile in 1918 in France. In 1940 he moved to the United States, where he lectured and wrote about Russian history at several universities until his death in 1970.

SEE ALSO

Bolsheviks; Lenin, Vladimir Ilich; Russia; Russian Revolution

FURTHER READING

Abraham, Richard. *Alexander Kerensky: The First Love of the Revolution.* New York: Columbia University Press, 1987.
Kerensky, Aleksandr. *The Crucifixion of Liberty.* New York: John Day, 1934.

Khmer Rouge

The Khmer Rouge is a Cambodian communist guerrilla movement that became the ruling political party in Cambodia between 1975 and 1978. (The French word for "red"—*rouge*—refers to the communism of this group of Khmers.) Khmer Rouge military forces, commanded by political leader Pol Pot, fought against the pro-Western royalist government, led by Prince Souvanna Phouma after 1964. In spite of U.S. military intervention, including the bombing of much of Cambodia by the U.S. Air Force and the invasion of eastern Cambodia by the U.S. Army in 1970, the Khmer Rouge captured the Cambodian capital, Phnom Penh, on April 17, 1975, putting an end to more than a decade of civil war between communists and royalists.

The Khmer Rouge removed almost the entire Cambodian population from all cities and towns and moved everyone except key industrial workers into the countryside. Former royalists, anticommunists, government soldiers, and others were sent to concentration camps and prisons, known later in the West as the "killing fields." As many as 1 million Cambodians (out of a national population estimated at 7 million) were executed in the Khmer Rouge's autogenocidal campaign, designed to purge Cambodian society of all "antirevolutionary" elements.

After a series of border clashes, Vietnam invaded Cambodia and occupied it in 1978, installing its own regime of communists. The new government condemned Pol Pot and other Khmer Rouge leaders to death for genocide, although these leaders fled to the jungle before being captured by the Vietnamese. The Khmer Rouge organized itself again as a guerrilla movement, this time against Vietnamese communists. Although it was a significant military force in the western provinces, its alliances with non-communist resistance groups were lukewarm and it was often involved in military conflicts with them. The Khmer Rouge supported itself by winning con-

trol of a gem mining area, by engaging in drug trafficking, and by smuggling consumer goods across the border with Thailand.

Under the leadership of Pol Pot (until his overthrow in 1997) and Khieu Samphan, his second in command, the Khmer Rouge in the 1990s remained a major destabilizing force against the Cambodian government, which had been elected in 1992 under the auspices of a United Nations multinational peacekeeping force. The Khmer Rouge attacked UN peacekeepers, launched attacks on government forces, and began a campaign of "ethnic cleansing" against the Vietnamese villagers living in Cambodia. The Khmer Rouge in the mid-1990s was confined to western Cambodia, where it engaged in smuggling gems and munitions across the border with Thailand, sometimes with the complicity of local Thai officials and military units.

In 1996 the Khmer Rouge split into two warring factions, with one leader, Ieng Sary, pledging allegiance to King Norodom Sihanouk after being sentenced to death by other Khmer Rouge leaders for embezzling profits from the smuggling of gems into Thailand.

SEE ALSO
Autogenocide; Cambodia; Ethnic cleansing; Pol Pot; Vietnam

Young Cambodian children sit next to the pile of skulls that constitutes the "killing fields" memorial outside Phnom Penh. It is estimated that the Khmer Rouge killed almost one-fifth of the entire Cambodian population.

FURTHER READING

Kiernan, Ben, ed. *Genocide and Democracy in Cambodia: The Khmer Rouge, the United Nations, and the International Community.* New Haven: Yale University Southeast Asia Studies, 1993.

"The Real Toll." *Economist*, April 6, 1996.

Khomeini, Ayatollah Ruhollah Mussavi

- *Born: May 17, 1900, Khomein, Iran*
- *Died: June 3, 1989, Qom, Iran*

Ayatollah Ruhollah Mussavi Khomeini was the religious leader of Iran from 1979 to 1989, after the overthrow of the shah. Although he was not formally part of the government, he was the most powerful political figure in Iran. Khomeini presided over the establishment of an Islamic republic and promoted the spread of Islamic fundamentalism into Middle Eastern Muslim nations such as Lebanon, Syria, and the Arab states of the Persian Gulf through the Party of God, a radical Islamic movement.

Born Ruhollah Hendi, the future spiritual leader of Iran adopted the name Khomeini ("from Khomein") in 1930. His maternal grandfather, his father, and one of his brothers were all ayatollahs (which means "reflection of God"), religious leaders of the Shiite Muslims. His father was assassinated when Khomeini was a baby. He attended religious schools in Khomein and Arak and studied at the religious center of Madresseh Faizieh in the holy city of Qom. While there, he studied Islamic law and philosophy and wrote poetry. As an *ulema,* or religious scholar, he was the author of many books, and he trained thousands of Islamic priests.

In the 1950s Khomeini became a critic of the shah of Iran, opposing land reforms that took away property from the Iranian Muslim clergy and the legal emancipation of women. In 1963, after Muslim student riots against the shah, Khomeini was put under house arrest for a year. He went into exile in Iraq and then France and called for strikes and demonstrations against the shah.

Because of political unrest and the threat of violent revolution organized by Khomeini's followers, the shah left Iran on January 16, 1979, leaving behind a reformist "regency council" to govern. Khomeini returned to Iran on February 1, and less than two weeks later the caretaker secular government resigned and the Council of the Islamic Revolution, dominated by mullahs (low-ranking religious leaders) loyal to Khomeini, named a provisional government. On March 31, Iranians voted in a plebiscite, or popular election, to establish an Islamic republic. The ayatollah returned to Qom, where he exercised dominant influence over the regime, announcing religious edicts, such as the imposition of the strict Islamic legal code, that had the force of supreme law in the new Islamic state.

In the 1980s Khomeini led Iran after it had been invaded by Iraq over a territorial dispute. With his approval, militant students took U.S. diplomats hostage and held them in the U.S. embassy in Tehran for more than a year. Also with his approval, Iran bought weapons from Israel and the United States in 1985 and 1986 to use in the war against Iraq. The United States and Israel agreed to sell arms to Iran in exchange for the release of other American hostages held by his supporters in Lebanon.

Khomeini's Islamic courts took a hard line against any deviation from *sharī'a,* Islamic law. After an Iranian religious court issued a *fatwa* (religious edict) calling for the death of British author Salman Rushdie, for alleged blasphemy against Islam in his book *The Sa-*

tanic Verses, Khomeini personally offered a reward on February 19, 1989, for anyone willing "to send Rushdie to hell." The Iranian government then offered a reward for Rushdie's death, forcing him into hiding.

With the Ayatollah Khomeini's death, strict adherence to Islamic law diminished in Iran. And as revolutionary fervor waned, Iran turned to Western nations (other than the United States, with which it maintained a hostile relationship) for economic investment.

SEE ALSO

Iran; Islamic fundamentalism

FURTHER READING

Bakhash, Shaul. *The Reign of the Ayatollahs.* New York: Basic Books, 1984.
Gordon, Matthew. *Ayatollah Khomeini.* Rev. ed. New York: Chelsea House, 1988.
Khomeini, Ruhollah. *Islam and Revolution: Writings and Declarations of Imam Khomeini.* Translated by Hamid Algar. Berkeley, Calif.: Mizan Press, 1981.
Khomeini, Ruhollah. *Islamic Government.* Translated by the National Technical Information Service. Washington, D.C.: U.S. Department of Commerce, National Technical Information Service, 1979.
Zonis, Marvin. *Khomeini, the Islamic Republic of Iran, and the Arab World.* Cambridge, Mass.: Center for Middle Eastern Studies, Harvard University, 1987.

Khrushchev, Nikita Sergeyevich

- *Born: Apr. 17, 1894, Kalinovka, Russia*
- *Died: Sept. 11, 1971, Moscow, Soviet Union*

Nikita Khrushchev served as first secretary of the Communist Party (1953–64) and as chairman of the Council of Ministers of the Soviet Union (1957–64). As the leader of the Soviet Union, he repu-

diated the terror of Joseph Stalin's dictatorship and opened an era of political liberalization at home and the beginning of a thaw in the cold war with the United States.

Khrushchev, the son of a miner, became a machine repairman in the coal mines. In 1918 he joined the Communist Party and served in the Red Army during the civil war (1918–21) against the Whites (anticommunist forces). He then became assistant manager of a coal mine. Khrushchev was sent by the Communist Party to the Donets Industrial Institute from 1922 to 1925 to learn about mining management. Upon graduation, he became district party secretary for four years. After this assignment, he studied engineering and Marxism at the Industrial Academy of Moscow in 1930 and became secretary of a Moscow party district in 1931. In 1935 he became head of the entire Moscow Communist Party.

Stalin sent Khrushchev to the Ukraine in 1938, where he participated in purges against party leaders and served as a lieutenant general on the Ukrainian front during World War II. He remained first secretary of the Ukraine until 1949, when he was named to the Politburo, the controlling committee of the Communist Party of the Soviet Union.

After the death of Communist Party leader Joseph Stalin in 1953, Khrushchev became first secretary of the Communist Party, sharing power briefly with several other leaders. In 1956, after consolidating his own power over the party, he made a secret speech to the 20th Party Congress in which he repudiated the crimes of Stalin, particularly his reign of terror against political opponents, and the forced collectivization policies in the 1930s that had led to the deaths of millions of peasants. The speech was kept secret from ordinary

Russians and from Western nations because Khrushchev was afraid that a public admission would weaken the legitimacy of the communist regime. Nevertheless, admission of the crimes of Stalin marked the first efforts to reform the Communist Party and eliminate totalitarian terror from the Soviet state. It is said that when a delegate to the Party Congress called out, "and where were you, comrade Nikita Sergeyevich, when these crimes were occurring?" Khrushchev angrily asked the delegate to stand and identify himself. When no one stood, Khrushchev remarked with an ironic smile, "I was then, comrade, where you are now."

In 1957 Khrushchev became chairman of the council of ministers, which administered government departments. He developed the Soviet space program, and he boasted that because of Soviet advances in science and technology, the grandchildren of U.S. political leaders would live willingly under a communist system. His erratic foreign policy ventures—including the disastrous introduction of ballistic missiles in Cuba in 1962, which created a confrontation with the United States—his failure to modernize Soviet agriculture, his division of the Communist Party organization into separate agricultural and industrial branches in 1962 (an unpopular decision that offended many party leaders who lost power in the shake-up), and a speech at the United Nations in which he took off his shoe and banged it on his desk for emphasis convinced his colleagues that he should be replaced. The Politburo, embarrassed by Khrushchev's image of a primitive Russian peasant and disturbed by the failure of his policies, engineered a coup against him in October 1964, forcing him into retirement.

Khrushchev was an emotional man, a self-described peasant, with the earthy language and the informal demeanor of a 19th-century American party leader. He established a close relationship with Fidel Castro, personally taking the Cuban leader around the Russian countryside for a hunting trip in the winter of 1963 after the Cuban missile crisis, as they worked to repair their relationship. Nevertheless, Castro always believed that Khrushchev had betrayed him by failing to stand up to the United States and by removing the missiles from Cuba after the United States quarantined the island.

Khrushchev eventually established a good relationship with U.S. president John Kennedy because the two of them had agreed to step back from the brink of nuclear war. On the other hand, Khrushchev never forgave President Dwight Eisenhower for ordering a U-2 spy plane on a mission over Russia just prior to the 1960 summit, at which they had planned to discuss nuclear arms limitations. In retaliation, Khrushchev broke up the summit in Paris, an act that Eisenhower believed was unforgivable, given the importance of slowing down the arms race.

Khrushchev was the first Soviet leader to show a human face to the world, the first to end the reign of terror in the Soviet Union, and the first to attempt a thaw in superpower relations. He boasted to Vice President Richard Nixon that "we will bury you," but by that he meant that the Soviet Union would overtake the United States in economic competition. But his own failures as an economic manager, particularly in the field of agriculture, laid the groundwork for the Soviet Union's stagnation in the decades to follow, and his boast turned out to be hollow.

SEE ALSO
Castro, Fidel; Cuba; Eisenhower, Dwight David; Kennedy, John F.; Soviet Union (Union of Soviet Socialist Republics)

FURTHER READING

Beschloss, Michael R. *The Crisis Years: Kennedy and Khrushchev, 1960–1963.* New York: Edward Burlingame Books, 1991.

Ebon, Martin. *Nikita Khrushchev.* New York: Chelsea House, 1986.

Kort, Michael. *Nikita Khrushchev.* New York: Franklin Watts, 1989.

Medvedev, Roy, and Zhores A. Medvedev. *Khrushchev: The Years in Power.* New York: Columbia University Press, 1976.

Rush, Myron. *The Rise of Khrushchev.* Washington, D.C.: Public Affairs Press, 1958.

Tompson, William J. *Khrushchev—A Political Life.* New York: St. Martin's, 1995.

Kiribati

REPUBLIC OF KIRIBATI

• *Capital: Tarawa*

Political history Located in the South Pacific, the Gilbert and Ellice Islands were originally inhabited around A.D. 1000 by the Micronesian A-Kiribati tribe. Many European trading ships visited the islands during and after the 16th century. The British established a protectorate in 1892 and annexed the islands as a colony in 1915. In 1941 they were captured by the Japanese, but the Allies retook the islands in 1943. In 1975 the Ellice Islands renamed themselves Tuvalu and severed their links with the Gilbert Islands. The Gilberts obtained independence in 1979 as Kiribati following a period of internal self-government under the United Kingdom begun in 1976.

Government institutions The president *(beretitenti)* is head of state and government and is elected by direct popular vote. The vice president and cabinet are appointed by an electoral college, whose members are elected from the legislature—the directly elected and unicameral Maneaba ni Maungatabu, which has 39 members. All judicial appointments are made by the president.

Parties and movements The Christian Democrats hold some seats in the legislature, but most candidates for office are not affiliated with a party. There are, however, loose groupings of like-minded legislators, the largest of which, after the Christian Democrats, is organized as the National Progressives.

Domestic issues The United Nations has warned that by the 21st century Kiribati may be completely submerged if ocean levels continue to rise due to global warming. Even a small rise might make the local water undrinkable if saltwater overruns the water table. As a result, Kiribati is one of the leaders of a group of Asian and Pacific nations calling for greater international cooperation on the environment.

Some politicians in the opposition have criticized the government for accepting too much foreign aid, particularly from Australia and China, because the government gave too much control to donor nations and brought in outside laborers.

International issues In 1985 Kiribati signed an agreement giving the Soviet Union exclusive fishing rights in its waters. The following year, however, it signed the South Pacific Regional Fisheries Treaty, which allowed U.S. tuna boats to fish there as well. Australia has been rebuffed in its attempt to lease a waste disposal site on the island of Banaba because of opposition from the local environmental movement.

SEE ALSO
United Kingdom

FURTHER READING
Sabatier, Ernest. *Astride the Equator.* New York: Oxford University Press, 1977.

Kohl, Helmut

- *Born: Apr. 30, 1930, Ludwigshafen, Germany*

Chancellor of West Germany from 1982 to 1992 and chancellor of Germany since 1992, Helmut Kohl unified East and West Germany at the end of the cold war. His insistence that East Germany join West Germany and adhere to its constitution and laws, rather than remain independent or loosely affiliated while maintaining its own economic and social systems, won out over the objections of the Soviet Union and the misgivings of France, the United States, and Great Britain.

Although Kohl is often considered by his fellow Germans to be a dull man with little insight or charisma, he has served as head of government far longer than any other Western or U.S. world leader. He has had a major impact on western European politics through his insistence that European economies be closely coordinated in the European Union and that Europe adopt a common currency.

As a teenager, Kohl was engaged in pre-military training for the German army just as World War II ended in 1945. He attended the University of Frankfurt and received a doctorate in political science from the University of Heidelberg in 1958. Between 1953 and 1966 he worked as a Christian Democratic Party leader and held minor local offices, then he became premier of the government of Rhineland-Palatinate, a state in western Germany, from 1969 to 1976. In 1976 he was defeated for the chancellorship by the Social Democrat Helmut Schmidt. But Kohl became chancellor in 1982 when the Free Democrats, the third most populous party in German politics, abandoned the Social Democrats to form a new majority coali-tion with the Christian Democrats.

Kohl was a centrist who made few policy innovations, and his cautious approach suited the voters. He won reelection in 1987. Kohl did move boldly on one issue: in 1990, as the East German regime crumbled, he called for the reunification of Germany, in spite of misgivings from the United States, Britain, France, and the Soviet Union, which feared the economic and possible military power of a reunited Germany. He won support in East Germany by promising currency reform that would provide hard currency deutsche marks to East Germans in exchange for their worthless currency. He strongly supported moving the federal capital back to Berlin from Bonn, which had been the capital of West Germany.

Kohl's political position later weakened as unemployment rose to massive levels in the east (after inefficient state enterprises were shut down) and taxes were raised in the west to pay the costs of reunification. Kohl's failure to vigorously condemn the rise of neo-Nazi extremists and their attacks on foreigners was condemned by many human rights activists.

SEE ALSO
East Germany; Germany; West Germany

FURTHER READING
Hämäläinen, Pekka. *Uniting Germany.* Boulder, Colo.: Westview, 1994.
Rosenfeld, Stephen S. "The Reassuring Chancellor." *Washington Post*, Nov. 1, 1996.

Korea, North

DEMOCRATIC PEOPLE'S REPUBLIC OF KOREA (CHOSUN MINCHU-CHUI INMIN KONGHWA-GUK)

- *Capital: P'yŏngyang*

Political history Located in the northern part of the Korean Peninsula, in northeast Asia, the portion of Korea north of the 38th parallel was occupied by the Soviet Union at the end of World War II. In November 1947 the Soviets refused to permit a United Nations commission access to their occupation zone, in order to prevent all-Korean elections authorized by the United Nations. Instead, the Supreme People's Assembly, controlled by the North Korean Workers' Party, was established by the Soviet Union to provide for self-government in the occupied area.

The following year, the nation declared its independence when the Soviets permitted it to elect the Supreme People's Soviet (the renamed legislature) and adopt a Soviet-style constitution.

Government institutions North Korea is a totalitarian dictatorship that, since its inception, has been ruled by the Kim family. Kim Il Sung, who was head of the Korean communists, ruled from 1947 until his death in 1994, when he was succeeded by his son, Kim Jong Il.

Under the 1972 constitution, the sovereign power is the unicameral, 687-member Supreme People's Assembly. Its members, however, are nominated by the president and run unopposed for four-year terms. In turn, under the constitution, the assembly names the president of the republic. The president nominates, and the assembly confirms, the members of the Central People's Committee, a body that appoints ministers to the Administration Council. The council conducts the actual day-to-day business of government under the leadership of a prime minister elected by the assembly. Because the president chooses who can run for the assembly, all political power rests in his hands.

The judiciary is under the control of the Communist Party. Local courts (People's Courts) hear petty civil and

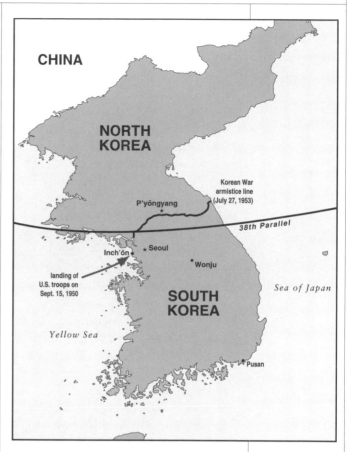

criminal cases. Serious cases are handled by the Courts of the Province. The Central Court is the court of last appeal and supervises the lower courts.

Parties and movements North Korea is a one-party communist state. The communist Korean Workers' Party dominates the Democratic Front for the Reunification of the Fatherland (a coalition of parties that, in addition to the Korean Workers' Party, contains two puppet parties designed to give the impression of multiparty rule). The Democratic Front provides voters with an approved list of candidates for elections.

Domestic issues The North Korean economy had a very high rate of growth in the 1980s. In the 1990s, however, it got into trouble because of the collapse of barter trading with the former nations of the Soviet Union; the economy contracted by 15 to 30 percent between 1980 and 1995. There have been shortages of food, fuel, and electricity, and summer storms damaged factories, roads, and communication systems, decreasing productivity and causing further harm to the economy, causing North Korea to abandon its policy of self-sufficiency and ask Japan, the United States, and other Western nations for emergency assistance. By 1997, North Korea was suffering extreme famine conditions.

International issues North Korea has been an implacable enemy of South Korea, which it invaded in 1950 in an attempt to reunify the country under communist rule. After its defeat in 1953, it set about attempting to weaken South Korea politically by engaging in acts of terrorism. In October 1983, 17 South Korean officials were killed in a bomb explosion in Rangoon, Myanmar (then called Burma), set by North Korean agents. In 1987, North Korea blew up a South Korean civilian airliner carrying 150 passengers. North Korea maintains its million-man military on alert near the border with South Korea.

In 1991 the two Koreas signed an Agreement on Reconciliation, Non-Aggression, and Exchanges and Cooperation that provided for the reuniting of families and other improvements in relations. Later that year, they signed an agreement to keep the peninsula free of nuclear weapons. The United States then removed from South Korea its nuclear weapons that had been stationed there to deter attack by North Korea.

Attempts by North Korea to develop its civilian nuclear power industry, however, have led to suspicions that under this cover it is attempting to build nuclear weapons in violation of this agreement. North Korea and the United States have held talks on improving access by international inspectors, but in 1993 North Korea barred access to inspectors from the International

Atomic Energy Commission to two of its plants at Yongbyon. U.S. intelligence sources believe that North Korea had possibly built at least one nuclear device by the end of 1993. In 1994 the United States and North Korea signed a Framework Agreement which provided that North Korea would close down a fuel reprocessing plant capable of producing weapons-grade plutonium. It would also send its existing radioactive fuel (capable of being made into bombs) out of the country. In return, the United States would supply North Korea with petroleum and would aid in the financing of two "light-water" nuclear reactors (whose spent fuel is not suitable for nuclear weapons) for electrical power. The United States also wants North Korea to sign the Nuclear Non-Proliferation Treaty, in which nonnuclear powers agree not to acquire nuclear weapons. In return for signing the Framework Agreement, North Korea received emergency food aid in the mid-1990s, channeled through the UN World Food Program.

North Korea is a major arms supplier to Third World nations, particularly those in the Middle East. It has developed a short-range ballistic missile that has enabled these nations to vastly increase the destructive power of their military forces.

Human rights Thousands of political prisoners, arrested for opposition to the communist regime, are held in labor camps or executed after trials conducted without due process of law. More than 150,000 Koreans working in Osaka, Japan (many in gambling parlors) are forced by North Korean agents working for the Chosen Soren (a Korean ethnic association in Japan) to hand over money in order to prop up the North Korean government.

SEE ALSO
Korea, South

FURTHER READING

Chua-Eoan, Howard. "Kim Jong Il: Now
It's His Turn." *Time*, July 18, 1994: 29.
Dae-Sook Suh. *Kim Il Sung*. New York:
Columbia University Press, 1988.
Lee, Chong-Sik, and Se-Hee Yoo, eds.
North Korea in Transition. Berkeley:
Institute of East Asian Studies, University
of California at Berkeley, 1991.
Smith, Hazel, et al., eds. *North Korea in the
New World Order*. New York: St.
Martin's, 1996.

Korea, South

*REPUBLIC OF KOREA
(TAEHAN MIN'GUK)*

• *Capital: Seoul*

Political history Located on the Korean
Peninsula in northeast Asia, Korea was
divided into three kingdoms from 57 B.C.
to A.D. 668—Koguryŏ in the north,
Paekche in the southwest, and Silla in the
southeast. Korea was united under the
Silla dynasty after 668; it was followed
by the Yi dynasty, which ruled between
1392 and 1910. China claimed Korea as
a sphere of influence (that is, an area under its domination) in the 15th century,
and the Yi rulers paid it tribute. In the
16th century they succeeded in eliminating Chinese influence, but when the
Ch'ing (Manchu) dynasty gained power
in China in the 1700s the Koreans resumed payments. China recognized
Korea's independence in 1895 after Japan had defeated China in a war that
year and established its own influence on
the peninsula.

Korea became a Japanese protectorate after the Russo-Japanese War of
1904–5 and was annexed by Japan in
1910. In 1945, after the Japanese defeat in World War II, the northern part
of the country above the 38th parallel
was occupied by the Soviet Union and
the southern part by the United States.

After negotiations to unify Korea
broke down in 1946, the Republic of
Korea was established in 1948. A
North Korean invasion of the south in
1950 was defeated by a U.S.-led coalition (which also included British,
Turkish, and Australian contingents),
acting under United Nations resolutions. A series of U.S. victories, led by
General Douglas MacArthur, resulted
in U.S. control over most of the peninsula. However, Chinese intervention
on the side of North Korea, its communist ally, then resulted in U.S. withdrawal back into the south and to a
military stalemate. An armistice was
declared in 1953, but no peace treaty
has been concluded, and the forces on
both sides remain on high alert.

The first president of the Republic
of Korea, Syngman Rhee, resigned in
1960 after mass demonstrations
against his autocratic rule. A military
regime took power in 1961 and eliminated all vestiges of democracy in
1972, when Park Chung Hee was
named President for Life and political
parties were outlawed. After Park was
assassinated by the Korean Central Intelligence Agency, allegedly in a coup
attempt by the head of the agency, another military leader assumed power.

*The Korean War
wreaked un-
imaginable dev-
astation on the
people of Korea.
Here, women
and children
search the
wreckage of the
city of Seoul for
anything that
can be burned as
fuel.*

Until 1988 South Korea was an authoritarian system, but mass public demonstrations forced the military to permit the nation's transformation into a multiparty democracy, although the military retains great influence. The first nonmilitary president, Kim Young Sam, was elected in 1993 on a reformist platform.

Government institutions The Constitution for the Sixth Republic of Korea was adopted in 1987 and provides for a semi-presidential system. The president is head of state and government and is directly elected by the people for a five-year term. The president appoints the State Council, consisting of government ministers and led by the prime minister. Legislative power is vested in the 299-member National Assembly, whose members are directly elected for four-year terms. Justices of the Supreme Court are appointed by the president; the chief justice appoints lower court judges.

Parties and movements The largest party is the New Korea Party, a coalition of the former Democratic Liberal Party (free-market and conservative) and three smaller reformist parties advocating reunification with North Korea and democratic reforms. It has had a majority in parliament since the April 1996 elections. The main opposition is the National Congress for New Politics, headed by former president Kim Dae-Jung. The United Liberal Democratic Party, the third largest, consists of pro-business politicians from the old Democratic Liberal Party who refused to join the New Korea Party.

Domestic issues The economy, led by its automobile, shipbuilding, construction, and consumer electronics sectors, has had one of the highest rates of growth in the world since the 1970s. South Korea has become one of the world's leading industrial powers. The exploitation of the work force, which labors under difficult conditions for low wages, has resulted in labor unrest that at times threatens the stability of the regime with protests and crippling strikes. Korea has also opened its domestic rice markets to the United States, prompting unrest among farmers because of lower prices.

In 1993, in order to placate Korean workers, the government began to take on the Chaebol, the large industrial conglomerates, calling for a freeze in their prices for consumer goods. Its Board of Audit and Inspection also began a campaign against the corruption that permeates Korean politics and the military. In 1995 the drive against corruption had implicated a number of high-ranking government and opposition party figures—including two former presidents put on trial for corruption—calling into question the stability of the multiparty system.

International issues The United States has been South Korea's main ally since its occupation began in 1945 and has safeguarded the regime militarily with 35,000 U.S. troops and with airplanes. Until the late 1960s the United States provided $1 billion in reconstruction aid annually, but the aid ended when the Korean economy "took off."

South Korea's main threat comes from the regime in North Korea, which invaded once and has threatened to do so again. U.S. president Bill Clinton warned the North Koreans in 1994 that an attack on the South "would be the end of their country." In 1997 under U.S. auspices, talks to reduce tensions on the peninsula resumed between North and South, and South Korea supplied food, fuel, and medical supplies to alleviate famine conditions in North Korea.

South Korea has expanded its trade with China and the former nations of the Soviet Union and the post-communist nations of eastern Europe since 1991. Relations with Japan improved after Japanese leaders apologized for the conduct of their armed forces during the Japanese occupation of Korea. Nevertheless, tensions remain high as the result of a territorial dispute with Japan over Tokto Island in the Sea of Japan (known as Takeshima Island in Japan). South Korea has occupied the island since 1953.

South Korea has become increasingly concerned by the effort North Korea has made to develop nuclear weapons. Talks on Korean reunification have been held periodically, but little progress had been made as of 1997.

Human rights Korean military and security forces brutally repressed worker and student demonstrations for political freedoms and better working conditions in the 1980s and massacred hundreds. Ex-President Chun Doo Hwan was sentenced to death in 1996 for ordering the army to shoot pro-democracy students in the southern city of Kwangju in May 1980. Another ex-president, Roh Tae Woo, was given 22 years for his part in the massacre.

In 1993 President Kim Young Sam granted amnesty to many people arrested by previous regimes. During the early 1990s as many as 1,500 prisoners were considered political prisoners by human rights groups. Laws providing for arrest and detention without trial and government regulation of speech, expression, association, and assembly were routinely used by the government in the mid-1990s against labor unions and human rights activists.

SEE ALSO

Korea, North; Rhee, Syngman

FURTHER READING

Cotton, James. *Politics and Policy in the New Korean State.* New York: St. Martin's, 1995.
MacDonald, Donald S. *The Koreans.* 2nd ed. Boulder, Colo.: Westview, 1990.
Savada, Andrea Matles, and William Shaw, eds. *South Korea: A Country Study.* 4th ed. Washington, D.C.: Federal Research Division, Library of Congress, 1992.
Whelan, Richard. *Drawing the Line: The Korean War, 1950–1953.* Boston: Little, Brown, 1990.

KOSOVO

Kosovo, a province of Serbia, is a flash point for Muslim-Serb conflict, which at any time could lead to a general war in the Balkans. It is populated by 2 million people, 95 percent of whom are Muslims of Albanian ethnicity. Its political leaders are Serbians and Eastern Orthodox in religion. Kosovo is regarded by Serbians as their ancestral homeland, and it is filled with ancient churches, shrines, battlefields, and burial grounds. It was the site of the first Serbian patriarchate, or religious leader, of the Eastern Orthodox church. At the Battle of Kosovo Polje (literally, "the field of black crows") on June 28, 1389, the Serbs

were defeated by the Ottoman Turks, which began a half millennium of Ottoman rule.

The Serbs took Kosovo from the Turks during the Balkan Wars of 1912–13. The area was incorporated into Serbia, and its Muslim population gained autonomy (self-government in local affairs) in the Yugoslav constitution of 1974. By 1980 Kosovo Muslims were calling for an end to Serbian rule and demanding the status of a republic within the Yugoslav federation. Feeling unwelcome, many Serbs left the area, but the Serbian government jailed Muslim dissidents. In 1989 Serbia revoked the autonomous privileges of the region, dissolved its parliament, dismissed its local police, and instituted martial rule in the capital, Priština. It closed Albanian-language schools and universities. That year, more than 2 million Serbs gathered at the battlefield of Kosovo to commemorate the Serbian loss 600 years earlier against the Muslim "infidels," symbolic of the Serbian desire not to relinquish the territory.

The Democratic League of Kosovo, a Muslim-led group, organized a referendum in 1990 in which most Kosovans voted for independence. In 1992 it held its own elections and declared a Republic of Kosova, but it remains under Serbian control. Serbs have attempted a "resettlement and return" program but, by 1996, few Serbs had returned and most of the Serbian population had left. However, the area contains lead, zinc, coal, silver, and gold, which the Serbs will not relinquish without a fight to Kosovo nationalists, organized in the Kosovo Liberation Army, founded in 1996. By 1997 the Yugoslav (Serbian) army had sent massive reinforcements to garrison the area and fight guerrillas attempting to establish an independent Republic of Kosova.

U.S. president George Bush warned Serbia in 1992 that if it were to use force in Kosovo, the United States would respond with force against Serbia to prevent a general Balkan war. A Serbian attempt at "ethnic cleansing" (removing or exterminating the Muslims) in Kosovo could bring Albania in to aid the local population, and Turkey, in turn, might aid Albania. In response, Greece and Serbia might ally, precipitating a larger conflict in the Balkans.

SEE ALSO

Albania; Ottoman Empire; Serbia; Yugoslavia

Kurdistan

Kurdistan is a territory that covers most of eastern and southeastern Turkey, northern Iraq, northwestern Iran, northeastern Syria, and the Zagros and Taurus mountain ranges. More than 20 million Kurds, a Sunni Muslim but non-Arabic ethnic group, live in this area: 11 million in Turkey, 6 million in Iran, and 4 million in Iraq.

Kurds have populated the area since the 1st century A.D. Kurdish kingdoms and principalities never united into a single nation, and the Kurds were conquered first by the Arabs and then by the Ottomans. The 1923 Treaty of Lausanne, signed by the European powers and Turkey, provided for the establishment of Arab states but denied independence to Kurdistan.

An independent Kurdish Republic in Mahābād, Iran, was established by Kurdish leader Mustafa Barzani after World War II, but it was crushed by the Pahlavi shahs, the rulers of Iran, after one year. The Islamic fundamentalist regime that later took over Iran also used

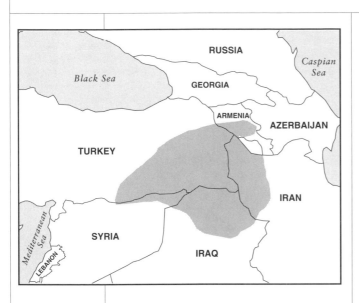

The shaded area shows where the Kurdish population is concentrated.

Kurds attempted to gain their independence. More than 750,000 Kurds were displaced as Iraqi forces attacked Kurdish villages after the war. A "safe zone" protected by U.S. warplanes was created in April 1991 north of Iraq's 36th parallel, and Kurds were fed and supplied by the United States through Operation Comfort. The U.S. emergency aid ended in 1992, but more permanent food aid and other relief for 700,000 Kurds costs the United Nations almost $500 million annually; UN guards from the World Food Program provide security for relief workers.

Kurdish leaders of the Patriotic Union of Kurdistan (led by Jalal Talabani) and the Kurdistan Democratic Party (under the leadership of Massoud Barzani, son of Mustafa Barzani) have established a de facto independent state, complete with a Kurdistan National Assembly (in which 50 seats are held by each of the two parties and 5 seats are given to Assyrian Christian Kurds) and a prime minister. Turkey, Iraq, and Syria have all warned the Kurds that a partition of Iraq or an independent Kurdistan would not be tolerated. They have used their armed forces against this Kurdish state in the 1990s and have relied on diplomacy to prevent nations from recognizing it.

military force against Kurdish guerrilla movements in the 1980s and 1990s. In Turkish Kurdistan, home to 10 million Kurds, the Kurdish Workers' Party began guerrilla warfare in 1984, but movements for Kurdish autonomy led by its 10,000 guerrillas have been defeated by 150,000 Turkish soldiers. The Turks have been helped by some Iraqi Kurds because Turkey controls their only supply route to the Western donor nations, who provide foreign aid to them.

In Iraq a Kurdish movement for autonomy, aided by the U.S. Central Intelligence Agency, began after the overthrow of the Iraqi monarchy in 1958. (The CIA cut off aid to the Kurds at the request of the shah of Iran in 1975, after Iran had reached an agreement with Iraq to defuse tensions.) During the Iran-Iraq War in the 1980s, the Iraqi Kurds were supplied by Iran, and Iraq used chemical weapons, bombs, and artillery shells against Kurdish villages. More than 180,000 people were killed, others were raped and tortured, and 4,000 villages were destroyed by the Iraqis in the Anfal (an Arabic word meaning "booty") campaign of genocide conducted between 1987 and 1989.

After the U.S. defeat of Iraq in the Persian Gulf War of 1991, the Iraqi

SEE ALSO
Iran; Iraq; Ottoman Empire; Syria; Turkey

FURTHER READING
Ghassemlou, A. R. *A People without a Country: The Kurds and Kurdistan.* Translated by Michael Pallis. London: Zed Press, 1993.
McDowell, David. *A Modern History of the Kurds.* New York: St. Martin's, 1996.
Miller, Judith. "Iraq: A Case of Genocide." *New York Times Magazine,* January 3, 1993: 12–17.
Randal, Jonathan C. *After Such Knowledge, What Forgiveness?* New York: Farrar, Straus & Giroux, 1997.

Kuwait

STATE OF KUWAIT (DOWLAT AL-KUWAIT)

• *Capital: Kuwait City*

Political history Located on the eastern part of the Arabian Peninsula, the area of Kuwait was ruled briefly by Alexander the Great in 323 B.C., when Greeks began to colonize the peninsula. Seleucids and Romans held sway until A.D. 500; then Arabian tribes settled in the area. The Anizal tribe of central Arabia took over the area in 1710. Kuwait's Al-Sabah dynasty began its rule in 1759, leading the Bedouin tribes that had moved from central Saudi Arabia to the Persian Gulf coast.

Kuwait became a British protectorate in 1897 as part of Great Britain's attempt to prevent Germany from gaining influence on the Arabian Peninsula. In 1914 Britain recognized Kuwaiti internal independence but continued to run its foreign relations and defense until 1961, when Kuwait achieved complete sovereignty. When Iraq threatened to invade later in the 1960s, British troops were called back, and then the Arab Legion, a military force trained and financed by the British and based in Jordan, provided its defense. Iraq invaded Kuwait in 1990 and annexed it, but the country was liberated in 1991 by a UN coalition led by the United States.

Government institutions Kuwait is a monarchy. Under the 1962 constitution, the head of state is the emir, chosen by and from the members of the ruling family. Governing power is exercised through the prime minister and a council of ministers. Legislative power is vested in the 50-member Majlis al-umma (National Assembly), whose members serve four-year terms. Voting rights are granted only to literate male Kuwaiti citizens, a small minority of the population.

In 1986 the government faced an attempt by pro-Iranian terrorists to topple it by sabotaging oil installations and plotting with political dissidents. The parliament was dissolved and the emir began to rule by decree. Four years later an appointed National Council of 75 members was established to provide a constitutional facade, but it had no power and could only advise the emir, so the country continued to exist under authoritarian rule.

An interim assembly was appointed by the emir in 1991 after the Iraqis were expelled from the country. On October 5, 1992, elections were held for the reinstated Majlis, and a large majority opposed to the Al-Sabah–appointed government was elected. The legislature launched investigations into the mismanagement of and corruption in government ministries. As a result, the council of ministers was reorganized in 1994, and the ruling family gave control of all ministries to the assembly, with the exception of foreign affairs, defense, and the interior.

Islamic law is the basis of Kuwait's legal system. The independent judiciary consists of Summary Courts to handle minor civil and criminal matters, a Court of First Instance to handle larger civil cases and serious criminal cases, a Court of Appeal, and a Court of Cassation to review decisions of the Court of Appeal. A State Security Court, responsible to the emir, handles cases involving sabotage, terrorism, and treason. The Constitutional Court, consisting of five judges, interprets the constitution and determines the constitutionality of laws passed by the parliament.

Parties and movements No political parties are permitted. Illegal political groups include the Constitutional Alliance, which seeks to convert Kuwait into a constitutional monarchy, and the

Facing ejection from Kuwait by a coalition of UN forces, defeated Iraqi forces set Kuwait's oil fields ablaze in the waning days of the Persian Gulf War.

Popular Islamic Congress, which seeks to install a fundamentalist regime.

Domestic issues Since the end of the Persian Gulf War in 1991, the main political issue has concerned the power of the monarchy. Because the government was unable to restore the country's economy quickly after the Iraqis were defeated, the council of ministers resigned. The emir then appointed a new council, dominated by pro-parliamentary forces who wish to convert Kuwait into a parliamentary regime by limiting the emir's lawmaking powers.

Corruption in Kuwait is rampant. Several members of the royal family have been accused of involvement in the embezzlement of more than $5 billion in public funds. These revelations have decreased the popularity of the Sabah family and have led to calls in the Majlis for reform.

International issues Kuwait has remained a close ally of the British since its independence. It has traditionally taken a hostile position toward Israel: Kuwait sent small contingents of forces to fight with Syria and Egypt against Israel in the 1973 war, condemned the Camp David peace agreements of 1978, and broke off diplomatic relations with Egypt between 1979 and 1987 after Egypt signed a peace treaty with Israel. During the Iraq-Iran war between 1981 and 1989, Kuwait sided with Iraq for reasons of Arab solidarity and because it feared that Iran would attempt to destabilize the government and install a pro-Iranian regime. The United States ensured the safety of Kuwaiti merchant shipping in 1987 after Iran declared a blockade of the Persian Gulf.

Iraq turned out to be the greater threat, however. It had traditionally considered Kuwait to be its 19th "lost" province. After the Iraqi army invaded Kuwait in August 1990 and then annexed it, U.S.-led forces entered Kuwait early in 1991 and liberated it.

Kuwait has been a mediator in regional disputes in the Persian Gulf involving Iran and Saudi Arabia, fearing that if hostilities break out, Iran would cross its borders in order to strike into Saudi territory or would close the Persian Gulf to its oil shipments.

Human rights The Al-Sabah regime has been charged with violations of legal rights in dealing with Kuwaitis accused of committing crimes during the Iraqi occupation. Some Palestinians who collaborated with the invading Iraqis were later abducted and tortured by security forces. Others were deported without due process. Most of the 350,000 Palestinian workers and their families who had been living in the country before the war were expelled from Kuwait after the Palestinian leadership sided with Iraq and backed its annexation of Kuwait.

Hundreds of thousands of other foreigners, who enjoy no civil or political rights, have taken their place in the Kuwaiti economy as teachers, office workers, and technical service workers. Foreign workers are forbidden to strike, and women workers are subject to abuse, rape, and assault without redress; more than 2,000 sought diplomatic protection in their home country embassies because their employers had abused them in the late 1990s.

SEE ALSO

Iran; Iraq; Islamic fundamentalism; Saudi Arabia

FURTHER READING

Crystal, Jill. *Kuwait: The Transformation of an Oil State*. Boulder, Colo.: Westview, 1992.
Crystal, Jill. *Oil and Politics in the Gulf*. New York: Cambridge University Press, 1995.
Mansfield, Peter. *Kuwait: Vanguard of the Gulf*. London: Hutchinson, 1990.

Kyrgyzstan

REPUBLIC OF KYRGYZSTAN (KYRGYZ RESPUBLIKASY)

• *Capital: Bishkek*

Political history Located in central Asia, Kyrgyzstan was conquered in ancient times by Mongols and Turkic tribes. The Kirgiz, a nomadic tribe, settled there be-
tween the 10th and 13th centuries A.D. Turkic tribes, Mongols, and Manchus from China dominated the area until 1876, when the Russians incorporated the Kirgiz Khanate into the czar's empire. After the Russian Revolution of 1917, Kyrgyzstan was incorporated as an autonomous district of the Russian Republic. It gained status as an autonomous oblast (regional government) in 1925, and in 1936 it achieved republic status within the Soviet Union. In 1991, after the attempted August coup by parts of the Russian military and security forces against Soviet leader Mikhail Gorbachev, it went along with the plan to dissolve the Soviet Union. Kyrgyzstan declared independence on August 31, 1991, and joined the Commonwealth of Independent States in 1992.

Government institutions Until 1991 the Kirgiz Soviet Socialist Republic was governed by a Supreme Soviet, an elected legislature whose local Communist Party members took orders from the party leaders in Moscow. In 1991 the name was changed to Kyrgyzstan and a presidential system was adopted. Under the 1993 constitution, the president is head of state and is elected by popular vote. The prime minister is appointed by the president and presides over the cabinet of ministers. There is a directly elected Zhogurku Kenesh (parliament), which makes the laws. It consists of a 70-member People's Assembly, which deals with regional issues, and a 35-member legislative assembly that deals with all other issues.

The judiciary takes direction from the president. Regional courts handle civil and criminal cases. Appeals are heard by the Higher Court of Arbitration, whose judges are nominated by the president and confirmed by the parliament. The Supreme Court hears appeals from the Higher Court of Arbitration; its justices are appointed by the president for 10-year terms. The Constitutional Court rules on the powers of the government and determines the constitutionality of laws passed by the parliament; its judges are appointed by the president and confirmed by the parliament for a term of 15 years.

Parties and movements Following the August 1991 attempted coup, the local Communist Party in Kyrgyzstan was disbanded as part of a purge of the party throughout the Soviet Union. New political groups include the Kyrgyzstan Democratic Movement and the Kirgiz Democratic Wing, two opposition parties, and National Unity, the movement that backs Kirgiz president Askar Akayev, a liberal and nationalist who is a non-communist and who won election unopposed in 1991, even before the collapse of the Soviet Union. He subsequently won a January 1994 referendum on the conduct of his presidency; he had initiated the referendum for a vote of confidence. In December 1995 Akayev, candidate of the National Unity Democratic Movement, won a second term with 71.6 percent of the vote. The reinstated Communist Party won 24.4 percent to become the country's second-largest party.

Domestic issues There are growing ethnic tensions between Kirgiz and Uzbeks. Russians are discriminated against, and 120,000 Slavs, mostly Russians and Ukrainians, have left since independence. In an effort to stem the flow of emigration, the government decreed in 1995 that Russian would be given the status of an official language in areas in which Russians constituted a significant presence.

The economy has suffered from the dissolution of the Soviet Union because Kyrgyzstan now has less trade with Russia. The economy produced 5 percent fewer goods and services by 1995 than it had in 1991. The main reason for the decline is the loss of Russian and Ukrainian markets for agricultural exports such as wool and cotton yarns and tobacco. Kyrgyzstan's markets for outmoded electronic goods also dried up, as Russia substituted more

advanced equipment from Asia and western Europe.

In 1993 the cabinet was dismissed for participating in the endemic corruption involving the nation's gold reserves. A national referendum conducted in 1994 backed the market reforms, including the encouragement of foreign investment and the protection of private property, instituted by the government in hopes of improving the nation's economy.

International issues Kyrgyzstan has a large Russian population and maintains close political and economic ties with Russia to counterbalance the possibility of a Chinese threat to its independence. It has established close cultural ties with Turkey and the other Turkic-language states in Central Asia.

Kyrgyzstan has tried to keep Tajiks from crossing into its territory in order to incite local Tajiks to join an Islamic revolution aimed at the secular governments of both Tajikistan and Kyrgyzstan. In the mid-1990s it also contributed troops to a peacekeeping mission organized by the Commonwealth of Independent States, designed to prevent the Tajiks from crossing into Afghanistan to join Tajik tribes there in the Afghan civil war.

The city of Osh is a transit point for opium grown in Tajikistan, Uzbekistan, and Afghanistan, and Kyrgyzstan is under international pressure by the United States and other Western nations to cut off the flow of drugs.

SEE ALSO

Commonwealth of Independent States (CIS); Russian Revolution; Soviet Union (Union of Soviet Socialist Republics)

FURTHER READING

Bremmer, Ian, and Ray Taras, eds. *Nation and Politics in the Soviet Successor States.* New York: Cambridge University Press, 1993.

Filipov, David. "From Collectivism to Capitalism." *Boston Globe*, March 25, 1997.

Hajda, Lubomyr, and Mark Beissinger, eds. *The Nationalities Factor in Soviet Politics and Society.* Boulder, Colo.: Westview, 1990.

Laos

LAO PEOPLE'S DEMOCRATIC REPUBLIC (SATHALANALAT PAXATHIPATAI PAXAXON-LAO)

• *Capital: Vientiane*

Political history Located on the Indochinese peninsula in Southeast Asia, the area was first settled by the Kha tribes, then by the Tai, people who migrated from southern China in the 8th century A.D. In the 14th century the first Laotian monarchy, the Lan Xang, was established with the aid of the Khmer tribes in what is now Cambodia. The Lan Xang ruled until Burma invaded in 1574. In 1637 the Burmese were expelled by the Lan Xang. In 1713 the area split into three kingdoms, Vientiane, Champassak, and Luang Prabang. The area was reunited by Siam (now Thailand), which converted the kingdoms into protectorates in the early 1700s and incorporated Vientiane as a Siamese province in 1800. Laos became a French protectorate in 1893 when the French took control of Indochina. The Japanese occupied Laos from 1941 until 1945 as part of their conquest of the Indochinese peninsula during World War II.

In 1947 the French reconquered Indochina and made Laos a constitutional monarchy with a puppet king. Later, in 1949, Laos became an autonomous state within the French Union, and in 1954, after the communists in Vietnam defeated the French army, Laos gained its independence under the Geneva Accords, which ended French control over all of Indochina. The communist Pathet Lao movement was permitted by the royal Laotian government to rule two northern provinces, based on an armistice accord of 1955. With North Vietnamese protection, Pathet Lao guerrillas, in violation of the armistice, fought against the royal government, which received help from the United States after 1961 in order to prevent a communist conquest of the entire nation. The communists continued to make gains on the battlefield. A provisional government incorporating the two sides was formed in 1974, and the Pathet Lao achieved full power the following year, after the United States ended its support for the provisional government and the communists defeated the government army. The 600-year-old monarchy was abolished by the communists.

Government institutions The 1991 constitution—written by a new generation of leaders whose goal was to modernize Laotian society—provides for a president of state with full executive powers. The president appoints a prime minister and a council of ministers, who run the government departments. Both the prime minister and the council must be approved by the legislature. The president also appoints provincial governors and mayors. The National Assembly, directly elected by popular vote, has legislative powers and meets twice a year

Pathet Lao forces in Laos rehearse a communist song. U.S. strategists originally believed that Laos, not Vietnam, would be the site of the most serious Southeast Asian conflict.

to approve the government's program.

The judicial system consists of the People's Supreme Court, district courts, and military courts, all of which function under government direction. All judges are appointed by the National Assembly.

Parties and movements Laos is a one-party authoritarian state. All political power is held by the Lao People's Revolutionary Party (LPRP), a Marxist-Leninist party formed from the Pathet Lao. The Lao Front for National Construction is an umbrella organization dominated by the LPRP, but it also contains members of several small ethnic groups not represented in the dominant party.

Domestic issues The Laos population consists of many different lowland, hill, and jungle tribes and ethnic groups, and beneath political ideology are regional and ethnic conflicts that must be mediated by the regime. One such conflict, for example, is between the Hmong in the hills and the lowland Lao, which led to an unsuccessful military mutiny by a Hmong commander in 1995 who had been passed over for promotion.

In an effort to spur economic growth, the government has permitted farmers to cultivate their own lands, overturning the prior communist policy of keeping all land in the hands of the state. In 1995 the government began allowing private companies to compete against some state enterprises and began to encourage foreign investment.

International issues Laos has close diplomatic relations with Vietnam and China, both of which supported the communists in the civil war. It had border clashes with Thailand, to the west, in the 1980s, but since then, economic investment from Thailand has helped relations. Laos has ended its barter system with Russia, China, and Vietnam, and although it is a communist state, it is becoming more integrated into the economy of Southeast Asia, with consequent pressure from foreign investors to liberalize its economy and adopt free-market reforms.

SEE ALSO
French Union; Indochina; Thailand; Vietnam

FURTHER READING
Committee of Concerned Asian Scholars. *The Indochina Story.* New York: Bantam, 1970.
Zasloff, Joseph, and Leonard Unger, eds. *Laos: Beyond the Revolution.* New York: St. Martin's, 1991.

Latvia

REPUBLIC OF LATVIA (LATVIJAS REPUBLIKA)

• *Capital: Riga*

Political history Located near the Baltic Sea in northeastern Europe between Estonia and Lithuania, the area was first settled by the Balts in the 6th century A.D. The area was conquered by the Vikings in the 9th century. Latvian tribes were ruled by the Knights of the Sword after 1230 and by the Order of Livonian Knights after 1237 (both groups were members of Teutonic tribes from Germany). In 1561 the knights ceded Latvian lands to Poland and Sweden after a short war. Russia gained control over all of Latvia between 1721 and 1795, and it was governed as part of the czar's empire in the 19th century.

In 1918, following the Russian Revolution, Latvia proclaimed its independence. German and British navies aided Latvia against Russia as part of

Soviet troops move in among demonstrators in the Latvian capital of Riga in March 1990. The following year, Latvia achieved independence after decades as a Soviet satellite state.

their effort to overturn the communist revolution there. The independent Latvian republic lasted from 1918 through the start of World War II in 1939, when the Soviet Union invaded and incorporated it as a constituent republic. When Germany invaded the Soviet Union in 1941, it occupied Latvia, but the Russians returned in 1943, and thereafter it remained a constituent republic of the Soviet Union. As the Soviet Union began to collapse in 1991, Latvia declared its independence and once again became a fully sovereign republic.

Government institutions In 1993 the 1922 constitution that had been written after Latvia first gained its independence from Russia was restored. The president is head of state and is elected by the legislature for a term of three years. Governing power is held by a cabinet of ministers, headed by a prime minister. The cabinet is accountable to a majority of the 100-member directly elected legislature, called the Saiema.

The judges of an independent supreme court are appointed by the president and confirmed by the Saiema.

Parties and movements In 1990 the Communist Party monopoly on political power ended, and the government permitted new parties to organize. After the dissolution of the Soviet Union and Latvian independence, the Latvian Communist Party itself was banned in 1991. The large Popular Front of Latvia spearheaded the independence movement but later dissolved after achieving its goal. As of October 1995, the largest party was the Democratic Party (center-left), which tried to preserve social welfare programs while at the same time dismantling the planned economy. It was followed closely by a new right-wing coalition of parties, in turn followed by the Latvian Way (center-right), which had been the majority party between 1993 and 1995.

Domestic issues One-third of the Latvian population is ethnic Russian, and only one-third of the population of the capital city of Riga is Latvian. Much of the domestic state-run industry is controlled by Russian managers and workers, who consider government attempts to privatize industry a threat to their control over the economy. Latvian conservative and right-wing parties use the continued Russian presence to fan ethnic nationalism and hope to force Russians to assimilate or emigrate.

International issues In the early 1990s Latvia pressured the Russians to withdraw from their naval facilities in the region and remove 57,000 Russian army forces. They withdrew in 1994 as part of an agreement brokered by the United States that allowed the Russians to retain control of an early warning radar system at Skrunda air base, in western Latvia, until 1998.

After the dissolution of the Soviet Union, Latvia was quick to join European international organizations and the United Nations. It is a member of the World Bank and works with the European Bank for Reconstruction and Development to make the transition to a capitalist economy. Latvia has joined with the other Baltic states, Estonia and Lithuania, to found the Baltic Assembly (to coordinate the work of parliaments) and the Baltic Council of Ministers (to coordinate economic and foreign policy). In 1992 Latvia joined with its Baltic neighbors and seven neighboring states to form the Council of the Baltic Sea States, to assist in the Baltic's transition to a free-market economy. In 1995 it was the first Baltic state to apply for membership in the European Union.

Human rights Laws restrict the rights of the Russian minority. Russians are ineligible for Latvian citizenship and therefore may not vote in the national elections.

SEE ALSO
Baltic states; Estonia; Lithuania; Russia; Soviet Union (Union of Soviet Socialist Republics)

FURTHER READING
Dreifelds, Juris. *Latvia in Transition.* New York: Cambridge University Press, 1996.
Hilden, John, and Patrick Salmon. *The Baltic Nations and Europe.* New York: Longman, 1991.

League of Nations

The League of Nations was an international organization of nation-states created after World War I under provisions of the Treaty of Versailles. Members of the league pledged not to go to war before submitting their disputes with other nations to arbitration, which could last up to nine months. Nations that did not do so would be subject to sanctions from the league, including economic and political boycotts.

The covenant of the league, its constitution, was a part of the peace treaties that the victorious allies signed with the defeated Central Powers at the end of the war. The League of Nations came into existence on January 10, 1920, and established its headquarters in Geneva, Switzerland. Because the U.S. Senate refused to ratify the peace treaties containing the league covenant, the United States was never a member. A total of 63 sovereign nations were members of the league, most from Europe and North and South America. Of these, Austria and Albania ended membership when they were annexed by Germany and Italy, respectively. Brazil, Chile, Costa Rica, El Salvador, Guatemala, Honduras, Hungary, Nicaragua, Paraguay, Romania, Spain, and Venezuela withdrew in the late 1930s when the league demonstrated its impotence as a peacemaking organization. The Soviet Union was expelled in 1939 for its aggression against Poland at the start of World War II.

Members of the League of Nations met in 1936 to discuss Germany's reoccupation of the Rhineland but took no action to stop Hitler.

The League of Nations consisted of an assembly, in which each nation had one vote, and a council, composed of the United Kingdom, France, Italy, and Japan (and Germany between 1926 and 1933), and 4 nonpermanent members (increased to 11 in 1936). A secretariat, or administrative office, staffed by international civil servants, was directed by a secretary-general chosen by the council.

The League of Nations created a Permanent Court of International Justice (known today as the World Court) to apply international law to disputes among nations, located at The Hague, Netherlands. The International Labor Organization, an autonomous organization within the framework of the league, promoted health and safety reforms for workers in industrialized nations. Today it continues its work under the auspices of the United Nations.

The League of Nations managed to settle several international disputes, including a territorial one between Sweden and Finland in 1921 and a struggle between Greece and Bulgaria in 1925. But its members were unable to deter Japanese aggression against China in 1931 and Italian aggression against Ethiopia in 1935. The league took no action when Germany reoccupied the Rhineland in 1936 or annexed Austria in 1938. It was powerless in the Spanish Civil War in 1936 and did nothing to stop the Italian conquest of Albania in 1939.

Japan withdrew from the league in 1932 after being condemned for its invasion of China. Germany left the league in 1933 and began a program of rearmament. Italy left the league in 1937 after its invasion of Ethiopia. Once World War II began, the league became defunct, as it became clear that the organization was ineffective in stopping aggression. It held its last meeting in December 1939, when it expelled the Soviet Union from membership for its attack on Finland. The League of Nations was superseded by the United Nations after World War II and formally went out of existence in 1946.

SEE ALSO
International Labor Organization (ILO); United Nations (UN); World Court (International Court of Justice)

FURTHER READING
Gilbert, Murray. *From the League to the UN*. Westport, Conn.: Greenwood, 1988.
Patterson, Charles. *The Oxford 50th Anniversary Book of the United Nations*. New York: Oxford University Press, 1995.
Scott, George. *The Rise and Fall of the League of Nations*. London: Hutchinson, 1973.
Walters, Francis. *A History of the League of Nations*. New York: Oxford University Press, 1965.

Lebanon

REPUBLIC OF LEBANON (AL-JUMHOURIYA AL-LUBNANIYA)

• *Capital: Beirut*

Political history Located in the eastern Mediterranean, the area that is now Lebanon was in ancient times ruled by Phoenicians, then by Romans. In the

11th century Lebanon was conquered by Christian Crusaders. Two centuries later, it was conquered by the Egyptian Mamluk empire. In 1516, the Ottoman Turks defeated the Mamluks and took control. Lebanon became part of the Ottoman Empire in the 16th century, divided into five districts inhabited primarily by Maronite (this refers to an Arabic rite affiliated with the Roman Catholic Church that originated in the 7th century A.D.), Greek Orthodox, and Catholic Christians, and Druze, Shiite, and Sunni Arabs. In 1920 these five districts were separated from Syria (with whom they had been joined by the Ottoman conquerors), formed into Lebanon, and administered by France as a mandate from the League of Nations. Lebanon achieved independence in 1941, and two years later a National Pact among various religious groups within the country gave a majority of the legislative seats to the Christians. In 1946 French troops that had been stationed there during World War II withdrew and the nation became completely independent. A succession of pro-Western governments provided the stability necessary to turn Beirut into a major financial and commercial center. The United States intervened with marines to save the regime from pro-Egyptian groups in 1958 who were attempting to install an anti-Western, Arab nationalist regime.

By the early 1970s hundreds of thousands of Palestinians had relocated to Lebanon from Jordan, including much of the Palestine Liberation Organization and its militias. In 1975 a civil war began, in which a coalition of leftist, Muslim, Druze, and Palestinian forces was pitted against right-wing, predominantly Maronite Christian groups. Beirut was divided into East (Christian) and West (Muslim) zones, and the rest of the country came under the control of local militias and warlords. In 1976 Syria, backing the Muslim side, sent troops into Lebanon to restore order. Six years later, Israel invaded Lebanon to root out Palestinian militias, which had been organizing attacks against Israeli-held areas. After briefly occupying Beirut, Israeli forces withdrew south and established a southern Lebanon security zone of 440 square miles, with its own independent Lebanese administration (run by Christians) and security force, the South Lebanon Army.

The 1989 Charter of National Reconciliation, known as the Taif Accords for the city in Saudi Arabia in which they were signed, paved the way for an end to the civil war and the creation of the Second Lebanese Republic. Since 1991 the country has been dominated by Syria, whose 40,000 troops, under the nominal designation of an Arab peacekeeping force, keep the Muslim and Christian factions in check and enforce the Taif Accords.

Government institutions Lebanon is a consociational democracy that provides specific representation for the various Muslim and Christian denominations in the government. Under the 1926 constitution, legislative power is exercised by the 108-member National Assembly. Seats are allocated by religion and, according to the Taif Accords, the legislature consists of an equal number

A Lebanese couple examines the rubble of their former home after an Israeli bombing raid in southern Lebanon. Throughout the 1970s and 1980s, Lebanon was one of the most wartorn regions on earth.

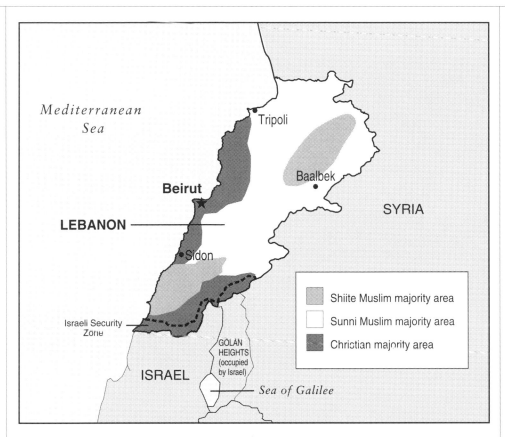

of Christians and Muslims. The president of the republic is the head of state and has traditionally been a Maronite Christian; the prime minister is a Sunni Muslim; and the president of the National Assembly is a Shiite Muslim.

Lebanon has a parliamentary system, in which a prime minister and cabinet (also formed along religious lines—half Christian and half Muslim) is responsible to the National Assembly. Under the Taif Accords, executive power was shifted from the Christian president to the Sunni Muslim prime minister and the Shiite Muslim president of the National Assembly.

The independent judiciary enforces laws drawn from Ottoman rule (criminal law) and French colonial rule (property, contracts, and civil procedures) and laws passed since the country gained independence (maritime law). The Court of Justice deals with national security issues. There are 56 district courts that deal with criminal and civil cases. There are 11 courts of appeal, each of which has 3 justices. The final appeals are heard by 4 Courts of Cassation, any one of which may reverse a lower court's decision and then try the case itself.

Parties and movements In Lebanon's multiparty system, political parties are organized along religious lines. The most powerful nongovernmental groups are the Lebanese militias (supported by the parties) and Palestinian political and military organizations. The radical Islamic group Hezbollah and its militia, the Party of God, are significant among Shiites in the south.

Domestic issues Since the end of the civil war in 1991, Lebanon has been engaged in economic reconstruction. It is once again an international banking and communications center and is attempting to establish itself as the gateway to the Middle East for European and American companies, some of which have established regional headquarters in the city. The Taif Accords call for a national commission to look into ways to eliminate religious-based representation in the parliament and cabinet, but as of 1997 there was no agreement on ending the system and replacing it with either proportional representation or single-seat contests. Christians are outnumbered 2-to-1 in the population, and the Phalange Party (Maronite) has threatened a renewal of civil war if the 50-50 power-sharing arrangement is ended.

International issues Lebanon is closely allied with Syria, which occupies much of the country with 35,000 troops and may have long-term plans for its annexation into a new "Greater Syria." In late May 1991 the two nations signed a treaty of "fraternity, cooperation and coordination" and established the Lebanese-Syrian Supreme Council to coordinate domestic and foreign policies.

Israel launched major attacks on Palestinian and Hezbollah bases in southern Lebanon in 1991 and 1993, but Lebanon remains a major staging area for guerrilla attacks by the 15,000 members of the pro-Iranian Party of God against settlements in northern Israel.

Human rights At least 17,000 Lebanese were seized by both sides as hostages during the civil war, and many remain unaccounted for. Pro-Iranian groups located in Beirut seized Western hostages, tortured and executed several, and exchanged others with the United States, France, and Germany for money and weapons in the early 1980s.

SEE ALSO

France; Iran; Ottoman Empire; Syria

FURTHER READING

Choueiri, Youssef, ed. *State and Society in Syria and Lebanon, 1919–1991.* New York: St. Martin's, 1994.
Collelo, Thomas, ed. *Lebanon: A Country Study.* 3rd ed. Washington, D.C.: Federal Research Division, Library of Congress, 1989.

Friedman, Thomas. *From Beirut to Jerusalem.* New York: Anchor, 1990.
Hanf, Theodore. *Co-Existence in War: Death of a State and Birth of a Nation in Lebanon.* New York: St. Martin's, 1994.
Khalaf, Samir. *Lebanon's Predicament.* New York: Columbia University Press, 1987.
Weinberger, Naomi. *Syrian Intervention in Lebanon.* New York: Oxford University Press, 1986.

Lenin, Vladimir Ilich

- *Born: Apr. 10, 1870, Simbirsk, Russia*
- *Died: Jan. 21, 1924, Gorki, Soviet Union*

Vladimir Ilich Lenin was the leader of the Bolsheviks during the Russian Revolution and head of the Russian government from 1918 to 1924. A brilliant intellectual, committed revolutionary, and fiery speaker, he rose to prominence by force of his personality, his ruthlessness, and his tactical genius in dealing with allies and enemies.

Under his leadership in the early 1900s the Bolsheviks renounced any possibility of peacefully seizing power from the czar and became a revolutionary party; as leader of Russia, Lenin enabled the Bolsheviks to consolidate their power after winning a civil war against

This contemporary painting shows Lenin addressing the citizens of Moscow on May 5, 1920. At the time, Russia was embroiled in civil war.

the counterrevolutionary armies. Under Lenin's regime, the communists began their reign of terror against "class enemies" and political dissidents—a legacy carried on and extended by Lenin's successor, Joseph Stalin, leading to the transformation of the Soviet Union from a radical revolutionary regime into a totalitarian dictatorship.

Lenin, whose surname was originally Ulyanov, was the son of a bureaucrat whom the czar had made a noble in recognition of his loyalty. (Lenin changed his name in 1900 to protect his family.) His older brother Alexander became a revolutionary and was hanged in 1887 after a failed plot to kill the czar. Lenin was expelled from the University of Kazan for his anti-czarist political activities but earned a law degree in absentia in 1891. Two years later, in St. Petersburg, he founded the Union for the Struggle for the Liberation of Labor, a revolutionary organization based on the Marxist idea that the czar's government was oppressing the workers and must be overthrown. In 1897 Lenin was arrested for his anti-government activities and spent three years in exile in Siberia, where he married and took the name Lenin.

In 1900 Lenin went to Munich, where he edited the newspaper *Iskra* (The Spark) and journals on Marxism and raised funds for his revolutionary activities. He also trained Russian revolutionaries in Paris. During this time Lenin wrote books and articles that set out his theory that communist intellectuals in Russia must guide the industrial workers, who would lead a revolution to end czarist rule. After the revolution, the workers would establish a "dictatorship of the proletariat" *(proletariat* is a term for "industrial workers"), with the Communist Party taking the leading role in guiding the revolution and the government that it would establish.

In 1903 Lenin's Bolshevik faction of the Communist Party split with the Mensheviks, the minority faction. (The names *Bolshevik* and *Menshevik* mean "majority" and "minority.") The Mensheviks believed that after the czar was overthrown, a multiparty social democracy patterned along Western lines, rather than a proletariat dictatorship, should be established.

Lenin opposed World War I and lived in exile in Switzerland, refusing to support Russia's stance against the German invaders. In the spring of 1917, after the czar's government had collapsed and a provisional government had been formed, the Germans arranged for a sealed railway car to take Lenin to St. Petersburg. The Social Revolutionaries, members of a moderate party favoring representative constitutional government, came to power, led by Aleksandr Kerensky. In October, however, Lenin and his Bolshevik followers launched a successful coup and seized power from Kerensky. They proclaimed the Russian Soviet Federated Socialist Republic. Lenin became chairman of the Council of People's Commissars, leading the new government. He signed a separate peace agreement with Germany, the Treaty of Brest-Litovsk, in 1918, which freed the government to concentrate on putting down opposition to the revolution.

Lenin consolidated power by defeating the counterrevolutionary White Russians, conservatives who supported the czar and whose white flag distinguished them from the Soviet Reds, in a civil war fought between 1918 and 1921. The Reds won in spite of military intervention on behalf of the Whites by the United States and other Western powers. To encourage postwar reconstruction, Lenin then relaxed communist dogma, which called for state control of all industry, and proclaimed a New Economic Policy, which liberalized the economy by permitting some private enterprise.

Lenin suffered a stroke in December 1922 that left him partially incapacitated. He died, never having fully recovered, in January 1924. Lenin's death plunged the new Soviet Union into a fierce struggle for power. His failure to establish a legitimate system of constitutional and democratic government, and his own participation in revolutionary acts of violence, paved the way for an even more ruthless communist regime after his death.

SEE ALSO

Bolsheviks; Communism; Kerensky, Aleksandr; Marxism-Leninism; Russia; Russian Revolution; Soviet Union (Union of Soviet Socialist Republics)

FURTHER READING

Haney, John D. *Vladimir Ilich Lenin.* New York: Chelsea House, 1988.

Lenin, Vladimir Ilich. *Introduction to Marx, Engels, Marxism.* New York: International Publishers, 1987.

Lenin, Vladimir Ilich. *The Lenin Anthology.* Edited by Robert C. Tucker. New York: Norton, 1975.

Pipes, Richard, ed. *The Unknown Lenin.* New Haven: Yale University Press, 1996.

Pomper, Philip. *Lenin, Trotsky, and Stalin.* New York: Columbia University Press, 1990.

Ulam, Adam. *The Bolsheviks.* New York: Collier, 1968.

Wolfe, Bertram. *Three Who Made a Revolution: A Biographical History.* 4th rev. ed. New York: Dell, 1964.

Lesotho

KINGDOM OF LESOTHO

• *Capital: Maseru*

Political history Located in southern Africa, the area known as Basutoland from 1818 to 1966 was originally in-

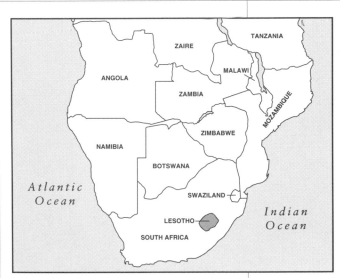

habited by the San (Bushmen) people. In the 18th century Zulus and then Sotho-speaking people moved into the area from East Africa. King Moshoeshoe negotiated a treaty of protection in 1843 with the British to stop the advance of Zulus in the south. In 1871 the British annexed it to the Cape Colony (later known as South Africa), whose territory completely surrounded it. In 1884 Basutoland became a British Crown Colony and was removed from Cape Colony jurisdiction. In 1966 it became an independent member of the Commonwealth of Nations under the name Lesotho.

The government of Chief (prime minister) Leabua Jonathan, who had ruled since independence, was overthrown in 1986 by Major General Justin Lekhanya. The army ousted the monarch, King Moshoeshoe II, in 1990 and installed his son, King Letsie III, as a figurehead for the military. Lehkanya, in turn, was deposed in 1991, and a new government held free elections and established a representative democracy within a constitutional monarchy. In 1994 an elected civilian regime took power for the first time, led by prime minister Ntsu Mokhele. In 1995 King Letsie III dismissed the elected government, however, as a prelude to reinstating his father, former King Moshoeshoe, which he did in 1995. After his death in a car accident in 1996, Letsie III was elected by the College of Chiefs to the throne.

Government institutions Lesotho is a monarchy in which the king is head of state. The College of Chiefs, consisting of tribal leaders, elects and deposes the monarch by majority vote. In 1990 the National Constituent Assembly was founded to draft a new constitution establishing representative institutions, which went into effect in 1993.

The constitution established a parliamentary system, with the king as head of state (without governing powers) and a prime minister and council of ministers accountable to a 65-member parliament elected by direct popular vote to run the government.

There is an independent judiciary. Judicial Commissioner's Courts try minor cases. Appeals are taken to the High Court, and the final appeal may be made to the Court of Appeal, which can also take original jurisdiction in any case.

Parties and movements Between 1986 and 1990 the military regime banned political parties. The Basotho National Party and Basotho Congress Party are the two largest parties today; the latter won the 1993 parliamentary elections and formed a government in 1994.

Domestic issues Lesotho remains unstable politically. King Letsie has been involved in attempts to dismiss the parliament and restore monarchical rule. Since 1993 there have been several coup attempts by officers in the armed forces, which were put down in 1994 by forces loyal to the government, and the military remains torn apart by factionalism.

International issues Lesotho is economically dependent on South Africa, whose industries and mines employ many workers from Lesotho. In 1986 Lesotho agreed to prevent raids into South Africa by members of the African National Congress (ANC) stationed in Lesotho. The ANC was engaged in armed struggle against the apartheid regime in South Africa at that time. Since the ANC came to power in South Africa in 1995, there remains considerable distrust between its leaders and the monarchy in Lesotho, which believes that South Africa may wish eventual incorporation into its territory.

The regimes signed accords late in 1995 to prevent cross-border smuggling and cattle rustling.

SEE ALSO
South Africa

FURTHER READING
Bardill, John, and James Cobbe. *Lesotho.* Boulder, Colo.: Westview, 1985.

Liberalism

Liberalism is a political theory whose proponents call for a secular state without an established religion; state-run secular schools instead of religious schooling; an end to monopolistic privileges in industry, trade, and finance; and the establishment of constitutional parliamentary government in place of monarchical rule.

Liberalism developed in 19th-century western Europe. Liberals tended to be merchants, industrialists, financiers, scientists, and educators who wished to end the privileges of the landowners and aristocrats allied with the hereditary monarchies. They called for free markets run by capitalist entrepreneurs rather than monopolies granted by the Crown to favored nobles. Liberals emphasized science and rationality rather than custom and tradition, and they promoted the positive law of public administration (that is, laws passed by legislatures to reflect the will of the people) rather than the natural law of the churches proclaimed by the clergy. Liberals emphasized civil rights and liberties and the rule of law as fundamentals of constitutional government. Liberal thought underlay the creation of the U.S. Constitution of 1787.

Liberal parties in the late 19th century opposed the socialist and communist parties then coming into existence in Europe because they would have nationalized (put under government control) the factories and financial institutions owned by supporters of liberal thought.

Liberals in Europe have not won the support of rural or urban workers because they have failed to offer them tangible benefits, and their base of support has shrunk in much of the 20th century and now typically consists of members of religious or ethnic minorities and affluent professional classes.

In western European politics most liberal parties are small, but they often hold the balance of power between larger parties to their right and left. As a result, their centrist position makes them suitable to participate in coalition governments. Outside Europe, liberals have sometimes won power on their own: the Liberal Party in Canada and the Democratic Party in the United States are the two largest and most powerful liberal parties.

In foreign economic policy, liberal parties tend to favor free trade rather than trade barriers and are in favor of regional integration, such as the European Union.

The Liberal International is a group of liberal parties—consisting of 16 European parties, 3 Latin American parties, plus the Canadian and Israeli parties— that meets to discuss liberal positions on issues such as tariffs and foreign investment. The Federation of Liberal, Democratic, and Reform Parties is a transnational group of liberals in the European Parliament and has member parties in 11 of the 12 nations of the European Union.

SEE ALSO

Capitalism; Communism; European Parliament; European Union (EU); Free trade; Parliamentary system

FURTHER READING

Bogdanor, Vernon, ed. *Liberal Party Politics*. New York: Oxford University Press, 1983.
Hall, John. *Liberalism*. Chapel Hill: University of North Carolina Press, 1988.
Hobhouse, L. T. *Liberalism*. New York: Oxford University Press, 1964.
Kirchner, Emil, ed. *Liberal Parties in Western Europe*. New York: Cambridge University Press, 1988.

Liberation theology

Liberation theology is a religious and political movement in Latin America that developed in the 1960s among Catholic priests and lay organizations. It emphasizes the need for Christians to empower the poor and oppressed by making the church responsive to their needs and by organizing Christian communities, by promoting communal and socialist activities rather than defending exploitive capitalism and, if necessary, by encouraging the poor to join in revolutionary movements against existing oppressive regimes. The liberation theologians assumed that it might be necessary to join with communist parties in revolutionary fronts against right-wing governments that were exploiting and oppressing the poor.

This grass-roots movement of priests gained some sympathy at various Latin American bishops' conferences, but the bishops condemned any alliance between Catholics and communists, whom they viewed as godless and amoral revolutionaries. They also condemned efforts to create "people's churches" outside of the institutionalized structure of parishes controlled by the church hierarchy.

Liberation theology played a role in the Sandinista defeat of the conservative Somoza regime in Nicaragua in 1979 as well as in the civil war in El Salvador (1981–93), where liberation priests allied themselves with the revolutionary movement Farabundo Martí National Liberation Front, named after an early 20th-century revolutionary figure in Central America. The Vatican, responding to the growth of liberation theology in Latin America, did not condemn the movement but in the 1980s it did insist that priests steer clear of alliances with Marxists and abandon the idea of class struggle and armed revolution.

In the 1990s liberation theologians emphasized building mass-based rural Christian communities along socialist lines, especially in rural areas. Liberation theology remains a strong force among many priests in rural Mexico and in much of Central America, those who minister to Indians in the Andes, and priests in the slums of Brazilian cities.

SEE ALSO
Capitalism; Communism; El Salvador; Marxism-Leninism; Nicaragua; Socialism

FURTHER READING
Gutierrez, Gustavo. *A Theology of Liberation.* Maryknoll, N.Y.: Orbis, 1988.
Novak, Michael. *Will It Liberate? Questions about Liberation Theology.* Lanham, Md.: Madison Books, 1991.
Sigmund, Paul E. *Liberation Theology at the Crossroads: Democracy or Revolution?* New York: Oxford University Press, 1990.

Liberia
REPUBLIC OF LIBERIA

• *Capital: Monrovia*

Political history Located in West Africa, Liberia was settled in 1822 by emancipated black slaves from the United States, with the financial support of the American Colonization Society, a group of whites that believed that slaves and free blacks in the United States should be encouraged to return to the continent of their ancestors. Jehudi Ashmun, a black Methodist minister, became the leader of the first colony, located at Cape Montserrado. In 1847 Joseph Jenkins Roberts became the first black governor, and he declared the settlement a sovereign state, which soon achieved international recognition from European nations and the United States. Roberts did what he could to stop the slave trade along the West African coast. In Liberia, the former slaves, known as Americo-Liberians, ruled over three indigenous African linguistic groups, the Mande, the Kwa, and the Mel, divided into more than 20 different tribes.

Liberia was ruled by a succession of authoritarian civilian leaders, descendants of the black freedmen from the United States who organized the True Whig Party and made Liberia into a one-party state. William Tubman, president from 1944 to 1971, was the last leader of the party to be president. He was also the last Americo-Liberian; subsequently, all Liberian leaders have been Africans. A military coup led by Samuel Doe overthrew the civilian government in 1980. Doe stocked the government with members of the Krahn tribe, leading to ethnic tensions threatening the military government's stability.

The first settle-ment established by emancipated American slaves in Liberia was this mission built by the American Colonization Society at Cape Montserrado in 1822.

In 1989 a civil war began when Charles Taylor and his National Patriotic Front movement (representing the Gio and Mano tribes) attempted to over-throw Doe, who was later captured and executed. Ethnic and factional fighting among many different groups ensued, and the violence claimed more than 150,000 lives. A peace accord was signed in July 1993 and is monitored by peace-keepers from other West African states. In 1995 the leaders of the three largest politi-cal factions—Charles Taylor, Alhaji Kromah, and George Boley—agreed to join the six-member National Council of State to govern Liberia until elections could be held. By 1996 the fighting among the three factions had renewed and the situation remained unstable. In 1997 the West African peacekeeping states picked a new interim president, Ruth Perry, a former legislator, and im-posed a new peace plan to end the civil war and arrange for elections in 1998.

Government institutions The con-stitution of 1986 provides that the presi-dent, who is directly elected to a six-year term, is head of state. The president also appoints the cabinet. A bicameral legis-lature consists of the 26-member Senate and 64-member House of Representa-tives, both popularly elected. A provi-sional government, run by the National Council of State, was formed in 1993 to prepare Liberia for free elections and a return to peace.

A five-member supreme court, com-posed of representatives of the major factions, was established in 1992. There are magistrate's courts for petty offenses and circuit courts for serious civil and criminal cases, but the system has not functioned during the civil war.

Parties and movements Liberia has a number of factions represented on the National Council of State, each of which exists simply to advance the political am-bitions of its leaders and the tribes that support them. The three largest factions are the National Patriotic Front of Liberia, led by Charles Taylor; the Ulimo-K faction, led by Alhaji Kromah; and the Liberia Peace Council, led by George Boley. The remnants of the mili-tary are represented by General Heze-kiah Bowen, chief of staff of the armed forces of Liberia.

Domestic issues Taylor and Kromah are the main contenders for power on the National Council of State, and until their power struggle has been settled, Liberia will remain impoverished and divided among tribally based mili-tias that have established their own fiefdoms, collect taxes and tariffs, and prevent any reconstruction of the shat-tered economy.

International issues More than 750,000 Liberians have been displaced into surrounding nations because of fight-ing in the countryside, and there have been incidents involving armed Liberian militias that have even invaded neighbor-ing states to attack rival groups that have fled. The 1995 peace agreement was ar-ranged by Ghana and Nigeria, acting on behalf of the Economic Community of West African States (ECOWAS), and these two nations have continued to inter-vene with military force in Liberia's cha-otic politics to prevent challenges to the authority of the National Council.

Human rights Guerrillas from Taylor's forces have been accused of atrocities and genocide against the Krahn and Mandingo tribes, who are mostly supporters of the former military regime. Alhaji Kromah, a Mandingo, has been accused by the Lofa Defense Force, a militia group, of massacring members of the Lofa tribe. More than 150,000 Liberians have been killed and 2.6 million left homeless because of the civil war.

FURTHER READING

Beyan, Amos. *The American Colonization Society and the Creation of the Liberation State*. Lanham, Md.: University Press of America, 1991.

Clapham, Christopher. *Liberia and Sierra Leone*. New York: Cambridge University Press, 1976.

Liebenow, J. Gus. *Liberia: The Quest for Democracy*. Bloomington: Indiana University Press, 1987.

Sawyer, Amos. *The Emergence of Autocracy in Liberia*. San Francisco: Institute for Contemporary Studies, 1992.

Libya

SOCIALIST PEOPLE'S LIBYAN ARAB JAMAHIRIYA (AL-JAMAHIRIYAH AL-ARABIYA AL-LIBYA AL SHABIYA AL-ISHTIRAKIYA)

• *Capital: Tripoli*

Political history Located along the southern Mediterranean between Egypt and Tunisia, Libya was settled by Berber tribes in ancient times, then by Phoenicians and Greeks in the 7th century B.C. Between the 2nd century B.C. and the 7th century A.D., the area was ruled by Carthage, Rome, the Vandals (a Germanic tribe), and the Byzantine Empire. It was conquered by Arabian tribes in the 7th century, who converted the people to Islam. In the 16th century Libya became part of the Ottoman Empire. The territory was granted au-

tonomy in 1711 but became an Ottoman *vilayet* (province) in 1835.

In 1911 Italy occupied Tripoli, a city on the coast, and settled more than 100,000 Italians there. The region was occupied by German forces during World War II until France and Britain occupied parts of Libya in 1943 and established their own colonial rule, governing it as a UN trusteeship after the war. Libya gained its independence from both Britain and France in 1951 under King Idris I. An army coup d'état abolished the monarchy and established a military regime under Colonel Muammar Qaddafi in 1969.

Government institutions In 1973 Qaddafi abolished the national government and established "people's committees" to administer public matters under his direction. In theory, Libya is ruled according to Qaddafi's concept of *jamahiriya,* which means "state of the masses," and is a direct democracy; in practice, however, it is an authoritarian state controlled by Qaddafi and his followers in several tribes.

Legislative power is vested in the 1,112-member General People's Congress. All Libyans are members of one of the 2,150 Basic People's Congresses (the "people's committees") organized around neighborhoods or occupations. Executive power is vested in

Libyan workers leave the chemical plant at Rabta. The plant became the object of international controversy in the late 1980s, when the United States claimed that it was designed to produce chemical weapons.

the General People's Committee, consisting of 22 secretaries appointed by Qaddafi who run the government departments.

The judiciary functions under the direction of the government. The People's Courts hear minor cases, and the Courts of First Instance hear serious civil and criminal cases. These cases are reviewed by the Courts of Appeal. Cases may be brought for final review to the Supreme Court, which is divided into circuits consisting of at least three justices. Libyan law must conform to rules of *sharī'a*, Islamic religious law.

Parties and movements Since 1971 Libya has banned all political parties. Two attempted coups by elements of the military, in 1986 and 1994, were put down by Qaddafi's revolutionary guards. Libya is governed through direct "popular assemblies" of citizens, which are guided by government officials who receive their instructions from Qaddafi.

Domestic issues Libya has, in the 1990s, permitted private enterprises to open and has privatized some state enterprises to encourage economic growth. The falling price of crude oil has hurt the Libyan economy, as has an international embargo on all flights in and out of the country, due to Libyan sponsorship of terrorism, though this has not created sufficient discontent to threaten the regime.

International issues Libya has attempted to export its brand of Arab nationalist, socialist, and revolutionary anti-Western politics to other states in Africa and the Middle East. In 1986 the U.S. State Department published a list of the terrorist movements Libya has sheltered, most of them involving radical Palestinian and Islamic movements.

Libya and Egypt fought several inconclusive border skirmishes in the late 1970s. Libya occupied large sections of Chad until driven back by French forces

in 1977 and the Chadian government in 1987. Libya claims sovereignty over the Aozou Strip, an area rich in minerals lying in Chad, adjacent to Libya, but in 1994 the World Court ruled that the territory belonged to Chad.

In 1987 Libya established close diplomatic links with Iran, which it viewed as an ally in its efforts to diminish U.S. influence in the region. Libya also has close ties with the Islamic regime in Sudan. A pro-Libyan government took power in Chad in 1990, militarily defeating a pro-Western faction favored by the United States and France.

The United States has had a number of conflicts with Libya. In 1986 it froze Libyan assets held in U.S. banks in reprisal for the suspected Libyan involvement in the bombing of a disco in West Berlin that killed 1 American and wounded 60 others. The United States retaliated with a bombing attack that injured several members of Qaddafi's family. The United States sent naval vessels into waters claimed by Libya to establish the U.S. right of passage and shot down several Libyan military planes that challenged U.S. fighters in the area. Attempts by the United States and other nations to foment popular discontent that might bring down Qaddafi have failed because of his popularity with Libyans, based in large measure on his anti-Western and pan-Arab rhetoric.

In 1989 Libya took the lead in establishing the Union of the Arab Maghreb, comprising Algeria, Libya, Mauretania, Morocco, and Tunisia, which is intended to promote economic and political cooperation but which has not served Qaddafi's ultimate aim of unifying the area under his leadership.

Human rights Libya was a pioneer in the use of state-sponsored terrorist activities against its enemies. It has funded terrorists who have bombed several airliners carrying civilian passengers, including the U.S. passenger plane over Lockerbie, Scotland, in 1988, in which all 258 passengers aboard, including 36 Syracuse University students returning from study abroad, were killed. It also bombed a French passenger plane the following year. The United Nations has imposed limited aviation sanctions on Libya until it hands over two terrorists accused in the Lockerbie bombing to British authorities for trial, but Libya has not done so.

SEE ALSO

Ottoman Empire; Qaddafi, Muammar al-

FURTHER READING

Anderson, Lisa. *The State and Social Transformation in Tunisia and Libya.* Princeton, N.J.: Princeton University Press, 1987.

Davis, John. *Libyan Politics.* Berkeley: University of California Press, 1987.

Fallaci, Oriana. "An Encounter with Colonel Qaddafi." *New York Times Magazine*, April 14, 1996.

Metz, Helen Chapin, ed. *Libya: A Country Study.* 4th ed. Washington, D.C.: Federal Research Division, Library of Congress, 1988.

Liechtenstein

PRINCIPALITY OF LIECHTENSTEIN (FURSTENTUM LIECHTENSTEIN)

• *Capital: Vaduz*

Political history Located in a valley between Austria and Switzerland, the area surrounding the city of Vaduz was originally inhabited by the Germanic Alemanni (a tribe) in the 6th century A.D. It became a part of the Holy Roman Empire in 1719, and in 1791 it was constituted as a principality (a province governed by a royal prince) by the Holy Roman Emperor Charles VI. Upon the dissolution of the Holy Roman Empire in 1806, it became a sovereign nation and joined the Rhine Federation, an alliance of Germanic principalities, during the early 1800s, when Napoléon dominated the European continent. In 1815, after Napoléon's defeat, Liechtenstein joined the German Confederation established by the victors at the Congress of Vienna (while remaining a sovereign state) and stayed within it until 1866, when it resisted the growing tendency toward German unification.

Economically and diplomatically, Liechtenstein was closely affiliated with Austria until 1919; as a result of Austria's defeat in World War I, however, Liechtenstein moved into the Swiss orbit. Today its currency and postal service are Swiss, although Liechtenstein issues its own stamps (avidly sought by stamp collectors); its medical services are affiliated with Switzerland and its citizens have access to Swiss doctors and hospitals; and it has a customs union with Switzerland that provides for uniform tariffs.

Although German is the official language of Liechtenstein, a dialect (Alemanni) is in wide use.

Government institutions Liechtenstein is a constitutional monarchy. The prince is the head of state. The 25

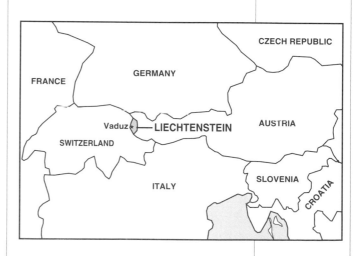

members of the unicameral parliament (*Landtag* in the German dialect) are elected for four-year terms. The monarch can veto legislation passed by the Landtag. A five-member government of ministers is elected by the Landtag and confirmed by the prince. The Supreme Court, Superior Court, and Constitutional Court are appointed by the government.

Parties and movements The two main parties are the Vaterländische Union and the Fortschrittliche Bürger Partei. Both are centrist and the differences between them involve personalities. They govern in a coalition, with the majority party controlling the council of ministers.

Domestic issues Because of its laws providing for confidentiality and its lax regulation of businesses, Liechtenstein is the nominal headquarters of many banks and corporations that seek to evade the strict regulations of other nations.

International issues Liechtenstein was not aligned with the West during the cold war but, like Austria and Switzerland, remained independent of all power blocs. It does participate in various European economic and security organizations: it is a member of the World Court, the Council of Europe, the European Free Trade Association, and the United Nations. It also participates in the Conference on Security and Cooperation in Europe.

SEE ALSO

Conference on Security and Cooperation in Europe (CSCE); Council of Europe; European Free Trade Association (EFTA); Switzerland; United Nations (UN); World Court (International Court of Justice)

FURTHER READING

Kohn, Walter S. G. *Governments and Politics of the German-Speaking Countries*. Chicago: Nelson-Hall, 1980.
Kranz, Walter, ed. *The Principality of Liechtenstein: A Documentary Handbook*. 4th rev. and enlarged ed. Vaduz:
Press and Information Office of the Government of the Principality of Liechtenstein, 1978.
Seger, Otto. *A Survey of Liechtenstein History*. Vaduz: Fürstlich Liechtensteinisches Pfadfinderkorps St. Georg, 1984.

Lithuania

REPUBLIC OF LITHUANIA (LIETUVOS RESPUBLICA)

• *Capital: Vilnius*

Political history Located near the Baltic Sea, the area was settled by Lithuanian tribes of Germanic origin in the 9th century A.D. As an independent kingdom, for a time after the 13th century, it acquired a vast swath of Russian, Polish, and Ukrainian land, from the Baltic to the Black Sea, holding sway over the large cities of Vilnius, Smolensk, Kiev, and Bratislava. In 1569 the grand duchy of Lithuania united with Poland in the Union of Lublin (named for a city in Poland). The grand duchy became a Polish and German counterweight to the expanding Russian state of Muscovy.

In 1795, following a series of military setbacks, Lithuania was annexed by Russia when Poland was divided between Russia and Prussia. It was occupied by

Independence supporters in Vilnius display a poster of the three Baltic republics (Lithuania, Estonia, and Latvia) cutting themselves free from Soviet rule. (CCCP is the abbreviation for U.S.S.R. in the Cyrillic alphabet.)

LITHUANIA IN 1462

SWEDEN

RUSSIA AND COLONIES

KHANATE OF KAZAN

Baltic Sea

Moscow ★

LIVONIAN KNIGHTS

Vilna ★

LITHUANIA AND ITS POSSESSIONS

KHANATE OF ASTRAKHAN

Warsaw ★

POLAND

CRIMEAN KHANATE

HUNGARY

CAUCASUS

Black Sea

BULGARIA

OTTOMAN EMPIRE

the Germans in World War I, then briefly by Poland after the war. It became an independent nation in 1918. A military coup d'état overthrew the democratic government and established an authoritarian dictatorship in 1926. In 1940, under Soviet pressure, Lithuania was occupied by the Red Army. It declared its independence in early 1991, an act recognized by Soviet leader Mikhail Gorbachev in late August 1991.

Government institutions Lithuania adopted a new constitution in October 1992, which established a parliamentary system. The head of state is the president, who is directly elected for a five-year term. Executive power is vested in a council of ministers, headed by a prime minister, appointed by the president with the consent of the legislature, the 141-member Seimas.

The judiciary consists of district courts, a Court of Appeal, and the Supreme Court. Justices of the Supreme Court are nominated by the president with the consent of the legislature. Judges of the Court of Appeal are nominated by a council of judges, subject to approval by the president and legislature. Lower court judges are appointed by the president. A constitutional court reviews the constitutionality of laws passed by the Seimas.

Parties and movements In 1991 the political movement called Sajudis, which had been the primary force fighting for an independent Lithuania, was defeated in the parliamentary elections after having mismanaged the postindependence economy. With its power diminished, it announced its transformation from a political party to a nonpartisan civic organization in 1992.

Lithuania in the mid-1990s had a multiparty system; the two main parties were the Democratic Labor Party of Lithuania (the former Communist Party) and the Conservative Party of Lithuania. Former Communists still wield considerable influence; the first president elected after independence, Algirdas Brazauskas, had been the leader of the Communist Party in the 1980s. The Democratic Labor Party under prime minister Adolfas Slezevicius formed the government after the parliamentary elections of 1992. The Conservative Homeland Party then won the 1996 parliamentary elections, with the Democratic Labor Party winning less than 10 percent of the vote because of its corruption and economic mismanagement.

Domestic issues The weakness of the post-Soviet economy, especially its rampant inflation and sharp drops in industrial and agricultural production (which resulted in high unemployment), led to the defeat of the first post-Communist government and a return to power of some former Communists in 1992. A Temporary Economic Crisis Committee was formed in 1992 to moderate the initial privatization efforts. In 1993 regulations forbidding foreigners to own property were lifted in a move to spur investment. With the control of inflation in 1994 and an increase in trade with the West, Lithuania was on the road to the development of a stable parliamentary democracy.

International issues Lithuania has a self-described foreign policy of "three plus five," which emphasizes close links with the other two Baltic nations (Estonia and Latvia) and with the five Nordic countries (Denmark, Finland, Iceland, Norway, and Sweden). Like the other Baltic states, Lithuania refused to join the Commonwealth of Independent States after the breakup of the Soviet Union. It has become a member of the Council of Europe and has sought economic ties with the European Union instead.

Lithuania signed a Declaration on Friendly Relations and Neighborly Cooperation with Poland in 1992 to recognize officially post–World War II borders and signed a treaty with Poland in 1994. The government of former Communists installed in 1993 worked to develop economic relations with states of the Commonwealth of Independent States. Russia withdrew the last of its troops in the summer of 1993. Lithuania has joined the Partnership for Peace, an association of eastern European nations hoping to join NATO, and has formally applied for membership in NATO.

Human rights In 1994 the government of Lithuania apologized to the Jewish community for the collaboration of Lithuanians during World War II in the Nazi genocide of 200,000 Lithuanian Jews and pledged that it would conduct prosecutions against those involved in these crimes.

Although 80 percent of the population is ethnic Lithuanian, 260,000 ethnic Poles live in the Vilnius area and there are also some ethnic Russians, constituting 9 percent of the population, who seek to preserve their own language and culture. Poland and Lithuania signed an accord in 1994 guaranteeing educational and cultural rights to the Polish minority.

SEE ALSO

Baltic states; Commonwealth of Independent States (CIS); Estonia; Latvia; Soviet Union (Union of Soviet Socialist Republics)

FURTHER READING

Clements, Walter, Jr. *Baltic Independence and Russian Empire.* New York: St. Martin's, 1991.

Senn, Alfred. *Lithuania Awakening.* Berkeley: University of California Press, 1990.

Lloyd George, David

- *Born: Jan. 17, 1863, Manchester, England*
- *Died: Mar. 26, 1945, Carnarvonshire, North Wales*

As prime minister of the United Kingdom (1916–22), David Lloyd George created the modern welfare state and then led his nation to victory in World War I, becoming the Earl of Dwyfor in recognition of his service to the nation.

Lloyd George was born in Manchester. He read law (studied under a lawyer) and became a solicitor (lawyer) in 1884. In 1890 he was elected to Parliament as a Welsh Nationalist. In 1905 he was chosen to head the Board of Trade and the following year he settled a bitter railroad strike. In 1908 he was made chancellor of the exchequer in Herbert Asquith's Liberal cabinet, the No. 2 post in the government. The following year he submitted a "war budget against poverty." Supported by Labour and Liberal members of Parliament, it was opposed by the heavily Conservative House of Lords. The Lords refused to approve the budget until there was a national parliamentary election, which would serve as a referendum on it. The election was

Known as the Welsh Wizard, Lloyd George was the architect of what was then the most progressive program of social legislation in British history.

held, the Liberals won, and Lloyd George was vindicated.

After another parliamentary election in 1910, King George V agreed to create enough new peers in the House of Lords to pass a bill reforming Parliament. As a result of the new law, the Lords would be unable to prevent implementation of bills passed by the House of Commons, though they would be permitted to delay them and could still propose modifications.

After this reform, which ended the veto power of the upper classes in Parliament and strengthened popular government, Lloyd George, as chancellor of the exchequer, introduced and got Parliament to pass major welfare-state legislation, including health insurance, old-age pensions, and unemployment insurance.

In 1914 Lloyd George won the support of the financiers in the City of London for British entry into World War I, and he devised a plan to maintain the solvency of the banking system during the war, at a time when the British government had to borrow heavily to pay for military expenses. In 1915 he became minister of munitions and oversaw development of the British war industry. He also pushed the cabinet to agree to conscription of men to fight in the war. In July 1916 he became head of the War Office. But in December he resigned because Prime Minister Asquith did not adopt his plans to coordinate the Allied armies and send troops to the east to aid Russia.

After Asquith's government fell in 1917, the king asked Lloyd George to form a cabinet. He established a unity government from all parties, and within it a small "war cabinet" to conduct the war. He made a key decision to send British and French troops into Italy to save it from the German and Austrian armies in 1917. Early in 1918, as the German army seemed about to make a breakthrough on the Western Front, Lloyd George convinced Woodrow Wilson to send U.S. forces (which were still being trained) into immediate service. He also forced the British generals to accept a combined Allied command under French marshal Ferdinand Foch. These decisions were crucial to the Allied victory of November 1918.

After the war Lloyd George won the 1918 election. But many Liberals broke with him, and his government remained in power only because it was supported by the Conservatives. In 1919 he participated in the peace negotiations at Versailles. He was the crucial mediator between U.S. president Woodrow Wilson and French premier Georges Clemenceau. He agreed with Wilson that there should be a League of Nations and agreed with Clemenceau on harsh peace terms for Germany.

After the war Lloyd George was also a mediator in domestic affairs. He helped fashion a settlement between unions and management in the 1919 railway and coal strikes. In 1921 he and Irish nationalist leaders settled the question of whether Ireland should be independent with an offer of dominion status for its Catholic counties.

Lloyd George fell from power in 1922 when Conservatives left his coalition cabinet. By 1924 his Liberal Party, now down to 40 members of Parliament, was reduced to being the third party in British politics, eclipsed by Ramsay MacDonald's Labour Party.

Lloyd George was an effective leader in war and peace, one of the most successful in British history. He was eloquent and witty, an effective administrator, yet he was known to be ruthless and overbearing and had no close friends. Perhaps the greatest irony in his distinguished career was that in spite of his successes in governing, by the end of his political career, his party had been eliminated as a major factor in British political life.

SEE ALSO
MacDonald, James Ramsay; United Kingdom; Versailles, Treaty of (1919); Welfare state; Wilson, Woodrow

FURTHER READING

Constantine, Stephen. *Lloyd George*. New York: Routledge, 1992.

Gilbert, Bentley B. *David Lloyd George: A Political Life*. 2 vols. Columbus: Ohio State University Press, 1987.

Pugh, Martin. *Lloyd George*. New York: Longman, 1988.

Rowland, Peter. *David Lloyd George: A Biography*. New York: Macmillan, 1976.

Shearman, Deidre. *David Lloyd George*. New York: Chelsea House, 1988.

Wrigley, Chris. *Lloyd George*. Cambridge, Mass.: Blackwell, 1992.

Lumumba, Patrice

- *Born: July 2, 1925, Onalua, Belgian Congo*
- *Died: Jan. 21, 1961, Elizabethville, Congo*

Patrice Lumumba was the leader of the Congolese independence movement and the first prime minister of the Republic of the Congo, known as Zaire from 1961 until 1997 and as the Democratic Republic of Congo since May 1997. Lumumba was a fiery speaker, passionate in his denunciations of colonial rule in Africa; his martyrdom in the cause of Congolese independence inspired a generation of African nationalists and black nationalists in the United States and the Caribbean.

After attending local missionary schools, Lumumba became a postal clerk in Stanleyville (now Kisangani). He organized a postal workers' union, then became a sales director for a brewery. Lumumba went to the capital, Léopoldville (now Kinshasa), and founded the National Congolese Movement, a group promoting independence. He was imprisoned in 1959 on charges of inciting riots. Because Lumumba spoke each of the Congo's major languages (Swahili, Kiluba, Linala, Kikongo) as well as French, he was able to organize a grassroots independence movement that crossed tribal lines.

In May 1960 his party won one-third of the seats in the National Assembly to become the largest political movement in the country. Reluctantly, the Belgian colonial authorities picked Lumumba to head the transitional government as prime minister. He immediately embarked on a radical policy of nationalizing European-controlled enterprises in an effort to create a socialist state. For this he was dismissed by President Joseph Kasavubu, acting with the complicity of the Belgians, shortly after the Congo declared its independence on September 5, 1960. The National Assembly, however, reinstated Lumumba, causing Colonel Mobutu Sese Seko to organize a coup d'état.

Lumumba was put under house arrest but escaped, heading toward Stanleyville. He was captured by government troops, and on January 18, 1961, he was taken into the province of Katanga (now Shaba) and executed by a military detachment acting under orders from a government minister. The United Nations was forced to intervene to restore order in Katanga and the rest of the Congo after Lumumba's death.

Mobutu then seized power and ruled autocratically for more than three decades. Lumumba had opposed Western colonial rule, but his assassination paved the way for Western corporations to invest in Zaire's vast mineral wealth on favorable terms. Lumumba's vision of a Congo free from Western influence and embracing African values rather than foreign culture and ideology died with him.

SEE ALSO

Zaire

FURTHER READING

Kanza, Thomas. *The Rise and Fall of Patrice Lumumba: Conflict in the Congo*. Boston: G. K. Hall, 1979.

Lumumba, Patrice. *Lumumba Speaks*. Edited by Jean van Lierde. Translated by Helen R. Lane. Boston: Little, Brown, 1972.

McKown, Robin. *Lumumba: A Biography*. Garden City, N.Y.: Doubleday, 1969.

Luxembourg

*GRAND DUCHY OF LUXEM-
BOURG (GRAND DUCHÉ DE
LUXEMBOURG [French];
GROSSHERZOGTUM LUXEM-
BURG [German])*

• *Capital: Luxembourg*

Political history Located in northwestern Europe, the city of Luxembourg was founded around A.D. 563 and became part of the empire of Charlemagne, the leader of the Franks (the Germanic tribe that conquered much of France and Germany in the 8th century). It became independent in 963 under Siegfried, a descendant of Charlemagne. In 1060 the city came under the jurisdiction of the House of Luxembourg, a Germanic noble family. After 1315 it was ruled by a succession of European powers, including the duke of Burgundy and Spanish, Austrian, and French monarchs. In 1815 it became a grand duchy ruled by the House of Orange-Nassau, which was also sovereign over the Netherlands. In 1839, after a revolt against the Netherlands failed, it lost the Walloon-speaking area in the north to Belgium, and what was left became a possession of the Dutch Royal House of Nassau. Luxembourg was granted internal autonomy by the House of Nassau in 1848, and in 1867 it became independent, governed by its grand duke (who was also the king of the Netherlands). Grand Duke Adolf of Nassau-Weilberg (a territory of Rhenish Prussia located near Luxembourg) came to the throne in 1890, ending the royal union that had existed with the Netherlands. Luxembourg was overrun by Germany in both world wars but was restored to independence each time after the Allies defeated Germany.

Government institutions Luxembourg is a constitutional monarchy. The grand duke is the head of state and is vested with executive power. He receives advice from his appointed 21-member Council of State. The duke appoints a separate council of ministers to run the government departments and a president of the government, who also serves as the prime minister. The ministers are accountable to the 60-member popularly elected Chamber of Deputies, whose members serve for five years. Judges are appointed for life by the grand duke.

The independent judiciary consists of justices of the peace who deal with minor civil, criminal, and commercial cases. Serious cases are handled by district courts. The Superior Court of Justice handles appeals from lower courts. Judges are appointed for life terms by the grand duke.

Parties and movements Three main parties vie for power in Luxembourg's multiparty system: the Social Christian Party (Christian Democrats), the Socialist Workers Party (socialist), and the Democratic Party (liberal).

Domestic issues Luxembourg's economy has relied on iron and steel production. Business owners, trade unions, and the government coordinate economic policy through tripartite committees. Luxembourg is devoted to maintaining high levels of employment, even as industrial enterprises modernize, because of the strength of its organized unions.

International issues Luxembourg is committed to European economic integration. It has a monetary pact with Belgium and is a member of the Benelux economic union, the European Union, and the North Atlantic Treaty Organization (NATO).

SEE ALSO

Belgium; Benelux; European Union (EU); Netherlands

FURTHER READING

Newcomer, James. *The Grand Duchy of Luxembourg.* Lanham, Md.: University Press of America, 1984.

Maastricht Treaty (1992)

The Maastricht Treaty is an agreement by the 12 members of the European Union (formerly known as the European Community) to promote European economic integration, including the development of a common currency to be introduced in 1999 called the Euro. The treaty was signed in the Dutch town of Maastricht on February 7, 1992. The accord built on the Single Europe Act of 1987, which had created a uniform internal European market within the European Community, including a common external tariff and customs union (so that goods within the European Community could move across borders without tariffs, while goods from outside, such as from Japan and the United States, would be charged a uniform tariff) and a common agricultural policy to prevent ruinous competition among European farmers, all of which had gone into effect by early 1992.

The Maastricht Treaty committed European Union members to a single European currency and to the creation by 1999 of a single central bank, the Economic and Monetary Union (EMU), to regulate it. The use of a single currency would save governments and businesses an estimated $30 billion or more annually. The EMU would then replace the existing Exchange Rate Mechanism (ERM), which had been created by the European Community in 1979 to maintain the value of member nations' currencies within a given fluctuating range.

Prospects that the treaty would go into effect, however, with all provisions intact (particularly the EMU), were not bright. France and Great Britain narrowly approved it, and in Denmark it took two referenda for the treaty to pass. Britain and Denmark won provisions allowing them to opt out of the common currency, which Britain then did in 1992. In 1993 a Germany First policy pursued by the Bundesbank (the German central bank) pushed interest rates up (a measure taken to stem the threat of inflation set off by massive expenditures to improve the economy of eastern Germany after reunification).

Meanwhile, France, Italy, and the Benelux nations engaged in deficit spending (that is, spending borrowed money) to stem their growing unemployment rates. And as their interest rates went down, Europeans rushed to put their money in German banks; as a result, the French franc and other European currencies lost value compared to the German deutsche mark. These currency flows revealed the weakness of the Exchange Rate Mechanism, which shifted in late 1993 from controlling currencies within a fluctuation range of 2.5 percent up or down to a range of 15 percent up or down. This wide range was evidence that the ERM had failed, that member nations would pursue their own monetary policies, and that the European Union would not be able to develop a common currency unless member nations were willing to give up autonomy in making fiscal and monetary policies.

By the late 1990s, European governments were still committed to implementing the treaty. But austerity policies in several countries, including France, Italy, and the United Kingdom, helped to topple the governments that had pursued such policies, and attempts to meet the treaty criteria for fiscal and monetary policies were proving far more difficult than European politicians had anticipated.

SEE ALSO

Central bank; European Union (EU)

FURTHER READING

Kenen, Peter B. *Economic and Monetary Union in Europe: Moving beyond Maastricht.* New York: Cambridge University Press, 1995.

Sbragia, Alberta, ed. *Euro-Politics: Institutions and Policymaking in the "New" European Community.* Washington, D.C.: Brookings Institution, 1993.

Macao

Macao consists of a peninsula on the Chinese mainland and two islands at the mouth of the Pearl River in China. It has a population of 480,000, one-fifth of whom hold Portuguese citizenship. Originally a part of China, Macao became a Portuguese colony and trading post in 1557. European traders settled there and traveled upriver to Canton, China, during the trading season from November to May to trade for silk and spices. Macao also served as a base for Portuguese trade with Japan.

By the 19th century Macao had become a center for gambling and other diversions that Hong Kong, its neighboring European enclave, had refused to legalize. By the 1850s, however, Macao's commercial role had been displaced by Hong Kong, and most Portuguese traders left. Today the major economic activity in Macao is gambling, which draws many people from Hong Kong.

From 1951 through 1974 Macao was an overseas province of Portugal; it then reverted to colonial status so that Portugal and China at that time could define it as Chinese territory under Portuguese administration. In 1987 Portugal and China agreed that Macao would be returned to Chinese control in 1999 and that its capitalist system would be maintained for the following 50 years, an arrangement for decolonization similar to

that which the Chinese negotiated with the British regarding the colony of Hong Kong. The transition is being overseen by the Sino-Portuguese Liaison Group, consisting of officials from both nations.

Until 1999 Macao is administered by a governor-general appointed by the Portuguese president with the informal concurrence of the Chinese government. Government department heads are also appointed by Portugal.

There is a 17-member Legislative Assembly, with 5 members appointed by the governor, 6 directly elected, and 6 chosen by charitable, educational, business, and labor groups in the colony.

SEE ALSO

China; Hong Kong; Portugal

St. Paul's church, built in 1602 with the help of Japanese Christians who had fled persecution, was destroyed by a fire in 1835. Only the stairway and facade of Macao's best-known landmark remain.

FURTHER READING
Guillen-Nuñez, Cesar. *Macau.* New York: Oxford University Press, 1984.

MacDonald, James Ramsay

- *Born: Oct. 12, 1866, Lossiemouth, Scotland*
- *Died: Nov. 7, 1937, at sea*

As prime minister of the United Kingdom (1924, 1929–31, 1931–35), Ramsay MacDonald was the founder of the Labour Party and led its successful effort to become one of the two major parties in British politics.

MacDonald came from a working-class family. He went to Drainie School, a state school in Scotland, then attended evening classes in London while working as a laborer. In 1875 he was elected to the London County Council, where he worked to improve housing conditions for the poor. In 1900 he helped found the Labour Party to represent the interests of working men and women. By 1911 he was the leader of the party in Parliament. In 1913 he was named to the Royal Commission on the Civil Service but resigned when he opposed British entry into World War I in 1914. In 1919, while out of the government, he wrote two books attacking the excesses of the communist revolution in Russia and defending the idea of parliamentary democracy and peaceful reform as effective means to achieve a socialist program.

In 1922, MacDonald was elected leader of the Labour Party. In the election held that year, the party eclipsed the Liberals to become the second largest group in Parliament. The following year his party became the largest, and in 1924 MacDonald was asked by King George V to form a cabinet.

As prime minister, MacDonald concentrated on foreign affairs. He settled the issue of German reparations to France and Italy (the cash payments that were punishment for World War I, which Germany claimed were too high), devising the London Settlement of 1924, which took the issue out of politics and into the hands of technical experts. But MacDonald's attempt to recognize the Russian revolutionary communist government was opposed by the Conservatives and Liberals, and his government fell.

In 1929 MacDonald won a plurality in the parliamentary election and formed his second government. One of his first decisions was to establish diplomatic relations with the communist regime in the Soviet Union. His policy toward Germany was conciliatory. He convinced France to end the Allied occupation of the Rhineland, which had been permitted under the terms of the Treaty of Versailles, which ended World War I. He attended the Washington Naval Limitation Conference in 1930, which resulted in an agreement among Japan, the United Kingdom, and the United States on limiting the number of warships in their navies.

With the United Kingdom's economy suffering as a result of the worldwide depression, MacDonald presided over a national unity government in 1931. Because his government was a coalition from the three parties, it could not take the drastic measures to stimulate the economy that a government formed solely from the Labour Party might have taken, and the nation remained mired in the depression. In 1935 MacDonald resigned for health reasons.

MacDonald's major contribution to British and world politics was the organization of a party of working men and women that condemned violence and concentrated on winning power through the ballot box.

SEE ALSO

Versailles, Treaty of (1919); United Kingdom

FURTHER READING

Marquand, David. *Ramsay MacDonald.* London: Jonathan Cape, 1977.

Morgan, Austen. *J. Ramsay MacDonald.* Manchester, England: Manchester University Press, 1987.

Macedonia

THE FORMER YUGOSLAV REPUBLIC OF MACEDONIA (REPUBLIKA MAKEDONIJA)

• *Capital: Skopje*

Political history Tribes known as Macedonians first settled the Balkan Peninsula north of Greece around 600 B.C. Under Alexander the Great, the kingdom of Makedon conquered Greece and then much of the eastern Mediterranean and Central Asia between 328 and 323 B.C. The area became a Roman province in 148 B.C. Slavs settled in the region beginning in the 6th century A.D., but the Bulgars conquered them in the 7th century to form the Macedo-Bulgar Empire.

Serbia took control of the area in the 14th century, and it became a part of the Ottoman Empire in 1355. In 1878, after defeating the Ottoman Empire in the Russo-Turkish War, Russia gave much of Macedonia to Bulgaria, a new Russian protectorate that had been carved out of Ottoman territories. Later that same year, at the Congress of Vienna (a meeting of European states to work out territorial adjustments), much of Macedonia was returned to the Ottomans at the insistence of the British, who wished to reduce Russian and Bulgarian influence in the Balkans. After the First Balkan War of 1912–13, the Eastern Orthodox nations of Greece, Serbia, and Bulgaria pushed the Muslim Ottoman Empire out of Macedonia. Most of Macedonia went to Serbia, and the remainder to Greece and Bulgaria. After the Second Balkan War of 1913, the Bulgarian portion was divided between Greece and Serbia. The Treaty of Versailles after World War I divided Macedonia once again among Greece, Bulgaria, and Yugoslavia (a larger, newly formed Balkan state that incorporated Serbia). In 1940 the Bulgarians occupied most of Macedonia, with the Greeks taking western territories. Macedonians fought against the Germans when the area was invaded in World War II.

When Marshal Josip Tito created modern Yugoslavia at the end of World War II, Macedonia became a constituent republic in its federal system and codified its Bulgarian southern Slav dialect as a separate language. Macedonia then offered assistance to Greek communists across the southern border during the Greek civil war in 1947 as part of Tito's plan to incorporate northern Greece into a large Macedonian province tied to Yugoslavia, but the defeat of the communist insurgency ended these plans.

Macedonia declared its independence from Yugoslavia in 1991, and the Yugoslav army withdrew peacefully. Because of a dispute with Greece over the name *Macedonia* (which also refers to a large part of northern Greece around Salonika), most nations refer to it as the Former Yugoslav Republic of Macedonia, or FYROM.

Government institutions Macedonia is a republic, with a president as head of state. Legislative power is exercised by a 120-member elected parliament (Sobranje).

Executive power is exercised by the prime minister and a cabinet of ministers, all of whom are elected by a majority vote of parliament.

The independent judiciary consists of district courts that handle civil and criminal matters. The Supreme Court

1069. Σκηναί καί τύποι της Μακεδονίας — Οἰκογένεια χωρικῶν
Scènes et types de Macédoine. — Famille de paysans.

Macedonian peasants pose in traditional clothing. In addition to its own heritage, Macedonia's culture draws on Greek, Serbian, Turkish, and Bulgarian influences.

handles appeals. The Constitutional Court considers the constitutionality of legislation. Judges are appointed and dismissed by the legislature, with the advice of a judicial council that consists of seven lawyers chosen by the legislature.

Parties and movements Former Communists dominate Macedonian politics, under the leadership of President Kiro Gligorov, a one-time Communist Party leader who led the nation to independence. He was elected twice to the presidency, in 1991 and 1995. Gligorov was gravely wounded in a car-bomb attack in October 1995, and the presidency passed to Liberal Party leader Stojan Andov, who ruled in coalition with the communist plurality in parliament. The two main opposition parties are the Democratic Party (social democratic) and the Alliance for Macedonia (right-wing nationalist).

Domestic issues One-quarter of the population is ethnic Albanian and Muslim, one-eighth is Greek, and the majority consists of ethnic Bulgarians (Macedonians) who are Eastern Orthodox Christians. The religious and linguistic diversity in the country has caused ethnic tensions, as the Albanian minority, led by its Party of Democratic Prosperity, has demanded local governing autonomy from the ethnic Bulgarians who control the national

government. The Albanians have also demanded the right to their own schools and the right to use their own language in government offices. The most radical Albanian group wants secession and is headquartered in the western town of Tetovo, near Albania.

International issues Greece believes that Macedonia has designs on its own northern province of Macedonia, which is peopled largely with Greek refugees from Turkey, which forced out ethnic Bulgarians (Macedonians) after World War II. Greece's objections to the use of the name *Macedonia* forced the nation to call itself the Former Yugoslav Republic of Macedonia in order to get into the United Nations and receive recognition from European nations and the United States. Macedonia agreed not to display its flag at the UN because of Greek objections to the design, which includes a 16-pointed star of the *Vergina,* a traditional Greek emblem but one that the Macedonians also claimed after its discovery in the mid-1960s at the tomb of Philip II, the father of Alexander the Great. Greece imposed a complete economic boycott on Macedonia in 1994, to enforce its own claim to the name *Macedonia,* with devastating results to its economy, but in 1995, after U.S. mediation, Greece agreed to drop the boycott in return for a Macedonian agreement to redesign its flag and drop all claims to territories beyond its existing borders.

Bulgaria recognizes Macedonia but because two-thirds of the Macedonian people are ethnic Bulgarians, there is some sentiment in Bulgaria for annexation. In western Bulgaria, also known as Macedonian Bulgaria, there is a contrary desire to secede and join with Macedonia.

Macedonia also has a tense relationship with Albania because of its treatment of ethnic Albanians near the borders. The United Nations sent 700 observers in 1992 as well as 560 U.S. peacekeeping forces to Macedonia's borders to ensure that Serbia, Bulgaria, Albania, and Greece do not attempt to destabilize the country and seize its territory. Although the United Nations imposed an economic embargo on Serbia in the mid-1990s because of its aggression against Bosnia, Macedonia has carried on an extensive and profitable trade in agricultural products with Serbia.

Human rights Macedonian police have used violence in the 1990s in clamping down on Albanian students in Tetovo who have promoted a secessionist movement.

SEE ALSO

Albania; Balkans; Bulgaria; Greece; Ottoman Empire; Serbia; Tito, Josip Broz; Turkey; United Nations (UN)

FURTHER READING

Danforth, Loring M. *The Macedonian Conflict*. Princeton, N.J.: Princeton University Press, 1995.
Kennan, George F., ed. *The Other Balkan Wars*. New York: Carnegie Endowment for International Peace, 1993.
Poulton, Hugh. *Who Are the Macedonians?* Bloomington: Indiana University Press, 1995.

Madagascar

DEMOCRATIC REPUBLIC OF MADAGASCAR (REPOBLIKA DEMOKRATIKA MALAGASY)

• *Capital: Antananarivo*

Political history Black and Semitic Africans and Malays originally inhabited this island, off the east coast of Africa, which was discovered for the West by the Portuguese explorer Diego Diaz in 1500. It was unified under the rule of the African Imerina monarchs after

1797. The island became a French protectorate in 1890 and a colony in 1895, when Queen Ranavalona III was sent into exile by the French. The British occupied it during World War II, after the Nazis took France. In 1946 it became a French Overseas Territory, then in 1958 achieved autonomy within the French Community as the Malagasy Republic. It gained independence peacefully in 1960. In 1973 a military coup ousted the civilian government, and successive military regimes with a socialist ideology ruled until 1991, when, under pressure from Western aid donors and lenders and the International Monetary Fund, an interim government was formed to prepare for the transition to multiparty democracy. In August 1992 the new constitution was approved by popular referendum.

Government institutions Madagascar is a constitutional republic. The president, elected by the people for a term of five years, is the head of state. Executive power is exercised by a prime minister, elected by a majority of the National Assembly. Government administration is supervised by a council of ministers, headed by the prime minister. Legislative power is exercised by a bicameral legislature. Two-thirds of the Senate are elected by an electoral college for a four-year term, and one-third is appointed by the president. The 138-member National Assembly is popularly elected for a four-year term.

There is an independent judiciary, consisting of special criminal courts to handle looting; Courts of the First Instance for routine civil and criminal cases, a Court of Appeal, and the Supreme Court. The Constitutional High Court rules on the constitutionality of laws and executive acts.

Parties and movements Until 1990 all politicians and top government officials had to become members of the National Front for the Defense of the Madagascar Revolution. In 1990, as part of the movement toward multiparty democracy, more than 30 parties were formed. The major ones are the Committee of Forces, the Movement for Proletarian Power, and the Militant Movement for Madagascan Socialism, all socialist parties of the left.

Domestic issues Madagascar is one of the poorest countries in the world, and the population growth outstrips its agricultural production. It has high inflation, a huge foreign debt, and high unemployment. The government implemented an austerity program in the 1990s in cooperation with the World Bank and International Monetary Fund. However, general strikes and labor unrest threaten its economic reform program, which is attempting to attract foreign investment and diversify its agriculturally based economy.

Madagascar has established several national parks that are home to unique plants and animals in an attempt to attract tourism.

International issues France provides foreign aid and is the major trading partner for its exports of coffee, vanilla, cloves, seafood, and cotton; ties are strained, however, because of a territorial dispute involving islands in the Mozambique Channel.

In the 1980s Madagascar had close ties with the Soviet Union, North Korea, China, Libya, and Algeria, but in the 1990s it turned toward the free-market economies, including France, Israel, South Korea, and South Africa, which could provide it with technology and investment capital.

Madagascar is a member of the Indian Ocean Commission, which promotes regional cooperation.

SEE ALSO
France; French Community

FURTHER READING
Covell, Maureen. *Madagascar*. London: F. Pinter, 1987.

Major, John

- *Born: Mar. 29, 1943, London, England*

John Major, who became prime minister of the United Kingdom in 1990, presided over the revival of the British economy in the 1990s. His successful economic austerity measures and attempts to further European integration weakened him as Conservative Party leader and paved the way for the revival of the British Labour Party.

The son of a circus acrobat and trapeze artist (whose act was called "Drum and Major"), John Major was born in a suburb in south London, attended grammar school in Rutlish, but had to leave at age 16 to go to work. He was a laborer, and when he was laid off, he received unemployment insurance for eight months. He was a clerk for the electric utility, was turned down when he applied to become a bus driver, and then became an accountant and worked in a London bank.

Major entered politics as a Conservative, and the party got him a job managing a public housing project in the suburbs as a reward for his campaign work. In 1974 he ran for Parliament and lost, but in 1976 he won a seat. He became assistant whip of the Conservative Party in 1983 (responsible for communicating messages from party leaders to the rank and file) and served in the Home Office in 1985 and as junior minister for the Department of Health and Social Security in 1986.

Major was appointed foreign secretary in 1989 and then chancellor of the exchequer at the end of the year, when Prime Minister Margaret Thatcher fired her chancellor and her chief economic adviser because they had gone public with their disagreements with each other. Major's rivals said at the time that he was appointed because Thatcher felt she could control him, and the newspapers called him "Thatcher's poodle." As chancellor, Major proposed a budget to squeeze inflation with tough measures such as high interest rates, saying "If it isn't hurting, it isn't working."

In November 1990, Conservatives deposed Thatcher because she had become unpopular with voters and had too many personal disagreements with party leaders, and Major, who was liked by all, became prime minister with her blessing. He quickly repealed an unpopular poll tax she had levied. And he broke with Thatcher to endorse a common European currency and greater integration of the European economies. Although he continued Thatcher's policies of deregulating the economy, he was not as ideologically conservative as she was, and kept to a middle ground in the Conservative Party.

In foreign affairs Major worked closely with the United States. He sent British troops as part of the U.S.-led force to end the Iraqi occupation of Kuwait in 1990, and in 1995 he sent forces to Bosnia as part of a multinational initiative to restore peace. Although he opposed German reunification, he maintained cordial relations with Chancellor Helmut Kohl. In 1993 he supported British ratification of the Maastricht Treaty, which provided for an eventual European currency. In 1995 he signed an agreement with the Irish government to provide a framework for settling the final status of Northern Ireland.

In 1996 Major became embroiled in a dispute with other nations in the European Union after most European nations banned British beef because many herds had been infected with "mad cow" disease. Major's government handled the quarantine and destruction of herds ineptly, lowering confidence around the world in one of Britain's primary exports. Major insisted that British beef was safe, but European health officials rejected his claim.

Although Major's party won the 1992 parliamentary elections, his poor performance in managing the economy had become an issue with middle-class Conservative voters. His party was drubbed in the 1996 local elections, and Major lost office in the 1997 national elections.

SEE ALSO
Maastricht Treaty (1992); Thatcher, Margaret; United Kingdom

FURTHER READING
Young, Hugo. "The Last Tory." *The New Yorker*, February 7, 1997, 56–67.

Malawi

REPUBLIC OF MALAWI (MALAW̑I)

• *Capital: Lilongwe*

Political history Originally inhabited by nomadic Bantu tribes, this territory in central Africa was developed by the British South African Company in the 1880s as a trading center for plantation agriculture. It became part of the British Central Africa Protectorate in 1891, then was separated into the Nyasaland Protectorate in 1907. In 1953 the British merged it into the Federation of Rhodesia and Nyasaland. Ten years later it became an autonomous self-governing state and in 1964 gained full independence and membership in the Commonwealth of Nations under the leadership of Hastings Kamuzu Banda, who had headed its independence movement. Malawi became a republic in 1966.

Government institutions The president is head of state, with a term of five years, and he is vested with executive power. Cabinet members are chosen by the president. The National Assembly consists of 112 members who are elected for five years.

Malawi has an independent judiciary. Magistrate's courts handle civil and criminal trials. The High Court hears appeals from magistrate's courts and also tries serious civil and criminal cases. The Supreme Court of Appeal hears cases from the High Court.

A constitutional amendment named Hastings Banda President for Life in 1971, but this provision was removed in 1993.

Parties and movements Malawi was a one-party authoritarian state between 1964 and 1994, under the rule of President Banda. He was a conservative nationalist who favored European investment and had a militantly anticommunist foreign policy. Membership in the Malawi Congress Party was compulsory for all adults. In 1993, under pressure from Western aid donors, the government sponsored a referendum and 63 percent of the voters rejected continuation of one-party rule and opted for a multiparty democracy.

In the presidential elections in May 1994, Banda was defeated by Bakili Muluzi, head of the United Democratic Front, a conservative party that assumed a leading role as the largest party in parliament. The second largest was the conservative Malawi Congress Party.

Domestic issues A weakening economy in the 1990s has led to industrial unrest and strikes by trade unions. A

power struggle between the army and the Malawi Young Pioneers, which is the armed movement of the Malawi Congress Party, ended when the militia group voluntarily disarmed in 1994. Ethnic friction was alleviated in 1994 when the new government ended a ban on use of the Tumbuka language, though it continues to favor use of Chichewa as the official "Malawi language."

International issues Malawi maintained diplomatic relations with South Africa when it was under white minority rule, which created tensions with the southern African nations of Tanzania and Zambia until the early 1990s, when a majority black government came to power in South Africa. Malawi remains economically and politically dependent on South Africa. Malawi has stationed troops in Mozambique to protect a strategic railway to the Indian Ocean from Mozambican rebels.

Human rights In 1995 former president Hastings Banda and two aides were charged by the government with the murder of four political rivals in 1983, after investigation by a special nonpartisan commission. Banda was acquitted in December 1995.

Carrying her child, a worker on a tea plantation casts a ballot to decide whether Malawi will return to democracy. In the 1993 election, an overwhelming majority of voters opted for multiparty elections.

FURTHER READING

Africa Watch. *Where Silence Rules: The Suppression of Dissent in Malawi.* New York: Africa Watch, 1990.

Williams, T. David. *Malawi: The Politics of Despair*. Ithaca, N.Y.: Cornell University Press, 1978.

Malaysia

FEDERATION OF MALAYSIA

• *Capital: Kuala Lumpur*

Political history This peninsula in Southeast Asia was ruled by Hindu and Muslim kings until the 15th century, when a Muslim empire based in the city of Malacca was established. The peninsula was taken over by the Portuguese in 1511 and by the Dutch in 1641. The British East India Company colonized the area around Penang in 1786 and gained Malacca after the Napoleonic Wars in 1815. Later, the British acquired the territories of Sabah and Sarawak (on the northeastern part of the island of Borneo) and in 1948, after putting down a communist insurgency, merged their peninsular possessions into the Federation of Malaya. The colony then gained its independence in 1957 after an anticolonial coalition of Malayans and ethnic Chinese won an overwhelming majority in the parliamentary elections. In 1963 Singapore merged with Malaya to form Malaysia, but Singapore's ethnic Chinese majority seceded from Malaysia in 1965.

Government institutions Malaysia has a federal system with 11 states and 2 federal territories. It is a constitutional monarchy and has a parliamentary democracy. The supreme head of Malaysia and head of state is the *Yang Di Pertuan Agong* (monarch). The nine hereditary sultans, or rulers, of the original Malayan states take turns serving as the monarch for a five-year term. The monarch acts on the advice of the prime min-

ister and cabinet members, who serve as heads of departments. They are chosen by, and are accountable to, the legislature. The parliament consists of the directly elected 192-member Dewan Rakyat (House of Representatives) and the 70-member Dewan Negara (Senate). A majority of senators are appointed by the monarch and the remainder by the 11 state legislatures.

The highest court is the Federal Court, which consists of the Lord President and the two chief justices of the high courts of Malaya and Borneo (the two territories that comprise Malaysia), along with six other judges.

Parties and movements Malaysia is a multiparty democracy. The largest party is the United Malays National Organization (UMNO), a party of the majority Muslim Malays, which is the mainstay of the ruling 14-party coalition, the Barisan Nasional. Opposition parties include the primarily Chinese Democratic Action Party, the Parti Bersatu Sabah (representing the state of Sabah), and the Muslim Unity Movement, an Islamic fundamentalist group.

In April 1995 the Barisan Nasional won a sweeping victory, obtaining 64 percent of the popular vote and winning 161 seats in parliament and control of 10 state legislatures. The nation has been ruled by prime minister Mahathir Mohammed, of the UMNO, since 1981.

Malaysia enjoys great reserves of wood and land, but unregulated harvesting and development have created significant environmental problems.

Domestic issues Malaysia has one of the fastest-growing industrial and trading economies in the world. It serves as a low-wage manufacturing location for foreign industries. Ethnic tension between Malays, who prevail in politics, and Chinese, who dominate banking and finance, has been reduced by regional development plans to benefit Malays.

Exploitive government logging and land development policies have aroused the ire of conservationists and environmentalists.

There is a movement for autonomy in Sabah, where the governing party's rule has weakened and parties representing local Sabah interests have gained power.

International issues Malaysia has supported many Third World international initiatives, including Chinese entry into the United Nations, diplomatic sanctions against Israel (for its rule over Palestinians on the West Bank) and South Africa (during the apartheid period), and the call for a New International Economic Order to benefit developing nations in world trade.

Malaysia is a major participant in the Association of Southeast Asian Nations (ASEAN), a regional forum for discussion of economic and political issues, but has opposed U.S. membership in the organization. It has close economic ties with Japan, which has invested heavily in Malaysian industry. Malaysia accepted a quarter of a million refugees from Vietnam in the 1970s after the communists seized power in Indochina but eventually closed its doors to more refugees and began efforts to repatriate them to Vietnam.

FURTHER READING

Lee, H. P. *Constitutional Conflicts in Contemporary Malaysia.* New York: Oxford University Press, 1995.
Means, Gordon. *Malaysian Politics.* New York: Oxford University Press, 1991.
Munro-Kua, Anne. *Authoritarian Populism in Malaysia.* New York: St. Martin's, 1996.

Maldives

REPUBLIC OF MALDIVES (DIVEHI JUMHURIYA)

• *Capital: Male*

Political history These 200 islands and atolls, located in the Indian Ocean, were settled by Buddhist fishermen from the Indian subcontinent around 500 B.C. They were governed as an independent sultanate (a Muslim monarchy) after the population converted to Islam in 1153. The Maldives came under the control of Ceylon (now Sri Lanka) in the 18th century, then became a British protectorate in 1887. Maldives became self-governing in internal affairs in 1953, and the sultanate was restored in 1954. It became fully independent and left the Commonwealth of Nations in 1965. Three years later, it became a republic and the sultanate was abolished.

Government institutions Maldives has a presidential system. The president is head of state and is directly elected after being nominated by the legislature; he serves for five years. The president appoints the cabinet, which is responsible to the legislature. The 48-member Majlis (Citizens' Council) has legislative power, with 8 of its members appointed by the president and the rest directly elected.

The judiciary consists of island courts on each of the 200 inhabited islands. Appeals are heard by the High Court. The judiciary is supervised by the Ministry of Justice and Islamic Affairs. The legal system is based on Islamic law.

Parties and movements No political parties or movements are permitted in Maldives. Several reformers in the Majlis received death threats from supporters of the regime, and all publications not sanctioned by the government were banned in 1990.

Domestic issues Maldives is one of the poorest and least developed nations in the world. Its fishing and agricultural economy is controlled by a small elite uninterested in economic modernization for the country. The main domestic issue involves the endemic corruption within the government ministries, and Maldives has established an anticorruption board to monitor its politicians.

International issues Maldives is a founding member of the South Asian Association for Regional Cooperation.

Indian troops guarantee the nation's political stability against outside coup attempts, especially those fomented by Sri Lankans, who wish to reduce Indian influence in the area.

Because none of its 1,190 coral islets rises more than six feet above sea level, the nation is acutely threatened by any potential rise in sea levels and therefore promotes international environmental efforts to prevent global warming.

FURTHER READING

Phadnis, Urmila, and Ela Luithui. *Maldives*. New Delhi: South Asian Publishers, 1985.

Mali

REPUBLIC OF MALI (RÉPUBLIQUE DU MALI)

• *Capital: Bamako*

Political history The Great Mali Empire of Western Africa along the Niger River dominated West Africa's gold and iron trade after the year 1200. It reached its height in the 15th century, when the city of Timbuktu was a world center for Islamic study. In 1591 the city was destroyed by the Moroccans, who pillaged it for its golden treasures, and the desert areas of the north were then governed by separate tribal monarchs, ruling over nomadic tribes, for the next four centuries. In the southwest, the area around Bamako and Ségou—a region of traditional Muslim architecture and learning—became the seat of the Bambara kingdom of the 1700s.

Mali was gradually annexed by France between 1881 and 1895, becoming part of French Sudan, itself a part of French West Africa. In 1958 it was granted autonomy within the French Community under the name Mali and then merged with Senegal to form the Federation of Mali, which became a sovereign state in 1960. Senegal seceded that same year.

Government institutions The constitution adopted in 1992 provides for a multiparty democracy and a presidential system. Executive power is vested in the president of the republic, who is elected by the people for a five-year term. The president appoints a prime minister, who then appoints a council of ministers. Legislative power is vested in the unicameral, 129-member National Assembly, whose members are elected for five-year terms. The Supreme Court, which takes direction from the governing party, is divided into civil, commercial, criminal, and social chambers (which handles divorce and child custody cases, for example).

Parties and movements Until 1991 Mali was a one-party authoritarian state. The Democratic Union of the Malian People, the sole political party, was dissolved in 1991 as a prelude to the creation of a multiparty system. The largest of the 40 or more new parties is the Alliance for Democracy (a social democratic party), followed by the National Congress for a Democratic Initiative (liberal). Since 1992 the Alliance for Democracy has dominated the government.

Domestic issues Mali is one of the five poorest nations in the world. Its agricultural efforts are hampered by drought, mismanagement, and corruption. The country suffers from regional conflict between pastoral Tuaregs in the far north and the majority Mande tribes. The Tuaregs briefly fought the central government in the early 1990s before agreeing to a pact for national reconciliation that granted their demands for a greater share of the national wealth and local self-rule.

The government is privatizing state enterprises and working with lender nations to reschedule its huge external debt payments in an attempt to improve the economy, which has been weakened by drought and desertification. Mali is also attempting to develop tourism. Its northern city of Timbuktu remains a destination for tourists seeking to learn about the ancient Islamic civilizations that border the Sahara. The Bandiagara Escarpment near the city of Mopti is the home of the Dogon people, who maintain a centuries-old life-style, and it has been declared a World Heritage site by the United Nations.

International issues Mali remains closely linked to France, which dominates its cotton trade and finances. In the 1960s Mali pursued a nonaligned policy, but in the 1970s it received aid from the Soviet Union, China, and Cuba, all seeking to reduce Western influence. By the 1980s it had shifted its orientation, and Western nations became the primary donors.

Mali had a border dispute with Burkina Faso, its neighbor to the south, over the Agacher Strip, which resulted in skirmishes in 1985. The two nations eventually agreed to split the territory.

SEE ALSO
French Community

FURTHER READING
Imperato, Pascal. *Mali: A Search for Direction*. Boulder, Colo.: Westview, 1989.

Malta

REPUBLIC OF MALTA (REPUBLIKKA TA' MALTA)

• *Capital: Valletta*

Political history Malta, an island off the west coast of Italy, was ruled by Phoenicians, Carthaginians, Romans, and Byzantines in ancient times. It was conquered by Arabs in the 8th century A.D. In 1090 Normans from Sicily conquered it and used it as a resupply base for the Crusades. In 1530 King Charles V of Spain gave the island to the Knights Hospitalers (thereafter known as the Knights of Malta) so that they would harass the Turkish navy to the east. The island was conquered by Napoléon Bonaparte of France in 1798, but it fell to the British fleet in 1800 and was annexed by Britain in 1814. Malta was granted limited self-rule in 1921. It gained its independence within the Commonwealth of Nations in 1964 and became a republic within the Commonwealth in 1974.

Government institutions The constitution adopted in 1974 provides for a multiparty democracy and a parliamentary system. The head of state is the president of the republic, elected by the people for a five-year term. The president appoints a prime minister, who then names a cabinet, which is responsible to the legislature for carrying out the policies the legislature enacts. Legislative power is vested in the unicameral, 65-member

House of Representatives, whose members are elected for a five-year term.

The judiciary consists of magistrate's courts and small claims courts for petty cases; civil and criminal courts for more serious matters; and a Court of Appeal and a Court of Criminal Appeal, which review lower court decisions. The Constitutional Court reviews laws passed by the parliament.

Parties and movements The two main parties are the Nationalist Party—a conservative party that is in favor of Malta joining the European Union and a supporter of privileges for the Catholic Church—and the Malta Labor Party, a social democratic party with a secular orientation.

Domestic issues One of the most important issues dividing the Maltese people is the role of the Catholic Church, which has the allegiance of most of the population. The church had vast properties on the island until the Labor Party passed a law in 1983 expropriating much of the property of the Catholic Church. It has also proposed an end to church schools.

Malta is attempting to industrialize its economy. It is a popular tourist destination because it retains much of the architecture and culture from the time of the Crusades.

International issues Malta was a key outpost for Britain during World War II, resisting German air attacks and enabling the British to maintain sea-lanes in the Mediterranean against German and Italian attacks. In 1971, however, under its leftist prime minister Dom Mintoff, it closed a NATO base and began a policy of nonalignment in the cold war. In 1978 the last of the British troops were withdrawn from the island.

Malta in the 1990s pursues a nonaligned policy and balances the influences of several world powers: it has an antiterrorism agreement with the British that prevents Malta from being used as a safe haven by Libyan-sponsored groups, although Libya remains an important trading partner; Italy guarantees Malta's neutrality.

Malta is preparing for European economic integration. It has associate status in the European Union and is considering an application for full membership. It has constructed a free port (through which goods can move to non-Maltese destinations without paying a tariff) and has opened a stock exchange, and it is liberalizing its trade and investment laws to allow more private investment.

SEE ALSO
Commonwealth of Nations; European Union (EU)

FURTHER READING
Thackrah, Richard. *Malta*. New York: Oxford University Press, 1985.

Mandate

Mandates were territories taken from Germany and the Ottoman Empire at the end of World War I and placed under the jurisdiction of the League of Nations by the victorious Allied powers who had occupied them. The league then assigned the territories to member nations, who were to prepare them for eventual independence. These territories included German colonies in Africa, mandated to Great Britain; German islands in the Pacific, north of the equator, mandated to Japan; and German Samoa, mandated to Great Britain. When the Ottoman Empire was dismantled after the war, Syria and Lebanon were assigned to France and Mesopotamia (Iraq), and Palestine to Great Britain. Belgium, Australia, New Zealand, and South Africa also gained mandates taken from German possessions.

An annual report was required of the administering nation on each mandate, to be submitted to the Permanent Mandates Commission of the League of Nations. Those appointed to mandates were in all cases either the occupying power or the beneficiary of one of the secret Allied treaties, concluded during and after World War I, that divided up some of the territories of the defeated Central Powers.

At the end of World War II, mandated territories were transformed into United Nations Trusteeship Territories, and they prepared for independence under the supervision of the United Nations Trusteeship Council. The last of the original mandates to gain independence was South-West Africa, now known as Namibia, in 1990.

SEE ALSO

League of Nations; Trust territories; United Nations (UN)

FURTHER READING

Hall, H. D. *Mandates, Dependencies, and Trusteeships*. London: Stevens, 1948.

Mandela, Nelson

• *Born: July 18, 1918, Umtata, Transkei, South Africa*

Nelson Rolihlahla Mandela was the leading opponent of the South African apartheid regime (the official policy of racial segregation introduced in 1948) and the president of the African National Congress (ANC), the movement

that transformed South Africa into a multiracial democracy. He became the first president of post-apartheid South Africa after the 1994 elections. A winner of the Nobel Peace Prize, he was one of the most influential world leaders in the 1990s because of his moral authority as a fighter for human rights.

Born of royal Thembu tribal lineage, Mandela grew up in the village of Qunu, and after his father died, he lived with his cousin, the chief of the region. Rolihlahla, his Thembu name, is translated as "he who brings trouble to himself," and Mandela's life fit his name. He attended Fort Hare University and Witwatersrand University, then practiced law in Johannesburg in 1941. He was a founder and national organizer of the ANC Youth League, a movement calling for the end of apartheid. In 1956 he and other ANC leaders were arrested and charged with treason, but he was acquitted and released in 1961. Mandela was arrested again in 1962 for anti-apartheid activities and sentenced to a five-year term; in 1963 he faced even more charges and was tried on a new treason charge in 1964. "I have cherished the ideal of a democratic and free society in which all persons live together in harmony and equal opportunities," he told the court. He added, "It is an ideal

Just released after 28 years of imprisonment, Nelson Mandela addresses the General Assembly of the United Nations in New York City in June 1990.

for which I am prepared to die." He was sentenced to life imprisonment and remained incarcerated on Robben Island from age 44 to 71.

While in prison, Mandela and his associates further developed their political theories and their plans for defeating the apartheid regime. Their education of a younger generation of militant ANC guerrillas imprisoned with them led them to refer to the prison as "Mandela University." While Mandela remained in prison, his wife, Winnie Mandela, continued his revolutionary work and was subject to arrest, detainment, and internal banishments (house arrest under rules prohibiting any contact with other people).

In 1990 Nelson Mandela was released by the white government of F. W. de Klerk as a first step toward negotiations with the ANC over sharing power and ending minority white rule. Mandela was elected president of the ANC upon his release from prison and participated in a national dialogue between the ANC and the government. These talks led to an agreement to begin the process of democratization and majority-rule elections for 1993. For their efforts, Mandela and de Klerk shared the Nobel Peace Prize in 1993. Two other South African blacks had previously won the prize for their opposition to apartheid: Chief Albert Luthuli of the Zulus in 1960, president of the ANC from 1952 to 1960, and Archbishop Desmond Tutu of the Anglican Church in 1984.

Mandela won the presidential election of 1994, and his party won an overwhelming victory in local elections in 1995, establishing it as the preeminent political force in post-apartheid South Africa.

Mandela in his 70s is a white-haired, dignified figure, with a ready smile and quick wit. He lives alone, since divorcing his wife because of her radical ideology and her involvement in forming a "Mandela Soccer Club" whose members were implicated in violent crimes. Mandela is known to black South Africans as Madiba (the Great One) because of his regal bearing and lineage. Because of his conciliatory attitudes and his willingness to concentrate on the future rather than on past injustices, he has been able to overcome white fears that a majority-rule government would leave whites no place in South Africa's future. He has received support from prominent white business leaders for his advocacy of multiracial policies. He was even able to neutralize the far-right Afrikaner groups (descendants of the 17th-century Dutch settlers), which called for an "all-white" homeland, by honoring a promise that the government would allow a commission to study the matter and issue a report on ways to preserve white culture in the nonracial but black-dominated South Africa.

At the 1995 Rugby World Cup, held in sports-loving Johannesburg, Mandela won the support of hundreds of thousands of fans, most of them whites, who cheered "Nel-son, Nel-son" as he strode across the field to wish the almost all-white Springbok team luck in the contest. In another gesture of goodwill, Mandela contributes one-third of his salary to the Nelson Mandela Children's Fund, which aids the poorest children in the nation.

SEE ALSO
Apartheid; de Klerk, Frederik Willem; South Africa

FURTHER READING
Hoobler, Dorothy, and Thomas Hoobler. *Mandela: The Man, the Struggle, the Triumph*. New York: Franklin Watts, 1992.
Mandela, Nelson. *Long Walk to Freedom*. Boston: Little, Brown, 1994.

Meer, Fatima. *Higher than Hope: The Authorized Biography of Nelson Mandela.* New York: Harper & Row, 1990.
Stefoff, Rebecca. *Nelson Mandela: A Voice Set Free.* New York: Fawcett Columbine, 1990.
Vail, John J. *Nelson and Winnie Mandela.* New York: Chelsea House, 1989.

Mao Zedong

- *Born: Dec. 26, 1893, Shaoshan, Hunan Province, China*
- *Died: Sept. 9, 1976, Beijing, China*

The Chinese revolutionary leader Mao Zedong was the leader of the Chinese Communist Party (1935–76) and the first leader of the People's Republic of China (1949–76). Mao was one of the most influential communist leaders of the 20th century. He brought a communist revolution to China that industrialized the nation, but the cost was high: millions of peasants died in famines, and the Communists established a totalitarian state that ruled through a combination of terror and party-sponsored corruption. Mao himself lived in seclusion, surrounded by sycophantic aides, and indulged himself in luxuries and vices denied to ordinary Chinese.

The son of farm workers, Mao Zedong began work in 1918 as a library assistant at Beijing University. He then became a schoolteacher in Hunan Province. In 1921 he was one of the founders of the Chinese Communist Party. Mao was assigned to coordinate the Communists in an alliance with the Kuomintang (Nationalist) Party, China's major political party, against warlords who wished to topple the republic. It was an uneasy alliance, and Mao was unable to make it work. By 1925 he had returned to Hunan to organize peasants in revolutionary activity against the Kuomintang.

After the Kuomintang began to arrest Communists in 1927, Mao organized the Jinggang Soviet (a group of revolutionary peasants) in a mountainous area near Hunan and later another base area soviet in Jiangxi. Mao also organized an army, but struggles within the party caused him to lose control over it to the party's central secretariat in Shanghai.

In 1935 Mao and other Communists embarked on the Long March from central China to Yanan in the remote northwest to escape Kuomintang armies. The veterans of the march would later form the core of the Communist Party leadership for the next four decades.

In 1935 Mao was elected to the leadership of the party Politburo, the governing council of the Communist Party, after defeating a party faction that looked to Joseph Stalin and the Communist Party in the Soviet Union for leadership.

In 1937 Mao agreed to an alliance with the Kuomintang against the Japanese, who had invaded China that year. In 1945, with Japan defeated, the Nationalists and Communists resumed their civil war. The Communists took power in 1949 as the Kuomintang leaders left mainland China in defeat and occupied the province of Taiwan.

During the civil war, Mao had managed to purge most of the Chinese communists who believed that the Chinese revolution should follow a Marxist model like the one Lenin had established in the Soviet Union. However, Mao himself cemented an alliance with the Soviet Union after he took power, relying on Soviet assistance during the Korean War (1950–53), when Chinese forces assisted North Korea in repelling the U.S. military forces from territory near China.

To defeat his pro-Soviet rivals a second time, in 1958 Mao launched the Great Leap Forward, a rural development program, and purged party leaders opposed to it. But its failure to improve the Chinese economy weakened Mao's prestige.

In the 1950s Maoism became an important ideology for revolutionary movements in the Third World. Mao's "Little Red Book" distilled the essence of his theories about the important role of peasants in revolutionary activity, the need for a "permanent" revolution from below to prevent the Communist Party from becoming too conservative, and the role of revolutionary communist parties in defeating the capitalist states of the West. The most radical communist revolutionaries in Europe and Latin America proudly took the label "Maoists."

In 1960 Mao split with the Soviet Union, in part because China was suspicious of Soviet efforts at "peaceful coexistence" with the West and in part because of Mao's distrust of Soviet economic advisers, whose advice, particularly in agriculture, had proven disastrous. With the help of the army and the Red Guards youth organization, in 1966 Mao launched the Cultural Revolution, a radical ideological movement designed to discredit his rivals within the party: the bureaucrats; those favoring détente, or peaceful relations, with the West; and those who wanted to emphasize economic growth at the expense of communist economic theory. Eventually, the army intervened to restore order after the Red Guard excesses, which included the virtual destruction of many institutions of higher learning and the incarceration of many scientists and intellectuals. In 1971 Mao fended off an attempted coup d'état by defense minister Lin Biao.

Mao ruled China as its uncontested leader with ideological fervor that gained him the support of revolutionary leaders in the party, especially each new generation of student activists. He used their support to discredit and destroy a succession of high-ranking party leaders, so that none of his rivals could ever accumulate enough power to successfully plot against him.

Throughout Mao's rule, the Chinese Communist Party treated him as a god. Huge portraits of Mao dominated the public squares, and his pictures could be found in every government office. His writings formed the core readings in the universities, and all schoolchildren were expected to memorize "the sayings of Chairman Mao." After Mao's death in 1976, his wife, Jiang Qing, and three confederates—known as the Gang of Four—plotted to seize power and continue the radicalization of the Chinese Communist Party. They were arrested preemptively by premier Hua Guofeng, who shortly thereafter became the Communist Party chairman. Party conservatives gained power by 1980, dramatically shifting China's economic policies from class struggle and a completely planned economy into a mixed economy (in which private enterprise would play a role) with significant investment from capitalist nations. The new generation of communist leaders dismantled the "cult of personality" that had surrounded Mao. Nevertheless, Mao continues to be honored as the founder of the communist state.

SEE ALSO

China; Communism; Marxism-Leninism; Soviet Union (Union of Soviet Socialist Republics); Stalin, Joseph

FURTHER READING

Ch'en, Jerome. *Mao and the Chinese Revolution*. New York: Oxford University Press, 1965.
Garza, Hedda. *Mao Zedong*. New York: Chelsea House, 1988.
Karnow, Stanley. *Mao and China: A Legacy of Turmoil*. 3rd rev. ed. New York: Penguin, 1990.
Mao Zedong. *Quotations from Chairman Mao Tsetung*. San Francisco: China Books, 1990.

- MARCOS, FERDINAND -

Poole, Frederick King. *Mao Zedong.* New York: Watts, 1982.

Salisbury, Harrison E. *The New Emperors: China in the Era of Mao and Deng.* Boston: Little, Brown, 1992.

Schwartz, Benjamin. *Chinese Communism and the Rise of Mao.* 2d ed. New York: Harper & Row, 1967.

Terrill, Ross. *Mao: A Biography.* 2nd ed. New York: Harper Collins, 1980.

Marcos, Ferdinand

- *Born: Sept. 11, 1917, Ilocos Norte, Philippines*
- *Died: Sept. 29, 1989, Honolulu, Hawaii*

Ferdinand Marcos was president of the Philippines from 1965 to 1986. He was the son of a local politician in Sarrat, in the province of Ilocos Norte, and earned a law degree from the University of the Philippines in 1939. That same year, he was acquitted of charges that he had murdered his father's chief political opponent. During World War II Marcos was an intelligence officer of the 21st Division of the U.S. Army, serving as a guerrilla leader fighting behind Japanese lines. After being captured by the Japanese, Marcos survived the 1942 Bataan Death March—a forced march of captive U.S. soldiers and Philippine troops and civilians, during which many were killed or died—and he was awarded a Silver Star Medal for his valor in battle. (Critics have charged that his wartime exploits were, for the most part, undocumented.)

After the war Marcos served on the staff of Philippine president Manuel Roxas. In 1949–56 he was a member of the Philippine House of Representatives and in 1956 became a member of the Senate, serving as its president in 1963. He was elected president in 1965 on the Nationalist ticket. He defeated President Diosdado Macapagal on the issue of graft, promising that he would restore honest and effective government.

Once in the president's office, Marcos turned out to be even more corrupt than his predecessor. Graft was rampant during his administration, and his personal cut of stolen funds from the Treasury and bribes for government contracts went into secret Swiss bank accounts, with the amounts involving billions of dollars.

In 1966 Marcos sent Philippine troops to serve in the war in Vietnam under U.S. command. For this, his nation received U.S. foreign aid, which was siphoned off by the military as part of a system of rampant corruption. By 1972 Marcos had become a dictator, imposing martial law, ruling by rigging elections and by using the security forces against his opponents. Confederates of Marcos in the military assassinated his principal political opponent, Benigno Aquino, in 1983. Protests against Marcos's rule increased, culminating in massive demonstrations that led to his ouster in 1986. He and his wife, Imelda, lived in exile in Hawaii until his death.

Benigno Aquino's widow, Corazon Aquino, who had been elected to the presidency in 1986, refused to allow Marcos's body to be returned for burial. Aquino's successor, Fidel Ramos, did, however, allow Marcos's body to be returned to the Philippines for burial in 1992. The Philippine government under Ramos has instituted legal actions in the United States and Switzerland for the return of billions of

Many Filipinos came to believe that the opulent way of life enjoyed by Ferdinand Marcos and his family was at the expense of the nation's well-being.

dollars in properties and bank accounts held by Ferdinand and Imelda Marcos.

SEE ALSO

Aquino, Corazon Cojuangco; Philippines

FURTHER READING

Bonner, Raymond. *Waltzing with a Dictator: The Marcoses and the Making of American Policy.* New York: Times Books, 1987.

Burton, Sandra. *The Impossible Dream: The Marcoses, the Aquinos, and the Unfinished Revolution.* New York: Warner, 1989.

Slack, Gordy. *Ferdinand Marcos.* New York: Chelsea House, 1988.

Thompson, Mark. *The Anti-Marcos Struggle.* New Haven: Yale University Press, 1995.

Marshall Islands

REPUBLIC OF THE MARSHALL ISLANDS (MAJŌL)

• *Capital: Majuro*

Political history The Marshall Islands, a group of about 30 atolls in the western Pacific, were initially claimed by Spain in 1592 but were never Spanish colonies and remained independent. They became a German protectorate in 1885 as part of the expansion of German naval power. During World War I they were occupied by the Japanese, who were awarded a mandate by the League of Nations in 1919. In 1944 the United States conquered them, and after the war they became part of the UN Trust Territory of the Pacific, administered by the United States. In 1986 the islands became an associated commonwealth of the United States under the Compact of Free Association with the United States, which granted it local self-government. Five years later, in 1991, the United States granted the Marshall Islands full independence.

Government institutions The constitution adopted in 1979 provides for a multiparty democracy and a presidential system. The head of state is the president, who is elected for a four-year term by the legislature. The 33-member directly elected parliament, called the Nitijela, has legislative power. The Council of Chiefs, or Iroj, representing tribal interests, is a consultative body to the president.

The judicial system consists of the Traditional Rights Court, which applies customary tribal laws; a district court for civil and criminal cases; the High Court of the Republic, which is a court of appeal; and the Supreme Court of the Republic, the highest court.

Parties and movements The main party is the Ralik Ratak Democratic Party, which is the organization used by the tribal chiefs to control island politics.

Domestic issues The islands suffer from severe drought, and poor weather has resulted in a food shortage in the 1990s. To alleviate its poverty, the government proposed in the 1990s that foreign nations be allowed to dump wastes on some atolls for a fee. There was opposition to this plan, however, because some of the waste was toxic, and islanders feared radioactive wastes might be included. Environmentalists have also opposed plans to generate energy by burning used car tires (which releases

On July 25, 1946, Bikini atoll was the site of an above-ground test of a U.S. atomic bomb. In terms of radioactive fallout, the test was one of the most damaging in the history of the U.S. nuclear weapons program.

pollutants into the atmosphere) and facilities to treat industrial waste from the United States.

International issues The republic is a member of the South Pacific Forum, a group of island nations in the region, and supports its opposition to drift-net fishing (a method that decimates fishing stocks by gathering up all available fish in whatever area the nets are dragged through) and its efforts to retard global warming. Global warming, which causes polar ice caps to melt and sea levels around the world to rise, threatens to put the Marshalls under water.

The islands have leased land to the United States for military facilities, which provide the main source of outside income. Kwajalein Atoll is used as a target for ballistic missiles fired from California.

Since the late 1980s, the Marshall Islands, with few natural freshwater supplies, have received technical assistance in water desalinization from Israel.

The Marshall Islands claim Wake Island, which remains part of the U.S. territory of Guam.

Human rights The Bikini and Eniwetok atolls were used as U.S. nuclear testing sites in the 1950s, and the United States has provided $150 million to compensate the victims of downwind radiation. The United States has also agreed to decontaminate Bikini Atoll. The inhabitants of Rongelap Atoll were relocated in 1985 to Mejato Atoll because of high levels of radiation. Rates of cancer due to fallout from these tests is high on many atolls.

Marshall Plan

The Marshall Plan was a U.S. foreign aid program that dramatically aided in the economic reconstruction of Europe after the devastation of World War II. It was devised by U.S. Secretary of State George Marshall, who announced it at the Harvard University commencement on June 5, 1947. Its purpose, Marshall said, was to revive "a working economy in the world so as to permit the emergence of political and social conditions in which free institutions can exist."

France and Great Britain organized European nations to respond to the U.S. offer of assistance by setting up coordinating committees to administer incoming aid. Although the United States emphasized that the Soviet Union could participate, the offer was conditional upon many requirements and was therefore rejected by Soviet leader Joseph Stalin, who suspected a Western plot to overthrow communist rule. Stalin organized his own Council for Mutual Economic Assistance (COMECON) to provide aid to war-torn Eastern Europe.

The Marshall Plan was then promoted by the Truman administration to the U.S. Congress and the American people as a means to contain Soviet expansion in Europe.

In the summer of 1947, Western European nations organized a committee to plan for economic recovery using U.S. aid. President Harry Truman offered $17 billion in aid, somewhat less than the $22.4 billion the Europeans had asked for. The U.S. Congress passed the Economic Cooperation Act in March 1948, and it appropriated $13.2 billion for four years (the equivalent of $80 billion in the 1990s).

To implement the Marshall Plan, 18 European nations created the Organization for European Economic Cooperation. By 1950 European industrial production was significantly

George Marshall was the architect of one of the most successful economic and social reconstruction plans ever devised.

higher than it had been prior to World War II, thanks in part to the U.S. aid.

SEE ALSO
Council for Mutual Economic Assistance (COMECON); Stalin, Joseph; Truman, Harry S.

FURTHER READING
Hogan, Michael. *The Marshall Plan.* New York: Cambridge University Press, 1987.
Milward, Alan. *The Reconstruction of Western Europe.* Berkeley: University of California Press, 1984.
Thomas, Evan. "The Plan and the Man." *Newsweek*, June 2, 1997, 36-39.

Marxism-Leninism

Marxism-Leninism is a set of political, economic, and social principles that serves as the foundation of all communist states. The central body of thought was developed in the mid to late 1800s by German political theorist Karl Marx and his lifelong collaborator, the English industrialist Friedrich Engels. It is a theory that intertwines history and economics and at its core predicts that in an industrial society there will always be a struggle between labor (working classes) and those with capital (business owners). Marxists believe that all value comes from labor and that capitalists exploit labor by taking the "surplus value" of what labor has produced. Marx believed that the working people must take political power in order to achieve a classless society and an end to exploitation.

These principles gained international attention when they were put into practice by Vladimir Lenin and the Bolsheviks, who gained control of Russia in 1917. Lenin agreed with Marx and Engels that the working classes (along with the peasants) must lead the revolution to a new society. Unlike Marx, however, Lenin also stressed the need for a revolutionary party that would be the vanguard of the proletariat (the working class); it would be an instrument of the working classes and a party that would have to take power through force.

But the Russian Revolution did not lead to the formation of an ideal state. Lenin established a state based on force, with a single party (the Communist Party) monopolizing political power. When Lenin died, Joseph Stalin assumed power and became the proponent of "Marxism-Leninism"—a term he coined—although, in reality, Stalin dismantled the original Bolshevik Party in the 1930s through his purges of party rivals. His totalitarian reign of terror put an end to any attempts to construct a true Marxist state in the Soviet Union.

In essence, Marxism attempts to explain the class struggle and to draw lessons from it. In *The Manifesto of the Communist Party* (1848), Marx and Engels suggested that everyone would benefit materially once competition and selfish motives are removed and that the elimination of privilege would lead to an enormous rebirth of true freedom, creativity, and culture among the oppressed. So far, however, no nation has achieved such an ideal state; certainly none based on Marxist-Leninist principles has done so.

SEE ALSO
Bolsheviks; Communism; Lenin, Vladimir Ilich; Russia; Russian Revolution; Soviet Union (Union of Soviet Socialist Republics); Stalin, Joseph

FURTHER READING
Balibar, Etienne. *The Philosophy of Marx.* Translated by Chris Turner. New York: Verso, 1995.
Berlin, Isaiah. *Karl Marx: His Life and Environment.* New York: Oxford University Press, 1996.
Feinberg, Barbara Silberdick. *Marx and Marxism.* New York: Franklin Watts, 1985.
Marx, Karl. *Karl Marx: The Essential Writings.* Edited by Frederic L. Bender. Boulder, Colo.: Westview, 1986.

Masaryk, Tomáš

- *Born: Mar. 7, 1850, Hodonín, Moravia*
- *Died: Sept. 14, 1937, Lány, Czechoslovakia*

Tomáš Masaryk was the founder of the nation-state of Czechoslovakia and served as its first president, from 1918 to 1935. He fought for the independence and self-determination of the people of eastern Europe, particularly the Czechs and Slovaks, after World War I, and his efforts helped to redraw the map of Europe.

He was the son of a Slovak father and Czech mother (of German descent); his father was a coachman on one of the imperial estates of the Austro-Hungarian Empire, which at that time ruled territory occupied by the Czech and Slovak peoples. Masaryk was educated at the University of Vienna and received a doctorate in philosophy in 1876. He lectured at the University of Vienna in 1879 and was then appointed to a professorship at the University of Prague. In 1899 Masaryk demonstrated great personal courage when he denounced the slanderous anti-Semitic myth that Jews engaged in ritual human sacrifice, a rumor that surfaced throughout Czech territory during a celebrated murder trial against a Jew accused of killing a Christian girl.

Masaryk was a scholar who always spoke up for what he believed. He attacked the Eastern Orthodox Church in Russia for what he thought were its efforts to prevent Western culture from modernizing the Slavic peoples. He was critical of the excesses of capitalism but opposed the revolutionary activities of communists, preferring the peaceful approach to socialism championed by the social democrats.

Wanting to do more than criticize the system, Masaryk decided to run for office. He served in the Austrian Reichsrat (parliament) from 1891 to 1893, then again from 1907 to 1914. He became part of a reform movement that attempted to transform the Austro-Hungarian Empire—which ruled over many different peoples, such as Austrians, Hungarians, Czechs, and Slovaks—into a multicultural democracy that would grant each people self-determination.

Masaryk became a Czech leader during World War I, when he became the leading advocate for Czech and Slovak secession from the Austro-Hungarian Empire. In return for Czech support of the Allied cause and the Allied use of Czech soldiers to fight against the Bolshevik Revolution in Russia, U.S. president Woodrow Wilson supported Masaryk's independence movement at the post–World War I peace conference at Versailles. Masaryk and Wilson favored the establishment of a number of small European states that would surround Germany with a *cordon sanitaire*, or buffer zone, and ensure a balance of power in postwar Europe.

On October 14, 1918, with Allied backing, Masaryk declared Czechoslovakia an independent nation, and on November 14 he was elected the first president. He served for 17 years, winning several free elections and working to make his nation a liberal democracy. Much of the time he mediated between the Czech majority and the less affluent Slovak minority, and his countrymen always considered him a fair arbiter of their disputes because of his judicious temperament and his utter fearlessness in speaking the truth. Masaryk retired in 1935 and died in 1937, just before Adolf Hitler's onslaught against Czechoslovakia temporarily ended its freedom and independence.

SEE ALSO

Austria; Austro-Hungarian Empire; Czechoslovakia; Germany; Hitler, Adolf

FURTHER READING

Capek, Karel. *President Masaryk Tells His Story*. 1934. Reprint, New York: Arno, 1971.

Lewis, Gavin. *Tomáš Masaryk*. New York: Chelsea House, 1990.

Mau Mau

The Mau Mau was the revolutionary organization that led Kenya to independence in the 1950s. Known formally as the Kenya Land Freedom Army, the name Mau Mau was the derogatory term used by the white settlers whom it fought. The Mau Mau was founded in 1952 after British colonial authorities had declared a state of emergency, arrested 200 Kenyan nationalist leaders, and banned their political party. Its goal was to overthrow the British colonial government and establish Kenya as an independent state. It consisted of members of the Kikuyu, Meru, and Embu tribes.

Mau Mau guerrillas murdered and mutilated white settlers in rural areas, especially in the white-settled Highlands, which contained the best farmland. The British army and colonial police forces combated the guerrillas, putting those they captured into concentration camps. As part of their "rehabilitation," the prisoners were subjected to "compelling force," a euphemism for torture, to obtain their confessions. In 1958, for example, 11 detainees at the Hola camp were killed during their interrogations. The Hola incident resulted in a change in British public opinion, which shifted toward granting Kenya its independence and removing the British military. The British government agreed to a constitutional convention to prepare the way for Kenyan independence.

Alleged Mau Mau guerrillas are rounded up in 1952.

In 1959 the Mau Mau disbanded as a prelude to Kenyan independence. Although they were known for killing white settlers, in fact less than 100 whites were murdered throughout the revolutionary period, while close to 2,000 black Africans were murdered by the Mau Mau. More than 11,000 Mau Mau guerrillas were killed by the British colonial forces in reprisals.

SEE ALSO

Kenya

FURTHER READING

Maloba, Wunyabari. *Mau Mau and Kenya*. Bloomington: Indiana University Press, 1993.

Mauritania

ISLAMIC REPUBLIC OF MAURITANIA (RÉPUBLIQUE ISLAMIQUE DE MAURITANIE)

• *Capital: Nouakchott*

Political history Located in northwest Africa, the northern part of Mauritania was inhabited by Muslim Arab nomads after the 7th century A.D., while the southern part belonged to the kingdom of Mali and traded with the advanced civilizations on the Niger River after the 9th century. The Portuguese began trading in the area in the 1500s, as did the French, Dutch, and British after the 1600s.

Mauritania became a French protectorate in 1903 and a French colony in 1920. It became an autonomous republic within the French Community in 1958 and then a sovereign independent state in 1960. Morocco claimed it as part of its sphere of influence but recognized Mauritanian independence in 1970. Mauritania was an authoritarian one-party state until 1978, when a coup d'état replaced the civilian government with a military regime. A 1991 constitution provided for the transition to a multiparty democracy.

Government institutions The 1991 constitution created a presidential system. The president of the republic, who is elected by the people for a five-year term, is the head of state and holds executive power. The president designates a prime minister as head of government. Legislative power is exercised by a 79-member National Assembly, whose members are elected for five-year terms, and a 56-member Senate, with members elected for six-year terms. The independent judiciary is headed by a supreme court.

Parties and movements The largest party is the Democratic and Social Republic Party (social democratic), which won most of the seats in the legislature in the 1992 elections. The main opposition party is the Union of Democratic Forces—New Era, a grass-roots organization that has won control of about one-fifth of the local government districts in the 1994 municipal elections.

Domestic issues Mauritania is divided between an Arab population in the north and a black population in the south; the government is dominated by the northerners, leading to great resentment in the south. Several political movements organized by the black Africans have been outlawed by the government on the ground that they promote divisive racial polarization.

International issues Mauritania has had conflicts with Senegal, its neighbor to the south, because livestock from Senegalese farmers have crossed the border to graze on Mauritanian land. It has also had border disagreements with Mali and Morocco over territorial demarcation lines. In 1989 Mauritania signed a treaty with Algeria, Morocco, Libya, and Tunisia providing for the establishment of the Union of the Arab Maghreb, a single nation-state, but as of the mid-1990s this organization had not actually unified these nations into a single political entity.

SEE ALSO
French Community

FURTHER READING
Handloff, Robert E., ed. *Mauritania: A Country Study.* 2nd ed. Washington, D.C.: Federal Research Division, Library of Congress, 1990.

Mauritius

REPUBLIC OF MAURITIUS

• *Capital: Port Louis*

Political history The islands in the southwestern Indian Ocean that make up Mauritius were settled originally by the Dutch after their discovery in 1507 and then by the French after 1721, when it became a French colony. Slaves from Africa and craftsmen from China and India were brought into the sugar plantations by the French. In 1810 the islands were taken by the British during the

Napoleonic Wars, and by the late 19th century the population was primarily of Indian descent.

Mauritius achieved independence in 1968 and is a member of the Commonwealth of Nations.

Government institutions Until 1992 Mauritius had a parliamentary system in which the head of state was the monarch of the British Commonwealth. In 1992 Mauritius approved a new constitution establishing a republic. The head of state is a president, elected by a majority of the National Assembly for a five-year term. Executive power is exercised by a prime minister, appointed by the president. Other ministers are appointed by the president on the recommendation of the prime minister.

Legislative power is exercised by a unicameral National Assembly, whose 62 members are popularly elected for five years. An additional 8 members are appointed to the legislature by the Electoral Supervisory System to provide some representation to minority groups, such as the Chinese.

Parties and movements Mauritius is a multiparty democracy. The largest party between 1978 and 1995 was the Alliance Party coalition, which includes the Labor Party (social democratic). In 1995 the coalition was ousted by the Opposition alliance, which won all 60 parliamentary seats with two-thirds of the vote, on a platform of providing for a fairer distribution of the national wealth.

Domestic issues Mauritius has attempted in the 1990s to diversify its economy from sugar production into manufacturing, particularly textile exports. A high rate of inflation, an increase in pollution, and the exploitation of the local labor force by foreign companies has led to political unrest, resulting in the turnover of government control in the 1995 elections.

On Mauritius, ethnic friction exists between speakers of Creole (a dialect of French) and Hindi speakers (the majority), and a backlash against the attempt to introduce the Hindi language into the schools accounted in part for the change in government in 1995.

International issues Mauritius has a territorial claim on the island of Diego Garcia, which is owned by the United Kingdom and leased to the United States for naval facilities.

SEE ALSO
Commonwealth of Nations

FURTHER READING
Bowman, Larry. *Mauritius*. Boulder, Colo.: Westview, 1991.

Meir, Golda

- *Born: May 3, 1898, Kiev, Ukraine, Russia*
- *Died: Dec. 8, 1978, Jerusalem, Israel*

Golda Meir served as prime minister of Israel from 1969 to 1974. She led Israel during the Yom Kippur War against Syria and Egypt in 1973 and was an effective spokesperson for the Israeli cause, enabling Israel to obtain crucial military assistance from the United States during and immediately after the hostilities.

Born Goldie Mabovitch in Kiev, a part of Ukraine then under Russian rule, she came to the United States with her family in 1906 to escape anti-Semitic pogroms. Later, she said that she became a Zionist in order to save Jewish children from the fear she felt as a youngster hiding from Russian cossacks. Her father became a railway worker in Milwaukee, Wisconsin, and she attended a teachers college and became active in socialist politics. In 1917 she married Morris Meyerson and, after meeting the Zionist leader David Ben-Gurion, the newly married couple emigrated to Palestine, where they worked on a kibbutz (a communal agricultural settlement) near Nazareth and changed their name to Meir, a version of Meyerson. They had two children and moved to Jerusalem. There she took in laundry to help support the family while her husband worked as an accountant. She divorced her husband in 1945.

Golda Meir became active in Zionist causes. She was a signer of Israel's Proclamation of Independence in 1948. During the war against five Arab nations that followed, she returned to the United States and raised millions of dollars for weapons and supplies. In 1949 she was elected to the Israeli legislature, called the Knesset, and became a cabinet member and ambassador to the Soviet Union. In Moscow, she attended religious services while 40,000 Jews rallied in the streets against repression by Soviet communist authorities. She then returned home and served in a variety of party and government posts. In 1969 she became Israel's fourth prime minister after being chosen by the Labor Party as its leader.

Golda Meir led the country during the Yom Kippur War of 1973, convincing the United States to resupply Israel with arms so that it could repel attacks by Egypt and Syria. Israeli forces crossed the Suez Canal and surrounded the Egyptian Third Army. Under U.S. pressure, Israel then accepted a ceasefire with Egypt and Syria. In 1974 Meir was forced from power by her own Labor Party leaders, who blamed her for a lack of preparedness that had cost a large number of Israeli casualties in the 1973 war.

Golda Meir was a strong leader who held her own among the tough men who dominated Israeli parliamentary politics. She wore no makeup, kept her gray hair in a bun, and rarely smiled or showed warmth in public, though she was capable of fixing late dinners for her aides after cabinet meetings that went on into the night. She was known as "Golda Shelanu" (Our Golda) to her supporters, who admired her tough stance against enemies of Israel. "If we have to have a choice between being dead and pitied, and being alive with a bad image," she once explained at the United Nations about her unyielding stance against the Western powers' insistence that she make concessions to its neighboring Arab states, "we'd rather be alive and have the bad image." Her life as a leader of the independence movement and as prime minister of an embattled nation serves as an inspiration for young Jewish women from many nations.

SEE ALSO
Israel; Zionism

FURTHER READING
Amdur, Richard. *Golda Meir: A Leader in Peace and War*. New York: Fawcett Columbine, 1990.
McAuley, Karen. *Golda Meir*. New York: Chelsea House, 1985.
Martin, Ralph G. *Golda: Golda Meir, the Romantic Years*. New York: Scribners, 1988.
Meir, Golda. *My Life*. New York: Putnam, 1975.

Mensheviks

The Mensheviks (Russian for "minority") were a faction of the Russian Social Democratic Labor Party (or Communist Party) that refused to accept Vladimir Lenin's leadership after the party Congress of 1903. Unlike the Bolsheviks, the majority faction that supported Lenin, the Mensheviks, led by a Jewish socialist named Martov, disagreed with Lenin's call for a highly disciplined "vanguard party" in which all members would be bound to carry out decisions once agreed upon, a principle Lenin called "democratic centralism." The Mensheviks believed that no such discipline should be required and that members should act according to their own principles and conscience. Martov and his followers did not believe that a political party should guide (that is, predetermine) the course of the revolution; instead, they argued that spontaneous uprisings by the masses of workers and peasants would eventually overturn the czar's regime and that these groups would then settle the question of how a new regime and society should be organized through grassroots democracy. Many Mensheviks believed that the revolution would occur in two stages: first, the workers would form a coalition with liberal capitalists to overthrow the czar's regime, and then a socialist system would emerge peacefully.

After the 1917 Russian Revolution ended the rule of the czar, the Mensheviks themselves split into two wings. One group was prepared to work with the revolutionary provisional government of Social Democrats headed by Aleksandr Kerensky (a government that Lenin dismissed as a "dictatorship of the bourgeoisie"), while the other tried to reunite with Lenin and the Bolsheviks. Many of the former group left the party after the Bolsheviks seized power by overthrowing the provisional government in November 1917. The Mensheviks who had tried to work with Lenin were purged from the Communist Party's Central Executive Committee in 1918 and from the local soviets, the assemblies of workers organized for revolutionary activities. Mensheviks were arrested in 1919 and again in 1921 for counterrevolutionary activities, especially protests and strikes in Petrograd (now St. Petersburg). The party itself was disbanded in 1923. The term *Menshevik* was thereafter used by the Bolsheviks to describe party members who refused to adhere to strict Communist Party discipline and the party line as set by its central committee.

SEE ALSO
Bolsheviks; Communism; Kerensky, Aleksandr; Lenin, Vladimir Ilich; Russian Revolution; Social democracy

FURTHER READING
Galili, Ziva. *The Menshevik Leaders in the Russian Revolution*. Princeton, N.J.: Princeton University Press, 1994.

Mexican Revolution

The Mexican Revolution encompassed a series of changes in the Mexican society and economy that began with the overthrow of the authoritarian regime of Porfirio Díaz in 1911 and led to a series of unstable regimes during the next two decades.

In 1910 Francisco Madero, a reformer from Coahuila State in Mexico, started the revolution against the government of Díaz—who was president of Mexico between 1876 and 1880 and again from 1884 to 1911—by calling for the restoration of the liberal constitution of 1857, land reform to benefit the Indians, and democratization of the government. Indians, mestizo (of mixed Spanish and Indian descent) farmers and urban workers, along with the mestizo middle class, fought against Díaz's corrupt and dictatorial government because it had favored large *criollo* landholders (descendants of the Spanish), foreign investors, industrialists, and the military. Madero insisted that Díaz honor a pledge not to run for reelection; when Díaz decided to run again, Madero fled

Seen here with his staff, Emiliano Zapata (seated, at center) came to represent the hopes of many Mexican peasants for genuine land reform and social change.

to the United States and proclaimed himself the legitimate president. With the help of Pancho Villa, a guerrilla leader based in Chihuahua State, Díaz was driven from power in May 1911 and Madero was then elected president in October.

The revolutionary government was unstable, however, because it was corrupt and ineffective, and it was opposed by the United States, which favored a more conservative government that would cooperate with foreign businesses. Madero was arrested and executed by General Victoriano Huerta in February 1913. This resulted in a three-sided civil war involving the new military dictator Huerta, the "constitutionalist" generals Venustiano Carranza and Álvaro Obregón, and two peasant leaders, Pancho Villa and Emiliano Zapata. Carranza became president in 1914; then Obregón defeated Villa in 1916 and Zapata in 1917. That year, the victorious leaders promulgated a progressive new constitution, which guaranteed land to Mexican peasants, ended the privileges of the Catholic Church, and guaranteed social welfare programs to the people. Carranza was betrayed and assassinated in 1920 by Obregón, who then assumed power until 1924, when he was succeeded by Plutarco Calles. In 1928, just as Obregón was about to assume office for another term,

he was assassinated by José de León Toral, a Catholic who resented Obregón's anticlerical policies. The following year, former president Calles, along with other revolutionary leaders, formed the Partido Nacional Revolucionario (National Party of the Revolution, or PNR), with the idea of ending the chaotic competition for power and channeling political ambition into peaceful politics. The new party was devoted primarily to consolidating its own power and ensuring a peaceful transition of the presidency. In 1946 its name was changed to Partido Revolucionario Institucional (Institutional Party of the Revolution), or PRI.

In 1934 President Lázaro Cárdenas instituted the last period of revolutionary activity by nationalizing railroads and oil fields, establishing many state industries, promoting labor unions, and breaking up large estates and redistributing land to the peasants. These actions gave the revolution a popular base of support among peasants and workers. Cárdenas was succeeded in 1940 as president by Manuel Ávila Camacho, who returned the PNR to the political middle, and foreign investment was encouraged in order to begin Mexico's rapid industrialization. By that time the Mexican revolutionary period had come to an end. The PRI after 1946 continued as Mexico's dominant political party, and, into the early 1990s, whoever it nominated for the presidency was almost guaranteed to win the election. It kept the nation from political chaos by allowing each outgoing president of Mexico to choose his successor from within the party's ranks.

SEE ALSO
Cárdenas, Lázaro; Mexico

FURTHER READING
Knight, Alan. *The Mexican Revolution.* New York: Cambridge University Press, 1986.

Mexico

UNITED MEXICAN STATES (ESTADOS UNIDOS MEXICANOS)

• *Capital: Mexico City*

Political history More than a thousand years ago, the Toltec and Mayan Indians had advanced civilizations in Mexico and much of Central America, but they were conquered by the Aztecs after the 12th century. The Spanish conquistador Hernán Cortés defeated the Aztecs in 1521, initiating three centuries of Spanish colonial rule.

In 1821 Mexico successfully fought against Spain for its independence. It lost Texas, however, to U.S. settlers in 1836. Mexico was then defeated by the United States in the Mexican-American War (1846–48) and lost all possessions north of the Rio Grande, including New Mexico, Arizona, and California. The church-supported regime of General Santa Anna was overthrown because he lost the war, and Benito Juárez took the vast landholdings of the Catholic Church and redistributed them to the peasants. In the 1860s Conservatives (landowning supporters of the church) allied with the French against Liberals (opponents of church influence). The French emperor Napoléon III sent an expeditionary force into Mexico in 1863, which conquered Mexico and installed a puppet emperor in 1864. When the Liberals won the ensuing civil war, the French withdrew, under U.S. pressure, and the emperor Maximilian was executed in 1867 by orders of Juárez.

Juárez was overthrown in 1876 by Porfirio Díaz, who assumed the presidency and ran Mexico through dicta-torship until 1911. Díaz allowed landowners to regain vast estates and mistreat their farm workers, policies that led to mounting discontent among the rural peasants.

The Mexican Revolution began in 1911 over the issues of corruption, land reform, and the perpetuation of dictatorial rule by Díaz. When Díaz relinquished power, a civilian government was formed under Francisco Madero. He, in turn, was overthrown by General Victoriano Huerta, and civil war ensued among various military factions. By 1930 an authoritarian one-party regime was established that ruled Mexico into the 1990s.

Government institutions The president, directly elected for a single six-year term, is the head of state and has executive power. The cabinet, whose ministers are appointed by the president, supervises government administration. Legislative power is vested in the bicameral Congreso de la Unión (National Congress), which is directly elected. The 128-member Senado (Senate) consists of four members from each state and the federal district; they serve six-year terms. The largest minority party is guaranteed at least one of the four seats from each state. The 500-member Cámara Federal de Diputados (Chamber of Deputies) is elected for three years, with 300 elected directly and 200 elected based on national votes for the parties.

Mexico has a federal system composed of 31 states and a federal district (Mexico City). Each state has its own constitution and is administered by a popularly elected governor. The 22 magistrates of the Supreme Court, who are appointed by the president and confirmed by the Senate, serve for six years.

Parties and movements Mexico is slowly moving toward multiparty democracy, due primarily to the electoral

Forces loyal to the rebel leader Pancho Villa enter the city of Juárez in triumph in the early days of the Mexican Revolution. Villa's exploits so alarmed the United States that President Woodrow Wilson sent troops to Mexico to apprehend him.

weaknesses of the dominant party, the Partido Revolucionario Institucional (Institutional Party of the Revolution), or PRI. Until the mid-1990s, the PRI rigged most state and federal elections, and there was widespread voting fraud in the 1988 contest: the ballots were burned by the army in 1991 to prevent investigation of the results that elected Carlos Salinas de Gortari. The Salinas regime was a disappointment to the Mexican people; posing as a reformer, Salinas continued the corruption in government.

By the mid-1990s Mexico was in a crisis of governance because corruption involving billions of dollars had reached the highest levels. In 1994, the last year of Salinas's term in office, the presidential candidate Luis Donaldo Colosio was assassinated at a campaign rally in Tijuana, and the head of the PRI, José Francisco Ruiz Massieu, was assassinated in Mexico City. Although individual assassins were arrested, most

Mexicans suspected that the killings were carried out to cover up criminality at the highest levels of the PRI, especially the opening up of Mexico to the largest of the world's drug cartels and financial manipulators.

In 1994 Ernesto Zedillo Ponce de León won the presidential elections; he was a PRI official but also a reformer who promised to root out corruption and end the alliance between top officials and *narcotraficantes* (drug dealers). His two predecessors, Salinas and Luis Echeverría, have both criticized him for weak leadership, but many in Mexico believe that the former leaders have been stung by government inquiries into corruption in their regimes. By 1995 the PRI was no longer in full control of Mexico, as opposition parties won significant proportions of seats in the national legislature and controlled several state governments. The main opposition parties in the 1990s were the conservative Partido de Acción

Nacional (National Action Party)—which controlled 4 state governments and 218 municipalities—and the socialist Partido de la Revolución Democratica (Democratic Revolution Party). The PRI lost control of the national legislature in 1997.

Domestic issues Mexico has privatized more than 1,000 state enterprises (worth more than $20 billion) and has encouraged foreign investment since the early 1990s. Still, much of the economy is controlled by the government, which fills jobs and awards contracts to those who will support the PRI. The Mexican Workers' Confederation, the largest national labor union, is dominated by the PRI and acts in accordance with government policies, even when they result in measures aimed at reducing workers' pay and benefits.

In the early 1990s Mexico followed an austerity program and emerged from a foreign debt crisis in which the annual inflation rate had reached more than 100 percent and real incomes had fallen by 40 percent. Although Mexico seemed poised for major growth, in 1994 the Mexican peso lost 30 percent of its value and the stock market fell, leading to a severe economic recession, a flight of capital from Mexico that reduced investment in new enterprises, and an inflation rate of 50 percent in 1995. The consequent precipitous drop in the standard of living for the peasants and urban middle class led many voters to desert the PRI in favor of the more conservative Partido de Acción Nacional.

On January 1, 1994, an armed Indian revolt, led by the 1,500 soldiers of the Zapatista National Liberation Army in the state of Chiapas, resulted in 145 casualties among the government troops and shook the Mexican political establishment. The rebels called for an end to PRI rule, free elections, land reform, and guarantees of cultural and linguistic rights for the indigenous Indian population. Although the Indians were chased from the towns of the state by the army and retreated to the Lancandón Forest near Guatemala, Indian activists continued to occupy many town halls. The PRI began negotiations with the Indians and their leader, Subcommander Marcos, culminating in a set of principles for reform in Chiapas reached in October 1995. The government also agreed to a series of national political reforms, including new limits on campaign finance contributions and a promise to hold completely fair elections.

International issues Relations between the United States and Mexico have been strained. In the 1930s Mexico seized control of U.S.-owned oil companies operating in Mexico. During the cold war, Mexico attempted to mediate disputes between the United States and left-wing governments in the Western Hemisphere, including Cuba and Nicaragua, which caused friction with the United States, which was not interested in compromise. In the 1990s the United States accused the Federal Judicial Police of providing protection for drug traffickers and of complicity in the murder of U.S. Drug Enforcement Agent Enrique Camareña in 1985. Large-scale illegal immigration from Mexico to the United States remains an issue between the two nations.

Mexico joined with the United States and Canada in the North American Free Trade Agreement (NAFTA) in 1994. NAFTA was supposed to improve the Mexican economy by providing new markets for the United States. But the overextended Mexican economy required a U.S. bailout of $18 billion to prop up the Mexican peso in 1994.

Human rights As political opposition to the authoritarian regime mounted in the 1990s, members of the

Mexican security forces and plain-clothes agents have suppressed dissent. Torture remains an instrument of the police and army, and it is sometimes used against journalists, opposition politicians, Indian dissidents, protesting students, and human rights advocates. A special Mexican investigating commission in 1995 accused the Mexican police of killing 17 peasants in Guerrero (the state where the resort of Acapulco is located) and accused state officials of covering up the crime.

SEE ALSO
Mexican Revolution

FURTHER READING

Camp, Roderic Ai. *Politics in Mexico*. 2nd ed. New York: Oxford University Press, 1996.
Castañeda, Jorge G. *The Mexico Shock*. New York: New Press, 1995.
Krauze, Enrique. *Mexico: Biography of Power: A History of Modern Mexico, 1810–1996*. Translated by Hank Heifetz. New York: HarperCollins, 1997.

Micronesia

FEDERATED STATES OF MICRONESIA

• *Capital: Palikir*

Political history Located to the northeast of Indonesia, Micronesia consists of a chain of islands and atolls in the western Pacific, comprising the island states of Yap, Truk, Ponape, and Kusaie, which were originally inhabited by fishermen who migrated from the Philippine and Indonesian islands. Spain acquired the Caroline Islands, as they were known in the 19th century, in 1885 and sold them to Germany in 1899. Japan occupied the islands at the start of World War I and in 1921 re-

ceived them as a League of Nations mandate. After their capture by the Allies in 1944, the islands became part of the United Nations Trust Territory of the Pacific Islands established in 1947 and administered by the United States.

Micronesia, comprising all the islands except for the Palau group (the westernmost islands), was established in 1979. In 1986 it entered into a Compact of Free Association with the United States, which retained sovereignty but permitted the islanders complete self-government. The agreement was terminated in 1990 when Micronesia became a sovereign state. It entered the United Nations in 1991.

Government institutions Micronesia is a federation with four states. The national government has a presidential system. The president and vice president are elected by the Congress from among the four senators at large in the Senate. The legislature consists of a 12-member unicameral Congress. Each state elects one senator for a four-year term and two other senators for two-year terms. The senators are influential tribal leaders.

Micronesia has an independent judiciary. Each of the states has a state court to hear civil and criminal cases and an appellate court. The final court of appeal is the Supreme Court.

Domestic issues Drought and Typhoon Owen in 1990 dislocated thousands of people, damaged most of the subsistence crops, and required the government to declare a state of emergency. Unemployment is high, as a result of the damage caused to so many farms and businesses by these natural disasters, but it is somewhat alleviated by public works projects such as construction of a new international airport.

International issues The United States has provided a substantial amount of foreign aid to help Micronesia cope with natural disasters.

Micronesia has a tuna-fishing agreement with Japan that limits the catch of Japanese fishing vessels to ensure the survival of the local fishing industry, but it has fishing disputes with Vietnam, which continues to overfish in its waters.

FURTHER READING

Kluge, Paul Frederick. *The Edge of Paradise: America in Micronesia*. New York: Random House, 1991.

Military regime

A military regime is a government controlled by military officers, whether or not they hold government positions. Usually the head of state is a member of the armed forces—such as Sani Abacha, general of the armed forces in Nigeria in the 1990s—and is often joined by a junta of officers who collectively exercise executive and legislative power and rule by decree. Sometimes, a nominal civilian government, with a civilian president as head of state, is actually controlled by a "strongman" from the dominant military service who holds no official public office but who wields power because of the military might he controls, such as Lieutenant General Raoul Cédras in Haiti in the early 1990s before his regime resigned due to U.S. pressure.

In some one-party states, a close alliance between party leaders and military officers provides for power sharing between civilian and military elites. In these nations, such as Iraq and China, the military controls state-owned corporations, enabling officers to profit from corruption. In some nations the military officers act as "guardians of the state," allowing civilians to rule but

setting guidelines beyond which a civilian government may not go in its social or economic policies. They reserve the right to overthrow the government if it goes too far with social reforms or if it elects a government formed from extremist parties. Algeria, Egypt, and Turkey are nations in which the military has made such claims in the 1990s.

Military governments do not permit free elections or multiparty competition until they are ready to return power to civilian rulers—which occurred in much of Latin America in the 1970s and 1980s—and they usually suspend civil liberties for the duration of their rule. Human rights abuses are common, because these military regimes feel that extreme methods, such as torture and execution, must be used to silence any opposition that might cause the people to revolt.

SEE ALSO

Algeria; China; Egypt; Haiti; Iraq; Junta; Nigeria; Turkey

FURTHER READING

Nordlinger, Eric A. *Soldiers in Politics*. Englewood Cliffs, N.J.: Prentice-Hall, 1977.
Perlmutter, Amos. *The Military and Politics in Modern Times*. New Haven: Yale University Press, 1977.

Mitterrand, François

- *Born: Oct. 26, 1916, Jarnac, France*
- *Died: Jan. 8, 1996, Paris, France*

Leader of the French Socialist Party after World War II and president of France between 1981 and 1995, François Mitterrand led his country into a role of leadership in Europe at the end of the cold war period. An austere and solemn man in public, Mitterrand was highly cultured and took great pride in planning massive public buildings, especially for the arts, that transformed the look of Paris.

Mitterrand was one of eight children whose father was an aviation executive. The young François attended a Roman Catholic school in Angoulême and then went to Paris to study law and political science. At first, he became a fascist, joining the paramilitary League of National Volunteers and associating with other right-wing nationalist groups. When World War II began, he joined the army as a sergeant and was wounded by an artillery shell in June 1940. He escaped from a German prisoner-of-war camp late in 1941. He went to Vichy and served as an official in the collaborationist French government, working with repatriated prisoners of war. He turned against the Vichy regime because of its discriminatory policies against French Jews and his realization that the Vichy regime could not promote French interests. He then went to London and in December 1943 to Algiers, when Charles de Gaulle assigned him to coordinate the Resistance movement against the Germans by former prisoners of war.

After the war Mitterrand abandoned his conservative philosophy. He served as the minister in charge of reintegrating former prisoners of war in the first postwar government. He was a Socialist deputy in the National Assembly between 1946 and 1958 and a senator from 1959 to 1962. Mitterrand served as minister of the interior from 1954 to 1955 and as minister of justice from 1956 to 1957. He was defeated for the French presidency in 1965 by Charles de Gaulle and in 1974 by Valéry Giscard d'Estaing, but Mitterrand defeated Giscard d'Estaing in a rematch in 1981 after the economy went into a recession. In 1986 he was reelected president, even though the rightist parties mustered a majority in parliament. Instead of resigning, he chose a conservative as prime minister, a system known as "cohabitation." In 1988 the leftist parties regained their majority and Mitterrand chose a fellow Socialist as prime minister. In 1993 he was once more, however, forced into a cohabitation arrangement after his party again lost its majority. His own popularity dropped dramatically, and with a serious illness he decided not to run for reelection. His party was defeated in 1995 when Jacques Chirac, a Gaullist, won the presidency.

Mitterrand transformed the political landscape in France. He formed a loose electoral alliance with the French Communists, which benefited the Socialists: while the Socialists became one of the largest parties, able to form a stable government and elect a president, the Communists declined, first becoming a junior partner in the coalition, then diminishing to a minor party altogether with almost no influence in French politics, as former Communist voters switched to support the programs of the Socialists.

Mitterrand was an ardent champion of domestic reform and modernization of government and the economy, presiding over an economy that was the fifth largest in the world. In one of his last efforts, he fought for French ratification of the Maastricht Treaty of 1992, which promoted the economic integration of western Europe, and furthered Franco-German economic and military integration, becoming one of the most influential statesmen in postwar Europe. He died of prostate cancer in 1996.

SEE ALSO
Chirac, Jacques; de Gaulle, Charles; France; Maastricht Treaty (1992)

FURTHER READING
Daley, Anthony, ed. *The Mitterrand Era: Policy Alternatives and Political Mobilization in France.* New York: New York University Press, 1995.

MacShane, Denis. *François Mitterrand, a Political Odyssey.* New York: Universe, 1983.

Mitterrand, François, and Elie Wiesel. *Memoir in Two Voices.* Translated by Richard Seaver and Timothy Bent. New York: Arcade, 1996.

Nay, Catherine. *The Black and the Red: François Mitterrand, the Story of an Ambition.* Translated by Alan Sheridan. San Diego: Harcourt Brace Jovanovich, 1987.

Ross, George, et al., eds. *The Mitterrand Experiment: Continuity and Change in Modern France.* Oxford: Polity Press, 1987.

Moldova

REPUBLIC OF MOLDOVA (REPUBLICA MOLDOVENEASCA)

• *Capital: Chişinău*

Political history The Ottoman Empire controlled the Bessarabia area in which Moldova lies (located to the east of Romania and west of Ukraine) until 1812, when it was ceded to Russia at the end of the Napoleonic Wars as one of the spoils of victory. Most of the population was ethnically Romanian, and by the end of World War I Russia was too weak to retain control of the entire territory. In 1918 Romania annexed the territory west of the Dniester River, and in 1924 the Soviet Union established the Moldavian Autonomous Soviet Socialist Republic on the eastern bank. It was merged with Bessarabia in 1940 to form the Moldavian Soviet Socialist Republic. Romania allied with Germany in World War II and occupied eastern Moldova, but the Soviet Union retook that territory in 1944. Moldova declared its independence in 1991 when the Soviet Union dissolved.

Government institutions In 1991 the Moldovan constitution was amended to establish a presidential system, replacing the prior rule by the Communist Party when Moldova was a Soviet republic. Under the new constitution, the president is the head of state and governs with an appointed council of ministers who run the government bureaucracies. A popularly elected, unicameral parliament exercises legislative powers. There is an independent judiciary that consists of district courts for civil and criminal cases. The Supreme Court handles appeals, and the Constitutional Court ensures that laws and government actions adhere to the constitution.

Parties and movements In 1991 Moldova was transformed from a one-party authoritarian Soviet republic into a multiparty democracy. The Communist Party of Moldova, which had been in power, was banned. Parties are organized partly along ideological and partly along ethnic lines; two-thirds of the population is ethnic Romanian, one-eighth is Ukrainian, and one-eighth is Russian. In the 1994 elections the Agrarian Democratic Party won almost half the seats in the parliament. In second place was the Socialist Bloc, giving pro-Russian parties a large majority in the legislature. The more nationalist and conservative parties, the Peasants' Party and the Christian Democrats, were far behind.

Domestic issues In 1991 Moldovan nationalists sought reunification with Romania (adopting that nation's flag and national anthem), but Romania's reluctance for an immediate merger then led to an upsurge of sentiment for Moldova to remain independent, followed in 1994 by a desire to move closer to Russia economically.

The region east of the Dniester River, populated by 800,000 ethnic Russians and Ukrainians, established its own Trans-Dniester Republic in 1992, with its capital at Tiraspol. The Russian 14th Army intervened to end hostilities between Moldova and the republic, which led to more than 500 deaths in 1993, and joint Russian and Moldovan peacekeepers patrolled the border, while the Russian army propped up the secessionist regime. Russia and Moldova agreed in 1994 on a three-year phaseout of Russian troops.

Moldova's economy collapsed as inflation and unemployment soared in the early 1990s, after the region left the Soviet Union and no longer benefited from its subsidies and low-cost imports. Since the mid-1990s Moldova has been selling off most of its state enterprises and embracing free-market policies, but its economy has remained weak.

International issues Moldova has romanized its alphabet (under Soviet rule it had used the Cyrillic alphabet of the Russian language), made Romanian its official language, and established close cultural ties with Romania. Western countries, the World Bank, and the International Monetary Fund (IMF) have pledged hundreds of millions of dollars in foreign aid to transform the Moldovan economy from a socialist to a market system.

SEE ALSO
Ottoman Empire; Romania; Russia; Soviet Union (Union of Soviet Socialist Republics); Ukraine

Monaco

PRINCIPALITY OF MONACO (PRINCIPAUTÉ DE MONACO)

• *Capital: Monaco*

Political history As a city in southeastern France, Monaco was first settled by Phoenicians and Greeks before the birth of Christ. In the Middle Ages it was ruled by the Italian city-state Genoa. Since 1297 Monaco has been an independent sovereign principality ruled by the House of Grimaldi, an Italian royal family. In 1815 the Congress of Vienna (a meeting of European states to work out territorial adjustments) placed it under the protection of the kingdom of Sardinia. In 1861 it came under the protection of France, as compensation for successful French intervention in the Sardinian efforts to unify Italy. The treaty with France explicitly reaffirmed the sovereignty of Monaco but allowed France to control its foreign policy. In 1911 Monaco became a constitutional monarchy, and in 1962 a new constitution vested sovereign power jointly in the monarch and the legislature. In the event that the Grimaldi dynasty becomes extinct, Monaco would become an autonomous protectorate of France and lose its sovereignty.

Government institutions The monarch—who since 1949 has been Prince Rainier III—holds executive power, which is exercised by the four-member Council of Government, headed by a minister of state (a French civil servant chosen by the prince from a list of three presented by the French government). Legislative power is exercised jointly by the prince and the unicameral 18-member National Council, whose members are directly elected for five-

The Pink Palace in Monaco is home to one of Europe's last ruling monarchies, the House of Grimaldi.

year terms. Laws passed by the National Council do not go into effect without the approval of the prince.

The independent judiciary includes Courts of First Instance for civil cases, the Crown Tribunal for criminal cases, and a High Court of Appeal. The Supreme Tribunal deals with cases involving civil liberties and administrative regulations that may abuse them.

Parties and movements Candidates for the National Council belong to the pro-monarchical Movement of the Democratic Union or the National and Democratic Union. The National and Democratic Union is the largest group, controlling almost all seats in the legislature. There is also a Socialist Party, which has not been able to win an election.

Domestic issues The economy is organized by the Société des Bains de Mer, a private financial and development corporation controlled by the prince. It has expanded the area of the tiny principality by one-fifth, by filling in harbor areas. Tourism (based on gambling), which is a primary source of income, has been heavily promoted

by the royal family. Many foreign banks and companies, which incorporate in Monaco because taxes are low and there is little government regulation, provide employment for numerous professional workers.

International issues Monaco is constrained by its treaty commitments to France, which conducts its foreign relations and controls its telecommunications and postal service, although Monaco does issue its own postage stamps, highly prized by collectors. Monaco is not a member of the European Union, but in 1993 it entered the United Nations as the smallest member state.

SEE ALSO
France

Monarchy

A monarchy is a political system in which the head of state is anointed or crowned in a religious ceremony and exercises the sovereign power of the nation-state for life. The word and the concept are old: *monarchy* comes from the Greek *monarkhia* (meaning "rule of one"), which became the Latin *monarchia*, then the French *monarchie* before passing into Middle English as *monarchie*. Usually, the monarch, known as a king or queen, succeeds to the throne through the principle of hereditary succession—that is, the throne is handed down through a family. In some European nations, including Denmark, Poland, the Holy Roman Empire, and Russia, monarchs were at times elected by the nobility.

In some societies, such as Egypt, the monarch was considered to be a god; in others, such as China and Japan, he was a descendant of the gods who combined priestly functions as head of the national religion with secular functions as head of state.

In medieval Europe the king was considered to be God's agent on Earth, a role recognized in the coronation ceremony. The doctrine of the divine right of kings specified that, as the agent of God, the king could do no wrong nor commit any crime. In England, the king was accountable only to God, not to courts or Parliament, although the king's ministers could be held accountable for the actions of the government.

Some European monarchs between the 13th and 18th centuries gradually recognized the constitutional rights of elected assemblies (parliaments) in matters such as lawmaking and taxation. Royal courts shared judicial power with courts established by the parliament. These nations, such as England, became constitutional monarchies. In other nations, such as France, Spain, Austria-Hungary, and Russia, monarchs organized state bureaucracies that gradually dominated political life at the expense of the nobility; these nations became

known as absolute monarchies because the laws of the state were determined by the monarchs.

In the nations that developed constitutional monarchies, cabinet government gradually appeared by the end of the 18th century: in such a system, the ministers appointed by the Crown to run the government had to command the confidence of parliament in order to pass legislation and implement their policies. By the mid-19th century the British Crown had assumed a primarily ceremonial role and political power was exercised by a prime minister and cabinet, who held office by virtue of their party's control of a parliamentary majority, obtained as the result of a victory in free elections.

At the end of the 20th century, Scandinavian nations, the Netherlands, and Great Britain all retain constitutional monarchs who possess no independent political power. The formal acts of the monarch are not his or her own but are the policies of the government. The monarch, at best, can influence the government by giving sound advice, often gained by a long-run perspective and experience in watching governments come and go.

Most of the absolute monarchies of the 18th century, such as those in France and Russia, were swept away by revolutions that transformed the nations into republics or totalitarian dictatorships in the 19th and 20th centuries. Occasionally, as in the case of Spain, a monarchy has been restored after a period of dictatorship, but it, too, conforms to the constitutional model.

African monarchs, who ruled over tribal kingdoms into the late 19th century, were incorporated into colonial governments by the European powers as territorial administrators. Although most African nations, after achieving independence, opted for presidential

In most nations that still maintain a vestige of monarchy, such as Great Britain, the institution serves as a unifying symbol of national tradition but possesses little political authority of its own. Here Queen Elizabeth leaves Buckingham Palace on the day of her coronation in 1953.

heads of state, many recognize tribal kings and queens as ceremonial rulers of ethnic groups within their nations, as in Nigeria and South Africa.

SEE ALSO

Austro-Hungarian Empire; Cabinet government; China; Denmark; Dictatorship; Egypt; France; Hirohito; Japan; Nigeria; Parliamentary system; Poland; President; Prime minister; Russia; South Africa; Sovereignty; Spain; United Kingdom

FURTHER READING

Gurney, Gene. *Kingdoms of Asia, the Middle East, and Africa*. New York: Crown, 1986.

Nicolson, Harold. *Kings, Courts, and Monarchy*. New York: Simon & Schuster, 1962.

Mongolia

STATE OF MONGOLIA (MONGOL ULS)

• *Capital: Ulan Bator*

Political history Mongolia, a landlocked nation in central Asia between China and Russian Siberia, was the center of the Mongol empire of Genghis Khan (1162–1227) and his successors. By the end of the 13th century, Mongols had conquered most of Eurasia and parts of eastern Europe. The Chinese Qing (Manchu) dynasty conquered Inner (southern) Mongolia, an area nearer to Beijing, China, in 1636 and Outer (northern) Mongolia in 1691. Mongolia was then ruled as a Chinese province until 1911, when it declared its independence; it was then forced, however, to become an autonomous province of Russia in the aftermath of the turmoil surrounding the Chinese Revolution. After the Russian Revolution of 1917, the territory became a staging area for anticommunist forces fighting to control the Trans-Siberian Railroad. In 1921, after the counterrevolutionary White Russians were expelled from the area, the communist Mongolian People's Revolutionary Party proclaimed a provisional "people's government" and declared its independence. It was quickly recognized by the Russian government, also under communist control, and returned to the Russian sphere of influence as the Mongolian People's Republic in 1924. China did not recognize the independence of Outer Mongolia until 1946. (Inner Mongolia remained a Chinese possession.) Mongolia gradually ended its status as a puppet state of the Soviet Union and became an independent communist state in the 1950s. In 1990, after a new nationalist movement, the Mongolian Democratic Union, held massive demonstrations in the capital in favor of democratization, the Communist Party decided to give up its formal governing power, and the nation was transformed into a multiparty democracy in 1992.

Government institutions Under the constitution instituted in 1992, Mongolia has a parliamentary system. The president is head of state and commander of the armed forces and is popularly elected for a four-year term. The 76-member Great Hural (parliament) exercises legislative power and appoints the prime minister and cabinet.

The independent judiciary consists of rural and urban district courts for civil and criminal cases. The Supreme Court handles appeals. The Constitutional Court ensures that laws adhere to provisions of the constitution. The General Council of Courts, consisting of high-level judicial officials, nominates members of the Supreme Court, who must be confirmed by the legislature.

Parties and movements Until 1990 Mongolia was an authoritarian one-party communist state, but in 1991, after massive demonstrations by pro-democracy students and workers, it began the transition to a multiparty social democratic state. The communist Mongolian People's Revolutionary Party was the largest political force, having won the free elections in 1992. Opposition reformist parties include the Mongolian Democratic Party, the New Progress Party, and the Social-Democrat Party, which formed a social democratic coali-

tion and elected a president in 1993, gaining control of the government.

A non-communist coalition, led by the Democratic Union, won a majority in the parliamentary elections in 1996, as a protest against the high unemployment rate and poverty. But in 1997 the Mongolian People's Revolutionary Party won the presidency, pledging to slow down radical economic reforms that had further increased unemployment.

Domestic issues Industrialization programs developed in the 1960s and 1970s with the help of the Soviet Union were too costly and left Mongolia bankrupt, with its factories burdened with obsolete equipment and unwanted products. However, the new constitution recognizes private property, which has speeded private investment and the transition to a free-market economy. The political parties disagree over the pace of reform, with the communists preferring a slower pace of privatization than the reformist parties.

International issues Mongolia serves as a buffer between Russia and China. Soviet troops served on the Mongolian-Chinese border until the 1980s, when they withdrew as part of an agreement between Russia and China to end their border disputes. China and Mongolia then signed a border treaty in 1988.

Russia is Mongolia's principal trading partner, though trade with China and Japan (involving industrial minerals) has increased in the 1990s.

In 1989 Mongolia joined the Group of 77, an organization of Third World nations concerned with economic development policies, and it has become a member of the International Monetary Fund.

SEE ALSO

China; Group of 77; International Monetary Fund (IMF); Russia; Soviet Union (Union of Soviet Socialist Republics)

FURTHER READING

Sanders, Alan. *Mongolia: Politics, Economics, and Society.* London: Frances Pinter, 1987.

Worden, Robert L., ed. *Mongolia: A Country Study.* 2nd ed. Washington, D.C.: Federal Research Division, Library of Congress, 1991.

Morocco

KINGDOM OF MOROCCO (AL-MAMLAKAH AL-MAGHRIBĪYAH)

• *Capital: Rabat*

Political history Located in North Africa, across the Strait of Gibraltar from Spain, Morocco was inhabited by Berbers, a mountain tribe, around 1000 B.C. It was ruled in ancient times by Carthage and Rome, and the area was invaded by the Vandals, a Germanic tribe, in the 5th century A.D. Arabs conquered Morocco in 683. In the 11th and 12th centuries a Moroccan Berber empire ruled most of North Africa and parts of Spain. By 1492, however, the Moroccans had been expelled from Spain. In the 16th century, the Berber empire collapsed and Morocco was divided into several small tribal kingdoms.

In the 1600s Morocco was reunited under the Alawid dynasty. In the 18th century, pirates from Barbary, on the Moroccan coast, won tribute from European powers, though the U.S. Navy in the early 1800s forced the pirates to cease their attacks on American shipping. Spain established colonies along the Moroccan coast and occupied Tangier in the 19th century.

By the Treaty of Fez, signed in 1912, Morocco became a French colony and Spain was given Moroccan territories to the south, which became known as Spanish Sahara. Tangier was put under international administration in 1923 as a free port. After World War II, an independence movement called the Istiqlal took up arms against the French, but was defeated. Nevertheless, a nationalist movement won the allegiance of Moroccans, and France prepared the colony peacefully for the transition to independence. In 1956 France granted Morocco, including the port of Tangier, its independence. The northern tip of Spanish Sahara was ceded to Morocco in 1958, and Spain returned the Ifni enclave (a territory surrounded by Morocco) in 1969. In 1976 Spain completely withdrew from Spanish Sahara and Morocco assumed control, renaming it Western Sahara. In 1991 Morocco agreed to hold a referendum in the area so that inhabitants could vote either for union with Morocco or independence, but by 1997 it was clear that Morocco would insist on unification with the territory.

In 1992, in an attempt to placate Islamic fundamentalists, the monarchy permitted fundamental constitutional reforms (including lowering the voting age to 20 and granting equal media access to all political parties), as well as multiparty elections.

Government institutions Under the constitution instituted in 1992, Morocco is a constitutional monarchy, with a hereditary king as head of state, functioning under Islamic law. Executive power is vested in the king, who appoints and may dismiss the prime minister and other members of the cabinet, who are also accountable to the legislature. Legislative power is exercised by a unicameral 306-member Chamber of Representatives; some of its members are directly elected and others represent professional groups and local governments.

Workers trench a road between Rafsai and Tabouda in the Rif region of Morocco. As in other nations of northern Africa, soil erosion and the encroaching desert threaten Morocco's agricultural foundation.

There is an independent judiciary that applies civil and Islamic law. Judges are appointed by the Crown after nomination by the Supreme Judicial Council, an advisory body chaired by the king. Courts of First Instance handle routine civil and criminal cases. Appeals from lower courts are heard by the Courts of Appeal. The High Court of Justice, whose members are selected from the parliament, deals with crimes committed by government officials. The Supreme Court supervises the judicial system and is the court of last appeal.

Parties and movements Morocco has a multiparty system. The largest parties are the Constitutional Union (pro-monarchical and conservative), the National Movement of Independents (conservative), the Popular Socialist Movement (social democratic), Istiqlal (the original independence party), and the Popular Movement (a breakaway group of Istiqlal).

Domestic issues In the 1990s Morocco has embarked on an economic austerity program designed to control its high inflation. This program, which has cut government jobs and benefits to workers, has resulted in high unemployment and strikes by unions. But the inflation rate has been controlled, foreign debt has been reduced, and state enterprises have been privatized. These changes, along with investment by foreigners, have fueled an expansion of the economy.

The unequal distribution of wealth in Morocco and high unemployment among the young have resulted in a grass-roots Islamic movement that was being repressed in the 1990s by the government. King Hassan II built the world's largest mosque in Casablanca in an effort to stem rising Islamic fundamentalist movements that were threatening his regime.

International issues Morocco annexed two-thirds of the former Spanish Sahara (now known as Western Sahara) in 1976; the remainder went to Mauritania, its neighbor to the south, but Mauritania renounced its claims under Moroccan pressure in 1979. Morocco has since then fought against the Polisario, a guerrilla movement seeking independence for Western Sahara. Polisario has received aid from Algeria, causing strains with Morocco.

In the 1990s Morocco has played the role of mediator in the Israeli-Arab dispute. King Hassan II has met openly with Israeli leaders to promote peace negotiations, and Morocco maintains low-level diplomatic relations with Israel. It has maintained cultural links with some of the 500,000 Jews of Moroccan descent who live in Israel.

Morocco joined the Union of the Arab Maghreb in 1989. The union is supposed to unite politically Morocco, Tunisia, Algeria, and Libya, but no concrete unification plans have been implemented, because Morocco has called for a "freeze" to protest Algerian interference with its plans for Western Sahara.

Morocco contributed to the international force that liberated Kuwait from Iraqi control in the 1991 Gulf War and in the mid-1990s remained a close ally of the United States.

Morocco in the 1990s was one of the largest suppliers of drugs to western Europe (mostly marijuana and hashish), and the European Union has pressed the king to step up eradication efforts.

Human rights The government of King Hassan II has arrested or placed under house arrest leading dissidents in order to avoid possible violent uprisings. These include Sheikh Abdulsalaam Yassine, founder of the Justice and Charity Movement, an Islamic welfare society; he was placed under house arrest in 1989.

SEE ALSO
France; Spain

FURTHER READING
Zartman, William. *The Political Economy of Morocco.* New York: Praeger, 1987.

Mozambique

REPUBLIC OF MOZAMBIQUE (REPÚBLICA DE MOÇAMBIQUE)

- *Capital: Maputo*

Political history Located in southeastern Africa, Mozambique was inhabited by Bantu peoples in ancient times. Arab merchants established trading settlements on Mozambique Island, off the northeast coast, in the 15th century. The Portuguese arrived in 1506 and ruled Mozambique as part of Portuguese India until they created a separate colony for the territory in 1752. Portuguese farmers created large sugar and cotton plantations in the late 19th century, when it became known as Portuguese East Africa. In 1951 Mozambique became an overseas province of Portugal.

After more than a decade of guerrilla war against the Portuguese, Mozambique won its independence in 1975. The independence movement then split into two factions, one supported by the Soviet Union and one by the United States. A bitter civil war ensued, which ended in 1991.

Government institutions The 1990 constitution provides for a presidential system. The president, directly elected for a five-year term, is the head of state. He holds executive power and governs with a council of ministers. Legislative power is vested in the 250-member Assembly of the Republic, whose members are directly elected for five-year terms.

Mozambique has an independent judiciary. There are district courts for civil and criminal cases, as well as customs, maritime, and labor courts. The Supreme Court, whose justices are appointed by the president, handles appeals. An administrative court reviews challenges to the legality of government actions and expenditures.

Parties and movements Mozambique was a one-party authoritarian state until the 1990s, when it began the transition to multiparty democracy. A Marxist-Leninist party called the Frente de Libertação de Moçambique (the Mozambican Liberation Front), or FRELIMO, was the sole party permitted before 1990. In 1991, as part of the agreement to end the civil war, other parties were permitted; a social democratic party and other opposition parties formed. In the fall of 1995 an anticommunist party, the Resistencia Nacional Moçambicana (Mozambique National Resistance), or RENAMO, which was formed out of a rebel guerrilla movement, boycotted the parliamentary elections, claiming that that they would be rigged; FRELIMO won the elections.

Domestic issues Mozambique suffered through a violent civil war between FRELIMO and RENAMO (which received support from the United States) from 1975 to 1992. In 1991 an agreement to end the civil war provided that RENAMO could become a legal political party after a general peace accord was signed. In the 1990s the party's guerrillas were integrated into a new, unified Mozambican army. The United Nations sent 7,500 peacekeeping troops to oversee the agreement.

In the mid-1990s the government relied heavily on Western donor nations, the International Monetary Fund, and the World Bank in its efforts to recover from the devastation of war. More than 4 million people were threatened with famine conditions in the early 1990s; more than 1 million Mozambican refugees who had fled the nation needed repatriation; and another million were in the nation's refugee camps.

Members of the government, including President Joaquim Chissano, renounced their communist ideology and in the mid-1990s practiced meditation and followed the teachings of Maharishi Mahesh Yogi.

International issues After gaining its independence, Mozambique was dominated by the communist faction of the independence movement and, as a result, developed close relations with the Soviet Union and other communist nations. But South Africa, Mozambique's neighbor to the south, supported the anticommunist RENAMO guerrillas in the 1980s. Two years later, South Africa and Mozambique signed the Nkomati Nonaggression Accord, but South African support for RENAMO continued.

In the late 1980s Mozambique began to shift to a pro-Western foreign policy, to go along with its move toward a free-market economy and increased political freedoms. In 1993 the United Nations sent a force of 7,500 peacekeepers to demilitarize the 20,000 guerrillas and 70,000 government troops and prepare the way for free elections after a peace accord. The United States spent $19 million to help with the conversion of FRELIMO and RENAMO from military movements into political parties for the 1995 elections and to provide the new parties with funds to build their local organizations and to run campaigns.

SEE ALSO
United Nations (UN)

FURTHER READING
Birmingham, David. *Frontline Nationalism in Angola and Mozambique.* Trenton, N.J.: Africa World Press, 1992.
Munslow, Barry. *Mozambique: The Revolution and Its Origins.* New York: Longman, 1983.

Mubarak, Muhammad Hosni

- Born: May 4, 1928, Kafr el-Moseilha, Egypt

As president of Egypt since 1981, Hosni Mubarak has maintained a pro-Western regime, continuing the policies of his predecessor, Anwar Sadat. He has been a force for moderation in Middle Eastern politics, vigorously opposing efforts by dictators such as Saddam Hussein in Iraq to destabilize the region and opposing the rise of Islamic fundamentalist movements in the Arab world. Mubarak has assisted the Palestinians in their autonomy negotiations with Israel and, at times when the negotiations went well, helped Israel end its isolation from the Arab world.

Born in a northern Egyptian village, Mubarak was educated at the Egyptian air force academy and became a fighter pilot. He fought in Yemen in 1964 and against Israel in 1967. He became air chief of staff in 1969 and commander in chief of the military from 1972 to 1975. In 1973, based on plans developed by Mubarak, Egypt and Syria launched an attack against Israel that enabled Egyptian forces to cross the Suez Canal and regain some territory they had lost in 1967.

In 1975 Mubarak was appointed vice president of Egypt by President Anwar Sadat, and in 1978 he helped organize the National Democratic Party, the main civilian prop for the military regime. Mubarak assumed the presidency after Sadat was assassinated by Islamic fundamentalists in 1981. A plainspoken military man, Mubarak was underestimated by most observers, who failed to see his intelligence and his political skills. He is not an inspiring speaker or leader, but he has been able to consolidate power and stabilize his regime against internal opposition. And he has demonstrated great personal courage in making public appearances in Cairo and the countryside after members of his government were assassinated by Islamic extremists.

In the 1990s Mubarak cracked down harshly on Islamic terrorists who were attacking the minority Coptic Christians and foreign tourists. He brought Egypt back into the Arab League, the regional organization of Arab states, as a leading member. By 1987 almost all Arab states had resumed diplomatic relations with Egypt, which had been cut after Sadat had signed a peace treaty with Israel in 1978. Mubarak was a leader in the Arab coalition that formed against Iraq after its attempted annexation of Kuwait in 1990, and he sent Egyptian forces to Saudi Arabia to assist in the liberation of Kuwait in 1991.

SEE ALSO

Arab League (League of Arab States); Egypt; Iraq; Islamic fundamentalism; Israel; Sadat, Anwar

FURTHER READING

Lippman, Thomas. *Egypt after Sadat.* New York: Paragon, 1989.
Solecki, John. *Hosni Mubarak.* New York: Chelsea House, 1991.
Springborg, Robert. *Mubarak's Egypt.* Boulder, Colo.: Westview, 1989.

Mugabe, Robert

- Born: Feb. 21, 1924, Kutama, Northern Rhodesia

Robert Mugabe was the leader of the independence movement in Zimbabwe, and he served as its first prime minister (1980–87) and first president (1987–).

Born to a carpenter in a Rhodesian village, Mugabe became a teacher in Ghana in the 1950s, then returned to

Rhodesia to organize a movement for independence from the British colonial authorities.

Between 1964 and 1975 Mugabe was placed under arrest for his political activities. Meanwhile, the white minority established its own independent Rhodesian state and denied political participation to the black majority. In 1975, Mugabe escaped from prison and went into exile in Mozambique, where he commanded the armed struggle against the white government, engaging in guerrilla warfare and sabotage of industry.

After an internationally brokered settlement to end the war, the nation was renamed Zimbabwe and the white government was dismantled. Mugabe became its first prime minister in 1980. Although he was a black nationalist, his policies emphasized cooperation with the white minority, especially the farmers on whom the nation's immediate prosperity depended. He was elected president in 1987. He had earlier founded the ruling party, called the Zimbabwe African National Union (ZANU), and served as its first secretary; ZANU drew most of its support from the Shona people, the majority population. Mugabe was reelected president in 1990 for a six-year term and elected again in 1996.

Mugabe is distrustful of Western-style multiparty democracy, and he is attempting to move Zimbabwe to a one-party system to consolidate his power, while much of the rest of sub-Saharan Africa is being transformed into multiparty democracies. In the 1990s he has become a controversial figure in southern Africa because of his condemnation of homosexuals and his claim that same-sex love is "un-African."

SEE ALSO

Zimbabwe

FURTHER READING

Eide, Lorraine. *Robert Mugabe.* New York: Chelsea House, 1989.

Gann, Lewis. *The Struggle for Zimbabwe.* New York: Praeger, 1981.

Mugabe, Robert. *War, Peace, and Development in Contemporary Africa.* New Delhi: Indian Council for Cultural Relations, 1987.

Worth, Richard. *Robert Mugabe of Zimbabwe.* Englewood Cliffs, N.J.: Messner, 1990.

Multiparty democracy

A multiparty democracy is a political system in which more than one political party legally exists and two or more parties have enough popular support to compete for state power. Multiparty democracy requires the following conditions in order to work: freedom of speech, press, and association, so that parties can form without fear of reprisal; honest elections, so that a party cannot steal an election through fraud or intimidation; and periodic contests for the important offices of the state, so that officeholders face the voters and are accountable for their performance. Under such circumstances, one set of political leaders can be replaced with others more in tune with popular preferences.

In a two-party system, each of the major parties is capable of winning a majority of the votes cast in an election and of obtaining a majority in the legislature. In most multiparty systems, however, there are several different parties competing for power, none of which is likely to achieve a majority by itself. Instead, parties win votes along regional, religious, ethnic, linguistic, class, or ideological lines. After the elections, several parties agree to form a coalition in order to create a parliamentary majority capable of supporting a government. They bargain with each other over which cabinet positions each party will receive and over policies the new government will adopt.

Multiparty systems have existed in much of western Europe, including France, Italy, the Benelux nations, and the Scandinavian countries. In the 1990s many former communist states in eastern Europe and some regimes in sub-Saharan Africa replaced their one-party regimes with multiparty systems.

SEE ALSO

Democracy; One-party state; Parliamentary system

FURTHER READING

Budge, Ian, and Hans Keman. *Parties and Democracy: Coalition Formation and Government Functioning in Twenty States.* New York: Oxford University Press, 1990.

Laver, Michael, and Norman Schofield. *Multiparty Government: The Politics of Coalition in Europe.* New York: Oxford University Press, 1990.

Mussolini, Benito

• *Born: July 29, 1883, Predappio, Italy*
• *Died: Apr. 28, 1945, Dongo, Italy*

Il Duce (the leader) of Italy from 1922 to 1943, Benito Mussolini led his country out of the ashes of World War I and into the fire of World War II. He gave Italians a sense of mission, but that mission, unfortunately, involved an alliance with Germany and Japan in a fruitless attempt at world conquest.

Mussolini's father was a blacksmith and his mother a teacher. He was expelled from several schools for fighting and was known as a bully. He was intelligent, however, and received a teacher's diploma in 1901, then taught secondary school in a local village. In 1904 he served in the Italian army. His early political orientation was socialist, and he called for a workers' revolution against the conservative government. In 1912 Mussolini made fiery speeches at a Socialist Party congress and, as a result, was made editor of the party newspaper, *Avanti* (Forward).

Mussolini was an opportunist, willing to embrace any ideology in order to gain political power. In 1914 he was expelled from the Socialist Party and created the Autonomous Fascist Movement to support the war policies of the government during World War I. Mussolini's Fascists emphasized nationalism, militarism, and protection of Italian corporations—the exact opposite of the Socialist positions he had previously espoused, which during the war emphasized the solidarity of workers in different nations, pacifism, and the nationalization of corporations. For Mussolini, political ideas were always less significant than the opportunity to win power.

During World War I, Mussolini again served in the Italian army and was wounded in 1917. After the war, he was defeated in his 1919 bid to be elected to parliament. His Fascist movement organized as a political party and won an electoral victory in 1921: he and 34 other Fascists became deputies in parliament. In October 1922 Mussolini organized a march on Rome and his newly formed street gangs, the Blackshirts, attacked communists, socialists, and trade unionists with the tacit support of corporate leaders, landowners, the monarchy, and much of the Catholic Church hierarchy. That same month King Victor Emmanuel III named Mussolini prime minister. The following year, however, Mussolini organized security forces loyal to his party rather than to the king. By 1924 his party had won an absolute majority in the parliament, due to his program promising full employment and social benefits for workers but at the same time promising to end strikes and restore order.

After the assassination of Giacomo Matteotti, a leading Socialist Party member of parliament, by Mussolini's Blackshirts in 1925, Mussolini declared a state of emergency, suspended civil liberties, and established a Fascist dictatorship. By 1926 all other parties were abolished and it was forbidden to form new ones. Because of Mussolini's popular support and the backing of the army and wealthy industrialists, the king acquiesced in the dictatorship. Mussolini concluded an agreement with the Vatican in 1926 that quadrupled church revenues from the state in return for papal recognition of the legitimacy of the Fascist regime.

Mussolini was a great orator who excelled at making speeches from his balcony to adoring crowds, chanting *Du-ce, Du-ce*. He originated the Fascist salute and always wore a military uniform. He announced grandiose projects and proclaimed the glories of the Italian nation, but his declarations were usually exaggerations of the truth. Mussolini claimed, for example, that Italy had 150 powerful army divisions, when actually it had only 10. When Italian forces were in combat, he always claimed great victories, even when his forces were being defeated. Truth was always the first casualty in his military adventures.

Mussolini used his governmental powers primarily for the benefit of Italian corporations, which increased their profits at the expense of workers, whose wages fell.

His Fascist state was anti-Semitic. He scapegoated the Jews to hide his economic failures; in fact, it was his military expenditures that caused hardships. He prohibited Jewish intermarriage and forbade Jewish children from attending the public schools. Jews were banned from many occupations, their property was confiscated by the state, and they were subject to forced labor in war factories after 1940.

Mussolini embarked on several imperialistic ventures during his rule, such as the successful invasion of Ethiopia in 1935. The following year, he helped the Spanish fascist general Francisco Franco achieve power in Spain by defeating the Loyalist government in a civil war. In that same year, Mussolini signed agreements with Adolf Hitler's Germany, establishing a pact called the Rome-Berlin Axis that would lead to a military alliance. In 1939 he annexed Albania, Italy's neighbor across the Adriatic Sea. After World War II began, Mussolini joined Hitler in war on France in 1940. But the tide soon turned against the Italian armies. Mussolini's invasion of Greece turned out to be a military disaster, and Hitler was forced to send in German divisions to complete the conquest. The Italians were defeated in North Africa by the British in 1941, when Hitler again had to send in German forces.

By 1942 the Italians were being beaten in Italy itself after the Allied invasion. Mussolini was deposed by the Grand Council of Fascism (the Fascist legislature) in 1943 after the Allies had swept into central Italy, and he became

Mussolini decorates the battle flag of the Italian Royal Air Corps. Like Hitler, Mussolini played on popular prejudices to institute a dictatorial regime.

nothing more than a puppet of Hitler's forces in northern Italy, where he organized the Italian Social Republic (or Republic of Saló). Mussolini acquiesced in the Nazi roundup of Italian Jews. Thousands of Jews were deported to concentration camps in Germany. More than 200 were murdered by the Germans and Italian collaborators.

In April 1945, after the German defeat, Mussolini was captured by anti-Fascist partisans as he was attempting to flee into Switzerland. He was killed by a firing squad on April 28, 1945, and his body and that of his mistress, Claretta Petacci, were left on public display in the Piazzale Loreto (one of the main public squares) in Milan.

Mussolini had promised to restore to Italy the glory and power of the ancient Roman Empire. His attempt to do so led Italy down the path of aggression and, ultimately, to devastation.

SEE ALSO

Axis powers; Dictatorship; Fascism; Hitler, Adolf; Italy

FURTHER READING

Collier, Richard. *Duce! A Biography of Benito Mussolini.* New York: Viking, 1971.
Lyttle, Richard B. *Il Duce, The Rise & Fall of Benito Mussolini.* New York: Atheneum, 1987.
Mussolini, Benito. *Fascism: Doctrine and Institutions.* 1935. Reprint, New York: Fertig, 1968.
Smith, Denis Mack. *Mussolini.* New York: Vintage, 1983.

Myanmar (Burma)

UNION OF MYANMAR (PYIDAUNGZU MYANMA NAINGNGANDAW)

• *Capital: Rangoon*

Political history Myanmar (known as Burma until 1988) is located in south-east Asia between Thailand to the east and India to the west. It was originally an independent kingdom of mountain tribes. It was conquered by the British East India Company during the Anglo-Burmese War of 1824–26. The British government, as part of a reorganization of its empire, took it from the company, put it under direct colonial administration, and annexed it to India in 1886. In 1937 Burma became a separate colony.

The Japanese occupied Burma in 1942, during World War II; it was reconquered by the Allies in 1944–45 and became independent in 1948, as the British decided to withdraw rather than wage a costly war against the Burmese independence movement. A communist rebellion and attempts by northern provinces to secede (so that local ethnic groups could control opium growing and arms smuggling) were crushed in 1968 by the central government. The country was renamed the Socialist Republic of the Union of Burma in 1974, as the government moved to a planned economy and closer ties with non-Western powers such as China. Its mismanagement of the economy resulted in a low growth rate and high unemployment, and Burma failed to join other Asian states as they became major industrial economies.

In 1988 demonstrations by students and workers forced the one-party state to agree to hold elections. Before democratic elections could be held, however, a military junta called the State Law and Order Restoration Council overthrew the civilian one-party state in 1988 and changed its name to Myanmar in recognition of the fact that the country contains ethnic groups other than the Burmese. (Myanmar is a local name for the territory and has no ethnic reference.) In the 1990 legislative elections, an opposition party, the National League for Democracy, won a majority of seats, but the election results were invalidated by the military regime.

Government institutions The State Law and Order Restoration Council exercises all executive and legislative power and rules by decree. It also appoints the chief judge and all other judges in the country's court system. The council stated in 1990 that it intended to rule for at least another decade. A constituent assembly was first elected in 1990, but opposition delegates were barred from serving and their parties were banned. In any event, the assembly has only advisory powers.

In 1992 the United Nations Committee on Social, Humanitarian, and Cultural Issues condemned the military regime for its failure to move toward democracy. A puppet convention of civilian party officials called by the regime in 1993 to revise the constitution (in order to placate the UN) was told by the council that the Tatmadaw (military forces) must retain the leading role in government under any new constitution. In 1995 the generals reiterated their demands, insisting that the military be given some of the seats in parliament.

Parties and movements The Burma Socialist Program Party was the only party permitted by the military ruler U Ne Win between 1962 and 1988, at which time he declared socialism a bankrupt ideology and recommended development of a multiparty system. When the other military leaders, with the tacit support of U Ne Win, took power in a coup that same year to forestall any movement toward democracy, they established the National Unity Party, a cosmetic effort to broaden their base of support, but it was without practical significance, because the party remained a tool of the military junta.

The party was defeated in the 1990 legislative elections by the opposition National League for Democracy, which won 80 percent of the vote. The opposition was denied the opportunity to take control of the government, however, and the ruling generals labeled it "subversive."

Domestic issues Military rule since 1962 and imposition by the junta of the "Burmese way to socialism," a system of military control over a backward economy, have left Myanmar one of the poorest nations in the world. The military regime has retaliated against attempts by students and intellectuals to democratize Myanmar and has, for example, sent troops to disperse unarmed demonstrators, killing thousands. In addition, the deteriorating economy, especially high food prices, continues to fuel popular discontent.

Ethnic conflict also threatens the integrity of the nation. The Karen tribe in the northeastern state of Kayah originally attempted to establish an indepen-

The Prince and Princess of Wales leave Sule Pagoda in the Burmese capital of Rangoon in 1906. At the time, Great Britain administered Burma as part of its Indian empire.

dent nation in the 1950s. Since the late 1980s, along with other tribes such as the southern Mon, it has called for a system of autonomous rule for the tribes. The Kachin tribe, however, ended its rebellion in the northern region in 1994, and the remaining communist rebels in the northeast have also negotiated a truce with the central government. The opium warlord Khun Sa and the United Shan Army (a group composed of ethnic Shans in the northern territories) controlled much of the opium trade in the north and resisted efforts by the military regime to take control of their territory and its opium trade. It is believed that some military officers, in fact, participated in the drug trade. In 1997 Khun Sa surrendered to government forces, putting an end to his Shan insurgency.

International issues Since putting down the democracy demonstrators in 1988, resulting in the loss of 3,000 lives, the military regime has been shunned by most of the world, though its immediate neighbors have tried to influence it through diplomacy. In 1997, however, the Association of Southeast Asian Nations agreed to admit Myanmar, a step that ended its isolation without forcing it to change its repressive policies.

Myanmar has no military alliances and remains neutral and nonaligned. It buys weapons from western European nations and from China, which has become its major supplier. In attempting to quell tribal rebellions organized by the Karen National Union along the border with Thailand, Burmese troops have entered Thai territory and, after occasional military confrontations with Thai troops, been forced back into Myanmar.

The central government's resettlement of Buddhists in the Muslim parts of the state of Arakan, to establish a counterweight to separatist Muslims, has forced Muslim Rohingyas (a tribal mountain people) into neighboring Bangladesh, and border incidents have led both nations to mobilize their military forces.

In an attempt to gain Western investment, the junta has promised to institute some political freedoms, but nothing concrete was forthcoming through 1997. Most Western donor nations have refused to provide development aid to Myanmar because of its military rule, but the country's high rate of AIDS in the 1990s has caused public health officials in international organizations to call for a reassessment of that policy.

Myanmar supplies more than half of the heroin sold in the United States but lacks any effective drug-control programs, although the United States has provided training and technical support for eradication programs.

Human rights Between 1988 and 1993 as many as 10,000 student protestors may have been killed in demonstrations against the military regime. More than 1,600 of the regime's political opponents were jailed or placed under house arrest, including Nobel Peace Prize–winner Aung San Suu Kyi, leader of the National League for Democracy. Many members of the democracy movement have been charged with treason, imprisoned in the political wing of Insein Prison, and forbidden to engage in future political activities. The military has killed thousands of civilian protestors, and refugees from Myanmar have charged the army with the rape and torture of dissidents.

SEE ALSO
Aung San Suu Kyi

FURTHER READING
Aung San Suu Kyi. *Freedom from Fear and Other Writings*. New York: Penguin, 1991.
Maung, Mye. *Totalitarianism in Burma*. New York: Paragon, 1992.

Namibia

REPUBLIC OF NAMIBIA

• *Capital: Windhoek*

Political history Located along the southwestern coast of Africa, the area was originally settled by the Khoikhoin (formerly known as the Hottentot), San (Bushmen), and Herero (Bantu) peoples by 1000 A.D. In the 15th century the Portuguese established coastal settlements to trade with these peoples. In 1876 the British annexed a small area called Walvis Bay as a naval base and trading station but refused requests by tribal leaders to establish a protectorate, because the land was arid and would cost more to defend than it was worth. Germany assumed control of the territory, then called South-West Africa, in 1884, at the request of local German missionaries and proceeded to exterminate much of the Herero and Nama tribes, who opposed German rule and revolted in 1903 and 1904. During World War I, British forces from South Africa occupied South-West Africa, and in 1920 the League of Nations mandated the region to the British dominion of South Africa.

In 1925 South Africa granted limited self-government to the European settlers, but the African peoples remained a low-paid labor force that toiled in diamond mines or on farms. After World War II the United Nations refused a South African request to annex the mandated territory. South Africa, as a result, refused to convert its mandate into a UN trusteeship and attempted to annex the territory anyway. In 1949 the white inhabitants were granted representation in the South African parliament, and in 1966 apartheid and security laws were extended to the mandate. In response, the United Na-

tions terminated the South African mandate, a formal gesture with no practical consequences. That same year, the South-West Africa People's Organization (SWAPO), a guerrilla organization representing blacks in the territory, began an armed revolution, operating from bases in Zambia and Angola.

After more than two decades of fighting, South Africa decided to grant independence to the territory in 1988, as it suffered military defeats at the hands of SWAPO and its Cuban and Angolan allies. In 1988 a Multiparty Conference established the Transitional Government of National Unity. The UN Transitional Assistance Group, with 7,000 peace-keepers, supervised elections in 1989, and in 1990 South-West Africa declared itself an independent republic under the name Namibia. It was the last country in Africa to shed its colonial status.

Government institutions The 1990 constitution provides for a presidential system. The president, directly elected for a five-year term as the head of state, holds executive power and governs with a council of ministers. Legislative power is vested in the 72-member National Assembly, whose members are directly elected for five-year terms. The judiciary consists of an independent supreme court and local magistrate's courts.

Parties and movements Namibia is a multiparty democracy that has held

This billboard in the city of Windhoek proclaims the joy of Namibians at finally attaining freedom in 1990. Namibia was the last African colony to achieve political independence.

two high-turnout, free elections since independence. SWAPO, transformed from a guerrilla movement into a social democratic political party, won a majority of seats in these elections. Its leader, Sam Nujoma, became the first president of Namibia in 1990. A coalition of whites, Hereros, San, and other tribal groups has organized as the Democratic Turnhalle Alliance, a liberal party that represents the interests of these minority groups against the dominant Ovambo tribe.

Domestic issues Namibia has mineral reserves, including valuable diamond mines, and an active commercial fishing industry. Yet it has an unemployment rate of 40 percent and a large external debt and is economically dependent upon South Africa, which controls its railroad links to the rest of Africa. Much of the economy is run by the 70,000 Afrikaans whites (the descendants of Dutch settlers in South Africa), and the redistribution of wealth to impoverished tribes is an important political issue. Although Sam Nujoma and other SWAPO leaders are professed socialists who welcomed aid from the Marxist nations of Cuba and Angola in their independence struggle, in the 1990s Namibia has pursued a moderate economic course and has welcomed foreign investment from Western nations in its mining industry.

International issues When Namibia became independent, South Africa and Namibia agreed that South Africa would administer the port of Walvis Bay and its 12 islands, which had been under South African rule since 1922. In 1994 South Africa agreed to turn over the bay to Namibia. In 1990 British military advisers began to train the Namibian Defense Forces, to preserve its independence from

any future South African or Angolan pressure. To offset its dependence on South Africa, Namibia is a member of the Southern African Development Coordination Conference, a group of black African states that meets to coordinate foreign policy.

SEE ALSO
Mandate; South Africa

FURTHER READING
Simon, David. *Independent Namibia: One Year On.* London: Risct, 1991.

Nasser, Gamal Abdel

- *Born: Jan. 15, 1918, Alexandria, Egypt*
- *Died: Sept. 28, 1970, Cairo, Egypt*

Gamal Abdel Nasser was the leader of the Egyptian revolution of 1952 and president of Egypt from 1956 to 1970. He was an important Arab nationalist who opposed Western influence in the Arab world. His fiery oratory inspired a generation of young Arabs, known as Nasserites, and helped topple governments supported by the West in Lebanon and Iraq.

Born in a poor section of Alexandria, Nasser moved as a child to a poor village in the Nile Delta, where his father ran the post office. Nasser attended the military academy in Cairo and graduated in 1938 as a second lieutenant. Beginning in 1943 he served as an instructor at the Army Staff College. During Egypt's 1948 war with newly independent Israel, Nasser fought with distinction in southern Palestine and became known as the "Lion of Faluja," because his battalion held a vital position in one of the few battles in which Arab armies performed well.

A Namibian villager sullenly displays the registration papers the colony's South African government forced all blacks to carry. In administering Namibia, South Africa also applied its apartheid system there.

After the war with Israel, Nasser and other young officers disillusioned with Egyptian corruption founded the Movement of Free Officers, which organized a coup d'état that overthrew King Farouk on July 23, 1952. Nasser chaired the Revolutionary Command Council, the group that took over the country, and was named minister of the interior. In 1954 he became prime minister and in 1956 was elected president. In his book *Philosophy of the Revolution*, published in 1954, he outlined his goal to unite the Arabs, then the African continent, and finally all Muslims, in an international movement that would end Western colonialism.

In 1955 Nasser refused to join the Baghdad Pact, which linked Turkey, Iraq, and Iran in a pro-Western alliance, signaling that he would not continue the pro-Western policies of the Farouk regime. He began to purchase arms from communist Czechoslovakia and accepted a Soviet offer to construct the Aswan Dam, decisions that upset the United States, France, and Great Britain, whose leaders believed that Egypt was siding with the Soviet Union in the cold war. In 1955 Nasser also announced that he was nationalizing the Suez Canal, which until that time had been owned and operated by a private European company. This move upset Western nations that did not wish to cede control to the Egyptians.

In 1956 Israel invaded the Sinai Peninsula to end cross-border guerrilla raids by Egyptians. The British and French governments used this as a pretext to invade Egypt in the name of protecting the Suez Canal. But the real goal was to topple Nasser and reassert Western influence. The United States and the Soviet Union, however, forced the expeditionary force to withdraw from the Suez Canal region and end the invasion, and they pressured Israel to withdraw its forces from the Sinai Peninsula. Nasser was then able to nationalize the canal, which increased his popularity with the Egyptian and Arab masses. In 1958 he organized a political federation (known as the United Arab Republic) with Syria in the name of Arab unity, but it dissolved three years later, because Syrians resented Egyptian influence.

In 1967 Nasser used his military forces to close the Strait of Tiran, located at the southern tip of the Sinai Peninsula where it meets the Red Sea, to Israeli shipping. This action precipitated the Six-Day War between Egypt and Israel, in which Egypt was badly defeated and lost the Sinai Peninsula. Nasser offered his resignation, but his regime organized massive demonstrations in his support, and he continued in office. Nasser died during the subsequent war of attrition against Israeli forces situated on the eastern bank of the Suez Canal.

Nasser was a dynamic figure who inspired the Arab people, but he failed to unite them or put Egypt's economy on the path of progress. His greatest domestic accomplishment, the Aswan High Dam, provided a better life for millions of Egyptians through irrigation projects and energy production but caused great ecological damage in the Nile Delta. Nasser replaced a corrupt and ineffective monarchy that was subservient to Western interests with an authoritarian state, but he missed the opportunity to advance Egypt technologically and bring new private investment to the country, and he spent too much money on weapons and fruitless conflicts with Israel.

SEE ALSO
Egypt; Israel

FURTHER READING
Beattie, Kirk J. *Egypt During the Nasser Years: Ideology, Politics, and Civil Society.* Boulder, Colo.: Westview, 1994.
DeChancie, John. *Gamal Abdel Nasser.* New York: Chelsea House, 1988.

Stephens, Robert. *Nasser: A Political Biography*. New York: Simon & Schuster, 1972.

Vatikiotis, Panayoitis. *Nasser and His Generation*. New York: St. Martin's, 1978.

Woodward, Peter. *Nasser*. New York: Longman, 1992.

Nationalism

Nationalism is a political theory whose core idea is that people who have racial, ethnic, religious, or linguistic characteristics in common should have an internationally recognized right to determine their own political destiny by forming a separate, sovereign nation-state. Nationalism developed in the 19th and 20th centuries in Europe. It challenged the validity of empires such as the Ottoman, Austro-Hungarian, and Russian empires, territories in which people of different races, religions, and ethnicities lived side by side. Ethnic nationalists argue that a single group or "nationality" should constitute the citizens of a nation-state. Minorities consisting of other ethnic, religious, or racial groups living in the country would be given the status of aliens, or, as citizens, they would enjoy fewer political and civil rights than those given to the majority group. The most extreme nationalists call for the expulsion of minorities by force or even (in the case of the Nazis in Germany) their extermination.

After the Great Powers (Great Britain, Russia, and Prussia) defeated the French emperor Napoléon Bonaparte and restored traditional empires at the Congress of Vienna in 1815, nationalism swept the European continent, eroding the legitimacy of the empires in central, southern, and eastern Europe.

In the late 19th century, nationalism led to the unification of the German principalities into a single German nation-state and of the Italian city-states into a single Italian nation-state.

After World War I, both Woodrow Wilson's Fourteen Points and the charter of the League of Nations called for national "self-determination"—that is, the formation of nation-states out of the various empires that had been defeated during the war, particularly the Austro-Hungarian Empire and the Ottoman Empire.

In the aftermath of World War II, nationalism drove the anti-Western, anti-imperialist independence movements in Africa and Asia. When India won its independence from Great Britain in 1947, for example, it split into two nations, Hindu India and Muslim Pakistan (each of which had many different ethnic groups linked by a common religion). In Africa, by contrast, newly independent nations retained their colonial boundaries, which lumped together members of different tribes, often with different racial and religious identities, making it difficult to forge a single national identity in these nations.

In the Soviet Union and Eastern Europe after World War II, nationalism conflicted with the communist ideology, which argued that class solidarity among the proletariat (workers) would transcend national differences. In fact, the Soviet Union was created out of hundreds of different groups in which Russians were a bare majority. With the collapse of the Soviet Union in 1991, these separate groups eventually broke up into 15 nation-states, many of them loosely joined in the Commonwealth of Independent States.

In Eastern Europe, nationalism was suppressed by Soviet military force but flared into open rebellion on several oc-

General Paul von Hindenburg, Kaiser Wilhelm II, and General Erich Ludendorff confer at German General Headquarters in the closing days of World War I. In the 20th century, Europe has twice been devastated as a consequence of aggressive German nationalism.

casions. In 1990, with the collapse of the Soviet-sponsored governments, nationalism became a potent political force. Czechoslovakia split into two nation-states, the Czech Republic and Slovakia. Yugoslavia split into several ministates based on ethnicity and religion. Minorities in various eastern European nations began to suffer repression, and anti-Semitism, frequently a rallying point for extreme nationalist movements, once again surfaced, even though most of these nations had hardly any Jewish populations to repress.

Nationalism today competes with two other territorial doctrines. One is the movement for regional unification, such as the European Union's attempt to integrate western European nations through its economic and monetary institutions and the Ba'ath Arab Socialist and Islamic fundamentalist movements, which seek to unite the Arab world and the Muslim peoples, respectively. The other is the movement for regional autonomy and decentralization, which involves minority cultural, linguistic, and religious communities within existing nation-states demanding recognition of

their own national identities, either by gaining autonomy or complete independence. These include the Scottish and Welsh demands for autonomy or independence (which Great Britain has recognized by granting them separate legislatures), the Breton and Corsican movements for cultural autonomy in France, the Basque separatist and Catalan autonomy movements in Spain, and the Quebec independence movement in Canada.

Finally, nationalism is threatened by the rise of technologically advanced and affluent "city-states" whose populations are responsible for the development of advanced urban economies that have more in common with urban centers in other nations than with their own hinterlands. These centers, such as Stuttgart in Germany, Milan in Italy, Lyon in France, and Barcelona in Spain, seek autonomy in making industrial policy and freedom to pursue their own version of foreign economic policy.

SEE ALSO
Austro-Hungarian Empire; Autonomy; Ba'ath movement; European Union (EU); Nation-state; Ottoman Empire; Soviet Union (Union of Soviet Socialist Republics); State

FURTHER READING

Greenfield, Liah. *Nationalism: Five Roads to Modernity*. Cambridge: Harvard University Press, 1992.

Hobsbawm, Eric. *Nations and Nationalism Since 1780*. 2nd ed. New York: Cambridge University Press, 1992.

Howe, Geoffrey. *Nationalism and the Nation-State*. Cambridge, England: Cambridge University Press, 1995.

Hutchinson, John, and Anthony Smith, eds. *Nationalism*. New York: Oxford University Press, 1995.

Kedourie, Eli. *Nationalism*. 4th ed. London: Blackwell, 1993.

Kohn, Hans. *The Age of Nationalism*. 2nd ed. Westport, Conn.: Greenwood, 1977.

Seton-Watson, Hugh. *Nations and States*. London: Methuen, 1977.

National Socialism

SEE Nazi Party

Nation-state

The term *nation-state* denotes both the government that possesses sovereign power over a defined territory and the people who live in that territory. Often the term *nation* is used to signify that most of the people share a common ancestry, racial and ethnic characteristics, language and religion, and customs and traditions. In that sense, there are few true nation-states because, in most cases, the peoples ruled by states have diverse racial and ethnic characteristics (and some are descended from mixed marriages), and they often have different languages and religions. Only half the nation-states today have a single group that comprises three-quarters or more of the population, and less than one-tenth of the nations have a single group that comprises more than 90 percent. Even in some of these countries, such as France,

Japan, and Germany, there are significant racial, linguistic, religious, or ethnic minorities who may not be granted citizenship but who live and work there, and sometimes have for generations. In nation-states such as the United States, Canada, Brazil, and Argentina, government immigration policies (and in some cases the importation of African slaves) have created a mosaic of different ethnic, religious, and racial groups, all of which are granted citizenship and identity as part of the "people" of the nation.

In some countries, especially those in Africa (where more than 1,000 different ethnic groups live) and Asia, dominant ethnic groups, even when they are a minority of the population, assume state power by force. They keep other groups in permanently subjugated positions, with only the prospect of civil war or revolution to ease their plight. In other nation-states, such as Spain and the United Kingdom, minority territorial communities have successfully pressed for forms of regional autonomy, creating "states within the state" to parallel their sense of "nations within a nation." The same process is occurring in the 1990s in Russia, which has become a federation that has a majority of ethnic Russians but also includes numerous other ethnic groups in their own geographic regions.

Consociational systems refer to nation-states in which two or more ethnic groups share power on equal terms, such as the Flemish-speaking and French-speaking communities in Belgium and the French, German, and Italian populations in Switzerland. The French-speaking inhabitants of Canada have pushed for such a system, claiming that Canada consists of two separate nations; their failure to convince English-speaking Canadians to accept this claim has led a majority of the French speakers in Quebec Province to vote for independence in referenda, though as of 1995 their efforts to win independence had not yet succeeded (because English-speaking Quebecers tended to vote against the measure, along with two-fifths of the French speakers).

Throughout the world in the 20th century, the quest for national identity and statehood has weakened and even destroyed existing states. Yugoslavia was fractured into separate states in 1991 when Serbs and Croats declared their independence. A part of Yugoslavia, Bosnia and Herzegovina, endured a four-year war as rival Bosnian Muslims, Serbs, and Croats fought over the territory. In Spain a separatist Basque movement seeks an independent state on the French border. Israel is faced with Palestinian and Israeli Arab demands for an independent Palestine. Sri Lanka has Tamil separatists.

The Soviet Union dissolved on the basis of regional national identities, and Russia itself has yet to come to terms with non-Russian nationalities such as the Tatars, who are seeking increased territorial autonomy or fully independent status, and the Chechens, who fought unsuccessfully against the Russian army between 1992 and 1996 for a state of their own. In Georgia the Muslim Abkhaz seek independence from the Eastern Orthodox Georgians. In Turkey and Iraq, separatist Kurds seek their own state. In the Sudan, the Muslim Arab government has fought against Christian black Africans in the south. Tibetan monks have sought independence since the 1950s from Chinese rule, but their revolt in 1959 was crushed. Indonesia ended a revolt on East Timor in 1975 and has put down separatist movements in North Sumatra.

SEE ALSO

Autonomy; Nationalism; Sovereignty

FURTHER READING

Deutsch, Karl, and William Folz, eds. *Nation-Building*. New York: Atherton, 1963.
Hobsbawm, Eric. *Nations and Nationalism Since 1780*. 2nd ed. New York: Cambridge University Press, 1992.
Tivey, Leonard, ed. *The Nation State*. Oxford, England: Martin Robertson, 1980.

Nauru

REPUBLIC OF NAURU (NAOERO)

• *Capital: Yaren*

Political history Nauru, an island in the South Pacific east of Indonesia, was originally inhabited by Polynesian, Micronesian, and Melanesian islanders. It was discovered by the English in 1798, who called it Pleasant Island because of its lush vegetation. One hundred years later, Germany annexed it after pressure from German farmers on Nauru to incorporate it into the nearby German Marshall Islands Protectorate. The Germans later surrendered it to Australia in 1914 during World War I.

The island was administered by Australia under a League of Nations mandate from 1920 to 1947, at which time it became a UN Trust Territory administered by Australia, New Zealand, and the United Kingdom. According to the terms of the trusteeship, Australia was to prepare the island for independence. By 1965 the islanders had created a governing tribal council and achieved local autonomy. Then Australia turned over the phosphate-mining operations, which was key to the island's economy, to the local tribal government in 1967. Nauru gained independence in 1968 and became an associate member of the Commonwealth of Nations in the following year.

Government institutions Executive authority is vested in the president of the republic, who is elected by the parliament. The president appoints six ministers who form a cabinet that administers the government departments and is collectively responsible to the parliament. Legislative power is vested in an 18-member parliament, whose members are elected for up to three years (although elections may be held before the terms are up). The Local Government Council represents the country's 14 districts and also runs enterprises such as the local shipping line. There is an independent judiciary.

Parties and movements The only registered party is the Democratic Party of Nauru, which is a creation of the tribal chiefs and which fills all positions on the Local Government Council.

Domestic issues Nauru has strip-mined its extensive phosphate deposits, leaving the island an environmental disaster. Four-fifths of the island has been ravaged and remains a pitted, uninhabitable area of limestone pinnacles. The narrow coastal strip suffers from drought because the mined area emits heat waves that prevent clouds from forming over the island. Nauru, however, has a $1 billion trust fund from its mining profits. Local politics involve control over the investment of funds and fears by some people that tribal leaders are squandering the money or being bilked out of it by outside swindlers. Nauru is developing a plan to rehabilitate an area that had been extensively mined, and Australia has agreed to pay $75 million in reparations for damage to an area that it had mined during its trusteeship. If the ecological damage on the island cannot be repaired, the tribal leaders are considering moving the entire population to another Pacific island, which would be purchased from one of its neighbors.

International issues Relations with Western Samoa, to the southeast of Nauru, are tense because it accused Nauru of secretly funding the opposition party in the Samoan elections of 1989. Nauru had hoped the opposition party would permit it to increase its investments on the island. In 1990 Nauru recalled its consul and sold all its assets in Western Samoa.

Nauru would be submerged by the rising sea levels if global warming occurs, and so it calls for attempts to decrease pollution levels in the industrial world.

SEE ALSO
Trust territories

Nazi Party

The National Socialist Workers Party (NSDAP, or Nationalsozialistische Deutsche Arbeiterpartei in German), better known as the Nazi Party, controlled Germany during the period of the Third Reich (1933–45). It was founded as the German Workers' Party in 1919 by Anton Drexler, a locksmith from Munich, and was run by Adolf Hitler after August 1921, when he renamed it the National Socialist German Workers Party. His 25-point platform opposed the Weimar Republic and what Hitler considered to be a humiliating peace treaty that Germany had signed to end World War I. The Nazis also called for government control of industry, efforts to reduce unemployment, and increased social welfare programs for workers.

In foreign affairs the party was expansionist, calling for *Lebensraum* (living space) for Germany in Europe at the expense of its neighbors. It argued that the German *Volk* (people) were Aryans, a race that was superior to the *Untermenschen* (inferior people) such as the Jews, the Slavs, and the Romanies

Germany's Nazi leaders—including Adolf Hitler (without hat), Hermann Göring (right of Hitler), and Heinrich Himmler (left of Hitler)—accept the accolades of their supporters at one of the Nuremberg rallies in the mid-1930s.

(Gypsies). The Nazi ideology drew upon fascism, calling for government control—but not ownership—of industry. In government, it emphasized rule by a *Führer* (leader) who would govern by decree.

The party attempted unsuccessfully to overthrow the Weimar Republic in a *Putsch* (revolt) in 1923 and was then disbanded. It was reorganized in 1925 but won only 2.6 percent of the parliamentary vote in 1928. During the depression it did better, winning 18.3 percent of the vote in the 1930 parliamentary elections. In July 1932 it won 37.4 percent, but in the November elections it won 33 percent. Backed by many of Germany's largest corporations, which saw the Nazis as their protectors against communists and socialists, the Nazis pressured President Paul von Hindenburg to name Hitler chancellor, which he did on January 30, 1933. The Nazis were now in power.

The party was transformed into an instrument of state power when other parties were banned in July 1933 by Hitler's decree. Under Hitler, the Nazis dominated the German economy and military and led the nation into its disas-trous policies of aggression against other nations in Europe and the Holocaust against the European Jews.

The Nazi Party was disbanded after the German defeat in World War II in 1945. The constitution of the Federal Republic of Germany banned it and neo-Nazi parties as well, though by the 1980s a small neo-Nazi movement existed in many German cities and engaged in terrorist attacks against immigrants and in incendiary "actions" against government offices.

SEE ALSO
Federal Republic of Germany; Germany; Hitler, Adolf; Holocaust; Neo-Nazis; Third Reich

FURTHER READING
Ebenstein, William. *The Nazi State.* New York: Octagon, 1975.
Fischer, Klaus P. *Nazi Germany: A New History.* New York: Continuum, 1995.
Kater, Michael H. *The Nazi Party: A Social Profile of Members and Leaders, 1919–1945.* Cambridge: Harvard University Press, 1983.
Kirk, Tim. *The Longman Companion to Nazi Germany.* New York: Longman, 1995.
Neumann, Franz. *Behemoth: The Structure and Practice of National Socialism, 1933–1944.* 2nd ed. New York: Octagon, 1972.

Nehru, Jawaharlal

- *Born: Nov. 14, 1889, Allahabad, India*
- *Died: May 27, 1964, New Delhi, India*

A leader of the Indian independence movement and the first prime minister of India (1947–64), Jawaharlal Nehru has been the most influential Indian leader since independence. He was a towering figure in world politics as a founder of the Nonaligned Movement during the cold war.

Nehru's father was a wealthy lawyer and politician, and Nehru was a member of the Brahman caste, the highest level of Hindu society. Nehru studied at Harrow, an elite private school in England, and at Cambridge University, and he became a lawyer in England in 1912. He began his political career as a Fabian Socialist, a member of a society of British intellectuals who believed in the peaceful transformation of the economy from capitalism to socialist rule through parliamentary democracy. When Nehru returned to India, he became active in the Home Rule League, an organization calling for dominion status, instead of colonial, for India within the British Commonwealth.

After the Amritsar Massacre of 1919, in which British soldiers gunned down unarmed Indian protestors (killing 379 and wounding more than 1,200), Nehru joined the Congress Party, which also advocated dominion status. He was imprisoned by the British in 1921 for civil disobedience, together with his father, Motilal Nehru. (The British imprisoned Jawaharlal Nehru nine times, and he spent more than nine years in jail between 1921 and 1945.)

In 1927 the younger Nehru became president of the All-India Trades Union Congress, an arm of the Congress Party. The following year he and other young Congress leaders opposed dominion status within the British Commonwealth for India, which had been the goal of the Congress Party, proposing instead full independence. Nehru became the intellectual leader of Indian youth, and the Congress leaders, recognizing the need to gain their support, named Nehru president of the All-India Congress Committee (the official name of the Congress Party). He negotiated the Government of India Act in 1935 with the British, a law that gave Indian provincial governments some local autonomy.

At the start of World War II the Congress Party launched a civil disobedience campaign against the British. After a year in prison, Nehru was released. In 1942 he and other Congress Party leaders again refused to accept dominion status, which the British were now offering, or support the British in World War II, and he and the other leaders were imprisoned by the British again until June 1945.

In 1947, when India finally achieved independence as a result of the continued struggle of the Congress Party leaders, Nehru became both prime minister and minister of external affairs. He was one of the many Indian leaders who accepted the partition of the former British colony into Muslim Pakistan and predominantly Hindu India. In 1951 Nehru led his Congress Party to an overwhelming victory, establishing it as the most important political force in the new nation. In domestic affairs he socialized much of the Indian economy. He believed in a secular India and opposed extremist Hindus who would have forced all Muslims out of the country. He promoted the modernization of Indian society and supported, for example, greater legal rights for women. In foreign affairs he promoted neutrality and was one of the organizers of the Nonaligned Movement at the Bandung (Indonesia) Conference in 1955. In practice, however, India maintained close ties with the Soviet Union (which India viewed as a deterrent against possible Chinese aggression) and somewhat chilly relations with the United States.

Nehru died in 1964 after a series of strokes. He had succeeded in holding India together after independence and in converting it from a collection of colonial states into the world's largest democracy. He had prevented the forces of Hindu nationalism from creating a parochial theocracy and had begun to modernize Indian society to take its place as one of the most influential nations in the world.

SEE ALSO
Commonwealth of Nations; India; Nonaligned Movement; Pakistan

FURTHER READING
Finck, Lila, and John P. Hayes. *Jawaharlal Nehru.* New York: Chelsea House, 1987.
Mehta, Vcd. *A Family Affair: India under Three Prime Ministers.* New York: Oxford University Press, 1982.
Nanda, B. R. *Jawaharlal Nehru: Rebel and Statesman.* New York: Oxford University Press, 1995.
Wolpert, Stanley. *Nehru: A Tryst with Destiny.* New York: Oxford University Press, 1996.

Neo-Nazis

Neo-Nazis are members of far-right political movements and parties who believe in the supremacy of the "Aryan" race (northern European whites) and the inferiority of other races. They wish to

Neo-Nazis have adopted the swastika as a symbol of their own anti-Semitic activities.

remove foreigners, immigrants, and Jews from their countries. Neo-Nazi organizations are located primarily in western and eastern Europe, the nations of the former Soviet Union, and in several nations in the Western Hemisphere, including Argentina, Canada, and the United States. Neo-Nazis glorify the Nazi leader Adolf Hitler, who had hoped to exterminate Jewish populations in Germany and other parts of Europe in the 1930s and 1940s. In Germany and other European nations, neo-Nazis have engaged in violence against immigrants and other foreigners; they have, for example, fire-bombed homes and worker hostels and beaten people to death.

In 1994, as a result of their violent activities, Germany banned seven neo-Nazi organizations, which together had approximately 40,000 members. Even so, because of high unemployment in the states of the former East Germany, the neo-Nazi movement has gained strength there.

In the United States, the neo-Nazi movement includes the Aryan Nation, a group whose headquarters is in Idaho, which it hopes to establish as the territory of a "white nation-state" free of the influence of America's racial and ethnic minorities. There are also a dozen or so "skinhead" groups (so named because their members shave their heads) such as the Fourth Reich Skinheads of Orange County, California, and the New Dawn Hammerskins of Massachusetts. People linked to neo-Nazi organizations killed 31 people between 1990 and 1995, with victims most likely to be African-Americans, Jews, and Latinos.

The neo-Nazi movement worldwide has approximately 70,000 members in 30 countries, according to the Anti-Defamation League, an organization that monitors anti-Semitic activities of these and other hate groups.

SEE ALSO

Anti-Semitism; Hitler, Adolf; Nazi Party

FURTHER READING

Anti-Defamation League. *The Skinhead International, a Worldwide Survey of Neo-Nazi Skinheads*. New York: Anti-Defamation League, 1995.
Eatwell, Roger. *Fascism: A History*. New York: Viking, 1996.
Hasselbach, Ingo, with Tom Reiss. "How Nazis Are Made." *The New Yorker,* January 8, 1996, 36–57.
Schmidt, Michael. *The New Reich*. New York: Pantheon, 1993.

Nepal

KINGDOM OF NEPAL (NEPAL ADHIRAJYA)

• *Capital: Katmandu*

Political history Located between northern India and southwestern China, the area that is now Nepal was first settled in the 3rd century B.C. by Mongols moving south and Indo-Aryans moving north. It was on a trading route by the 3rd century A.D. Between the 10th and 18th century, the area was ruled by the Buddhist Malla dynasty. In the 15th century it split into three separate Malla kingdoms. The three principalities of Nepal were united under the Gurkhas, a northern Indian warrior group, who conquered the area in 1769. The British gained trading rights with the kingdom in 1792, when Nepal came under British protection. In 1923 Britain recognized Nepal's sovereignty and ended its protectorate as part of the effort to decolonize after World War I.

From the mid-19th century until 1951, power in Nepal had been in the hands of nobles, and the monarch was only a figurehead. Between 1951 and 1991, however, Nepal was ruled by King Mahendra, who, with the support of the Indian government, proclaimed an absolute monarchy in 1951, seizing governing power from the prime minister, who had represented the nobles. Mahendra banned political parties in parliament in 1960, after the cabinet sought to limit the power of the king. In a referendum in 1980, voters approved the monarchical system (now under Mahendra's son Birendra) and kept the ban on political parties. After the military fired on unarmed demonstrators protesting the rule of the monarchy in 1990, King Birendra attempted to defuse the public uproar by agreeing to convert Nepal from absolute rule to a constitutional monarchy with a multiparty parliament.

Government institutions Under provisions of the 1990 constitution, executive authority is vested in the monarch. Legislative power is vested in a bicameral parliament, consisting of a 205-member House of Representatives, whose members are elected for five-year terms, and a 60-member National Council, with members elected for six-year terms. There is an independent supreme court consisting of a chief justice and six other judges.

Parties and movements Political parties were banned until 1990, when the king proclaimed a multiparty system and 21 parties were organized. Following elections in 1991, the Nepali Congress Party won the most seats in parliament, followed by the Communists. In 1995 the Communist Party (United Marxist and Leninist), led by Man Mohan Adhikary, won the parliamentary elections (by winning 88 seats, a plurality but not a majority) and formed a government, which became the first elected communist government in Asia. The Nepali Congress Party came in second, with 83 seats, followed by a monarchist party, the New Democratic Party, with only 20 seats. The Communists promised to uphold multiparty democracy.

Domestic issues In the 1990s government corruption, unemployment, inflation, and economic austerity programs imposed by the government have caused demonstrators to clash with police and engage in strikes and anti-government protests. The sale of state-owned enterprises to private investors, who made exorbitant profits, was a controversial policy pursued by the Congress Party in an attempt to revitalize the economy while consolidating its power, and it was one of the reasons for its 1995 defeat. The failure of the Congress Party to redistribute land to poorer peasants, as the party leaders had promised, was also a factor in its loss. The Communists have, however, confiscated large landholdings and forced the sale of land to peasants by absentee landlords, policies that are popular in the countryside among poorer farmers, who provide the base of support for the party.

International issues Nepal had close relations with India until 1993, but they were strained when Indian police entered Nepal in pursuit of Gurkha Liberation Front militants in 1993. Nepal has bought weapons from China and accepted Chinese domination of Tibet to counterbalance Indian influence.

In response to Nepal's friendship with China, India in 1990 closed its border crossings to Nepal and restricted trade. The following year, new treaties between India and Nepal resolved most of the frontier issues and allowed Nepal to share its water resources and hydroelectric power with India.

Due to unrest in nearby Bhutan in the Himalaya Mountains, more than 20,000 Bhutanese of Nepali origin have been repatriated to Nepal.

SEE ALSO
India

FURTHER READING
Hutt, Michael, ed. *Nepal in the Nineties.* New York: Oxford University Press, 1994.
Majracharya, B. R., and S. R. Bakshi, eds. *Political Development in Nepal.* New Delhi: Anmol, 1993.

Netanyahu, Benjamin

• *Born: Oct. 21, 1949, Tel Aviv, Israel*

As prime minister of Israel, Benjamin Netanyahu has been a fierce foe of international terrorism. He was elected in June 1996 to renegotiate the terms of peace between Israel and the Palestinian Authority, the governing body for Palestinians in the West Bank and Gaza.

Netanyahu (the name means "God's Gift") spent his high school years in Philadelphia, where his father, a distinguished scholar of Jewish history, was teaching. He learned to speak English flawlessly. Netanyahu returned to Israel and joined an elite antiterrorism unit of the Israeli Defense Forces, the Sayeret Matkal. In 1972 he and others in his unit rescued passengers from a hijacked jet in Israel. Netanyahu returned to the United States and earned a B.S. in architecture in 1974 and a master's degree in business in 1976 from the Massachusetts Institute of Technology.

Netanyahu's brother Jonathan was killed leading a daring raid in Entebbe, Uganda, to free an Israeli plane and hostages held by terrorists in 1976. Benjamin and his family organized the Jonathan Institute, which conducts research about terrorist groups. He worked in the furniture business in Tel Aviv for several years.

Netanyahu became active in politics and was named deputy chief of Israel's mission to the United Nations in 1982, becoming ambassador to the UN in 1984. He became an effective and articulate spokesperson for Israel on American television programs. In 1988 he returned to Israel and won a seat in the Knesset (parliament) as a member of Likud, the party favoring a tough stance in negotiating peace with Arab states and Palestinians. He was deputy foreign minister from 1988 to 1991 and then became deputy minister in the prime minister's office, serving as Israel's chief spokesperson during the Gulf War.

In 1992 Netanyahu was one of a group of legislators who successfully promoted a change in Israeli election law: henceforth, the prime minister would be directly elected by the people rather than chosen by the Knesset. The following year Netanyahu was chosen to head Likud. In June 1996 he beat Shimon Peres of the Labor Party in the nation's first popular election and became the prime minister of Israel. At 46 he was the youngest prime minister ever elected in Israel; all his predecessors had been over 60.

Netanyahu's actions in his first years created great controversy. He announced that he would renegotiate the Oslo Accords with the Palestinians, deals to which Israel had already signed

agreement, guaranteeing that Israel would transfer control of much of the West Bank to Palestinian self-rule. He delayed a meeting with Yasir Arafat, president of the Palestinian Authority, which led Palestinians to suspect he was not interested in peace. He refused to release female Palestinian prisoners under the terms of the Oslo Accords, and also refused to allow construction of an access road linking Palestinian-controlled areas in Gaza and the West Bank. He opened a new entrance to a tunnel adjoining the Temple Mount, one of Islam's holiest sites.

In response to these hard-line policies, Palestinians demonstrated, and rock throwing escalated to automatic rifle fire between Israeli and Palestinian police. Later, Netanyahu announced new plans to build housing at existing settlements and in the Palestinian sector of Jerusalem, leading Palestinians to believe that he would increase Jewish settlement in areas they expected to govern as part of the final peace accords. He also refused to commit his cabinet to the second and third stages of troop pullbacks in the West Bank that had been agreed upon by the previous Labor government.

Netanyahu's efforts to renegotiate these agreements widened the divisions in Israeli society between those who wanted a final settlement with the Palestinians that would effectively divide Palestine into Jewish and Arab states and those who hoped that Israel could continue to dominate the West Bank, leaving Arabs some autonomy to manage local affairs. His government's actions were met in Arab states with hostility, and the cooperation in diplomatic and economic relations that had occurred under the Labor government ground to a halt in 1996.

In 1997, due in part to pressure from the United States and western Europe and to a drop in foreign investment that had weakened the Israeli economy, Netanhayu modified his hard-line stance. Negotiations with Arafat resulted in an Israeli pullout from Hebron, although Israeli settlers would remain under military protection. All of the women prisoners were released, and the peace process resumed.

Netanyahu's zigs and zags in dealing with the Palestinians reflected divisions in Israeli public opinion and his precarious position within his political party. If he made too many concessions to the Palestinians, his party might depose him as leader and cabinet defections might bring down his government. If he made too few concessions, the peace process would founder, foreign allies would withdraw support, Israel would once again be isolated in the region, and Israeli voters might turn to another leader in the next elections.

SEE ALSO

Arafat, Yasir; Israel; Palestinian Liberation Organization; Peres, Shimon

FURTHER READING

Netanyahu, Benjamin. *A Place Among the Nations: Israel and the World.* New York: Bantam, 1993.
Netanyahu, Benjamin, ed. *Terrorism, How the West Can Win.* New York: Farrar, Straus & Giroux, 1986.

Netherlands

KINGDOM OF THE NETHER-LANDS (KONINKRIJK DER NEDERLANDEN)

• *Capital: Amsterdam*

Political history The Low Countries (parts of present-day Belgium and the Netherlands) were inhabited by Celtic and Germanic tribes before the birth of Christ and were conquered by Julius Caesar for Rome in 55 B.C., though the Romans lost them to invading Germanic tribes in the 5th century A.D. These territories became part of Charlemagne's European empire in the 8th century, but after the end of his reign they were divided among various Germanic princes. The Netherlands were conquered by the Spanish Habsburgs in the 16th century, when the Spanish empire was expanding because of increasing wealth as the result of gold found in its colonies in the New World.

William of Orange, the German count of Nassau, a province of the Netherlands, led its Protestant inhabitants to fight for independence from Catholic Prince Philip II of Spain in the 1570s. Dutch rebels prevented the Spanish Armada from transporting the duke of Parma's army from the Netherlands to invade England, then joined with British ships to fight the Spanish Armada and disperse it in the first week of August 1588.

The Netherlands became a great maritime trading power in the 17th century. British attempts to curtail its trade led to war between the Dutch and the British from 1652 to 1654, in which the British triumphed; thereafter, the British supplanted the Dutch as the major sea power in the world. In 1688 the British Parliament invited the Dutch ruler, William of Orange, with his English wife, Mary Stuart, to rule England as constitutional monarchs, replacing the absolute monarchy. As William III and Mary II, they combined the naval resources of Britain and the Netherlands to keep French maritime power at bay.

In 1795 the French revolutionary armies took over the Netherlands and formed the Batavian Republic. They were expelled in 1813 after the defeat of Napoléon, and the Netherlands became a unified nation under King William I in

In the 17th century, Dutch maritime prowess extended the power of the Netherlands from Europe to the far reaches of India and the Orient, as this illustration from the period portrays. For a time, this small lowlands country was one of the most powerful nations in the world.

1815. Part of its southwestern territory seceded in 1830 and became known as Belgium. The Dutch declared themselves neutral in European conflicts, particularly those involving Germany and France between 1870 and 1945, but they were invaded, nevertheless, and occupied by Germany during World Wars I and II. At the end of World War II, after being liberated by Allied armies, the Dutch abandoned their traditional neutrality and joined NATO and other organizations of the integrated European community.

Government institutions The Netherlands is a constitutional monarchy that actually functions as a parliamentary democracy. The head of state is the hereditary monarch. Executive authority is exercised by a council of ministers, led by the prime minister, who is responsible to the legislature. Legislative power is vested in the bicameral States-General. The 75 members of the First Chamber are elected by the 12 provincial councils and serve for six-year terms; the system is staggered so that half of the First Chamber members are elected every three years. The 150 members of the Second Chamber are directly elected

for four-year terms by voters who select a party from a list: the parties are awarded seats in the Second Chamber based on the proportion of votes they receive. The judges of the High Court are appointed by the sovereign from a list prepared by the Second Chamber.

Parties and movements The Netherlands is a multiparty democracy. The four main parties are the Christian Democratic Appeal (Christian democratic), the Labor Party (social democratic), the People's Party for Freedom and Democracy (liberal), and the Democrats '66 (reformist).

Domestic issues Since the 1980s the government has attempted to cut spending without sacrificing generous social welfare benefits. Cabinets have collapsed over taxing and spending issues when one of the parties in the government coalition balks at supporting cutbacks unpopular with the voters.

International issues The Netherlands is a member of NATO and the Benelux Economic Union (with Belgium and Luxembourg) and was a founding member of the European Community (now the European Union). During the Persian Gulf War of 1991 it sent naval warships to the gulf and missiles to Turkey as part of the U.S.–led allied effort to defeat Iraqi leader Saddam Hussein after he had invaded and annexed neighboring Kuwait.

The Netherlands was part of the United Nations peacekeeping force during the Bosnian civil war in the 1990s, but its small and outgunned force was unable to prevent Serbian atrocities against Bosnian Muslims in the area assigned to it. With the end of the cold war the government has significantly reduced its defense expenditures.

Human rights During the German occupation of the Netherlands during World War II, the Dutch attempted to protect the Jewish population from Nazi atrocities. When the Nazis ordered the Jews to wear yellow stars of David, the first star was worn by Queen Wilhelmina in a symbolic gesture of defiance.

SEE ALSO

Belgium; Benelux; European Union (EU)

FURTHER READING

Gladdish, Ken. *Governing from the Center: Politics and Policymaking in the Netherlands.* London: Hurst, 1991.
Tash, Robert. *Dutch Pluralism: A Model in Tolerance for Developing Democracies.* New York: Lang, 1991.

New Hebrides

SEE Vanuatu

New International Economic Order (NIEO)

The New International Economic Order was a set of political and economic demands on Western industrial nations

(known as the First World) presented by developing nations (known as the Third World) at the United Nations General Assembly session of 1974. These included a demand for protection against fluctuations in the price of goods exported to industrial nations; preferential tariffs that would provide for lower rates for Third World industrial goods exported to the West; protection for Third World enterprises and services against foreign competition in Third World nations; increases in foreign aid; rescheduling of debt payments; and transfers of technology to developing nations.

These demands were pressed by the Group of 77, an association of developing and nonaligned nations, at meetings of the United Nations Committee on Trade and Development (UNCTAD). They were rejected by the West, which has preferred policies that allow Western investment in Third World countries without onerous government regulations.

SEE ALSO

First World; Group of 77; Third World

New Zealand

• *Capital: Wellington*

Political history The Dutch navigator Abel Tasman was the first European to encounter the Maori, the indigenous people of New Zealand, in 1642, when he discovered the islands during his explorations of Australia. The islands to the east of Australia that are now known as New Zealand were further explored by the British captain James Cook in 1769. After 1800 the western side of the islands harbored British whaling settle-

Maori dancers perform a tribal ceremony. The Maoris are the aboriginal inhabitants of New Zealand.

ments and trading stations that supported Australian settlers coming from New South Wales. In 1840 New Zealand became a British colony, and British wars against the indigenous tribes lasted until 1847, when the Maori were subdued. New Zealand was granted internal autonomy (for white settlers) in 1852 under the New Zealand Constitution Act, but tribal peoples were not given any political rights. Between 1860 and 1877 the Maori fought a new war against the British settlers but once again were defeated.

In 1876 the island's provinces were abolished by British colonial administrators, and New Zealand became a unitary state. New Zealand became a British dominion in 1907, when white-dominated colonial territories held by Great Britain were made partners in its imperial policies. It was granted full autonomy in 1931 by a Statute of Westminster. Since 1947, it has been a sovereign state within the Commonwealth of Nations.

Government institutions New Zealand is a parliamentary democracy. The head of state is the monarch of the Commonwealth, represented on the islands for ceremonial purposes by a governor-general. A prime minister and executive council supervise the govern-

ment departments. Legislative power is vested in the 97-member House of Representatives, whose members are directly elected for three-year terms, with four seats reserved for Maori representatives. There is an independent judiciary, headed by the Court of Appeal.

Parties and movements New Zealand has a multiparty system. The dominant parties are the National Party (liberal) and the Labour Party (social democratic). Smaller parties include the New Labour Party (left-wing), the Green Party (ecological concerns), and New Zealand Party (reformist). By the mid-1990s several small parties, organized as the Alliance in combination with the Maori, had won almost one-fifth of the vote.

In 1993 New Zealand ended its system of electing members of the legislature in single-winner races and instead decided to institute a system of proportional representation. Starting in 1995, voters chose 65 members in district elections but selected another 65 members in a national proportional contest, in which seats were allocated to party representatives based on the percentage of the vote that their party won.

Domestic issues In the early 1990s the government attempted to cut spending for the nation's generous social welfare benefits, which included payments to cover medical bills, free hospitalization, maternity benefits, disability insurance, old-age pensions, and free higher education. A coalition of minor parties challenging these cuts has gained popular support. The Maori tribes have pressed their land claims (much of their land was forcibly taken from them in the 19th century by Australian settlers) in the Maori Land Court established by the government. The government has allocated $1 billion to settle these land claims.

In the mid-1990s a movement in New Zealand called for an end to its membership in the Commonwealth of Nations and its transformation into a republic in which a president would become the head of state. This position was supported by the prime minister in 1994, who called for the transformation by the year 2000.

International issues Australia is New Zealand's major military and diplomatic ally. The two nations signed a trade agreement in 1983 providing for economic cooperation involving trade and technology.

In 1986 New Zealand prohibited U.S. warships with nuclear weapons from visiting its ports, and the United States responded by suspending the ANZUS treaty, a collective security arrangement with New Zealand and Australia. It also cut off arms sales to New Zealand in 1987.

Relations with France deteriorated after a 1985 incident in which the *Rainbow Warrior,* a ship manned by environmentalists protesting French nuclear testing in the Pacific, was blown up by French agents in a New Zealand harbor. A French promise to suspend nuclear testing in 1992 improved relations, but when France decided to explode six atomic weapons in the South Pacific in 1995, New Zealand launched strong diplomatic protests. New Zealand is also a strong proponent of bans on international whaling and drift-net fishing.

SEE ALSO

ANZUS Treaty; Australia; Commonwealth of Nations; United Kingdom

FURTHER READING

Mulgan, Richard. *Politics in New Zealand.* New York: Oxford University Press, 1994.
Palmer, Geoffrey. *Unbridled Power.* New York: Oxford University Press, 1979.
Rice, Geoffrey W., ed. *The Oxford History of New Zealand.* 2nd ed. New York: Oxford University Press, 1992.

Ngo Dinh Diem

- *Born: Jan. 3, 1901, Hue, French Indochina*
- *Died: Nov. 2, 1963, Saigon, South Vietnam*

The first president of South Vietnam (1955–63), Ngo Dinh Diem became a dictator whose corrupt and ineffectual rule enabled a communist insurrection to gain ground in the early 1960s, eventually leading to military intervention by the United States in order to combat the communists.

Diem was the son of a government minister. He graduated from the School of Public Administration in Hanoi and became a provincial governor. In 1933 he briefly served as minister of the interior in the French colonial government, but he resigned in protest against French policies, because he realized that France did not intend to grant Vietnam independence. After World War II he refused an offer to serve as minister of the interior in the communist regime of Ho Chi Minh.

After a stay in Europe, Diem returned to Vietnam in 1954. With U.S. assistance, he won election as president in a contest held in South Vietnam in 1955, then declared it a sovereign nation and republic. Diem refused to participate in the scheduled 1956 all-Vietnam elections, whose purpose was to pave the way for the reunification of North and South Vietnam, fearing defeat by Ho Chi Minh.

After the communist Viet Cong guerrillas began a civil war in the South, Diem turned to authoritarian rule. His forces fired on Buddhist demonstrators in the city of Hue, which turned much of the population against him, in part because of his own Catholic faith. The U.S. government did not dissuade generals in the South Vietnam army from carrying out a coup d'état, and Diem was overthrown and killed by government soldiers on November 2, 1963.

Diem's assassination ushered in a period of prolonged political instability, as military leaders plotted and executed various coups. The weakness of the South Vietnamese government and army led to great gains by the Viet Cong in 1964. In response, the United States began a military escalation and replaced military advisers and antiguerrilla forces with regular military forces in 1965.

SEE ALSO
Ho Chi Minh; Vietnam

FURTHER READING
Hammer, Ellen. *A Death in November, 1963.* New York: Dutton, 1987.

Nicaragua

REPUBLIC OF NICARAGUA (REPÚBLICA DE NICARAGUA)

• *Capital: Managua*

Political history Located in Central America, the area that is now Nicaragua was first settled by peoples from South America and Mexico. The Spanish established settlements under the direction of the explorer Francisco Fernández de Córdoba in the 1520s. The indigenous peoples were conquered in 1552 by Spain, which established agricultural plantations. In the 17th and 18th centuries the British established settlements on the North Atlantic coast and imported African slaves for their plantations. Pirates also made their bases in the area. The British established a protectorate

along the east coast of Nicaragua known as the Mosquito Coast between 1740 and 1786, when the area was taken over by the Spanish.

In 1821, as part of the movement for independence throughout the European colonies of Central and South America, the Spanish were driven out of the cities of León and Granada, which briefly united with Mexico (1822–25) and then, under the name Nicaragua, became a province within the United Provinces of Central America (1826–38). Nicaragua became independent in 1838 as the United Provinces dissolved into separate states because of resentment over Guatemala's domination. Mosquitia, the former British protectorate centered around San Juan del Norte, remained a separate kingdom on the Atlantic Coast until 1860.

U.S. Marines occupied Nicaragua several times in the early 1900s, because of political instability and the consequent threat to U.S. investments, and they propped up the Conservative Party, which favored U.S. investment. The marines finally departed in 1933, leaving behind Anastasio Somoza y García, the head of the National Guard, as dictator. His regime was headed after his death in 1956 by his son Luis, and then after his death in 1967 by his other son, Anastasio. The Somoza regime was overthrown on July 19, 1979, by the Sandinistas, a Marxist-Leninist movement that established an authoritarian state. The ruling junta was led by a youthful Sandinista guerrilla, Daniel Ortega, and his brother Humberto Ortega, who became defense minister. An 11-year civil war ensued between the Sandinistas and the contras, a group initially composed of former Somoza supporters that later broadened to include those disaffected with Sandinista political and religious repression of farmers in the northern provinces and people favor-

Vendors sell plantain and beverages on a street in Managua while their fellow Nicaraguans lounge beneath a campaign poster in February 1990. The elections that followed marked an end to the country's civil war and an end to the rule of the Sandinista party.

ing a democratic regime and opposed to discrimination against Indian tribes. The United States and Honduras supported the contras with food, supplies, and military equipment.

Exhausted by the fighting that was destroying the nation's economy, the Sandinistas and contras eventually realized that the war could not be won. Eventually, the civil war was ended by a compromise negotiated under the auspices of several Central and South American nations. The United States ended its support for the contras, and the Sandinistas agreed to hold free elections. The Sandinista regime ceded power to an anti-Sandinista party coalition after free elections in 1990.

Government institutions Under the constitution revised in June 1995, Nicaragua has a nominal presidential regime but one in which most governing power is exercised by the legislature. Executive power is vested in the president, who is elected by popular vote for a six-year term and who appoints a cabinet to run the executive departments. Legislative power is vested in the 92-member National Assembly, directly elected by a system of proportional party representa-

tion. There is an independent judiciary headed by the five-member Supreme Court, appointed by the legislature.

Parties and movements Between 1980 and 1990 Nicaragua was a modified one-party state. According to the 1980 constitution, the Frente Sandinista de Liberación Nacional (Sandinista National Liberation Front) was recognized as the governing party, and it organized both the armed forces, which became known as the Sandinista People's Army, and security forces as branches of the Sandinista movement. Other parties were permitted to exist but were not allowed to threaten the Sandinista control of the state.

In 1990, the Sandinistas agreed to permit a multiparty system as part of the compromise to end the civil war. The Sandinistas lost the subsequent election to the Unión Nacional Opositora (UNO), an electoral alliance of 14 parties. Violeta Barrios de Chamorro, head of the UNO, became president, replacing the Sandinista Daniel Ortega. In a conciliatory gesture, she agreed that a Sandinista could remain as head of the armed forces. In 1992 the UNO repudiated President Chamorro for her conciliatory position, and by 1993 she was relying on Sandinista and minor party votes for her progressive legislative program, while conservatives boycotted legislative sessions. In 1995, under pressure from the United States, the Sandinistas agreed to give up their control over the military, which assumed the name Nicaraguan Army after the resignation of Humberto Ortega.

In 1996 a rightist candidate, José Arnoldo Alemán Iacayo, a lawyer, coffee grower, and mayor of Managua in the early 1990s, defeated Daniel Ortega for the presidency. His victory consolidated the power of a right-of-center coalition and left the Sandinistas as the major opposition party.

Domestic issues After the 1990 elections, more than 75,000 government troops and 22,000 contra guerrillas were demobilized, leaving an army of only 16,000. In 1993 some 14 bands of rearmed contras in the north began political protests against the slow pace of land distribution to former guerrillas (which had been promised to them in 1990) and the death of 200 former contra leaders, attributed to the army, since the peace accords. Some Sandinista former soldiers (known as *recompas*, or "those who have returned"), also began to rearm. They demanded pensions from the government because of their forced retirement from the military, threatening a resumption of factional fighting.

The devastation of the civil war, combined with a disastrous earthquake that leveled Managua in 1972, has kept economic performance low, and unemployment is at 50 percent. Foreign investment is limited, and though some privatization has occurred, inflation is high and the standard of living has declined. As a result, the government lacks popular support.

International issues Until the Sandinista takeover, Nicaragua was a close ally of the United States. Under the Sandinistas, it received arms from Cuba and economic assistance from the Soviet Union because these nations had hopes of fostering a communist government there. The United States, opposed from the beginning to the Sandinista economic program, financed and armed the contra opposition, and the U.S. Central Intelligence Agency even helped the contras mine the harbor of Corinto to destroy merchant ships. In the mid-1980s the Contadora Group, consisting of Colombia, Panama, Mexico, and Venezuela, met to find ways to end the fighting. In 1989 these nations signed the Tela Agreement (named for the city in which they met), which provided for the demobilization of Sandinista troops and repatriation of contra exiles. The Meskito Indians also agreed to renounce their armed struggle against the Sandinista government. As part of the overall agreement, the Sandinista government dropped a lawsuit against Honduras (for its support of the contras) at the International Court of Justice.

A teenage Sandinista checks his rifle in Managua in 1979. Frequently, young fighters join civil wars in the Third World.

Since the 1990 elections, Nicaragua has pursued closer relations with the United States. Because of growing Sandinista influence in the Chamorro regime, however, the United States suspended more than $100 million in foreign aid to Nicaragua in 1992. Other international aid donors provide Nicaragua with about $600 million in grants and loans annually.

Human rights Under the right-wing Somoza dictatorship, political dissidents were routinely imprisoned, tortured, and executed. Indians were oppressed in the same way, and their land was expropriated. Independent trade unions were not permitted to exist. A leading publisher of an independent newspaper was assassinated in an attempt to end freedom of the press.

Under the Sandinistas most of these abuses were ended, although democratic government was not permitted. Peaceful critics of the regime faced arrest and sometimes physical abuse by the security forces.

Since the peace accords, the Permanent Commission for Human Rights (a Nicaraguan monitoring group) has accused the Nicaraguan military of murdering at least 13 former contra soldiers who were going to a demobilization site to turn in their weapons.

SEE ALSO

Chamorro, Violeta Barrios de; Marxism-Leninism; Ortega, Daniel

FURTHER READING

Gilbert, Dennis. *Sandinistas: The Party and the Revolution.* New York: Blackwell, 1988.
Morley, Morris. *Washington, Somoza and the Sandinistas.* New York: Cambridge University Press, 1994.
Wright, Bruce. *Theory in the Practice of the Nicaraguan Revolution.* Athens: Ohio University Center for International Studies, 1995.

Niger

REPUBLIC OF NIGER (RÉPUBLIQUE DU NIGER)

• *Capital: Niamey*

Political history Niger, a landlocked nation located in West Africa just north of Nigeria, was part of several ancient and medieval black African Is-lamic empires, including the ancient kingdom of Mali in the 13th century and the Fulani empire from the 16th through the 18th century. Europeans discovered it in the 18th century and France occupied it between 1883 and 1889 as part of the French conquest of West Africa. Niger became a French military territory in 1901, then part of French West Africa in 1904, and a separate colony in 1922. Niger became an autonomous republic in the French Community in 1958 and won full independence in 1960.

In 1974 Niger's civilian president was overthrown in a military coup d'état. The military remained in control in the late 1980s, although it governed through nominally independent civilian politicians. In 1991 Niger approved a new constitution and began the transition to a multiparty democracy under the leadership of an interim civilian prime minister, Amadou Cheiffon. In March 1993 Niger held free multiparty elections and chose Mahamane Ousmane of the Social Democratic Convention Party to be president. His rule was ineffectual, and in 1995 opposition parties won 42 of the 82 seats in the National Assembly. In 1996 Ousmane was ousted by an army coup led by Colonel Barre Ibrahim and Niger returned to a military dictatorship.

Government institutions Niger was ruled by its military between 1974 and 1993. A 1991 national conference of military rulers and civilian leaders dissolved the existing organs of government. The High Council of the Republic, an interim governing body controlled by the military, drafted a new constitution that went into effect in 1993. The head of state was the president, popularly elected for a term of four years. A council of ministers, headed by a prime minister, supervised government administrative departments. Legislative power was exercised by a National Assembly. These institutions were suspended by the army in its 1996 coup.

Parties and movements Until 1991 Niger was a one-party state. The military organized the sole legal party, the National Movement for Social Development (NMSD). In 1991 other parties were legalized. By 1992, 37 parties were registered. The leading parties are the Social Democratic Convention Party and the NMSD (pro-military socialist). Political party activity, however, was banned after the 1996 coup.

Domestic issues The transitional government in the 1990s introduced austerity measures and attempted to increase the amount of land under cultivation in order to promote exports for foreign exchange. A movement to provide autonomy to several regions led to negotiations between rebel Tuaregs in the northern region and the central government in 1992. But the civilian regime was unstable because of ethnic tensions between the Djerma tribe, which constituted less than 10 percent of the population but dominated the military, and the majority Hausa, which dominated civilian politics. The military officers justified their 1996 coup by pointing to a deadlock between the parliament and the president, which in their view had led to paralysis in policy-making.

International issues Niger maintained close economic and cultural ties with France, which provided it with foreign aid until the 1996 coup. At that time, France, the United States, and other Western nations cut off economic and military aid to protest the military takeover.

Japan purchases Niger's uranium for nuclear power and is an important trading partner. Libya has attempted to gain influence in the north so it can develop its mineral resources; its support for the Tuareg minority in northern Niger has strained relations between Libya and Niger.

SEE ALSO
French Community; French West Africa; Libya

FURTHER READING
Fuglestad, Finn. *A History of Niger, 1850–1960*. New York: Cambridge University Press, 1983.

Nigeria

FEDERAL REPUBLIC OF NIGERIA

• *Capital: Abuja*

Political history Located on the coast of southwestern Africa, Nigeria was the site of the Nok civilization, one of the most ancient cultures in the world. In medieval times the empire of the Yoruba was established, with its advanced woodworking and metalworking techniques. By A.D. 1000 the northern areas had been converted to Islam by the Kanem, who in the next four centuries traded throughout Africa, the Middle East, and southern Europe. In the 15th and 16th centuries the northern area was dominated by the Hausa and then by the Fulani kings, who established a Muslim caliphate. In the south, the Yoruba established an empire by A.D. 1000. From the 15th to the 18th century, the civilization at Benin became known throughout Africa and Europe for its bronze and ivory artwork.

Portuguese and British slave traders began their trafficking in humans and stolen artwork in the region in the 16th century. The British asserted their influence gradually over separate kingdoms in the north and south, and by 1861 the area around Lagos became a British colony. In 1906 the British conquered an area east of Lagos from the Ibo and called it the Protectorate of Southern Nigeria. In 1946 the British divided Nigeria into the Southern, Northern, and Eastern regions, each with limited local rule by an elected tribal assembly. In 1954 these areas were united into the Nigerian Federation, which remained a British colony with an autonomous central government, headed by a Nigerian prime minister. In 1960 Nigeria became an independent sovereign member of the Commonwealth of Nations. The following year the northern part of British Cameroon became part of Nigeria (while the southern part was ceded to Cameroon).

In 1964 Nigeria became a republic, and civilian and military governments have alternated in power since then. Between 1966 and 1995, seven coups occurred and three leaders were assassinated. In 1967 the Eastern Region, with its rich mineral resources, seceded and formed the independent state of Biafra, but it was reincorporated into Nigeria in 1970 after a civil war in which more than 1 million Biafrans were killed.

In 1987 a transitional program to civilian rule was announced, and a new constitution took effect in 1992. Elections in 1993 were annulled by the military, however, after millionaire businessman Moshood Abiola was elected. The military rulers rejected the election results, arrested political opponents (including Abiola), banned political parties, and governed by military rule into the late 1990s.

Government institutions Nigeria has a federal system comprising 21 states, each of which is administered by a military governor and state executive council. At the national level, the military ruled until 1993 through the Armed Forces Ruling Council, chaired by a president who is the head of state and commander in chief. The Ruling Council appointed a council of ministers, also headed by the president, to run the actual day-to-day affairs of the government. In 1993, after the June 12 presidential elections were an-

On the docks of the Nigerian capital of Lagos, relief workers unload emergency medical supplies donated by the United States. Nigeria's size and natural resources make it potentially one of the richest and most powerful nations of Africa, but corruption has hampered its economic development.

In June 1993, presidential candidate Moshood Abiola casts a vote for himself in the first free election held in Nigeria in several decades. Abiola won, but the military annulled the election and reinstated itself as Nigeria's ruling power.

nulled by the military, a Transitional Council was installed by the army to supervise a cabinet of civilian appointees. It was deposed in a coup d'état, however, and the new military ruler, Sani Abacha (who had previously served as the defense minister), appointed his own 25-member Provisional Ruling Council, consisting entirely of military officers, to oversee the government. The government rules by decree, and the decrees may not be challenged in the courts. In 1995 Abacha announced that he would restore elected civilian rule but had not done so as of 1997.

Parties and movements Until 1989 political parties were not permitted in Nigeria. That year, the military rulers established two political associations, the National Republicans and the Social Democrats (both conservative parties), after denying 13 parties permission to register. The military controlled both parties, writing their platforms, appointing party officials, and providing public funding. Nevertheless, it refused to abide by the election results in 1993, which had resulted in the election of businessman Moshood Abiola as president, and once again banned political parties. The ban was lifted in June 1995.

Domestic issues After the presidential elections of 1993 were annulled, widespread demonstrations by prodemocracy groups (including a general strike) and the unpopularity of an economic austerity program led to a coup d'état by Defense Minister Sani Abacha late in the year.

Nigeria's economy has been hurt in the 1990s by low prices for oil, the country's primary export. The unemployment rate is high, and the inflation rate reached 100 percent in 1995. The currency has become worthless. Per capita income has fallen from $1,000 in 1980 to $250 in 1995. Corruption, smuggling, and organized crime are major problems, and the country is now the center of the drug trade in Africa. Many of the top government leaders receive payoffs when they award contracts for exploitation of the oil reserves. A government commission revealed in 1994 that officials could not account for $12.2 billion in oil sales made to Western nations during the Persian Gulf War.

The World Bank and International Monetary Fund have worked with Nigeria in the 1990s on developing an austerity plan that would involve rescheduling its $30 billion debt. By relieving pressure from foreign lenders, this would allow Nigeria to use its funds to address domestic problems.

The economic weakness of the country, and the resulting unpopularity of the rulers, has led to political instability. The military rulers have dissolved the national parliament and state legislatures, disbanded labor unions, shut down newspapers, banned political movements, and arrested dissidents. The regime has even dismissed hundreds of army officers in purges in an attempt to silence any opposition to its policies.

Ethnic conflict in Nigeria also threatens the stability of the state. There are 250 different groups, but the three largest regional groupings—the Hausa and Fulani in the Muslim north, the Yoruba in the southwest, and the Ibo in the southeast—account for three-fifths of the population. The northern tribes have dominated the military since independence and, for most of Nigeria's existence, have used the military to control the government. Muslims, who constitute half the population and are concentrated in the north, have demanded the imposition of Islamic law.

A former military leader of Nigeria, General Olusegun Obasanjo, was arrested by the regime in 1995 after he attempted to create an alliance between the Yoruba and Ibo, because the military rulers, from the North, felt threatened by any coalition of these southern tribes.

International issues Nigeria has been a leader in African affairs, because of its size, its population (the largest in Africa), and its natural resources. However, it has had problems with Ghana, because it expelled illegal Ghanian immigrants, and it has had border disputes with Chad and the Cameroons. Nigeria participated in the military force of West African nations that attempted to put an end to the Liberian civil war in 1993–95. Earlier, in 1991, Nigeria had deployed troops in Sierra Leone to protect that nation against Liberian rebels. It also intervened unsuccessfully in Sierra Leone in 1997 to try to put down a coup against the elected civilian government.

In 1995 the United States and Great Britain cut off foreign aid to Nigeria to protest the excesses of the military regime.

Human rights Hundreds of pro-democracy demonstrators were killed and imprisoned in Lagos, and tight controls on the media were imposed by the military regime in 1993. Members of the Campaign for Democracy, which led protests against the annulment of the elections, have been imprisoned.

The regime has used its Mobile Police Force to put down all protests by the Ogoni tribe protesting exploitation of their oil fields in the Niger Delta; the police razed 27 villages and killed 2,000

Ogoni. On November 10, 1995, the military government executed Ken Saro-Wiwa, a playwright and environmentalist, along with eight other men of the Ogoni tribe, who had been leaders of the Movement for the Survival of the Ogoni People. The government claimed these Ogoni had murdered political opponents, but the Ogoni believed that they had been executed because of their opposition to government plans to develop the oil deposits in Ogoniland. In response to the executions, the World Bank halted a $100 million loan to Nigeria to develop liquefied natural gas, and South Africa's president Nelson Mandela condemned the executions as a "heinous act." The Commonwealth of Nations suspended Nigeria indefinitely because of the executions in 1995, the first time the Commonwealth had ever suspended a member state. The United States ended arms sales, denied visas to Nigerian officials and their families to visit the United States, and voted against loans to Nigeria in the World Bank. The United States did not, however, ban new American investment in the Nigerian economy, as some human rights advocates proposed. The Organization of African Unity also criticized Nigeria.

SEE ALSO

Cameroon; Commonwealth of Nations; Liberia

FURTHER READING

Achebe, Chinua. *The Trouble with Nigeria*. London: Heinemann, 1984.
Ihonvbere, Julius. *Nigeria: The Politics of Adjustment and Democracy*. New Brunswick, N.J.: Transaction, 1994.
Metz, Helen Chapin, ed. *Nigeria: A Country Study*. 5th ed. Washington, D.C.: Federal Research Division, Library of Congress, 1992.
Peters, Jimi. *The Nigerian Military and the State*. New York: St. Martin's, 1995.
Saro-Wiwa, Ken. *Ogoni: Moment of Truth*. Port Harcourt, Nigeria: Saros, 1994.
Zartman, I. William. *The Political Economy of Nigeria*. New York: Praeger, 1983.

Nixon, Richard Milhous

- *Born: Jan. 9, 1913, Yorba Linda, Calif.*
- *Died: Apr. 22, 1994, New York, N.Y.*

Richard Nixon was the 37th president of the United States (1969–73) and the only U.S. president to resign his office. He was only the second president (after Andrew Johnson) ever to be involved in impeachment proceedings by the House of Representatives. A hard-line anticommunist who made his reputation by attacking Democrats for "losing" China and being "soft" on the Soviet Union, Nixon nevertheless claimed a place in American history as a diplomat for establishing friendly relations with communist China and concluding arms control agreements with the Soviet Union.

Trained as a lawyer, Nixon served in the navy in World War II, then was elected as a Republican to the U.S. House of Representatives in 1946 and to the U.S. Senate in 1948. He established a reputation as a highly partisan campaigner who would not hesitate to attack the patriotism of his Democratic opponents. He served as Dwight Eisenhower's vice president from 1953 to 1961 but was defeated for the presidency by John Kennedy in the 1960 election. He was elected president in 1968 on a Republican platform calling for an end to the Vietnam War.

Early in 1969, Nixon stated his principles regarding future uses of U.S. armed forces, a statement that became known as the Nixon doctrine. He made three points: the United States would honor all treaty commitments, it would provide a nuclear "umbrella" for U.S. allies against threats by other nuclear powers, and it would provide weapons

With his wife, Pat, U.S. president Richard Nixon poses on the Great Wall of China during his groundbreaking visit to the communist People's Repubic of China in 1972. The diplomatic opening to China is one of the undeniable achievements of Nixon's controversial presidency.

and assistance to friendly nations but would not commit U.S. forces to localized conflicts that did not involve the superpowers or the vital interests of the United States.

Nixon "Vietnamized" the war (that is, had South Vietnam do the fighting) and removed most of the 500,000 U.S. ground combat forces from Vietnam. Soon, U.S. combat casualties were sharply reduced. In 1970 he ordered the invasion of neighboring Cambodia in pursuit of Vietnamese communist forces, an action that led to widespread protests and demonstrations in the United States. By 1972 almost all U.S. forces had been removed from South Vietnam, and on January 21, 1973, after a Christmas bombing campaign against North Vietnam, the United States came to an agreement with the North Vietnamese. A cease-fire was proclaimed, U.S. prisoners of war were returned, and U.S. military involvement in the Vietnam War ended. Air Force bombing continued against the communists in Cambodia, however, until Congress overrode a Nixon veto and ordered a halt to the bombing by August 15, 1973. Congress then passed the War Powers Resolution of 1973, also over Nixon's veto, which said that Congress must approve of any military action by a president within 60 days or the forces must be withdrawn.

Although Nixon had made his career in the cold war as a hard-line anticommunist, he reversed his long-standing opposition to seating China in the United Nations in 1971. Then, in February 1972, he became the first U.S. president to visit the People's Republic of China. He established low-level diplomatic relations with that nation, naming George Bush to head a "mission" to Beijing, though without instituting formal diplomatic recognition of its government or an exchange of ambassadors.

In May 1972 Nixon made a trip to the Soviet Union and completed a significant arms-control agreement involving limitations on intercontinental ballistic missiles. He made a televised speech to the people of the Soviet Union, reassuring them that the United States did not have aggressive intentions against them. This summit ushered in a period of détente (the relaxation of cold war tensions) between the two superpowers, who signed numerous other agreements on science, space, technology, and trade over the next two years. In 1973 Nixon sent arms to Israel during the Yom Kippur War against Syria and Egypt, and after the cease-fire, the United States was instrumental in obtaining an Israeli pullback from the Sinai Peninsula and establishing a demilitarized zone there.

In domestic affairs Nixon was a moderate conservative, but many of his lasting initiatives, including environmental protection laws, the food stamp program (which provides food for low-income people), and the improvement of welfare programs, were passed with the cooperation of the Democratic Congress, because they were considered lib-

eral measures. He also won passage of a revenue-sharing measure that provided $5 billion annually to state and local governments, and a "bloc grant" program that gave these governments greater flexibility in spending money on health, education, training, and social service programs. When Nixon tried to institute conservative policies, such as a ban on busing children to schools (which had been put in place to overcome racial segregation in public schools) or dismantling social service programs to aid the poor, he was blocked by Congress.

Nixon won a landslide reelection victory in 1972. Early in his second term, however, it was revealed that operatives working for the Committee to Re-Elect the President had burglarized the Democratic National Committee headquarters in the Watergate office complex during the 1972 presidential campaign. Nixon resigned his office on August 9, 1974, shortly after the House Judiciary Committee voted to recommend three articles of impeachment to the full House.

In retirement, Nixon wrote many books on foreign policy. He gradually assumed a role as a senior adviser to Republican presidents in foreign policy. Nixon died on April 22, 1994, in New York City. His funeral, held at his birthplace in Yorba Linda, California, was attended by four U.S. presidents and leaders from many nations, evidence that to some extent he had rehabilitated his image through his conduct as an ex-president.

Nixon was one of the most influential U.S. politicians in the post–World War II period, active in national politics for more than four decades. He was one of the architects of the militant anticommunism that characterized U.S. foreign policy through the 1960s, and then as president fashioned the policy of détente that replaced it with a more sophisticated way of responding to the challenges posed by Soviet foreign policy. Unfortunately for him and for the nation, his "take no prisoners" approach to elections led him to cover up criminal activity committed by his staff in the White House, a scandal that paralyzed his government for more than a year and led to his forced resignation.

SEE ALSO

Bush, George; China; Cold war; Eisenhower, Dwight David; Kennedy, John F.; Soviet Union (Union of Soviet Socialist Republics); Vietnam War

FURTHER READING

Ambrose, Stephen. *Nixon.* 2 vols. New York: Simon & Schuster, 1987.

Nixon, Richard. *RN: The Memoirs of Richard Nixon.* 2 vols. New York: Warner, 1978.

Parmet, Herbert. *Richard Nixon and His America.* Boston: Little, Brown, 1990.

Pious, Richard M. *Richard Nixon: A Political Biography.* Englewood Cliffs, N.J.: Silver Burdett, 1992.

Ripley, C. Peter. *Richard Nixon.* New York: Chelsea House, 1987.

Nkrumah, Kwame

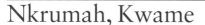

- *Born: Sept. 21, 1909, Nkroful, Gold Coast*
- *Died: Apr. 27, 1972, Bucharest, Romania*

Leader of the Pan-African movement and the first prime minister (1957–60) and president of Ghana (1960–66), Kwame Nkrumah was one of the most influential African political thinkers and politicians during the transition to post-colonial rule. A self-styled Christian Marxist, he was an original thinker and a dynamic speaker, with a natural gift for political organization.

Baptized Francis Nwia Nkrumah, he was educated in Catholic mission schools and at a government teachers

college. He then studied history and philosophy in the United States, first at Lincoln University in Pennsylvania, where he earned bachelor's and master's degrees in 1939, and then as a graduate student in philosophy at the University of Pennsylvania, where he also earned an M.A. While in graduate school, Nkrumah became active in politics and was president of the African Students' Organization of the United States and Canada.

In 1945 he was a co-organizer of the Pan-African Congress in London, a meeting that laid the groundwork for the national liberation movements in many West African nations. Many African students and intellectuals who had studied in Europe and the United States attended the Congress.

After returning to his country in 1947, Nkrumah became general secretary of the United Gold Coast Convention, a movement seeking independence for Ghana (known also at that time by its colonial name Gold Coast). He was jailed in 1948 by British colonial authorities after riots broke out in Accra to protest continued British rule. In 1949 he became the leader of the Convention People's Party (CPP), breaking with his former organization because it was too conservative and would not endorse militant action. In 1951 the CPP won the elections for the legislature, and the British released Nkrumah from jail so that he could take office as the leader of the government under British administration. The following year, he became prime minister of the colonial government that prepared the country for independence.

In 1957 the Gold Coast won independence and changed its name to the African one of Ghana. After a 1960 plebiscite converted it into a republic, Nkrumah was elected its first president. He gave himself the title *Osagfeyo,* or "redeemer." He established an authoritarian one-party state based on what he called "Nkrumaism." This philosophy, which he espoused in 10 volumes of works about Africa and its struggles for independence from the West, was a blend of Marxism, Maoism, and Pan-Africanism (a movement that called for the liberation of all colonies on the African continent).

Government corruption and a deteriorating economy led Nkrumah's opponents to make several attempts on his life. After a coup by the army in 1966, he was exiled to Guinea. He later moved to the Ivory Coast. Nkrumah died in Bucharest, Romania, where he had gone to receive medical treatment in 1972.

Nkrumah was one of the founders of modern post-colonial Africa. Through the force of his personality, he organized an independence movement, but he was too much of an ideologist to understand the practical workings of the economy. He failed to improve Ghana's economy or transform its institutions—schools, agriculture, and the civil service, for example—to meet the rising expectations of the people. He consolidated his rule by establishing a one-party authoritarian state, based on a cult of personality, on "the leader who never dies," rather than by bringing democratic institutions and practices to Ghana.

SEE ALSO

Ghana

FURTHER READING

Davidson, Basil. *Black Star: A View of the Life and Times of Kwame Nkrumah.* Boulder, Colo.: Westview, 1989.

Kellner, Douglas. *Kwame Nkrumah.* New York: Chelsea House, 1987.

Nkrumah, Kwame. *The Autobiography of Kwame Nkrumah.* Edinburgh: T. Nelson, 1959.

Nkrumah, Kwame. *Dark Days in Ghana.* New York: International Publishers, 1969.

Nonaligned Movement

The Nonaligned Movement is an informal association of more than 100 developing nations (located primarily in Africa, Asia, and the Middle East) that staked out a neutral position during the cold war between the United States and the Soviet Union. Its founders were Indian prime minister Jawaharlal Nehru, Yugoslav president Josip Broz Tito, and Egyptian president Gamal Abdel Nasser. The first summit meeting of nonaligned heads of state was held in Belgrade, Yugoslavia, in 1961; since then, summits have been held at three-year intervals.

In the 1960s the focus of the movement shifted from the cold war toward Third World economic development. The Coordinating Bureau of Nonaligned Countries was established in 1973 with headquarters in Algiers, Algeria. It promoted the idea of a New International Economic Order, a set of demands by developing nations on the Western industrial nations that called for favorable terms of trade, lenient debt payment schedules, and other economic advantages.

The Nonaligned Movement grew to include almost all of the non-Western developing nations. It became the most influential voting bloc in the United Nations and other world organizations in the 1970s. Although its economic goals—including calls for technology transfers from developed to developing nations—were sidetracked by the opposition of the Western nations, it played a constructive role in ending colonial rule in southern Africa, in pressing for international recognition of Palestinian claims for autonomy and statehood, and in protecting the global environment.

SEE ALSO

Nasser, Gamal Abdel; Nehru, Jawaharlal; New International Economic Order (NIEO); Third World; Tito, Josip Broz; United Nations (UN)

FURTHER READING

Singham, A. W., and Shirley Hune. *Non-Alignment in an Age of Alignments.* London: Zed, 1986.

Nordic Council

The Nordic Council was founded in 1952 by Denmark, Finland, Iceland, Norway, and Sweden. It promotes economic, social, and political cooperation among these nations. The Annual Council consists of 87 members elected by the parliaments of the Nordic nations, with their political parties proportionately represented. Each nation is represented on the presidium, which directs the work of the council. The presidium proposes coordination among the Nordic nations on issues involving energy, fisheries, women's rights, refugees, tourism, anti-drug policies, and transportation policies; its recommendations are often adopted by its member states.

SEE ALSO

Denmark; Finland; Iceland; Norway; Sweden

FURTHER READING

Wendt, Frantz. *Cooperation in the Nordic Countries.* Stockholm: Almqvist & Wiksell International, 1981.

North American Free Trade Agreement (NAFTA)

NAFTA is a comprehensive trade agreement put into effect by Canada, Mexico, and the United States in 1993. The pact is designed to eliminate most tariffs and trade barriers on industrial and agricultural goods and on services, creating a regional economy (rather than one limited by national borders) that lowers the costs of doing business for companies operating in North America. Most tariffs are being phased out over 15 years, starting in 1993. Immigration requirements for corporate executives and professionals wishing to transfer between North American countries have been eased.

A side agreement, called the Agreement on Environmental Cooperation, negotiated in 1993 called for fines of up to $20 million for violations of labor and environmental laws and for limited trade sanctions on governments that permit such violations. The U.S.–Mexico Border Environmental Commission monitors compliance. The North American Development Bank loans up to $3 billion for environmental protection projects on the U.S.–Mexican border.

An Agreement on Labor Cooperation permitted investigations of labor abuses involving worker safety, use of child labor, and minimum-wage standards. Government leaders hold annual meetings to consider policies for industries that suffer greatly from competition.

Opponents of NAFTA in the United States charged that businesses would move their operations to Mexico to take advantage of its lower labor costs and regulatory laxness and that the United States would be flooded with cheap foreign imported goods that would wipe out domestic industry. Proponents, such as U.S. president Bill Clinton, claimed that the United States would gain jobs and revenues for the government through the expansion of the North American economy and argued that the agreement would create a huge new market of 80 million Mexicans for U.S. products and that companies intending to use Mexican labor did not need NAFTA in order to relocate.

The first two years of implementation, 1993–95, had mixed results for the United States. Many industries, such as automobile manufacturers, benefited economically from NAFTA, but others did relocate to Mexico to take advantage of cheap labor. The Mexican and Canadian economies both suffered severe recessions, which led them to import fewer goods than expected. Instead of running a large trade surplus with Mexico, the United States in 1994 actually began running a trade deficit (that is, importing more goods from Mexico than it exports). Moreover, NAFTA did nothing to stem the tide of illegal immigration from Mexico to the United States, because the additional jobs created in Mexico by NAFTA were more than offset by increasing unemployment due to its recession.

NAFTA, however, has spurred other nations in the Western Hemisphere to conclude similar agreements. In 1993 the presidents of Argentina, Brazil, Uruguay, and Paraguay agreed to phase out all regional tariffs by the end of the year. Bolivia, Colombia, Ecuador, and Venezuela also knocked down their tariff barriers in the 1990s. These regional agreements have been very successful in stimulating growth in Latin America in the 1990s.

FURTHER READING

Belous, Richard, and Jonathan Lemco, eds. *NAFTA as a Model of Development.* Albany: State University of New York Press, 1995.

Doran, Charles. "Building a North American Community." *Current History* 94 (March 1995): 97–101.

Krueger, Anne. *American Trade Policy: A Tragedy in the Making.* Washington, D.C.: American Enterprise Institute, 1995.

McGraw, Dan. "Happily Ever NAFTA?" *U.S. News & World Report*, Oct. 28, 1996, 46–49.

North Atlantic Treaty Organization (NATO)

NATO is a collective security alliance founded in 1949 for the defense of Western Europe, Canada, and the United States. It was designed to deter the prospect of aggression by the Soviet Union and its Warsaw Pact allies in Eastern Europe against the democratic nations of Western Europe. Western nations believed that the Soviets might launch a massive ground invasion through Germany, and NATO was designed to counter that potential threat. Under Article 5 of the NATO treaty, the parties agreed that "an armed attack against one or more of them shall be considered an attack against them all."

NATO's 16 member nations as of 1996 were Belgium, Canada, Denmark, France, Germany, Greece, Iceland, Italy, Luxembourg, the Netherlands, Norway, Portugal, Spain, Turkey, the United Kingdom, and the United States. France was not part of NATO's military structure between 1966 and 1995, refusing to put its troops during that time under the joint military command but otherwise remaining a member of the organization committed to its principles of collective security.

The North Atlantic Council is NATO's highest authority, and each member nation sends one representative. The council may meet at the level of heads of state, heads of government, or foreign ministers. The military chiefs of staff of all member nations (including France since 1996) meet twice a year, and a military committee is in permanent session to coordinate training exercises for NATO forces.

NATO MEMBERS IN 1997

French forces were not integrated into the NATO command structure between 1966 and 1995.

The military arm of NATO consists of a European Command, an Atlantic Ocean Command, and an (English) Channel Command. These units develop defense plans and hold combined military exercises. Member nations determine their own contributions to NATO forces. In the 1990s, with the end of the cold war, several nations, including the United States, reduced their commitments of forces. In 1992 France and Germany organized their own joint force with two divisions outside of NATO, though Germany kept its remaining forces under NATO command.

NATO served purely as a deterrent force, and because the Soviet Union and its Warsaw Pact allies remained on their side of the Iron Curtain, it was never once engaged in military action between 1949 and 1991.

With the collapse of the Soviet Union and the ending of the Warsaw Pact in 1991, the nations of eastern Europe regained their freedom of action in foreign affairs. Several asked for NATO membership, but in 1993 Russia warned that an expansion of NATO into eastern Europe would force Russia into "fundamental" military countermeasures, perhaps triggering a renewal of the cold war. In December 1994, NATO foreign ministers agreed on a "parallel track" approach, in which they would gradually expand the alliance while encouraging the Russians to cooperate.

In 1994 the eastern Europeans accepted a NATO offer to join an auxiliary organization known as the Partnership for Peace, which involved cooperation with, but not formal membership in, the NATO alliance. Initially, even Russia planned to join the partnership, but in early 1995 it suspended these plans, claiming that NATO continued to pursue expansion in the east, which it viewed as a hostile act. In June 1995 Russia agreed to continue with the partnership but warned that it would suspend its participation if NATO admitted new members.

The Russians have urged NATO to convert itself from a military alliance to a political organization open to all European nations. As of 1996, 12 nations in the Baltic region and eastern Europe had all asked to join NATO, but none had been admitted. The nations most likely to be admitted in the late 1990s were Poland, Hungary, and the Czech Republic, because of their commitment to democratic multiparty systems.

In 1997 the Russians reluctantly acquiesced to NATO expansion. Russia and NATO agreed that Russia would be consulted on any NATO decisions, though it would not have a veto. The NATO powers agreed not to put nuclear weapons in the territories of new member states. These understandings were formalized in the NATO-Russia Founding Act of 1997.

In the summer of 1995 NATO military forces were used for the first time in combat when they bombed Bosnian Serb forces in retaliation for attacks against United Nations–designated "safe zones." In late 1995 NATO sent 50,000 troops (including 20,000 U.S. troops) to Bosnia to replace the UN peacekeeping force with an "implementation force" (IFOR) to see that the Dayton peace agreements to end the civil war were implemented—the first time that NATO ground forces had been used in an actual military mission since the creation of the alliance.

SEE ALSO

Cold war; Soviet Union (Union of Soviet Socialist Republics); Warsaw Pact

FURTHER READING

Kelleher, Catherine, and Gale Mattox. *Evolving European Defense Policies.* Lexington, Mass.: Lexington Books, 1987.

Papacosma, S. Victor, and Mary Ann Heiss, eds. *Does NATO Have a Future?* New York: St. Martin's, 1995.
Talbott, Strobe. "Why NATO Should Grow." *The New York Review of Books,* August 10, 1995, 27–30.

Northern Ireland

Northern Ireland consists of six counties (known collectively as Ulster) with Protestant majorities that were partitioned into a separate administration under Great Britain's Government of Ireland Act of 1920. They remained within the United Kingdom when Ireland (Eire) became independent in 1922. Northern Ireland was granted internal autonomy that year, but the British Parliament reserved to itself the powers to raise taxes and to handle Northern Ireland's external affairs.

At that time, and into the 1970s, Protestants, who constituted three-fifths of the population in Northern Ireland, dominated the government through the Ulster Unionist Party and the Royal Ulster Constabulary (police force). Catholics, who typically voted for the Nationalist Party and the Social Democratic Labor Party, had little representation in the government and faced economic discrimination from the Protestant majority in Ulster. The Protestants, in turn, feared that someday they would be forced to unite with Ireland (which had never given up its claims to the six counties) and would suffer discrimination under a Catholic majority.

In 1969, after a period of violent sectarian conflict between the Protestants and Catholics, due in large measure to anti-Catholic preachings by the Protestant minister Rev. Ian Paisley,

A young sup-
porter of Sinn
Féin urges an end
to the "troubles"
that have devas-
tated the six
counties of
Northern Ireland
since 1969. The
region's Catholic
minority tend to
regard them-
selves as Irish,
while the Protes-
tant majority
pledges political
allegiance to
Great Britain.

the British government sent in troops to restore order and protect Catholics from Protestant attacks. In 1972 the British established a system of direct rule and abolished the government in Northern Ireland, hoping that it could provide an impartial administration that would win support from both sides. Instead, British troops were subjected to guerrilla attacks, primarily from Catholic gunmen who hoped the British could be induced to leave Northern Ireland entirely. Terror campaigns waged against each other by the Irish Republican Army (IRA)—a Catholic paramilitary organization (known in Gaelic as Oglaigh na hÉireann) that seeks a united Ireland—and Protestant paramilitary groups (the Ulster Freedom Fighters and the Ulster Volunteer Force) claimed the lives of more than 3,100 people between 1969 and 1993 and wounded more than 35,000. Bombings and political assassinations conducted by the IRA disrupted normal life in English cities as well.

In 1985 Ireland and the United Kingdom signed an agreement stating that there would be no change in the status of Northern Ireland without the consent of a majority of its people. This agreement "softened" the provision (that is, allowed for some change) in Articles 2 and 3 of the Irish constitution, which defines the national territory of Ireland to include the six northern counties, a provision that had put the Irish government in conflict with the British policy of fostering an independent Northern Ireland. In turn, the British government asked the Irish government for help in finding a solution to the sectarian conflict.

Talks among British and Irish officials and the leaders of the Northern Irish communities were inaugurated in 1991. The IRA and its political arm, Sinn Féin (We Alone), led by Gerry Adams, proposed that after a cease-fire is in place the British pull out their 17,000 troops from Northern Ireland and negotiate for a gradual unification of the six counties with Ireland. The Irish government proposed a period of joint Anglo-Irish sovereignty over the counties, a proposal that was rejected by the British government. The leading Protestant politician, James Molyneux, the head of the Ulster Unionists, split with the more militant Rev. Ian Paisley, the head of the Democratic Unionists, and indicated that hc was prepared to negotiate with the Irish government.

Late in 1993 British prime minister John Major and Irish prime minister Albert Reynolds agreed to pursue talks based on a new "declaration of principles" to resolve the Northern Ireland question. As of 1994, the two sides agreed in the Downing Street Declaration that the Sinn Féin party could participate in peace talks if the IRA halted its terrorist activities. On August 31, 1994, the IRA declared a cease-fire, the Protestant gunmen responded in kind in October, and an uneasy peace ensued.

Through 1994, 3,173 victims had died in the conflict. In November 1994 Reynolds gave assurance to the Protestants in Northern Ireland that they would never be forced into a united Ireland against their will. Early in 1995 peace talks began between some of the moderate Northern Irish political leaders, who had renounced violence, and the British government, though Sinn Féin, which had not renounced violence, was not included. In late 1995, the International Body on Disarmament, a three-member international mediation panel (with members from the United States, Canada, and Finland) began efforts to work out an agreement between the British government and Sinn Féin that would lead to the disarmament of the IRA and to Sinn Féin participation in the peace talks that might determine the future of Northern Ireland. Hostilities resumed in 1996 after peace talks stalled, but with the election of a more conciliatory Labour government in the United Kingdom in 1997, talks were likely to resume.

SEE ALSO

Ireland; Irish Republican Army (IRA); United Kingdom

FURTHER READING

Harkness, David. *Ireland in the Twentieth Century.* New York: St. Martin's, 1996.

Keogh, Dermot, and Michael Haltzel. *Northern Ireland and the Politics of Reconciliation.* New York: Cambridge University Press, 1994.

McGarry, John, and Brendan O'Leary. *Explaining Northern Ireland.* Oxford, England: Blackwell, 1995.

McGarry, John, and Brendan O'Leary. *The Future of Northern Ireland.* New York: Oxford University Press, 1991.

Teagu, Paul. *Beyond the Rhetoric: Politics, the Economy, and Social Policy in Northern Ireland.* London: Lawrence & Wishart, 1987.

North Korea

SEE Korea, North

North Vietnam

SEE Vietnam

Norway

KINGDOM OF NORWAY (KONGERIKET NORGE)

• *Capital: Oslo*

Political history Located on the western side of the Scandinavian peninsula, Norway was settled by Vikings in the 7th century A.D. Harold the Fairhaired, the first Norwegian monarch, came to power in 872. He and his successors promoted Viking settlements and raids through much of northern Europe, Iceland, and Greenland and sent discovery expeditions to North America. The Vikings were converted to Christianity after the year 1000 under King Olaf II. In 1397 Norway was united with Denmark and Sweden in the Kalmar Union, controlled by the Danish kingdom. Norway was governed by the Danes until 1814, when Denmark, which had been allied with Napoléon, was forced by the allies who had defeated Napoléon to give it up to Sweden. In 1815, after an attempted Norwegian secession had been put down, the Swedes recognized Norway as an independent state under the Swedish Crown. In 1905 Norway declared its independence and Sweden acquiesced rather than go to war. Norway decided to continue with a monarchical form of government, and Prince Charles of Denmark agreed to become king of Norway, under a system of parliamentary government in which he was to be the nominal head of state.

Norway remained neutral during World War I, but Germany occupied the nation during World War II and established a puppet government under the Norwegian collaborator Vidkun Quisling. With the Allied victory, King Haakon VII (formerly Prince Charles of Denmark), who had led a government in exile in London, returned the nation to constitutional rule.

Government institutions Norway is a constitutional monarchy with a parliamentary system of government. Sovereignty is vested in the monarch. Executive power is nominally held by the monarch but is actually exercised by the council of ministers, led by the prime minister. The council is appointed by the monarch in accordance with the will of the legislature, to which it and the prime minister are accountable. Legislative power is held by the unicameral 165-member Storting, which is directly elected on the basis of proportional representation, in which parties are awarded seats depending on how many votes they receive. The Storting then

chooses one-quarter of its members to form the Lagting (upper house), and the remainder form the Odelsting (lower house). There are 18 Supreme Court justices, and cases are heard by panels of five. There are five appellate courts as well as district courts. Judges are appointed by the government with the approval of the Storting.

Parties and movements Norway is a multiparty democracy. The main parties are the Norwegian Labor Party (social democratic) and the Conservative Party, followed by the Socialist Left Party and the Centre Party (liberal). The Conservative Party, when in power, has attempted to trim back the generous welfare-state benefits, a policy opposed by the Labor Party and Socialist Left Party.

Domestic issues Norway attempts to protect domestic industries from foreign competition and tries to limit access to its fishing waters in order to ensure an adequate supply of fish for its own fishermen.

International issues After World War II, Norway abandoned its traditional neutrality (which had not protected it from German invasion) and became a member of the North Atlantic Treaty Organization (NATO). Norway, however, refused to join the European Community in 1972. After Finland and

Off Norway's coast, fishing trawlers ply the waters of the Lofoten Islands for codfish, a staple of the Norwegian diet and economy. Norway remains a seafaring nation whose economic well-being is heavily dependent on maritime endeavors.

Sweden decided to enter in 1993, Norway could not afford to remain isolated economically in the region and in 1993 it decided to seek admission, pending approval by referendum. Norway became the only country to turn down membership when its citizens voted against it by a narrow margin in 1994. With huge oil fields being developed in the Norwegian Sea near the Arctic Circle, the voters saw no need to share their prosperity.

Norway is embroiled in disputes with several neighboring nations over environmental issues. Its relations with Sweden deteriorated in the 1980s over the culling (killing) of seals by Norwegian hunters, which led to a Swedish boycott of Norwegian fish. Denmark also had a dispute with Norway over fishing and mining rights. Norway has attempted to keep Spanish and Portuguese fishing boats from overfishing in its waters. Norway's resumption of commercial whaling, in violation of an international ban, has earned it worldwide condemnation.

Norway has protested against nuclear emissions from Russian power plants that have left radioactive residues in its reindeer herds. The United States and Norway agreed in 1996 to provide technical assistance and financing to help Russia dispose of nuclear wastes in the Arctic region and to control radioactive emissions in the Barents and Kara seas. Norway has also protested against British industrial emissions that have damaged Norwegian forests.

SEE ALSO
Denmark; European Union (EU); North Atlantic Treaty Organization (NATO); Sweden

FURTHER READING
Olsen, Johan. *Organized Democracy: Political Institutions in a Welfare State—The Case of Norway.* New York: Columbia University Press, 1983.

Nuclear arms

Nuclear arms are weapons of mass destruction in which the energy is nuclear, rather than mechanical or chemical, as in the weapons used before World War II. The first nuclear weapon was designed in Los Alamos, New Mexico, in 1945 by a team of scientists led by the physicist J. Robert Oppenheimer. Sponsored by the U.S. government, this secret research effort was called the Manhattan Project. The bomb the scientists created derived its energy from fission, the splitting of atomic nuclei. In 1952 American scientists developed the hydrogen bomb, a more modern nuclear weapon based on fusion, the joining together of atomic nuclei at very high temperatures.

The actual explosive device in a nuclear weapon is contained within the weapon's warhead. Nuclear weapons are divided into four categories, according to the way the warhead is delivered to its target: intercontinental ballistic missiles (reentering the atmosphere from space), submarine-launched ballistic missiles (launched from submarines), bombers (dropped from aircraft), and cruise missiles (delivered by missiles flying close to the ground).

Only two nuclear bombs have been detonated during wartime. During World War II, U.S. president Harry S. Truman decided to drop an atomic bomb on the Japanese city of Hiroshima. He justified the nuclear attack by explaining that the alternative was a U.S. invasion of Japan that might cost as many as 1 million American lives. On August 6, 1945, the B-29 bomber *Enola Gay* dropped the bomb on Hiroshima. The effect was devastating. Three-fourths of the buildings were demolished; 118,661 people were killed, 30,524 seriously injured, and 48,606 slightly injured. Many people suffered horribly disfiguring radiation burns, and many children born to women who were exposed to the radiation suffered severe birth defects. The Second Japanese Army, headquartered in the city, was completely eliminated.

A second bomb was dropped on Nagasaki three days later. In both cases, the explosion produced high levels of radiation, a by-product of the uranium and plutonium used in the nuclear reaction. Radiation is very harmful, and often fatal, to humans, animals, and plants. It causes long-term ecological damage and is the frequent cause of severe birth defects in children. Radioactive particles from the debris of a nuclear explosion can be carried great distances by wind and may even fall on the country that detonated the nuclear weapon.

Most nuclear weapons are in the hands of five nations: the United States, Russia, China, France, and Great Britain. In addition, several other nations may possess nuclear weapons. These include India, Pakistan, Israel, and South Africa.

Nuclear arms development and proliferation occurred mainly in the United States and in the Soviet Union. In the 1940s and 1950s, the United States had an overwhelming nuclear superiority. Throughout the 1960s, however, the Soviet Union built up its nuclear stockpile, so that it had virtually the same nuclear strength as the United States by the end of the decade, and it pulled ahead of the United States in the 1970s.

This balance in power led to a state of "mutual assured destruction" (MAD) in which either country's society could be destroyed and still possess sufficient nuclear force to retaliate against the enemy. In this situation, each side pursued a strategy of deterrence by continuing to build nuclear arsenals in order to deter the enemy from attacking. Deterrence is successful when each party convinces the other that it can, and will, strike back when attacked.

The specter of nuclear warfare was at the forefront of international attention during the cold war, which lasted roughly from 1947 to 1989. The cold war was an ideological conflict primarily between the United States, upholding democracy and capitalism, and the Soviet Union, which was committed to communism. During the cold war, the United States extended its nuclear protection to Western Europe through the North Atlantic Treaty Organization (NATO), while the Soviet Union gave its protection to Eastern Europe through the Warsaw Treaty Organization (Warsaw Pact). Britain and France began to develop their own nuclear weapons as well. The British integrated theirs into the NATO system, while the French pursued a go-it-alone approach to nuclear deterrence.

Some political theorists argue that the cold war actually promoted peace. Because both East and West were afraid of the effects of nuclear war and of retaliation from the enemy, neither was willing to launch the first missile. The balance of power created by MAD prevented aggression. It also made the United States and the Soviet Union realize how much they both relied upon the stability of deterrence to ensure their own security. Concerned about the prospect of one country possessing the ability to attack the other without fear of retaliation, the two nations began to discuss various arms control proposals in the 1960s.

In August 1963 U.S. president John F. Kennedy and Soviet leader Nikita Khrushchev signed the Limited Test Ban Treaty, which prohibited nuclear testing in the atmosphere, outer space, and the

The wreckage of Hiroshima in September 1946, one year after the atomic bomb was dropped there, attests to the terrible power of nuclear weapons. Although several nations have attained nuclear-weapons capability since 1945, the bombs the United States dropped on the Japanese cities of Hiroshima and Nagasaki during World War II are the only ones that have actually been used in warfare.

oceans. Only underground testing, which presented no risk of radioactive fallout, would be permitted.

In 1968, international negotiators wrote the Nuclear Non-Proliferation Treaty (NPT) to prevent the spread of nuclear weapons to other countries and to oversee the development of peaceful forms of nuclear technology. The United States and the Soviet Union agreed to several strategic arms limitation agreements (SALT I in 1972 and SALT II in 1979) and several test-ban treaties.

In 1983 U.S. president Ronald Reagan pursued a new defensive strategy and announced his plan for the Strategic Defense Initiative (known as Star Wars), which he hoped would protect the United States by creating a military shield in space. The U.S. defense buildup brought the Soviet Union to the negotiating table in a position of weakness. In 1987, Reagan and Soviet leader Mikhail Gorbachev agreed to the Intermediate-Range Nuclear Forces Treaty, which provided for gradual dismantling of all

Soviet and U.S. medium- and short-range missiles in Europe. The negotiations, along with the collapse of the Soviet Union in 1991, spelled the end of the cold war nuclear arms race. In the 1990s both sides reduced the number of missiles and warheads, and each stopped targeting the other's cities.

Nuclear testing has remained a controversial issue, however. Because the radiation effects of nuclear weapons can spread very far from the actual testing site, countries around the world have called for complete bans on nuclear testing, even underground. Many fear the far-reaching negative impact of radiation on the earth's water, soil, animals, and plant life. An international anti-nuclear movement sprang out of the peace protests of the 1960s. To this day, many people around the world oppose the production, proliferation, and use of nuclear weapons. Still, specialists fear that the 21st century may witness one or more nuclear wars, particularly in the Third World or in former Soviet countries, where regulation of nuclear technology has proven difficult and where weapons may be sold to or stolen by terrorists, Third World states, or guerrilla movements. Such wars would not only be locally devastating but would also cause ecological damage throughout the world.

SEE ALSO

Cold war; North Atlantic Treaty Organization (NATO); Reagan, Ronald; Truman, Harry S.; Soviet Union (Union of Soviet Socialist Republics); United States of America; Warsaw Pact

FURTHER READING

Cozic, Charles, and Karin Swisher, eds. *Nuclear Proliferation: Opposing Viewpoints*. San Diego, Calif.: Greenhaven, 1992.

Gregory, Donna Uthus, ed. *The Nuclear Predicament: A Sourcebook*. New York: St. Martin's, 1986.

Herken, Gregg. *The Winning Weapon: The Atomic Bomb in the Cold War, 1945–1950*. New York: Vintage, 1981.

Hersey, John. *Hiroshima*. New York: Bantam, 1975.

Sanford, James, Jr. *Nuclear War Diary*. Byron, Calif.: Front Row, 1989.

Sayle, Murray. "Letter from Hiroshima." *The New Yorker* (July 31, 1995): 40–61.

Smoke, Richard. *National Security and the Nuclear Dilemma: An Introduction to the American Experience in the Cold War*. New York: McGraw-Hill, 1993.

Smoke, Richard. *Think about Nuclear Arms Control: Understanding the Arms Race*. New York: Walker, 1988.

Talbott, Strobe. *Deadly Gambits: The Reagan Administration and the Stalemate in Nuclear Arms Control*. New York: Knopf, 1984.

Nuremberg trials (1945–46)

The Nuremberg trials in 1945–46 established the principle that the international community has a responsibility to punish leaders of nations for crimes against humanity. At the end of World War II the victorious Allied powers established the International Military Tribunal, headquartered in Berlin, to try Nazi leaders for war crimes (including the decision to wage aggressive war in Europe) and crimes against humanity (including the extermination of Jews, Slavs, Gypsies, homosexuals, and people with disabilities). Most trials took place in Nuremberg, Germany, which had been the location of several Nazi Party congresses in the 1930s. (Other trials of low-level officials were held by U.S. military courts elsewhere in Germany.)

The decision to try Nazis for war crimes was ratified by the Allies in the London Agreement for the Prosecution and Punishment of the Major War Criminals of the European Axis, which was signed by France, Great Britain, the United States, and the Soviet Union on August 8, 1945. Based on the initial findings of the United Nations War Crimes Commission in London that crimes had been committed, including crimes against peace (planning an aggressive war), war crimes (atrocities committed during the war), and crimes against humanity (genocide), 21 Nazis were indicted by October 1945 and stood trial in Germany. Each of the four victorious Allied powers—France, Great Britain, the Soviet Union, and the United States—sent one judge and one alternate. The judges relied on established principles of international law regarding admissible uses of force and the treatment of prisoners of war and civilian populations.

Although the Nazi defenses consisted largely in arguing that there was no legal precedent for such trials, the tribunal rejected that argument and proceeded with the trials, which took 10 months. Eleven Nazis received the death sentence and were executed; three

The planner of the Nazi death camps, Albert Speer (standing between soldiers in back row), testifies before the tribunal at the Nuremberg trials at the end of World War II.

were to be imprisoned for life; two were given 20 years in prison, one was given 15 years, and one was given 10 years. Three were found not guilty.

Adolf Hitler, the Nazi leader, had already committed suicide rather than be taken prisoner in Berlin, but many other top Nazi leaders were convicted. They included, among others, Hermann Göring (who committed suicide before his execution), the head of the Luftwaffe (the German air force) that had begun the practice of bombing civilian targets; Joachim von Ribbentrop, the Nazi foreign minister who had created the Axis alliance; and Albert Speer, an architect and planner of labor and death camps.

Four organizations in the German Third Reich were declared criminal organizations. These included the Schutzstaffel, or SS, the elite unit of the Nazi Party. The SS controlled the secret police and intelligence services of the Nazi state and the concentration camps in which genocide occurred. The other or-

ganizations included the Brownshirts (a paramilitary arm of the Nazi Party), the Gestapo (the secret police), and the Leadership Corps of the Nazi Party, which consisted of its top civilian and military leaders.

The Allied Control Council, in charge of governing postwar Germany, ratified all the sentences. Then, through Control Council Law No. 10 of December 20, 1945, it authorized the Allies to establish other "appropriate courts" to try less important war criminals. After the Nuremberg trials, 177 other war criminals were tried, including doctors, lawyers, judges, generals, SS officials, and military contractors. Of these, 24 were sentenced to death, 20 to life imprisonment, and 98 to prison terms of up to 25 years. Eleven of those sentenced to death had their sentences reduced to life imprisonment. In 1951 many of the sentences were reduced by the U.S. High Commissioner to Germany, John McCloy, as part of his policy of permitting low-level Nazis to cooperate with the U.S. occupation authorities in administering the reconstruction.

SEE ALSO
Hitler, Adolf; Nazi Party; War crimes

FURTHER READING
Conot, Robert. *Justice at Nuremberg.* New York: Harper & Row, 1983.
Marrus, Michael R., comp. *The Nuremberg War Crimes Trial, 1945–46: A Documentary History.* Boston: Bedford Books, 1997.
Taylor, Telford. *The Anatomy of the Nuremberg Trials: A Personal Memoir.* New York: Knopf, 1992.

Nyerere, Julius

• *Born: Mar. 1922, Butiama, Tanganyika*

President of Tanzania from 1962 to 1985, Julius Nyerere was the political theorist who formulated the doctrine of African socialism (*Ujamaa*). Though born in a small village in Tanganyika, he was educated at Makerere College in Kampala, Uganda, where he received a B.A. degree in history in 1945. While there, he met many of the young African leaders of independence movements, and he became politically active in opposition to British colonial rule in East Africa. After teaching at a Catholic secondary school in Tanganyika, Nyerere studied British history and politics at the University of Edinburgh in 1952. He then was elected president of the Tanganyika African National Union, an independence movement, in 1954, and negotiated with the British about the terms under which Tanganyika would become independent.

Nyerere became prime minister of Tanganyika when it became independent in 1961, assuming the post of president the following year when the nation

became a republic. In 1964 he joined Tanganyika with Zanzibar, its predominantly Arab island neighbor to the east, to create Tanzania. Nyerere created the self-help program of *Ujamaa* (a Swahili word meaning "togetherness"), which he developed in the late 1960s. This form of African socialism emphasized establishment of rural collectives instead of private ownership of property, and it called for the nationalization of important sectors of the economy. It was a popular program because of its principles, but Tanzania's economy lagged behind that of neighboring Kenya, which was more hospitable to Western development and private enterprise. Tanzania remained committed to *Ujamaa* anyway.

Nyerere was known as Mwalimu (teacher) by leaders of liberation movements that made their headquarters in Dar es Salaam, the capital of Tanzania. After 1975 he chaired the "frontline" states (Angola, Botswana, Mozambique, Tanzania, Zambia, and Zimbabwe) that assisted anti-apartheid forces in their struggle against South Africa's racist regime. In 1978, after Uganda had attacked Tanzania (for supposedly harboring a Ugandan exile force), Nyerere invaded Uganda, removed the bloodthirsty dictator Idi Amin from power, and helped Ugandans gain a semblance of normal life. He continued to

Nyerere meets with President Jimmy Carter of the United States in August 1977. As a supporter of liberation movements in Africa, Nyerere shared a common interest with Carter, who had made human rights the focus of U.S. foreign policy.

champion African socialism and the cause of Third World nations, becoming a leading proponent of the New International Economic Order to adjust trade patterns to benefit Third World nations, a critic of the World Bank and International Monetary Fund (which he believed set onerous terms for aiding African nations), and a leading participant in the Nonaligned Movement, which had been established by developing nations to pursue a course of peace and neutrality during the cold war.

Nyerere was a regal figure who dressed in traditional tribal regalia and constantly toured the countryside, exhorting workers and peasants to advance African socialism. He was revered in Tanzania and was elected president four times. In 1985 he voluntarily gave up power—a rarity in Africa—but remained head of his political party (renamed Chama Cha Mapinduzi [Revolutionary Party of Tanzania]) until 1990, when he retired.

SEE ALSO

New International Economic Order (NIEO); Nonaligned Movement; Socialism; South Africa; Tanzania; Third World; Uganda

FURTHER READING

DuBois, Shirley Graham. *Julius K. Nyerere: Teacher of Africa*. New York: Messner, 1975.
Hatch, John. *Two African Statesmen: Kaunda of Zambia and Nyerere of Tanzania*. Chicago: Regnery, 1976.
Nyerere, Julius. *Crusade for Liberation*. New York: Oxford University Press, 1978.
Nyerere, Julius. *Freedom and Development. Uhuru na Maendeleo. A Selection from Writings and Speeches, 1968–1973*. New York: Oxford University Press, 1973.
Pratt, Cranford. *The Critical Phase in Tanzania, 1945–1968*. New York: Cambridge University Press, 1976.
Smith, William Edgett. *We Must Run While They Walk: A Portrait of Africa's Julius Nyerere*. New York: Random House, 1972.

Oligarchy

Oligarchy (from the Greek words *oligos*, meaning "few," and *arkhes*, meaning "rule") is rule by the few. Oligarchy can be contrasted with rule by the many (democracy) or rule by one (monarchy). The term was used by the Greek philosophers Plato and Aristotle, who distinguished oligarchy (rule of the wealthy few) from aristocracy (rule by the excellent few), because the oligarchs ruled in their own interest rather than for the benefit of society as a whole.

An oligarchy also differs from a kleptocracy, in which government officials seek to amass their fortunes by stealing from the treasury and extorting money from the wealthy.

The typical 20th-century oligarchy consists of large landowning families, their allies within the clergy of an established church, military officers, and agents of the security forces. The oligarchy rules a nation indirectly, by dominating one or more conservative political parties. Oligarchies have been especially influential in most of the Central and South American states, such as Guatemala, Honduras, and Chile, as well as in some of the non-communist states of Asia, such as the Philippines.

Oligarchies have many opponents. Radicals are enemies of the oligarchy because they believe that political power should not be linked to an established church. So are liberals, who prefer free-market capitalism to the state-controlled enterprises and markets rigged by oligarchs to favor their interests as producers. Socialists, social democrats, and communists call for the nationalization of industrial enterprises and large landholdings and for the redistribution of land to poor farmers, all of which make them enemies of the oligarchs.

When an oligarchy faces strong domestic opposition, the military and security forces may engage in intimidation, terror, and torture and rely on death squads to eliminate political opponents. Oligarchies are sometimes overthrown by revolutionary movements after civil wars. During the cold war, the United States often propped up anticommunist oligarchies, such as ones in the Philippines, Malaysia, Thailand, and South Vietnam, against leftist and communist movements, which usually received arms, financing, and military training from the Soviet Union, China, Cuba, North Korea, or other communist states.

A related use of the term *oligarchy* involves Western political parties in multiparty systems. According to the "iron law of oligarchy," formulated by the early-20th-century German sociologist Robert Michels, these political parties—even the social democrats and socialists who advocate democracy and equality—have a tendency to be ruled by a few bosses rather than according to democratic principles.

SEE ALSO

Communism; Conservatism; Democracy; Liberalism; Monarchy; Radicalism; Social democracy; Socialism

Oman

SULTANATE OF OMAN (SALTANAT 'UMAN)

• *Capital: Masqat*

Political history Oman is located in the southeast corner of the Arabian Peninsula. From ancient times, the Omani tribesmen traded with and were some-

This postage stamp proclaims 1993 the "year of the youth" in Oman, which was also enjoying its 23rd year of independence from Great Britain. Oman is one of the few remaining absolute monarchies in the world.

times part of Persian empires until the area was taken over by Portugal from 1507 to 1659, when the Ottoman Turks incorporated it into their holdings. In 1741 it was conquered by the Yemeni Al-Busaid dynasty. During the 19th century, Oman became an important military power, controlling much of the southern Arabian coast, Zanzibar (a trading island off the eastern coast of Africa), the southern coast of Iran, and some of the coast of Baluchistan (southern Pakistan). In the latter part of the 19th century, all these territories freed themselves militarily from Oman's rule.

In 1891 Oman became a British protectorate. It gained its full sovereignty through a treaty of friendship with Great Britain in 1951, though it remained under British military protection. It was known as the Sultanate of Muscat and Oman until 1970, when the British withdrew their military forces—after finding the cost of maintaining a military presence in the Middle East prohibitive—and it assumed the name Oman.

Government institutions Oman is an absolute monarchy. The monarch, known as the sultan (since 1970, Qaboos bin Said), appoints a cabinet that exercises executive power. There is a consultative council (the Majlis-ash-

Shoura) composed of representatives, appointed by the sultan, from each tribal clan; the council advises the sultan on his decrees and regulations and represents the interests of the 59 *wilayats* (districts). Sultan Qaboos is unmarried, has no royal heirs, and as of the mid-1990s had devised no mechanism for succession. The most likely candidates to succeed him are three royal cousins.

Parties and movements There are no legal parties or movements permitted by the sultan. The opposition groups have organized into the Popular Front for the Liberation of Oman (PFLO), a clandestine movement that seeks the overthrow of the sultan and the establishment of a popular regime.

Domestic issues Oil is Oman's main source of revenue. The country is trying to diversify its economy, however, in case the oil runs out and to protect itself from oil price fluctuations. Fifteen percent of oil revenues are allocated to a General Reserve Fund, which makes investments for the government. Under Sultan Qaboos, Oman has transformed itself from an isolated and backward nation into a prosperous one, as the government has built schools, roads, hospitals, and modern housing. Women have been granted civil rights and permitted to join the work force. Slavery, not uncommon in the 1960s, has been abolished.

Oman's oil reserves will be depleted by 2015, and the prospect of losing its main source of revenue has created political instability. More than 100 high-ranking officials were arrested in 1994, charged with plotting to overthrow the sultan. The sultan has been criticized for lavish spending and for building up the military with unneeded equipment. The World Bank has criticized Oman for squandering its oil revenues on unneeded projects.

International issues Two-thirds of the oil from the Middle East (and 40 percent of the world's oil) passes through the Strait of Hormuz, between the Arabian Peninsula and Iran, giving Oman—whose northern tip forms one edge of the strait—strategic importance for the West. In 1980 the United States and Oman signed a defense agreement providing for U.S. bases in the sultanate, which enabled Oman to resist Soviet and Iranian pressure to pursue an anti-Western foreign policy. Since 1991, Oman has permitted the United States to base C-130 transport planes and equipment for the U.S. Rapid Reaction Force (designed to arrive within days of a crisis situation to project U.S. force) in the Middle East.

Oman and Yemen cut relations in the 1970s because of Yemeni support for a leftist guerrilla movement in Oman's southern Dhofar Province, but in the late 1980s trade and cooperation resumed.

Oman, viewing Iraq as a threat to its own security, supported the international force that liberated Kuwait from Iraqi occupation in 1991.

SEE ALSO
Sultanate

FURTHER READING
Allen, Calvin. *Oman: The Modernization of the Sultanate*. Boulder, Colo.: Westview, 1987.
Skeet, Ian. *Oman: Politics and Development*. New York: St. Martin's, 1991.

One-party state

A one-party state is a nation-state in which political power is exercised by a single political party. No opposition parties are permitted. Within the single party, contests may be held for nomi-

Polish communists proclaim their loyalty to the Soviet Union at a party conference in Warsaw in October 1956. After World War II, communist governments established dictatorships in much of Eastern Europe.

nations to public office, which permit various factions or tendencies within the party to test their strength.

In the general election, there is only one slate of candidates for the offices to be filled. Elections at best are votes of confidence in the regime: low turnouts, spoiled ballots (those defaced by the voter), or write-in votes are the only ways to indicate dissent. To combat such forms of dissent, totalitarian states mobilize their electorates and require that everyone vote and then usually report favorable votes in the 99 percent range.

Fascist and communist movements established one-party totalitarian states upon attaining power in Russia, Italy, and Germany between 1917 and 1933. In Africa and the Middle East, the nationalist independence movements that gained power after World War II transformed themselves into parties and then monopolized political power. The military regimes that overthrew many of the civilian governments in Africa, Asia, and Latin America also organized parties or movements that allowed no opposition, such as the regime of Augusto Pinochet in Chile or the military junta that took power in Myanmar in 1988.

In some states a single party plays a dominant role but permits minor parties to exist, provided they do not challenge its political power. In Poland and

Hungary, for example, peasant parties were permitted in "popular front" coalitions with the Communist Party when the Communists took power after World War II.

Most one-party states began transforming themselves into multiparty democracies in the 1990s, partly as a result of the collapse of the Soviet Union, its withdrawal from Eastern Europe, and its loss of influence in Africa and Asia. To some extent, these transformations involved modest concessions to the demands of First World nations providing foreign aid, but in many cases these new governments emerged because of the pro-democracy demands made by students, trade unionists, and intellectuals.

SEE ALSO

Communism; Democracy; Fascism; Multiparty democracy; Totalitarianism

FURTHER READING

Zolberg, Aristide. *Creating Political Order: The Party States of West Africa.* Chicago: University of Chicago Press, 1966.

Organization for Economic Cooperation and Development (OECD)

The OECD was founded in 1961 by the First World industrial democracies to promote their economic prosperity. It succeeded the Organization for European Economic Cooperation, created in 1948, that had used U.S. economic aid under the Marshall Plan to reconstruct Western Europe after World War II. By the early 1990s the OECD consisted of the following European nations: Austria,

Belgium, Denmark, Finland, France, Germany, Greece, Iceland, Ireland, Italy, Luxembourg, the Netherlands, Norway, Portugal, Spain, Sweden, Switzerland, and the United Kingdom. It also included the following non-European nations: Australia, Japan, Mexico, New Zealand, Turkey, and the United States. The OECD has named Hungary, Poland, the Czech Republic, and Slovakia as "partners in transition," because these nations have adopted free-market economies and have multiparty democratic political systems. The OECD in 1995 signed a cooperation agreement with Russia that permits the exchange of economic data and allows Russia to benefit from OECD expertise in economic forecasting.

Each nation is represented on the OECD Council, which in turn has a 14-member Executive Committee to prepare its agenda for the coordination of economic and social policies. A secretariat based in Paris administers OECD programs.

The OECD has more than 200 committees and special agencies, assisted by a staff of close to 2,000 economists. The most important unit is the Economic Policy Committee, consisting of central bankers and economic policymakers in each nation. It attempts to coordinate fiscal and monetary policies. The Development Assistance Committee meets to coordinate economic development aid to Third World nations. The Group on North-South issues deals with conflicts between First and Third World nations, especially proposals for a New International Economic Order, proposed by Third World nations. The OECD was instrumental in the creation of the International Energy Agency, which stockpiles oil reserves used to intervene in markets when the Organization of Petroleum Exporting Countries (OPEC) oil cartel

attempts to raise prices. Under U.S. prodding, the OECD in the 1990s has turned to the study of international trade issues, corporate pollution in manufacturing, and the rights of labor to organize.

SEE ALSO

First World; Marshall Plan; New International Economic Order (NIEO); Third World

FURTHER READING

Camps, Miriam. *First World Relationships: The Role of the OECD.* New York, Council on Foreign Relations, 1975.

Organization of African Unity (OAU)

The OAU was founded in 1963 by the independent nations in Africa (except for the apartheid regime in South Africa) to promote peace and stability on the African continent, improve living standards, defend the sovereignty and territorial integrity of African states, and eradicate colonial and white-minority rule in Africa. South Africa is now a member of the OAU. In 1984 Morocco withdrew from the organization in protest over the admission of the Sahrawi Arab Democratic Republic (also known as Western Sahara), a territory occupied by Morocco.

The OAU Assembly of Heads of State meets annually, and resolutions must be passed by a two-thirds majority. Its Council of Ministers meets twice a year. The General Secretariat is located in Addis Ababa, Ethiopia.

In 1964 the OAU rejected appeals by the Pan-Africanist Kwame Nkrumah, prime minister of Ghana, to promote the creation of a "United States of Africa" as a political confederation. It limited itself to working instead for "solidarity and cooperation." The OAU has mediated disputes between warring nations on the continent (Ethiopia and Somalia), settled boundary disputes (Morocco and Algeria), attempted reconciliation of factions in civil wars (Nigeria and Liberia), formed an African Anti-Apartheid Committee to promote a boycott of South Africa, and attempted to work out debt-reduction agreements with Western nations. The OAU has adopted an African Charter of Human and People's Rights but has not attempted to protect human rights when regimes violate them, because it will not violate the sovereignty of member states.

SEE ALSO

Nkrumah, Kwame

FURTHER READING

El-Ayouty, Yassin, and William Zartman, eds. *The OAU after Twenty Years*. New York: Praeger, 1984.

Organization of American States (OAS)

The OAS was created in 1948 in Bogotá, Colombia, at the Ninth International Conference of American States. Its purpose is to promote unity and cooperation among the nations of the Western Hemisphere. The OAS was the successor to the International Union of American Republics (known as the Pan-American Union), which had been founded in 1890.

The OAS consists of 35 nations in the hemisphere. Cuba is a member, but its communist government was suspended from OAS activities in 1962 be-

cause of its subversive activities against other countries in the hemisphere. The OAS General Assembly meets annually to set policy. The ministers of foreign affairs of the member nations hold "meetings of consultation" when needed to consider urgent problems. The Permanent Council, which meets regularly at OAS headquarters in Washington, D.C., consists of each nation's ambassador to the OAS.

The OAS implements the Inter-American Treaty of Reciprocal Assistance (Rio Pact) signed in Rio de Janeiro, Brazil, in 1947, which requires nations of the hemisphere to act in concert to repel outside aggression. A two-thirds vote of the OAS may trigger sanctions or military action against an aggressor, something which was done in 1962 when the OAS backed the U.S. quarantine of Cuba after that nation had accepted nuclear missiles from the Soviet Union. The OAS also implements the Charter of Punta del Este, signed in Uruguay in 1961, which pledged inter-American efforts to advance social and economic progress in the hemisphere and which was followed by the creation of the Alliance for Progress.

The OAS maintains specialized councils, conferences, organizations,

The OAS has its headquarters in Washington, D.C. Over the years, the organization has struggled to balance the sometimes opposing interests of the United States and the countries of Latin America.

and committees. The Inter-American Economic and Social Council promotes efforts at regional economic integration; the Inter-American Council for Education, Science, and Culture promotes exchanges of scholars and researchers; the Inter-American Commission on Human Rights reports on human rights abuses in the Western Hemisphere; the Inter-American Court of Human Rights, based in San José, Costa Rica, hears complaints by member states; the Inter-American Defense Board plans for the common defense and operates the Inter-American Defense College to train military officers of Latin American nations; and the OAS Verification Commission monitors elections and in 1989–90 aided in the transition from Sandinista rule to multiparty democracy in Nicaragua.

The OAS often serves as a sounding board for Latin American complaints against the United States, including protests over U.S. military intervention and calls for renegotiation of debts owed by Latin American nations to U.S. banks. But the OAS also serves the purposes of the U.S. government. The OAS has backed the United States on some foreign policy issues, including the U.S. quarantine of Cuba during the Missile Crisis of 1962 and the invasion of the Dominican Republic in 1965 by U.S. Marines to install a government favorable to U.S. interests. However, U.S. invasions of Grenada in 1982 and Panama in 1989 were not sanctioned by the OAS, because the OAS considered these invasions to be interference in the internal affairs of member states, although the organization took no actions opposing the invasions in order not to antagonize the United States. The OAS was unable to take action against the U.S.-backed contras in their civil war activities against Nicaragua in the mid-1980s, due to the opposition of the United States to the Sandinista regime.

SEE ALSO
Pan-American Union; United Nations (UN)

FURTHER READING
Scheman, L. Ronald. *The Inter-American Dilemma*. New York: Praeger, 1988.
Vaky, Viron. *The Future of the Organization of American States*. New York: Twentieth Century Fund, 1993.

Organization of Central American States (OCAS)

The OCAS is a regional association founded in 1951 that promotes economic, political, and cultural cooperation among Central American states. OCAS was founded in 1951 by Costa Rica, El Salvador, Guatemala, Honduras, and Nicaragua. It has its headquarters in San Salvador, El Salvador.

Members' heads of state and foreign ministers meet to discuss issues involving national security and regional development. The Legislative Council, consisting of representatives from each nation's parliament, meets to promote uniform commercial laws. The Court of Justice decides cases submitted by member nations. The Cultural and Educational Council promotes cultural exchanges; the Defense Council provides a forum for defense ministers to consult on matters of mutual concern; and the Central American Bureau, headed by a secretary-general, serves as a secretariat and organizes ministerial and presidential conferences.

The OCAS serves as a forum for discussion, but like most regional organizations, it does not actually do anything concrete.

Organization of Eastern Caribbean States (OECS)

The Organization of Eastern Caribbean States was founded in 1981 by seven newly independent island nation-states that had formerly belonged to the West Indies Associated States. In addition, the British Virgin Islands is an associate member.

The OECS attempts to coordinate foreign policy and domestic economic development. Policy is set by the Authority of Heads of Government, and there are committees of ministers for foreign affairs, defense policy, and economic affairs.

In 1982 the OECS formally requested U.S. intervention in Grenada, one of its member states then in the midst of a civil war between two military factions, to restore order and preserve lives and property. Members did so because they were concerned about Marxist political parties and movements in the Caribbean, which they viewed as a threat to the existing pro-Western island regimes.

Organization of Petroleum Exporting Countries (OPEC)

OPEC was established in 1960 to coordinate export and production policies among petroleum-exporting nations. Members in the early 1990s included Algeria, Gabon, Indonesia, Iran, Iraq, Kuwait, Libya, Nigeria, Qatar, Saudi

Arabia, the United Arab Emirates, and Venezuela. (Ecuador was a member but resigned in 1983. Iraq's oil exports were embargoed by the United Nations after it invaded Kuwait in 1990.)

OPEC establishes production quotas for its members in an attempt to stabilize prices by keeping supply on the world market in balance with demand. It also sets a pricing schedule to which OPEC nations pledge adherence, although member nations frequently ignore the quotas (by producing and exporting greater amounts) and the prices (by offering lower prices to gain market share).

The OPEC Conference is the highest authority, consisting of the petroleum ministers of each nation. The Board of Governors manages the organization. The OPEC Economic Commission conducts studies on pricing policies and recommends changes. The OPEC news agency provides the media with its point of view on issues. At times, OPEC takes advantage of the world demand for oil to post huge price increases, as in 1973 and 1979, when oil prices tripled. At other times, as in 1983, sharp decreases in demand for oil due to conservation measures or industrial recessions have led to production cutbacks. These are controversial, and some members cheat on their quotas, offering buyers hidden

Flanked by advisers, Ahmed Zaki Yumani, the Saudi oil minister, considers a price hike at the 1980 meeting of OPEC. The organization includes nations from Africa, South America, and the Middle East.

discounts, or even threaten to withdraw from the organization. Because OPEC has no way to impose sanctions against violators, its efforts to control prices have been unreliable.

In the 1970s OPEC controlled more than half of the world's oil production; in the 1990s it was down to less than 40 percent. This has reduced its influence on petroleum prices, which in the early 1990s were considerably lower than in the late 1970s.

OPEC is dominated by Saudi Arabia, the largest exporter of oil in the world. Its dependence on the United States for security assistance and its excessive spending on military weapons and grandiose development projects have given it an incentive to expand production, which serves to moderate world oil prices, against the wishes of Iran, which has attempted to restrict output and raise prices.

SEE ALSO
Saudi Arabia

FURTHER READING
Ahrari, Mohammed. *OPEC: The Failing Giant*. Lexington: University of Kentucky Press, 1986.
Cook, William J. "Why OPEC Doesn't Matter Anymore." *U.S. News & World Report*, Dec. 13, 1993, 73.
Skeet, Ian. *OPEC: Twenty-five Years of Prices and Politics*. New York: Cambridge University Press, 1988.

Ortega, Daniel

• *Born: Nov. 11, 1945, La Libertad, Nicaragua*

Daniel Ortega was the leader of the Sandinista National Liberation Front, a guerrilla movement that overthrew the dictatorship of Anastasio Somoza in Nicaragua in 1979. Ortega headed the junta that assumed power between 1979 and 1984 and served as president of Nicaragua from 1984 to 1990.

Ortega's father had been a peasant soldier in the rebel army of César Augusto Sandino, a patriot who had fought against U.S. military occupation of Nicaragua in the 1930s. Daniel Ortega was educated at schools in Managua, then briefly attended Central American University there. He dropped out when the secret police began investigating him for radical activities.

In 1963 Ortega joined the Sandinista National Liberation Front, an organization attempting to overthrow the Somoza regime by force, and headed its urban wing in Managua. He was captured in 1967 for taking part in a bank robbery (in order to provide funds for his movement) and imprisoned until 1974, when he was released in exchange for hostages taken by the Sandinista guerrillas. Ortega went briefly to Cuba for training in guerrilla warfare, then slipped back into Nicaragua to rejoin the Sandinistas. He was instrumental in forging a broad-based coalition of religious, business, and labor leaders in opposition to the dictatorial Somoza regime.

In 1978 Ortega became one of the nine *comandantes* leading the revolution. After the overthrow of the Somoza regime, Ortega became one of the five members of the ruling junta, quickly assuming the role of leader. He established ties with Cuba and the Soviet Union and was soon embroiled in a struggle with the administration of Ronald Reagan in the United States and the counterrevolutionary force, or contras, in Nicaragua that it supported.

In 1984 Ortega became the coordinator of the revamped three-member junta and government council, and he was elected president in elections held that year. He was interested in economic development, but through most of his presidency his major efforts were devoted to repelling attacks by the contras, a paramilitary force organized and financed by the United States that sought the overthrow of the Sandinista regime. Though he was defeated in the 1990 presidential election by Violeta Chamorro, a moderate former member of the junta who was now backed by the United States, Ortega remained the leader of the Sandinista National Liberation Front.

Ortega was idealistic and courageous as a military *comandante,* and his efforts to rid Nicaragua of a cruel dictator were successful because he had the backing of the vast majority of the Nicaraguan people. But his unwillingness to permit a real multiparty democracy—however understandable in the context of a bitter civil war—and his inability to master the intricacies of postwar economic reconstruction and development prevented him and his colleagues from institutionalizing their revolutionary movement and converting Nicaragua from a traditional oligarchical system into a modern and progressive democracy.

SEE ALSO

Chamorro, Violeta Barrios de; Nicaragua

FURTHER READING

Booth, John. *The End and the Beginning: The Nicaraguan Revolution.* Boulder, Colo.: Westview, 1985.
Cockcroft, James D. *Daniel Ortega.* New York: Chelsea House, 1991.
Miranda, Roger. *The Civil War in Nicaragua: Inside the Sandinistas.* New Brunswick, N.J.: Transaction, 1993.

Ottoman Empire

The Ottoman Empire was created from what is now Turkey, Central Asia, and the Balkans in the 14th century by Turkic-speaking Islamic tribes from Central Asia led by Osman I and his successors. They expanded their territories in the aftermath of the collapse of the Christian Byzantine Empire. Led by Osman's heirs Murad I and Bayezid I, the Ottomans conquered all of Anatolia (now Turkey) between 1300 and 1402, moving as well into Thrace and Macedonia (Greece), Bulgaria, and Serbia. The empire, under Murad II and Mehmed II, consolidated its rule in the Balkans south of the Danube River by 1453. In the early 1500s the Ottomans, led now by Selim I and then Süleyman I, doubled the size of their empire by seizing what is now Syria, Palestine, Egypt, and Algeria, which had been ruled by the Mamluks (descendants of Turkish military slaves who had established their own empire based in Egypt). The Ottomans also conquered Hungary and moved down the Euphrates River to conquer Iraq and through the Mediterranean to take control of Tripoli. By the end of the 17th century, the Ottomans had won Caucasia (Armenia, Azerbaijan, and Georgia).

In the 19th century the Ottoman Empire began its territorial decline. In 1878, after the first Russo-Turk War, the Congress of Berlin forced the Ottomans to give up Romania, Serbia, Montenegro, Bulgaria, Cyprus, and other territories. In 1882 the British replaced the Ottomans as the dominant power in Egypt by intervening to remove a reformist government that had taken power from the ruling pashas. By 1913 the Ottomans had been expelled from the remainder of the Balkans.

The Ottomans sided with Germany during World War I, and after the war its Arab possessions were transferred to Great Britain and France to be ruled as mandates under the League of Nations; these included Lebanon, Syria, Iraq, Palestine, and Transjordan. The Ottomans

OTTOMAN EMPIRE 1 5 2 9 – 1 7 8 9

retained their rule only on the Anatolian peninsula—in what is now Turkey.

The Ottoman emperor Mehmed VI was overthrown by revolutionaries led by Kemal Atatürk in 1922. The new regime ended the religious caliphate, the office of the Islamic religious leaders who had supported Ottoman rule, and created the modern secular nation-state of Turkey.

SEE ALSO

Atatürk, Ghazi Mustafa Kemal; Balkans; Imperialism; League of Nations; Turkey

FURTHER READING

Inalcik, Halil. *The Ottoman Empire: The Classical Age, 1300–1600.* New York: Praeger, 1973.
Kinross, Patrick. *The Ottoman Centuries.* New York: Morrow, 1977.
Palmer, Alan. *The Decline and Fall of the Ottoman Empire.* New York: M. Evans, 1992.
Wheatcroft, Andrew. *The Ottomans.* London: Viking, 1993.

Pakistan

ISLAMIC REPUBLIC OF PAKISTAN (ISLAM-I JAMHURIYA-E PAKISTAN)

• *Capital: Islamabad*

Political history The Harrapan civilization flourished in the northern Indus Valley, located in southern present-day Pakistan, between 4000 and 2500 B.C.; the Harrapans also settled at Mohenjo-Daro to the southwest. After 1500 B.C. Aryan-speaking invaders from the Indian subcontinent established Hindu civilizations, which were later conquered by the Persians, Greeks, and Sassanids from the west. The Indus Valley was conquered by Alexander the Great, then incorporated into the Mauryan empire of Aśoka, the Bud-

These Pakistani soldiers are members of the famed Khyber Rifles regiment, which dates back to the period of British rule of Pakistan.

dhist king of India who controlled most of the Indian subcontinent in the 3rd century B.C.

Islam was introduced after the Arab invasion of the subcontinent in 712, and the local populations converted. Muslim Moguls conquered most of the Indian subcontinent after 1526, but the British East India Company controlled the Indus Valley by 1760.

Hindus became the dominant population in central India, while in the northwest and southeast of the subcontinent much of the population was Muslim. In 1867 both Hindu and Muslim areas came under direct colonial administration as part of the British India Crown Colony. After World War I the newly formed Muslim League—an organization devoted to the advancement of the Muslim population—began to push for a separate Islamic state for the Muslim parts of the subcontinent. Although Hindu leaders in India wished for a single state, advocates of partition won the day.

The Muslim League and the predominantly Hindu Congress Party joined forces against British colonial rule, and by 1947 the British had agreed to end their rule and partition the subcontinent. Pakistan, the Muslim area, was constituted as a dominion within the British Commonwealth in 1947 under provisions of the Indian Independence Act; it consisted of two widely separated provinces, East and West Pakistan, with the western province dominating the government because of its larger population. Pakistan became a republic within the Commonwealth of Nations in 1956. In 1971, after chafing under the autocratic rule of West Pakistan, the province of East Pakistan declared its independence as the People's Republic of Bangladesh.

Through much of Pakistan's history, the country has been governed in an authoritarian way by military rulers. Since 1988, however, after the death in a plane crash of General Zia-ul-Huq (who ruled between 1977 and 1988), it has made the transition to a multiparty democracy. The military still considers itself to be a stabilizing force, ready to step in if a civilian politician cannot maintain order and provide effective government.

Government institutions Pakistan is a federal state with four provinces, a federal capital district, and tribal areas administered by the central government. But with provincial governors appointed by the central government, it has become more unitary than federal in practice.

When not run by the military, Pakistan has a semi-presidential system. The president is the head of state, and a prime minister and cabinet responsible to parliament (since 1988) run the government. Legislative power is exercised by a bicameral parliament consisting of a 73-member Senate, elected by the provincial assemblies, and a 217-member National Assembly, to which Muslims elect 207 members and religious minorities choose 10. An attempt by prime minister Nawaz Sharif to limit the powers of president Ghulam Ishaq Khan and establish a parliamentary system was defeated in 1993, when the army insisted that both the president and prime minister resign and new elections take place.

Parties and movements When Pakistan is not run by military rulers, it has a multiparty democratic system. The main parties are the Islamic Democratic Alliance (a conservative party based in the populous southern province of Punjab) and the Pakistan People's Party (liberal) based in the province of Sind. The Islamic Democratic Alliance favors a parliamentary system, whereas the Pakistan People's Party prefers a strong presidential system. The latter party won the parliamentary elections in 1993 (though it did not obtain a majority) with the army ensuring a fair election. Benazir Bhutto— the daughter of a former Pakistani prime minister who was executed by the military—assumed power as prime minister. She was forced to resign in 1996 amid charges of political corruption.

In 1997 Bhutto's Pakistan People's Party (PPP) was defeated by the Muslim League, which won 140 seats in the 217-seat National Assembly, while the PPP won only 25. Led by Prime Minister Nawaz Sharif, the Muslim League hoped to form a government that could complete a full five-year term—something no cabinet in Pakistan has achieved since independence in 1947.

Domestic issues Pakistan is home to many different ethnic groups that speak a variety of languages (with English and Urdu the official languages). The Punjabis, in the northeast, are the largest group, followed by the Pashtuns in the northwest and the Sindhis in the southeast. Smaller groups include the Baluchis in the southwest and the Muhajirs (Muslims who fled from India in 1947) living around Karachi. Pakistan suffers from ethnic unrest in the Sind and Baluchistan provinces. The introduction of the Islamic legal code called *sharī'a* (laws based on Islamic religious principles) in 1991 has been criticized by Bhutto and the Pakistan People's Party.

Government corruption and poor economic performance have marked rule by both major parties and the prior military regimes. A militant Islamic movement, the Mohajir Qaumi Movement, centered in Karachi, engaged in a terror campaign in the mid-1990s to secure the civil rights of the Muhajirs. There is also conflict between the majority Sunni Muslims and minority Shiites. The militant Sipah-e-Sahaba group of Sunnis has pressured the government to declare the Shiites a non-Muslim minority; it is opposed by the Sipah-e-Muhammed (a Shiite group). In response to armed clashes between these groups, the government cut funding to all religious schools in 1996.

International issues Pakistan has fought a number of wars with India since the partition, one of which resulted in independence for Bangladesh. It looks to China and the United States, as counterweights against India, to provide it with weapons and diplomatic support. Armed border conflict in the Kashmir region between India and Pakistan has threatened to erupt into major war for decades, and at times the two nations have engaged in military skirmishes in the area using ballistic missiles, heavy artillery, and other strategic weapons to strike villages across the Line of Control separating the two sides. Pakistan has threatened to build ballistic missiles if India continues to develop its medium-range Prithvi-2 missile, which can carry nuclear warheads.

The United States opposes Pakistan's efforts to become a nuclear power. The United States suspended foreign aid to Pakistan in 1990 because it had not signed the Nuclear Non-Proliferation Treaty, which pledges signatories to refrain from developing atomic weapons. Discussions resumed in 1993 on ways to end the impasse, and transfers of U.S. military equipment resumed in July 1996. The United States provided assistance to Pakistan in closing down bases of more than 1,000 Islamic terrorists in the North-West Frontier Province after members of these groups were linked to terrorist attacks in western Europe and the United States, including the 1993 bombing of the World Trade Center in New York City and the deaths of two U.S. diplomats in Karachi.

Pakistan served as a major base for anticommunist Islamic rebels fighting against the Soviet occupation of Afghanistan in the 1980s; it accepted many Afghan refugees and backed Afghanistan's interim coalition government. In the mid-1990s Pakistan supported the Muslim government in Bosnia and Herzegovina and the UN peacekeeping efforts there. In 1972 Pakistan withdrew from the Commonwealth of Nations but rejoined it in 1989 after returning to democratic rule.

Human rights Pakistan in the 1990s permitted thousands of children to work in factories, producing goods for U.S. markets, including soccer balls and handwoven carpets. Children have been sold by their parents into industrial slavery, then branded and beaten into accepting factory work conditions.

Pakistan's Commission on Human Rights estimates that 11 million children under the age of 14 work in factories or fields and that one-quarter of the work force consists of children. The median age of children entering the work force is 7.

SEE ALSO

Bangladesh; Bhutto, Benazir; Commonwealth of Nations; India

FURTHER READING

Burki, Shadid J. *Pakistan.* 2nd ed. Boulder, Colo.: Westview, 1991.
Iftikhar, Malik. *State and Civil Society in Pakistan.* New York: St. Martin's, 1996.
Jalal, Ayesha. *Democracy and Authoritarianism in South Asia.* New York: Cambridge University Press, 1995.
Jalal, Ayesha. *The State of Martial Rule: The Origins of Pakistan's Political Economy of Defence.* New York: Cambridge University Press, 1990.
Schanberg, Sydney. "Six Cents an Hour." *Life* (June 1996): 38-42.

Palau

REPUBLIC OF PALAU (BELU'U ERA BELAU)

• *Capital: Koror*

Political history Located in the western Pacific Ocean, Palau is a chain of 200 islands. The first inhabitants, the Belau, came from Indonesia and the Philippines in approximately 1500 B.C. The first European to visit was the Portuguese navigator Ferdinand Magellan in 1521. The island was a British trading stop in the 17th and 18th centuries. It was a Spanish colony between 1885 and 1899, when Spain sold the islands to Germany, which wanted to mine its phosphate deposits. Japan occupied the islands in 1914; they were later captured by the United States during World War II.

The United States administered Palau as a UN trusteeship from 1947 until October 1994, when Palau voted to become a sovereign nation—the last of the 11 UN trusteeships to do so.

Government institutions Palau is a republic and the head of state is the president, who has all executive powers. There is a bicameral Olbiil Era Kelulau (congress) that exercises legislative powers. The independent judiciary is headed by a supreme court.

Parties and movements The two main parties are the Coalition for Open, Honest, and Just Government, which favored political reform and an end to corruption, and the Ta Belau Party, which favored continuing commonwealth status with the United States.

Domestic issues Palau has engaged in an austerity program since gaining independence. But the main domestic issue involves political corruption.

International issues The United States, which has two naval bases in the islands and exclusive naval access to Palau's territorial waters, is responsible for Palau's defense. In addition, the United States and Japan provide most of Palau's foreign aid and private investment.

SEE ALSO
Trust territories

Palestine

Palestine, the territory in southwest Asia lying between the Jordan River and the Mediterranean Sea, was known as the Land of Canaan by the early tribes in the 15th century B.C. Jews fleeing the pharaohs in Egypt settled in the area around 1200 B.C. and established the Kingdom of Israel. That kingdom split into two separate kingdoms, Israel and Judaea, after the death of King Solomon.

Israel was conquered by the Assyrians in 722 B.C. and Judaea by the Babylonians in 586 B.C. In the late 4th century the area was conquered by Alexander the Great. A Jewish revolt against Greek rule led to establishment of an independent Jewish state in 141 B.C. But the Jews were conquered by the Romans in 70 B.C., who established the provincial administration of Palestine, ruling the local Jewish population through kings of the Herodian dynasty.

In A.D. 66 a rebellion was crushed, and in 70 the Romans destroyed the Temple at Jerusalem and expelled many Jews. A second rebellion was ended by force in 132. By the 4th century A.D. Palestine had become a province of the Byzantine Empire and a center for Christian monasteries and pilgrimages. It was conquered by the Arabs and became part of the Arabian Empire in 636; it was then governed by the Muslim religious leaders, or caliphate, at Damascus after 661 and by the caliphate at Baghdad after 762.

In 1099 the Crusaders from western Europe attempted to reintroduce Christianity, and they established the Latin Kingdom of Jerusalem, but they were driven out by the Muslims within two decades. Palestine was conquered by the Mongols in 1258, but they were driven out by the Egyptians in 1260, and the territory was then ruled as part of the Mamluk Empire from Cairo. In 1516 it was conquered by the Ottomans.

After World War I, Palestine became a British mandate under the auspices of the League of Nations. The British government had already stated in the Balfour Declaration of 1917 that it viewed "with favour the establishment in Palestine of a national home for the Jewish people . . . it being clearly understood that nothing shall be done which may prejudice the civil and religious rights of existing non-Jewish communities."

Jews began to immigrate to Palestine from Russia and eastern Europe, fleeing acts of anti-Semitism in the late 19th century. In 1921 a proposed constitution for a Palestinian state was rejected by the Arabs in the region, because it would have permitted massive Jewish immigration and other concessions to the Zionist movement (organizations of Jews in Europe and North America supporting a Jewish homeland in Palestine). The proposed state was also rejected by the Jews, because they would be outnumbered by Arabs. Civil unrest between the growing Jewish community and the Arab majority broke out in the 1920s and in 1936 and lasted through 1939. The Arabs then rejected a plan for the partition of Palestine recommended by a British Royal Commission.

In 1939 the British changed course. They now called for power sharing between the 750,000 Arabs and 450,000 Jews in a unified Palestinian state to be established by 1949. Their policy limited Jewish immigration to 75,000 annually through 1944. These limits were ignored by Jews fleeing Nazi persecution and concentration camps during World War II, who entered Palestine illegally. At the end of the war the League of Arab States, consisting of most of the states in the Middle East, insisted that Palestine be given independence and be controlled by the Arab majority. The Jewish Agency, a Zionist organization responsible for establishing Jewish institutions in Palestine, supported partition so that the Jews could control their own state. The British turned the issue over to the

United Nations. A majority of the nations then members were sympathetic to the Jewish cause because of the genocide committed against Jews in the Holocaust; as a result, resolutions of the UN General Assembly in 1947 recommended a partition plan.

Jews proclaimed the State of Israel on May 14, 1948, in the territory granted to them by the United Nations. Refusing to accept partition, five Arab armies (from Egypt, Jordan, Iraq, Syria, and Lebanon) invaded Israel with the objective of establishing an Arab state of Palestine over the entire area. The Israelis repulsed the invasion and gained additional territory not contemplated in the UN plan. Of the remaining lands that the UN allotted to the Palestinians (the Arabs living in the partitioned area), the territory around Gaza (a strip of land on the Sinai Peninsula) came under Egyptian administration (and became known as the Gaza Strip), while areas of Palestine west of the Jordan River and East Jerusalem (together known as the West Bank) were incorporated into the Hashemite Kingdom of Jordan. More than 700,000 Arabs fled or were expelled from Israel during the conflict; many went to refugee camps in Gaza, the West Bank, and surrounding Arab countries. Only 160,000 of the original 750,000 Palestinians remained in Israel

Palestinian children listen as a teacher reads to them in a tent school established for refugees in the Gaza Strip in 1951. Almost half a century later, many Palestinians still live in refugee camps throughout the Middle East.

after the armistice of 1949. Within the next decade, hundreds of thousands of Jews in Egypt, Morocco, Yemen, and other Arab states immigrated into Israel, many after being pressured to leave by the Arab states that had opposed the creation of Israel.

In 1964 the Palestine Liberation Organization (PLO) was created by the Palestinian refugees to work for the establishment of a Palestinian state on the territory of Israel. In the late 1980s Palestinians in the territories occupied by Israel in the 1967 Six-Day War engaged in acts of civil insurrection known as the *intifada* (which means "uprising").

In the early 1990s Israelis and Palestinians sought a compromise that would end their conflict. After secret negotiations in Oslo, Norway, Yasir Arafat, chairman of the PLO, wrote a letter of recognition to Israeli prime minister Yitzhak Rabin, stating that "the PLO recognizes the right of the State of Israel to exist in peace and security." The two men signed a Declaration of Principles late in 1993 calling for negotiations on an Israeli withdrawal from West Bank lands. After further negotiations, on May 4, 1994, the PLO and Israel agreed on the Framework for Peace, involving a transitional period in which autonomy would be granted to the Gaza Strip, the area around the town of Jericho, and other towns, all of which would be administered by a Palestinian Authority. The Israeli-Palestinian Interim Agreement, signed in Washington, D.C., on September 28, 1995, specified how the Framework for Peace would be implemented as the Israelis withdrew. It also provided for Israeli protection of the 130,000 settlers on the West Bank and the 3,300 Israelis in the Gaza Strip. By 1996 most of the large towns on the West Bank—including Jenin, Tulkarm, Nablus, Qalqilya, Ramallah, Bethlehem, and Jericho—and the Gaza Strip were controlled by the Palestinians. Further negotiations would be held on water rights in the area, on the future of Jerusalem (which Jews wished to keep undivided but Arabs wanted to partition), and the possibility of a sovereign Arab state in Palestine. A permanent accord was to be negotiated and implemented by September 1998, though that timetable was abandoned after negotiations stalled in 1997.

In 1996 the Palestinian Authority held its first elections. Yasir Arafat won 88.1 percent of the vote for president, defeating Samiha Khalil, an opponent of the accord with Israel. The legislative branch of the Palestinian Authority, the Palestinian Council, was dominated by Arafat's followers, who won 66 of the 88 seats on the council. The militant Islamic movement Hamas boycotted the elections, claiming that the peace process itself was flawed and that peace could not be achieved with the Israelis. The Authority consolidated its power in 1996 by establishing a 9,000-person police force (many of whom had been veterans of the Palestine Liberation Army, which had been based in Egypt and Tunisia) as well as the Palestinian Protective Security Service, based in Jericho, which arrested a number of human rights activists and independent journalists. It also issued a decree in Gaza that no religious leader in the area's 200 mosques could make a political statement without the Authority's advance approval.

The prospects for peace between Israel and the Palestinian Authority dimmed in the early months of 1996 as the armed wing of Hamas engaged in a series of suicide bombings in Jerusalem and Tel Aviv that left hundreds of Israelis dead or injured. In response, the Israelis sealed off the Palestinian territory and demanded that the Authority take swift action against the terrorists. If it did not, Israel reserved for itself the right to engage in all-out war on Palestinian terrorists. Israel also demanded that the Authority make changes in the PLO Charter, which continued to call for the destruction of Israel.

SEE ALSO

Anti-Semitism; Arafat, Yasir; Holocaust; Israel; Jordan; Ottoman Empire; Palestine Liberation Organization (PLO); United Nations (UN); Zionism

FURTHER READING

Khalidi, Walid. *Palestine Reborn*. New York: St. Martin's, 1992.
Said, Edward. *The Question of Palestine.* New York: Vintage, 1992.
Sayigh, Rosemary. *Palestinians, from Peasants to Revolutionaries*. London: Zed, 1979.

Palestine Liberation Organization (PLO)

The Palestine Liberation Organization (PLO) was founded at an Arab League summit meeting held in Cairo on January 16, 1964, to represent the interests of Palestinians displaced by the formation of the state of Israel. The PLO has as its goal the creation of a nation-state in part or all of the land that constitutes Israel and its occupied territories. The PLO is financed by members of the Arab League, by contributions from Palestinians, and by the returns on its own investments, which are administered by the Palestine National Fund. Overall policy is made by the Palestine National Council, a 600-person parliament representing the Palestinian people, and is executed by the PLO Executive Committee, which consists of representatives from various other Palestinian organizations. Since 1967, the chairman of the PLO has been Yasir Arafat, who is the head of the main Palestinian guerrilla organization, al-Fatah (the Victory).

On June 2, 1964, the Palestine National Council adopted a Palestine National Charter. It stated that Palestine is an indivisible territorial unit whose boundaries are the same as the British mandate of Palestine. It defines as Palestinians those who lived in Palestine prior to 1947, including those who were evicted or emigrated after the founding of Israel, as well as Arabs who took Israeli citizenship or who live in areas occupied by Israel. The covenant stated in Article 9 that "armed struggle is the only way to liberate Palestine" and in Article 15 that "the elimination of Zionism in Palestine" (that is, forbidding the establishment of a Jewish homeland) is a national duty and a legitimate form of self-defense against Jewish aggression. Indeed, it declared the 1917 Balfour Declaration, in which Great Britain called for the establishment of a national homeland for the Jews, to be "null and void." And it stated that the establishment of the state of Israel was an illegal act, to be treated as "null and void." The PLO rejected "all solutions which are substitutes for the total liberation of Palestine." However, many of these articles have since become invalid, especially since the PLO recognized a two-state solution—Israel and Palestine—in 1988, but these articles have not been formally repealed.

The PLO created a Palestine Liberation Army based in Syria. It was decisively defeated by the Israeli Defense Forces during the Six-Day War in 1967, and thereafter the PLO engaged in guerrilla warfare against Israel rather than rely on conventional military forces. In 1969 the PLO declared that peace would be possible in the area only "in a democratic free Palestinian state where

His face covered to prevent identification, a demonstrator waves a Palestinian flag during a demonstration over the status of territory on the West Bank of the Jordan River. Israel, Jordan, and the Palestinians have all made claims to the West Bank.

all Palestinians, Christians, Moslems and Jews will be equal and free from Zionist racism." In 1970 the PLO launched an armed attempt to topple the monarchy in Jordan, hoping thereby to take control of that state, whose population is majority Palestinian. It was defeated by the Jordanian army and forced to flee.

In the 1970s the PLO established itself in Lebanon, where it mounted guerrilla operations against northern Israeli settlements, and it engaged in hijackings of airplanes and other acts of international terrorism in order to bring attention to its cause. On October 29, 1974, in Rabat, Morocco, the Arab heads of state recognized the PLO as "the sole legitimate representative of the Palestinian people." Jordan thereafter gave up its claims to administer the territory of the former British mandate as well as its claim to represent the interests of Palestinians there, ceding both claims to the PLO. On November 22, 1974, the United Nations General Assembly adopted a resolution recognizing the PLO as the representative of the Palestinian people and granting the PLO permanent observer status at the General Assembly. It became a member of the Nonaligned Movement in 1975 and, in 1976, a full member of the Arab League (all Arab states) and the Organization of the Islamic Conference (all Islamic states).

The PLO condemned the peace agreements between Israel and Egypt concluded in 1978. It refused to participate in talks involving "autonomy" for Palestinians on the West Bank of the Jordan River, as called for in the agreements, insisting on its right to liberate territory and establish its own sovereign state. After the PLO stepped up guerrilla attacks against Israel for several years, the Israelis invaded southern Lebanon, occupying that area and much of Beirut in June 1982. The Israelis withdrew from most of Lebanon after the evacuation of the PLO leadership and many of its fighters to Cyprus and from there to several Arab nations in September 1982.

Since the early 1980s the PLO has been hampered in its struggle by severe internal divisions, which at times have led to outright warfare between various factions and often involved assassinations of key leaders. In 1988 the PLO renounced terrorist activity against Western interests or in the West, although it reserved the right to continue its armed struggle against Israel. In 1989 moderates endorsed UN resolutions that recognized Israel's right to exist. Rejectionists, however, who abandoned the PLO, refused to go along with this position.

In the 1990s the PLO was challenged for primacy within the Palestinian movement by Hamas, an Islamic fundamentalist group organized in the Gaza Strip and West Bank. In an effort to retain its leadership of the Palestinian national movement, the PLO agreed in 1991 to participate in Middle Eastern peace talks sponsored by the United States. Israel, for the first time, agreed to negotiate with a Palestinian delegation; before, it had insisted on negotiating only with a joint Palestinian-Jordanian delegation. Although Israel still refused to deal directly with the PLO, it knew that the members of the Palestinian delegation to these talks were known to be PLO supporters and understood that their negotiating positions were cleared by the PLO Executive Council. In 1993 the delegates to the peace conference became officials of the PLO, and Israel decided for the first time to negotiate openly with the organization. Between January 1993 and November 1995 the PLO negotiated an agreement with the Israelis for a withdrawal from much of the West Bank and from the Gaza Strip, and for administration of these areas to be turned over to the newly established Palestinian Authority, the agency that would administer the territory under Israeli sovereignty during the interim negotiations.

Since the late 1980s the PLO has suffered from lack of funds, especially after its sympathy for Iraq in the Persian Gulf War led Saudi Arabia and other wealthy Arab states to cut off their financial contributions. After signing the Peace Accords with Israel, the Palestinians were promised more than $2 billion in aid from Western donors, Japan, the United States, and countries in the Persian Gulf. As of 1997, most of these funds had not been given to the Palestinian Authority, because donor nations were concerned about corruption and mismanagement by Palestinian officials.

SEE ALSO

Arab League (League of Arab States); Arafat, Yasir; Egypt; Intifada; Islamic fundamentalism; Israel; Jordan; Lebanon; Palestine; Syria; United Nations (UN)

FURTHER READING

Cobban, Helena. *The Palestine Liberation Organization.* New York: Cambridge University Press, 1984.
Misahl, Shaul. *The PLO under Arafat.* New Haven: Yale University Press, 1986.
Rubin, Barry. *Revolution until Victory? The Politics and History of the PLO.* Cambridge: Harvard University Press, 1994.

Panama

REPUBLIC OF PANAMA (REPÚBLICA DE PANAMÁ)

• *Capital: Panama City*

Political history Located on the Central American isthmus just to the north of South America, Panama was originally settled by Indian tribes. Christopher Columbus visited the area in 1502, and the Spanish explorer Vasco Núñez de Balboa traveled there in 1513; the Spanish soon established colonies, starting with Panama City in 1519. Spanish treasure galleons traveling from Panama back to Spain and filled with precious metals were attacked by British priva-

An aerial view of the Panama Canal, which is approximately 50 miles long. Still an important shipping thoroughfare, the canal is scheduled to revert to Panamanian control at the end of the 20th century.

teers such as Francis Drake (between 1672 and 1695) and Edmund Morgan (between 1668 and 1672), whose daring exploits cost the Spanish empire much of its New World treasure.

Panama became a province of New Granada (the northern part of South America) in 1739. It was incorporated into Gran Colombia when that nation gained its independence from Spain in 1821. Panama fought a war of independence against Colombia between 1899 and 1902. During the war, Panamanian leaders agreed to permit the United States to build a canal linking the Atlantic and Pacific oceans (which would halve the duration of a sea voyage from New York to San Francisco) in return for help from a U.S. fleet in preventing Colombia from reinforcing its military by sea, thus enabling the Panamanians to win independence. Subsequently, a 1904 treaty permitted the United States to use and occupy the Panama Canal Zone, a strip of land that would be adjacent to the canal. The United States then built the canal, which opened in 1914. The United States treated Panama as a protectorate, sending troops there in 1918 to put down internal unrest against a

government friendly to the United States. In 1936, as part of its hemispheric "good neighbor" policy, the United States dropped its claim to have the right to intervene to protect U.S. lives and property in the city of Colón and Panama City.

In 1964, after Panamanian students engaged in anti-American protests against the occupation of the Canal Zone, claiming that it was an infringement on Panamanian sovereignty, the United States and Panama began negotiations to abolish it. A 1978 treaty between the two nations provided for Panamanian operation of the canal by 1999, ended U.S. occupation of the zone, and established Panamanian sovereignty over the Canal Zone after a brief transitional period.

Under the Panamanian constitution, the canal is to be operated by the Panama Canal Authority, whose 11 members serve for terms of nine years. They are nominated by the president and confirmed by the legislature. A merit system determines appointments to the work force that runs the canal. Toll rates are set by the Panama Canal Authority and are subject to approval by the cabinet.

In 1997 the U.S. military withdrew from Panama and moved the headquarters of the U.S. Southern Command to Miami.

Panama has alternated between corrupt civilian regimes supported by a financial oligarchy and populist authoritarian military rulers who steal most of the public treasury. In 1989 a civilian regime was installed by the United States after the military government led by strongman Manuel Noriega annulled elections in which opposition Social and Christian Democrats had won a majority over military-sponsored candidates. The new civilian government had little popular support, however, and in 1992 its package of 58 constitutional amendments was overwhelmingly rejected by the voters as a protest against its corruption. New elections were held in May 1994, leading to a democratic government headed by Social Democratic businessman Ernesto Pérez Balladares.

In 1996 the government sentenced Noriega in absentia to 20 years in prison for ordering the killing of nine of his own soldiers involved in a coup attempt. The sentence (as well as two previous convictions in Panamanian courts for other murders) could not be carried out, because Noriega was serving a sentence in the United States for being part of a ring smuggling drugs into the United States.

Government institutions Panama has a presidential system in which the president is the head of state, chief executive, and commander in chief. The president, along with two elected vice presidents, is elected for five years. The president appoints the provincial governors. Legislative power is vested in the 67-member Legislative Assembly, whose members are elected for five-year terms. The Supreme Court consists of nine justices appointed by the president. The president also appoints the judges of the district courts.

Parties and movements Panama has a multiparty system in which coalitions vie for power. The largest coalition is the Alianza Democrática de Oposición Civilista (Democratic Alliance of Civil Opposition), made up of Christian Democratic and Social Democratic parties, followed by the conservative Coalición de Liberación Nacional (National Liberation Coalition). Until 1994 the largest single party was the conservative Partido Revolucionario Democrático (Revolutionary Democratic Party), which had won the presidential election in 1990. In 1994 the party formerly headed by Noriega, the Revolutionary Democratic Party, now completely reconstituted as a social democratic party, won the presidential election and control of the legislature, although the party renounced Noriega's leadership and his corrupt dictatorial rule.

Domestic issues In the early 1980s lax financial regulations made Panama a home for offshore foreign banks and a transit point for illegal drugs bound from Colombia to the United States. Much of the drug money was deposited in Panamanian banks, fueling a brief period of prosperity that ended when the United States unseated the military regime.

The Strategy of Development and Economic Modernization put into place by the civilian government in the early 1990s relied on U.S. aid to create a free-market economy. In 1991, to satisfy foreign aid donors and investors, the government introduced austerity measures, including a reduction in public expenditures, a reformed tax system, and privatization of state enterprises. The armed forces were abolished by presidential decree and an elections tribunal was established to prevent election fraud. In 1992 the voters defeated a constitutional amendment that would have permanently abolished the army.

International issues Since its independence, Panama has been dominated by the United States, which until 1936 regarded it as a protectorate, financed its government, trained its National Guard, and used the country as its major military base of operations in Latin America. In the late 1980s the regime of General Manuel Noriega began to distance itself from the United States after a U.S. grand jury indicted him on a charge of drug smuggling. In 1989 a U.S.–sponsored coup to unseat Noriega failed. But after Noriega's forces killed a U.S. Marine, the United States invaded in Operation Just Cause. Noriega was taken to the United States to stand trial on drug charges, where he was convicted of eight charges of conspiracy to distribute cocaine.

In 1991 Panama and the United States signed an agreement providing the United States with information about offshore banks based in Panama in order to combat their drug-money laundering activities.

Human rights The military regime of General Manuel Noriega used torture in its Cárcel Modelo (the so-called Model Prison) and murder to silence or eliminate its political opponents. After his overthrow, more than 100 of his military officers were arrested on charges ranging from homicide to drug running. After the 1994 election victory of Noriega's party, however, all were pardoned by the newly elected president Balladares. In 1996 the Cárcel Modelo was dynamited to bits.

SEE ALSO
United States of America

FURTHER READING
Buckley, Kevin. *Panama: The Whole Story*. New York: Simon & Schuster, 1991.
Meditz, Sandra W., and Dennis M. Hanratty, eds. *Panama: A Country Study*. 4th ed. Washington, D.C.: Federal Research Division, Library of Congress, 1989.
Ropp, Steven. *Panamanian Politics*. New York: Praeger, 1982.

Pan-American Union

The Pan-American Union was an organization created to promote economic development in the Western Hemisphere and to coordinate foreign and defense policies in the hemisphere. The first International Conference of American States was held in Washington, D.C., in 1889. The delegates rejected the U.S. proposal for a customs union (an agreement to eliminate tariffs on goods traded by member nations) and an arbitration treaty, which would have required that certain disputes be submitted to binding international arbitration. The conference did establish the International Union of American Republics to collect commercial information for export-oriented businesses. The agency to collect the data was named the Commercial Bureau of the American Republics; it was located in Washington and supervised by the U.S. State Department. After the first meeting, international conferences were held approximately every five years.

In 1910 the Commercial Bureau was renamed the Pan-American Union, and the conference became known as the Pan-American Conference. The member nations were Argentina, Bolivia, Brazil, Chile, Colombia, Costa Rica, Cuba, the Dominican Republic, Ecuador, El Salvador, Guatemala, Haiti, Honduras, Mexico, Nicaragua, Panama, Paraguay, Peru, the United States, Uruguay, and Venezuela.

At the Santiago Conference of 1923, held in Chile, the Pan-American Union negotiated the Gondra Treaty, which created arbitration machinery for the peaceful settlement of disputes among member nations. At the 1928 Havana conference, the United States was condemned for its military interventions to prop up pro-U.S.

leaders in the Dominican Republic, Haiti, Honduras, and Nicaragua. At the 1933 conference in Montevideo, Uruguay, the United States joined in the Convention on the Rights and Duties of States, which declared that "no state has the right to intervene in the internal or external affairs of another." Shortly thereafter, President Franklin D. Roosevelt announced a Good Neighbor policy, withdrew U.S. troops from Haiti, and renounced the right to intervene in the affairs of Cuba.

Several Pan-American Conferences were held during World War II. In the 1940 Act of Havana, the delegates agreed on measures to keep French territories in the hemisphere out of German hands. They also affirmed in a Declaration of Reciprocal Assistance and Cooperation that an attack on any nation in the hemisphere would be taken as an attack on them all. These measures superseded the Monroe Doctrine of 1823, in which U.S. president James Monroe, acting alone, had warned European nations against further colonization or other intervention in the Western Hemisphere. In 1948, under provisions of the UN Charter, the Organization of American States replaced the Pan-American Union as the regional organization for the Western Hemisphere.

SEE ALSO

Organization of American States (OAS)

FURTHER READING

Inman, Samuel. *Problems in Pan-Americanism*. New York: Doran, 1921.

Papua New Guinea

INDEPENDENT STATE OF PAPUA NEW GUINEA

• *Capital: Port Moresby*

Political history Located on the eastern part of the island of New Guinea, just north of Australia, the area that constitutes Papua New Guinea has been settled by indigenous Papuans and Melanesian Islanders for 10,000 years. The Dutch claimed the western half of New Guinea in the early 19th century and it later passed to Indonesia, which rules it under the name of Irian Barat. On the eastern side, the Germans took the northern part and the British took the southern part in 1884. The British transferred their share to Australia in 1905. In 1914, during World War I, Australia captured the north from the Germans and administered it after the war as a League of Nations mandate. After 1949, the two territories on the eastern half were jointly administered by Australia, then given self-government in 1973 and complete independence within the Commonwealth of Nations in 1975.

Government institutions Papua New Guinea is a parliamentary democracy. The head of state is the monarch of the Commonwealth of Nations, represented on the island by a governor-general. The head of government is the prime minister, who presides over the National Executive Council (cabinet), which is accountable to the elected 109-member National Parliament. The independent judiciary, which is headed by a supreme court, includes district and local courts.

Parties and movements The largest parties in Papua New Guinea's multiparty system are the Pangu Pati (Papua Unity Party), which led the nation to its independence as a nationalist movement, and the People's Democratic Movement, formed in the 1980s out of a dissident wing of Pangu leaders concerned about political corruption.

Domestic issues In response to a secessionist movement in Bougainville—a small island that is part of Papua New Guinea and is located next to the Solomon Islands chain—the Revo-

Seated under umbrellas to shield them from the tropical sun, UN and Dutch officials listen as authority over Papua New Guinea is officially transferred from the Netherlands to the United Nations on October 1, 1962. The transfer was a first step toward complete independence for the island nation.

lutionary Army, the nationalist movement on Bougainville, has sabotaged copper mines owned by Australian companies. Copper is one of the largest exports; the Papuan economy was weakened when the copper mines were shut by secessionist rebels in the early 1990s. The government is plagued by corruption at the highest levels. Crime is high, with much of it involving disputes between members of different tribes, and the death penalty has been reintroduced.

International issues Indonesia, which administers the western half of the island, and Papua New Guinea created a border commission to regulate immigration and control smuggling in 1990, and they signed a security agreement in 1992. Indonesian troops in the mid-1990s have gone across the border in pursuit of members of the Melanesian Free Papua Movement, which seeks to unify the entire island.

Relations with the neighboring Solomon Islands deteriorated after Papuan forces raided its territory to search for Bougainville rebels.

Papua helped form the Melanesian Spearhead Group to win independence for New Caledonia, an island chain to its southeast controlled by France.

SEE ALSO
Australia; Commonwealth of Nations; Indonesia; Solomon Islands

FURTHER READING
Griffin, James. *Papua New Guinea: A Political History*. Richmond, Australia: Heinemann Educational Australia, 1979.

Paraguay

REPUBLIC OF PARAGUAY (REPÚBLICA DEL PARAGUAY)

• *Capital: Asunción*

Political history Located in central South America, Paraguay was originally inhabited by the Guarani, Tupian, and Guaycuru Indians. Spain conquered and settled the area in 1535 as a line of defense against Portuguese settlements in Brazil. For the next two centuries, Jesuits established missions to convert the Indians to Christianity, while a European elite established plantations, logging operations, and silver mines requiring Indian labor. Paraguay became independent in 1811, then repulsed attempts by Buenos Aires (Argentina) to annex it. For most of the 19th century it was ruled by dictators who had the backing of wealthy elites.

Paraguay intervened to prevent Brazil from dominating its southern neighbor Uruguay and lost much of its territory to Brazil, Uruguay, and Argentina in the War of the Triple Alliance, named after its opponents, which occurred between 1865 and 1870. Almost half of the Paraguayan population was killed in that war. Paraguay, however, won territory from Bolivia in the Gran Chaco War (1932–35).

In the 20th century Paraguay continued to be ruled by a succession of dictators and military regimes. The last dictator was Alfredo Stroessner, who ruled from 1954 until 1989,

During Alfredo Stroessner's reign, Paraguay earned a dubious reputation as a haven for Nazi war criminals.

District courts try civil and criminal cases. The Supreme Court has five members, appointed by the president and confirmed by the Senate.

Parties and movements The military leaders who ran Paraguay until 1993 permitted a multiparty system to compete for legislative seats, but in fact all elections were rigged and the outcomes preordained. The prevailing party since 1947 has been the conservative Partido Colorado (Colorado Party), which also triumphed in the first free elections in 1993. The Partido Liberal Radical Auténtico (Authentic Radical Liberal Party) is its major opposition, as well as the reformist Asunción Para Todos (Asunción Belongs to All).

Domestic issues Paraguay is one of the poorest nations in Latin America. In the 1980s inefficient state enterprises were sold to individual investors and in 1993 an austerity program designed to lower inflation was introduced in cooperation with the International Monetary Fund and the World Bank. The Paris Club (a group of Western nations that set policies about how to deal with debtor nations) agreed to renegotiate debt payments after Paraguay was unable to pay interest on its foreign debts in 1988. In the 1990s the United States and other industrial nations have invested billions of dollars to develop the Paraguay and Paraná rivers to stimulate Brazilian-Paraguayan commerce.

A peasant movement in the 1990s has demanded land reform and the breakup of large farms into smaller plots. Labor unions in the mid-1990s called for very large wage increases and conducted several unsuccessful general strikes. Paraguay's poor economic performance and consequent political unrest have left the civilian government unstable and without the

when he was deposed by the military. A civilian government was established in 1993.

Government institutions Under the 1967 constitution, established to provide a veneer of legitimacy to a dictatorial regime, Paraguay has a presidential system. The president is the head of state and exercises executive power, governing with an appointed council of ministers. Legislative power is granted to a bicameral, popularly elected National Congress, composed of a 36-member Senate and a 72-member Chamber of Deputies.

authority to govern effectively. In 1996 the civilian government barely managed to avoid a military coup d'état, with pressure exerted by the United States and Paraguay's neighbors.

International issues Paraguay was allied with Argentina and sympathetic to the Axis powers during World War II, and it was a haven for Nazi war criminals after the war. Thereafter it became allied with Brazil and established close relations with the United States during the cold war, in order to receive foreign aid to prop up its ailing economy. In 1991 Paraguay joined its neighbors Argentina, Brazil, and Uruguay in forming the Common Market of the South (MERCOSUR), and trade barriers among them were lowered progressively through 1994. In 1991 the United States ended tariff sanctions against Paraguay, which had been imposed in 1987 to punish the nation for its human rights abuses.

Human rights The dictatorial regime of General Alfredo Stroessner operated as a police state, using torture and murder against political opponents. In 1989 the Chamber of Deputies approved the San José Pact on Human Rights adopted by the Organization of American States, and the government began prosecution of former officials charged with such abuses. Since 1992, military officers have been subject to the jurisdiction of civilian courts.

SEE ALSO
Argentina; Axis powers; Bolivia; Brazil; Uruguay

FURTHER READING
Hanratty, Dennis M., and Sandra W. Meditz, eds. *Paraguay: A Country Study.* 2nd ed. Washington, D.C.: Federal Research Division, Library of Congress, 1990.
Miranda, Carlos. *The Stroessner Era.* Boulder, Colo.: Westview, 1990.

Paris Club

The Paris Club is an informal group of creditor (lender) nations that meets in Paris when necessary to negotiate changes in payment schedules and interest rates with debtor (borrower) nations. Its members are Canada, France, Germany, Italy, Japan, the United Kingdom, and the United States.

Between 1956 (when it was founded) and the late 1970s, the Paris Club dealt primarily with Latin American debt renegotiations. In the 1980s, rescheduling the debts of African governments took priority. The negotiations may include outright cancellation of some debt; a "debt for nature" swap, which involves reducing debt in return for conservation measures (such as saving a rain forest); extension of repayment periods; a reduction in interest rates on debts; or a "grace period" in which no debt payments need to be made. Debtor nations are normally required to conclude an economic adjustment agreement with the International Monetary Fund (IMF) and conduct a discussion of development goals with the World Bank before a meeting with creditor nations occurs.

The Paris Club negotiations involve only government loans and credits, not loans extended by private banks. Negotiations between debtor governments and these private organizations are conducted by the London Club, an informal group of the same nations that meets in London, which tends to provide terms comparable to Paris Club agreements.

Because the Paris and London Clubs require developing nations to engage in austerity programs sponsored by the IMF and World Bank, nations with large debts often find themselves obliged to cut social welfare programs and tolerate high unemployment to control inflation. As a result of these policies, many Third World politicians in Africa and Asia, such as the leaders of Myanmar and Nigeria, do not believe that it is possible to have democratic regimes and at the same time meet the demands of the creditor nations. Instead, they argue that economic growth is possible only for those nations with authoritarian regimes that do not have to follow mass public opinion, which tends to oppose the economic programs required by the clubs.

SEE ALSO

International Monetary Fund (IMF); Third World; World Bank (International Bank for Reconstruction and Development)

FURTHER READING

Echengreen, Barry, and Peter H. Lindert, eds. *The International Debt Crisis in Historical Perspective.* Cambridge: Harvard University Press, 1989.

Parliamentary system

A parliamentary system is a structure of government in which legislative and executive powers are fused. The ministers of the cabinet retain their office only if they have the support of a majority of the members of the legislature. The ministers—including the prime minister, who serves as head of government—are themselves elected to parliament, sit in its sessions, and lead its debates. As a collective cabinet, they take responsibility for passing legislation; as ministers, they implement the laws.

The parliamentary system may be contrasted with the presidential sys-

tem, in which the president exercises executive power and a congress exercises legislative power. In a presidential system department heads may not serve in the legislature and members of the legislature may not serve as executive officials.

A government loses power in a parliamentary system when it loses majority support. This may happen in one of four ways. The least common method is the "vote of no confidence," in which the parliament explicitly refuses to vote "confidence in the ministry." This was the way the Fourth French Republic (1946–58) and post–World War II Italian governments were brought down, for example. Alternatively, a government that is defeated on a vote on an important issue may assume that it has lost its majority in parliament and may resign. In that case, new elections may be called, or the head of state may call upon another member of parliament to try to put together a government that can win support of a parliamentary majority. This often happens in a multiparty system such as Italy's, when a minor party that belongs to a majority coalition deserts the coalition to bring down the government and

In London, the annual opening of Parliament in 1978. England's Parliament is justifiably proud of its status as the oldest deliberative governmental body in the world in terms of continuous service.

provoke a reshuffling of cabinet positions or a change of policy.

A third way in which a government can fall is by an intra-party "coup" against its leader. The majority party simply replaces its leader with someone else it finds more congenial to its purposes, and the cabinet is reconstituted under this new leadership. This method is often used in Canada, Germany, and Great Britain. The final and most common way a government can fall is by losing its parliamentary majority in an election.

A parliamentary system distinguishes between the operational part (the prime minister and cabinet) and the symbolic part (the head of state, usually a president or monarch). The role of the head of state is to preside over the formation of a cabinet accountable to the legislature and to formally assent to the appointment of the prime minister and other ministers. To the extent that the head of state is granted governmental powers and prerogatives by the constitution, these are exercised on the recommendation of, and according to the policies formulated by, the prime minister and cabinet. In the British system, for example, the monarch has the right to be consulted, the right to advise, and the right to caution the cabinet about a course of policy. But the monarch may not impede the government in its course of action.

Parliamentary systems exist in many nations, including the United Kingdom, Canada, Japan, India, Israel, and most states in western Europe.

SEE ALSO
Presidential system; Semi-presidential system

FURTHER READING
Bagehot, Walter. *The English Constitution.* 1867. Reprint, Ithaca: Cornell University Press, 1966.
Caraley, Demetrios, ed. *Presidential and Parliamentary Systems: Which Work Best?* New York: Academy of Political Science, 1994.
Lijphart, Arend, ed. *Parliamentary Versus Presidential Government.* New York: Oxford University Press, 1992.

Peace Corps

The Peace Corps is an agency of the United States government that sends volunteers to developing nations to assist in educational, scientific, and community development programs. The Peace Corps was established by President John F. Kennedy in 1961 with a threefold objective: to gain friends for the United States during the cold war; to assist in the development of friendly nations; and to give volunteers a greater understanding of the world they live in. Its first director was Sargent Shriver, Kennedy's brother-in-law, whose enthusiasm for the program enabled it to grow to more than 10,000 volunteers within a three-year period. It is similar to the British Volunteers in Service Overseas and programs run by France and the Scandinavian nations of Norway, Sweden, and Denmark.

Peace Corps volunteers are expected to live in conditions similar to those of local residents, and they are paid a modest stipend. Initially, a large number of volunteers were recent college graduates who taught English or other academic subjects. In response to requests from host nations, the mix of volunteers soon shifted to include more older people with technical expertise and business or farming experience. In recent years, volunteers have worked in the post-communist nations in eastern Europe to help entrepreneurs set up private busi-

A Peace Corps worker in Venezuela shows children how to graft a tree. Although the Peace Corps has always maintained that its mission is nonpolitical, it has often been the focus of anti-American sentiment.

nesses as well as in the Third World; in Africa, for example, volunteers have helped eradicate Guinea-worm disease. The National Council of Returned Peace Corps Volunteers is an organization that lobbies the U.S. Congress for adequate funding for the organization.

Although many nations have welcomed Peace Corps volunteers, the program is often criticized by anti-American politicians who claim that it is a front for U.S. intelligence agencies, the U.S. military, or U.S. corporations. At times, Peace Corps volunteers have had to be removed from some Asian and African countries, such as Iran and Kenya, when relations with the United States have deteriorated.

The Peace Corps has spawned several domestic government programs to assist poor communities in the United States, including Volunteers in Service to America (established in 1964 as part of President Lyndon Johnson's War on Poverty) and the Americorps Volunteers, created in 1993 by President Bill Clinton. These programs have also been controversial, with Democrats defending them as useful for poor communities and Republicans criticizing them as a waste of taxpayers' dollars.

SEE ALSO
Kennedy, John F.; Third World

FURTHER READING
Ashabranner, Brent K. *A New Frontier: The Peace Corps in Eastern Europe.* New York: Cobblehill, 1994.
At Home in the World: The Peace Corps Story. Washington, D.C.: Peace Corps, 1996.
Redmon, Coates. *Come As You Are: The Peace Corps Story.* San Diego: Harcourt Brace Jovanovich, 1986.
Schwarz, Karen. *What You Can Do for Your Country: An Oral History of the Peace Corps.* New York: Morrow, 1991.
Weitsman, Madeline. *The Peace Corps.* New York: Chelsea House, 1989.

Perestroika

SEE Gorbachev, Mikhail

Perón, Juan Domingo

- *Born: Oct. 8, 1895, Lobos, Argentina*
- *Died: July 1, 1974, Buenos Aires, Argentina*

Juan Perón was president of Argentina from 1946 to 1955 and from 1973 to 1974 and founder of the Peronista political movement that dominated Argentine civilian politics for five decades after World War II. He was a handsome man, tall and athletic, and a dynamic speaker who had the ability to rouse his audiences to a fever pitch, whether speaking in person or broadcasting on the radio. Widely read in history and in political theory, Perón attempted to transform Argentina into a fascist state with populist trappings and twice led his nation into political chaos. As a young military officer in the 1930s, Perón openly admired the fascist governments of Italy and Germany because of their seeming discipline and ability to recover from the worldwide economic depression.

Perón helped to organize the Group of United Officers to overthrow Argentina's corrupt civilian government in 1943. They were successful and Perón was appointed secretary of labor; he won support from the unions by raising wages and providing social welfare programs. In 1945, Perón was appointed vice president and minister of war. Fearing his ambition, the government arrested him in 1945, but backed by massive street demonstrations, he forced the authorities to release him within a day. Perón was elected president in 1946 with strong labor support.

His program of Peronismo (also known as Justicialismo, or the Justice Movement) involved government regulation of the economy, the establishment of state enterprises, and social welfare benefits for workers. Banks, railroads, utilities, and communication systems were converted into government corporations. The nationalization of these industries reduced foreign influence over the Argentine economy, a move that was popular with nationalistic Argentines. Although workers benefited from Perón's reforms, the lack of foreign investment and the mismanagement of the economy led to a period of stagnation that reduced one of the wealthiest economies in Latin America to a shambles.

A sympathizer of the Nazis during World War II, Perón by 1947 had given safe haven to almost 100,000 Nazi and fascist war criminals fleeing Europe after the Allied victory. Two German submarines sent Nazi art treasures and gold to Argentina for safekeeping in 1945. In return for his help, the Nazis rewarded Perón with a Swiss bank account and a mansion in Cairo, Egypt.

Perón allowed multiple political parties to exist, but he exerted strict press censorship and closed down opposition newspapers. He won reelection in 1951 after amending the constitution so that he could serve a second consecutive term. His second term was marked by unremitting hostility to the Catholic Church, which he accused of trying to overthrow him. In 1955, at Perón's instigation, the legislature passed laws separating church and state. Late that year a military coup d'état overthrew Perón's regime, and the new military junta gave him safe conduct to Paraguay, fearing a backlash if he were arrested. He later went into exile in Spain.

In 1973 Perón returned to Argentina and won the presidency in a free election. After his death in 1974, his movement split between right and left wings. His second wife, Isabel, who had succeeded him as president, was unable to maintain her rule and was herself overthrown by the military in 1976.

The Peronista political movement remains a potent force in Argentinean politics. An avowed Peronista, Carlos Saúl Menem, was elected president of Argentina in 1989, although his liberal, free-market approach to the economy repudiated most of the Peronista economic legacy. Nevertheless, the impact of Peronismo remains strong in Argentina and much of Latin America, because Juan Perón was the first South American leader to attempt to empower the poor and the workers and give them some sense of dignity and worth in modern Latin American society.

SEE ALSO

Argentina; Perón, María Estela Martínez de (Isabel); Perón, María Eva Duarte de

FURTHER READING

Barager, Joseph. *Why Perón Came to Power.* New York: Knopf, 1968.
DeChancie, John. *Juan Perón.* New York: Chelsea House, 1987.

Turner, Frederick, and Jose Miguens, eds. *Juan Perón and the Reshaping of Argentina.* Pittsburgh: University of Pittsburgh Press, 1983.

Perón, María Estela Martínez de (Isabel)

• *Born: Feb. 4, 1931, La Rioja, Argentina*

Isabel Perón, the second wife of Juan Domingo Perón, was the first woman to be elected president of Argentina (1974–76). As a child, she quit elementary school to study music, and later became a piano teacher and then a ballerina. While on tour in Panama in 1956 she met former Argentine president Juan Perón. She resigned from the ballet company to become his personal secretary and companion, living with him in Madrid. They were married in 1961.

Juan Perón regained political power and was elected president of Argentina in 1973; Isabel was elected vice president. Late that year, gravely ill, Perón delegated governing power to her. When he died the following year, she succeeded to the presidency, becoming the first woman to be president of a Latin American nation. To combat the civil insurrection of leftist guerrillas, she imposed a state of emergency. Her accompanying economic austerity measures led the unions to call a general strike. In 1976 she was overthrown by a military junta, kept under house arrest until 1981, and now lives in exile in Spain.

SEE ALSO
Argentina; Perón, Juan Domingo

Perón, María Eva Duarte de

• *Born: May 17, 1919, Los Toldos, Argentina*
• *Died: July 26, 1952, Buenos Aires, Argentina*

Eva Perón was the first wife of Argentine president Juan Perón and a key organizer of the Peronista movement that had catapulted her husband to the presidency in 1946. A beautiful and dynamic First Lady, she seemed to symbolize for many Argentineans the style and flare of a new generation. Her efforts on behalf of the poor made her a cult figure among the downtrodden and throughout Latin America.

Eva Duarte was originally an actress who performed in radio soap operas. She met her future husband, Colonel Juan Perón, in 1944 after a performance, because he was entranced with her voice. When the government imprisoned him in 1945 (because fellow officers believed he was about to instigate a coup), she organized demonstrations demanding his release and helped in his court fight against imprisonment. Perón was released almost immediately, and four days later, on October 21, they were married. Eva then worked on Perón's 1946 presidential campaign by making speeches and organizing union support.

As First Lady of Argentina, she was instrumental in getting the congress to pass a law granting women the right to vote. She organized the Eva Duarte de Perón Foundation, which disbursed funds for social welfare programs in the slums of Argentina's large cities. She influenced the work of the government departments dealing with labor, health, and education by using government jobs and contracts to gain support for the Peronista movement. She was also instrumental in allowing ex-Nazis and members of the Croatian fascist regime to settle in Argentina and transfer vast wealth and looted works of art from Europe to Argentina.

Evita, as she was known, planned to run for vice president with her husband in the 1951 campaign, but her ill health prevented it. She died of cancer the following year, mourned and beloved by most of the poor and working people of Argentina (500,000 people attended her funeral), for whom she had become a national hero.

SEE ALSO

Argentina; Perón, Juan Domingo

FURTHER READING

Dujovne Ortiz, Alicia. *Eva Perón*. Translated by Shawn Fields. New York: St. Martin's, 1996.
Fraser, Nicholas, and Marysa Navarro. *Eva Perón*. New York: Norton, 1981.

Peru

REPUBLIC OF PERU (REPÚBLICA DEL PERU)

• *Capital: Lima*

Political history Located in the northwestern part of South America, the area that is now Peru was the site of several ancient civilizations, including those of the Chancay and Moche on the coastal Pacific, that of the Tiahuanaco on Lake Titicaca, and the enormous empire of the Incas in the 15th century. The area was conquered and settled in 1531–33 by the Spanish conquistador Francisco Pizarro, whose small army defeated a large Incan army and killed the Incan emperor Atahualpa in 1532. The viceroyalty of Peru was established in 1544 to administer all of the Spanish colonies in South America, and the city of Lima quickly became the largest and wealthiest settlement in the Americas. The Spanish completed their conquest by defeating the Incan King Tupac Amarú in 1571. During the next 250 years, Peru's gold and silver mines provided wealth for Spain.

Peru became independent in 1821 when Simón Bolívar, the liberator of much of South America, led his armies to victory over the Spanish colonial army at the battles of Junín and Ayacucho. Peru's attempts to control the region failed when Ecuador resisted annexation in 1829 and a federation between Peru and Bolivia collapsed in 1839. Thereafter, Peru was ruled by a succession of military leaders through much of the 19th century. After Chile defeated Peru in a territorial conflict, the War of the Pacific (1879–83), the Civilista movement arose in Peru, calling for civilian government to reform Peru's economy and institute progressive reforms. In 1895 a civilian democracy was inaugurated after the military had failed to solve Peru's economic problems. President Augusto Leguía extended his term unconstitutionally and established a dictatorship in 1925. In 1930 Leguía was overthrown by the military, which resumed control of the nation.

After 1930, as the popularity of democratic leaders dropped during the depression, Peru seesawed between outright military dictators and authoritarian civilian leaders.

A new period of civilian democracy started in 1939, but in 1968 the military again took over and relied on an alliance with Marxist labor unions to maintain power. In 1980 a civilian president assumed power after the military retired from politics, and in 1985 Fernando Belaúnde Terry became the first presi-

Though he is still revered as the liberator of Peru and much of the rest of South America, Simón Bolívar was destined to see his hope of a great South American federation—to rival the United States—never come to pass.

dent to turn power over peacefully to his elected successor. In 1992, however, President Alberto Fujimori declared a state of siege, dissolved Congress, and cracked down on Sendero Luminoso (Shining Path) guerrillas, a radical Maoist revolutionary movement that had engaged in terrorist activities.

Government institutions Peru has had more than 20 constitutions in its history. Under the most recent one (1979), Peru has a presidential system. The president is the head of state and exercises executive power, governing with an appointed council of ministers. Legislative power is granted to a bicameral National Congress composed of a popularly elected 60-member Senate and a 180-member Chamber of Deputies. The Supreme Court has 13 members, who are appointed by the president and confirmed by the Senate, as are the judges of lower district courts.

Parties and movements The main parties are the conservative Frente

Democrático (Democratic Front) and the Alianza Popular Revolucionaria Americana (American Popular Revolutionary Alliance, or APRA, which is composed of Social Democrats and Christian Democrats), followed by Cambio 90 (Change for the 90s), another conservative party. In 1990 and 1995 Cambio 90 won the presidential and congressional elections by large margins. The party welcomes foreign investment, free trade, and liberalization of the economy through deregulation and the selling off of state enterprises. Its support for voluntary birth-control measures, however, has put it on a collision course with the Catholic Church in Peru.

Domestic issues President Alberto Fujimori won the 1990 election on the Cambio 90 ticket, but lacking a parliamentary majority, he resorted to rule by decree. He suspended the constitution in April 1992 and later announced a timetable for the restoration of democracy, with elections for a new Congress and a proposal to draft a new constitution. His public approval rating soared to more than 80 percent, because his actions were designed to end terrorism promoted by Sendero Luminoso in the 1980s and early 1990s. Its 8,000 guerrillas have assassinated government officials and village peasants, sabotaged industrial facilities, blown up banks and hotels, and financed themselves by collecting taxes on cocaine growers in the Upper Huallaga Valley. Their terrorism and the military efforts to repress it resulted in more than 26,000 deaths and injuries and $25 billion in damages by the end of 1992. That year its leader, Abimael Guzmán Reynoso, was captured by government troops, who killed or arrested most of its leadership. A military court sentenced Reynoso to life imprisonment. The Sendero Luminoso Sixth Military Plan was timed to disrupt congressional elections in late 1993, but the Peruvian military succeeded in eliminating much of the terrorist group.

In 1995, 23 leaders of the Túpac Amaru Revolutionary Movement, another guerrilla group that had specialized in attacks on Western embassies and corporations, were arrested, and the government proclaimed victory over terrorism. In 1997 the group seized hostages at the Japanese ambassador's residence in Lima in an attempt to force the government to free its members from prison. Fujimori eventually ordered a military operation to rescue the hostages, which succeeded in doing so with only one hostage killed but all the guerrillas killed. Fujimori's successful antiterrorism operation increased his popularity.

Other than trying to control terrorism, Peru's main problem is its economy. Per capita income remains at the same level as in the 1960s, and runaway inflation may erode support for the Fujimori regime. More than half the population lives in poverty, and more than 80 percent of the labor force is underemployed (without full-time work). Foreign companies have invested in the country since 1990, but Peru's external debt has greatly increased, and it ran a high trade deficit in the 1990s.

To improve its poor economic performance, in the 1990s Peru privatized its extensive state enterprises, including mines and telephone and electric companies. As a result, by the mid-1990s it had the highest growth rate in Latin America. Government funds were being directed toward new social programs and public works in the poorest regions to blunt the appeal of guerrilla groups to poor peasants.

International issues Peru played a major role in the creation of the Andean Pact of 1969, in which it linked its economy with Bolivia, Colombia, Ecuador, and Venezuela. The resulting Andean Free Trade Zone eliminates tariffs among these nations.

In 1992 Peru agreed to give landlocked Bolivia access to the Pacific Ocean in exchange for its own access to the Atlantic via rivers through Bolivia.

In 1989 U.S. armed forces were stationed in Peru to aid in apprehending drug traffickers. All U.S. foreign aid and military assistance ended, however, when President Fujimori suspended the constitution. With the inauguration of a new Congress in 1992, aid was resumed.

In 1993 Peru repaid its debts to the World Bank and became eligible for new loans after six years of refusing to pay interest on its existing debts. Because of its own budget concerns, the United States cut its budget for antidrug assistance to Peru and other Andean nations in 1995. At Peru's request, the United States maintains a 10-person observer force on the Peru-Ecuador border at the Yaupi-Santiago border post to prevent a territorial dispute (which began in 1981) from escalating into a military confrontation.

Human rights In the 1990s the Sendero Luminoso guerrilla movement engaged in bombings and assassinations of civilians in its terrorist campaign to destabilize the government, a guerrilla war in which more than 30,000 civilians were killed by both sides between 1980 and 1995.

Peru's military has been charged with human rights abuses in villages and shantytowns harboring Sendero Luminoso guerrillas. Peru led the world in recorded disappearances of prisoners after their arrest (more than 100 each year from 1980 to 1993).

Several lawyers who defended Sendero Luminoso leaders before military courts were themselves sentenced to life imprisonment. Reporters have also been jailed, as well as schoolteachers sympathetic to Sendero Luminoso. Under the "Law of Repentance" enacted in 1993, many guerrillas have received amnesty after surrendering. In 1995 Peru's government approved a broad amnesty law that absolved the military of all human rights abuses committed between 1980 and 1995.

FURTHER READING

Cameron, Maxwell. *Democracy and Authoritarianism in Peru.* New York: St. Martin's, 1994.

Masterson, Daniel. *Militarism and Politics in Latin America: Peru from Sanchez Cerro to Sendero Luminoso.* Westport, Conn.: Greenwood, 1991.

Palmer, David. *The Shining Path of Peru.* New York: St. Martin's, 1992.

Rudolph, James. *Politics in Peru: The Evolution of a Crisis.* Stanford, Calif.: Stanford University Press, 1992.

Philippines

REPUBLIC OF PHILIPPINES (REPUBLIKA NG PILIPINAS)

• *Capital: Manila*

Political history The Philippines is an archipelago of more than 7,000 islands off southeastern Asia that were originally settled thousands of years ago by Malayans and others from the Asian mainland. Filipinos traded with Indians, Chinese, and Arabs prior to the European discovery of the islands in 1521 by the Portuguese navigator Ferdinand Magellan, who was sailing for Spain. Magellan died there in a battle with the native inhabitants. The islands were conquered in 1565 by Spain, which established colonial rule from the capital city of Manila. The Spanish established sugar plantations, converted the inhabitants to Christianity, and used the islands as a transit point for trade be-

tween their South American colonies and China.

Spain ceded the Philippines to the United States at the end of the Spanish-American War in 1898. After a guerrilla war for independence led by the nationalist leader Emilio Aguinaldo was put down by U.S. forces between 1898 and 1905, the United States ruled the Philippines as a colony and built naval bases there. The country was granted internal self-government as a commonwealth in 1935. In 1942 the islands were conquered by Japan during World War II, but they were recaptured by U.S. and Filipino forces in 1944–45.

In 1946 the United States granted the Philippines independence but negotiated a treaty that allowed the U.S. military bases to remain. The Philippines became a republic, but its democratic government gave way to the authoritarian rule of President Ferdinand Marcos, elected in 1966. His corrupt government siphoned billions from the Treasury for himself and his cronies. Marcos ordered the murder of a leading rival, Benigno Aquino, when Aquino returned from exile in 1983 to challenge Marcos's rule. The assassination sparked the resistance to his rule that eventually led to his defeat by Corazon Aquino, widow of the slain rival, in the 1986 presidential elections. After making a brief attempt to prevent the transfer of power, Marcos bowed to the "people power" of millions of citizens in the streets demanding his ouster, as well as to pressure from the United States, which opposed his attempts to set aside the election results. Marcos, who had long been a U.S. ally, went into exile in the United States. Aquino became president and served through 1992, when her chosen successor, defense minister Fidel Ramos, was elected president.

Government institutions Under provisions of the 1987 constitution, the

Philippines has a presidential form of government. The president is the head of state, chief executive, and commander in chief. The president may invoke martial rule but Congress may revoke it. Elected for a single six-year term, the president appoints a cabinet with the approval of the Commission on Appointments, which is drawn from both chambers of Congress. Legislative power is exercised by a 24-member Senate, whose members are directly elected for six years, and a 250-member House of Representatives, of which 50 members are chosen by the president from minority ethnic groups and the rest are popularly elected.

Parties and movements The Philippines is a multiparty democracy. In presidential elections the parties form coalitions. The majority coalition since 1986 has been the Laka ng Bayan (National Union Party), composed of the Liberal Party, the Labor Party, and the progressive party PDP-Labon (Fight of Democratic Filipinos).

Domestic issues The Philippines is wracked by conflict between the democratic government and the communist New People's Army (NPA). The government has made only limited land reform efforts to deal with the insurgency and has failed to win over peasants that support the NPA.

On the island of Mindanao, an Islamic fundamentalist group, the Moro National Liberation Front, seeks autonomy. The government signed a cease-fire with the group in 1994, but talks broke down in 1996. The extremist Islamic fundamentalist Abu Sayyaf has threatened to renew a civil war for complete independence. The island is considered the Muslims' ancestral home but now contains a majority of Christians who oppose autonomy.

The economy has stagnated, with high unemployment and income in-

equality causing social unrest in the 1990s. The country has not kept technological pace with leading nations in Southeast Asia and remains a low-wage manufacturing center for textiles and toys. The country is burdened with a large external debt, but much of the borrowed money was siphoned off by Marcos and his cronies. A 1990 earthquake, the eruption of Mount Pinatubo in 1991, and other natural disasters have also hurt the economy. Fidel Ramos instituted an austerity program in cooperation with the World Bank and International Monetary Fund in 1992.

International issues Since gaining its independence, the Philippines has been an ally of the United States and served as a staging area for the U.S. military during the Vietnam War. In 1992 the United States accepted Philippine demands that it withdraw from Clark Air Force Base and Subic Bay Naval Station. These facilities have since been leased to private companies as an industrial park.

The Philippines has a territorial dispute with China over the Spratly Islands, located between the archipelago and the mainland in the South China Sea. The dispute is important because gaining control of the islands means having access to rich off-shore oil deposits.

Human rights The Marcos regime engaged in intimidation, torture, and

Filipino peasants at work in rice paddies. Though the capital city of Manila has become one of the world's largest cities, much of the Philippines, especially the smaller islands, is still rural and poor.

assassination of political opponents and communist guerrillas. It imposed martial rule in 1972 and established a dictatorship, with no freedom of speech or assembly against the regime. In 1986 Aquino ended martial rule, freed political prisoners, and restored civil liberties. In 1990, under the Aquino regime, a special court convicted 16 military officers of the murder of Benigno Aquino.

SEE ALSO

Aquino, Corazon Cojuangco; Islamic fundamentalism; Marcos, Ferdinand

FURTHER READING

Bresnan, John, ed. *Crisis in the Philippines: The Marcos Era and Beyond*. Princeton, N.J.: Princeton University Press, 1986.
Dolan, Ronald E., ed. *Philippines: A Country Study*. 4th ed. Washington, D.C.: Federal Research Division, Library of Congress, 1993.
Karnow, Stanley. *In Our Image: America's Image in the Philippines*. New York: Random House, 1989.
Thompson, W. Scott. *The Philippines in Crisis*. New York: St. Martin's, 1991.

Pluralism

Pluralism is a political theory which claims that the fundamental interests in society are represented by factions and interest groups and that the greater the number of factions, the more stable the society. If there are many different groups, no permanent majority will be able to form and govern solely in its own interest. The theory asserts that no majority will oppress the minority in a pluralist system, provided the factional competition is conducted peacefully at the ballot box. Pluralist politics promotes the civil liberties of the right to association and petition and of freedom of speech and the press, so interest groups such as labor unions, corporations, religious organizations, civil rights groups, and others have access to the government and the media in order to influence public opinion.

In a pluralist system political parties are actually loose coalitions of groups and serve their interests. Elected representatives pay particular attention to interest groups that finance part of their campaigns for office. (In the United States, special interest groups lobby representatives on their behalf.) Instead of a single governing majority, coalitions will form in the legislature, and on each issue a differently constituted majority may have its way, even if only temporarily.

Each individual in a pluralist society belongs to many different groups (racial, ethnic, religious, regional, occupational), none of them controlled by the state. Each person has a diverse set of interests, and overlapping memberships often moderate one's views on issues. A homeowner, for example, may wish to see the pollution levels in his community reduced but may also, as a business owner, be inclined to resist restrictive pollution-control measures that increase his costs. Pluralism fosters moderation in each citizen as well as a balance of interests in the society as a whole.

The case against the establishment of a pluralist society is twofold: In a society in which the wealthy are outnumbered by the less affluent, the wealthy may use their money to gain more influence over government than any other group can. Pluralism in this case would not balance out the different interests, and the wealthy, with more power than the rest, would form an oligarchy. At that point, there might still be many groups in society, but government would take its orders from those with a preferred position, such as the large corporations. Alternatively, in a society in which most of the population is part of the middle class, most people may belong to many different groups that speak to their interests, but the least educated and the poor could remain unorganized. This may lead to what the 19th-century French theorist Alexis de Tocqueville referred to as a "tyranny of the majority" against those most in need of protection and help from the state, even in a society with pluralist interests.

The main contribution of pluralist theorists is their insight that in order to maintain a free society, most associations and groups should form in a voluntary manner rather than be organized by the government. There should be no official church, nor should the government organize workers into its own trade unions and professionals into its own associations. If these groups are not created by the government, they will remain free from coercion or direction by the state—unlike the situation in communist or fascist totalitarian and authoritarian regimes. Independent associations can communicate their own preferences for public policy to the government rather than follow "the party line" given to them by government leaders. When post-communist political theorists in eastern Europe and the former nations of the Soviet Union refer to their attempts to create a "civil society," they are talking about creating pluralism and ending just such organizations created and funded by the state.

SEE ALSO

Authoritarianism; Communism; Fascism; Totalitarianism

FURTHER READING

Dahl, Robert. *Dilemmas of Pluralist Democracy*. New Haven: Yale University Press, 1982.
Truman, David. *The Governmental Process*. New York: Knopf, 1951.

Poland

REPUBLIC OF POLAND (RZECZPOSPOLITA POLSKA)

• *Capital: Warsaw*

Political history Poland, located in northeastern Europe, was settled by a Slavic tribe known as the Polonians, and a Polish kingdom was founded in A.D. 966. The Poles accepted Christianity at the same time their kingdom was recognized by the Catholic Church and other European nations. Poland joined with the neighboring Kingdom of Lithuania in 1386, and the Commonwealth of Poland-Lithuania became a great power, with territories stretching through southeastern Europe. It reached the height of its power in the 17th century, when King Jan (John) III Sobieski stopped the advance of the Ottoman Empire into central Europe just south of Vienna. Thereafter, Poland grew weaker because of its corrupt nobility, and in a series of wars it was partitioned among Russia, Austria, and Prussia between 1772 and 1795. Napoléon revived a Polish state by establishing the puppet Grand Duchy of Warsaw. After his defeat, the European powers in 1815 permitted the Kingdom of Poland to exist as a state within the Russian Empire. The Russians spent the next 100 years attempting to introduce Russian language and culture and Orthodox religion into Poland, with little success.

Poland was reconstituted as a sovereign state after World War I, when Polish and Lithuanian forces fought against the revolutionary government in Russia until the Bolsheviks agreed in 1921 to accept Polish independence. At first a republic, Poland became a fascist-style dictatorship under Marshal Józef Pilsudski in 1926. After his death in 1936, a parliamentary facade remained, but the government was controlled by the military.

In 1939 Poland was invaded and partitioned by the Soviet Union and Germany. A government-in-exile in London organized Polish resistance forces, the Polish Home Army, to fight with the Allies against Germany during World War II. In 1941 Germany took over the Soviet territory of Poland, and from there the largest Jewish population in Europe was deported in the next three years to concentration camps.

At the end of World War II, Poland was occupied by the Soviet Red Army, which supported Polish communists against the government-in-exile in London. With the help of the Soviet Union, Poland became a communist puppet state. Some of its eastern territories were incorporated into the Soviet Union, according to agreements made by the Soviet Union, the United States, and the United Kingdom at the Potsdam Conference in Germany in August 1945. Poland was given some German territory in compensation, and the German population left the area. When elections were held in 1947, the Communist Party won a majority, and in 1949 the Communist Party took over all independent cultural and professional organizations, consolidating its power in a totalitarian regime. The Communists did permit the Catholic Church to continue its religious activities.

In the 1980s the regime's authority and legitimacy were challenged by the underground Solidarity movement, a labor union not recognized by the Communists, when it conducted strikes at the Gdańsk shipyards for higher pay, better working conditions, and no layoffs. In 1981, when Solidarity announced that it would hold its own referendum on the regime, President Wojciech Jaruzelski declared martial law and imprisoned many Solidarity leaders. Throughout the 1980s, the Catholic Church in Poland attacked the moral authority of the Communist rulers and allied itself with Solidarity.

In 1988 the Communist government negotiated with both the union and the church to try to end the impasse. The government agreed to permit Solidarity to compete in elections. In the 1989 elections Solidarity won control of both houses of parliament, although the agreement permitted the Communists to retain control of the lower house in spite of the election results. Jaruzelski remained president, but Solidarity leader Tadeusz Mazowiecki became prime minister. In 1990, as national movements across Eastern Europe challenged the presence of Soviet troops, the Polish Communists agreed to disband, and Jaruzelski resigned from the presidency. A new constitution was drafted. Solidarity leader Lech Wałęsa, who had replaced Mazowiecki and headed a coalition of labor and Catholic Solidarity members, was elected president and an era of multiparty democracy was inaugurated.

Government institutions Under provisions of the 1952 constitution (amended in 1989) Poland has a semi-presidential system. The president, directly elected for a five-year term, is the head of state and holds executive power. The president appoints a council of ministers and its chairman, or prime minister. The council is responsible to the legislature and to the president.

Legislative power is exercised by a bicameral National Assembly consisting of a 100-member Senate, with two senators elected from each province, and a 460-member Sejm (lower house), whose members are elected by proportional representation, with seats allocated to each party depending on what proportion of overall votes it receives. Members of the legislature serve for a four-year term.

The destruction of Warsaw in 1939. That year, Poland was invaded by both Germany and the Soviet Union, which divided up its territory.

The judiciary is composed of an independent supreme court, intermediate courts of appeal, and district courts.

Parties and movements Until 1989 Poland was a one-party state led by the Communist Party, officially named the Polish United Workers' Party. In 1989 an agreement with Solidarity (Solidarność in Polish) led to free elections but provided that the Communists would automatically retain a majority in the lower house of parliament for five years. In 1990, after an accord between the Communists and Solidarity, Communist president Wojciech Jaruzelski resigned, and Lech Wałęsa, the head of Solidarity, was elected president.

By the fall of 1990 Solidarity, no longer united by its opposition to the Communists, had splintered into numerous political parties, representing narrow constituencies in Polish society. In 1991 a 29-party parliament was elected and a weak coalition government was formed. In 1992 Hanna Suchocka was named Poland's first woman prime minister, heading a new multiparty coalition government. In the 1993 parliamentary elections, the centrist Democratic Union Party (free-market liberals), led by

Suchocka, were turned out of office. A coalition of communists, former communists, and socialists in the Democratic Left Alliance won a majority and formed a social democratic government along with the social democratic Polish Peasants' Party.

In the 1995 presidential elections, Wałęsa was narrowly defeated by Aleksander Kwaśniewski, a former editor of the Communist Party youth newspaper under the Jaruzelski regime and founder of the Left Democratic Alliance, a party of ex-Communists. The president, in turn, appointed a maverick former Communist, Włodzimierz Cimoszewicz, to head a coalition cabinet of leftist political parties.

Domestic issues Poland is making a transition from a centrally planned socialist economy to a free-market economy. Its radical transformation has resulted in hardship, including inflation and unemployment, but it posted the greatest economic gains in eastern Europe in the mid-1990s. More than half the labor force now works in private enterprises. Nevertheless, in spite of economic gains, several cabinets have been toppled by the legislature, and the

Solidarity movement has split over some of the antiunion measures taken by the government.

The liberal government of Hanna Suchocka, advised by Western economists, introduced high taxes and devalued the currency to stimulate exports just before the 1993 elections—a poor decision in political terms. The elections were a wake-up call to Polish leaders to moderate the pace of their free-market reforms. By 1994 voters were accusing the governing coalition, continuing with free-market reforms, of betraying its election mandate, and the coalition of communist and peasant parties was frayed with dissension over the pace of economic reform. The communist government that assumed power in 1996 intended to continue with economic reforms and encouraged Western investment in Poland's economy. It also pledged continued cooperation with the International Monetary Fund program for Polish economic development.

International issues Poland was a member of the Warsaw Pact and the Council for Mutual Economic Assistance, and its military forces and economy were dominated by the Soviet Union between 1947 and 1989. It participated in the 1968 Soviet invasion of Czechoslovakia that restored that country's hard-line communist regime.

In the 1990s Poland is no longer an ally of Russia, although it looks to both Russia and the United States to deter German territorial claims on its western borders. In addition, Poland is becoming integrated into western European institutions. It became a member of the Council of Europe and the Conference on Security and Cooperation in Europe. The Paris Club had canceled or renegotiated much of the Polish external debt in an attempt to stimulate the Polish economy. Poland was also a member of the Partnership for Peace of the NATO alliance. It asked to join the European Union and NATO and supported the bid of its neighbor Lithuania to join NATO, in spite of objections from Russia, which feared NATO troops on its borders.

Human rights More than 25,000 captured Polish officers were killed in the Katyn Forest by the Soviet Union in 1940 to pave the way for the Communist takeover. In 1956 a Polish attempt to free itself from Soviet domination was ended with a show of Soviet military force that prevented the Poles from exercising their right to self-determination. In 1981 the independent trade union Solidarity was banned and its leaders were arrested by the Polish government.

Under the Communists, Poles endured several periods of martial rule.

SEE ALSO

Solidarity (Solidarność); Soviet Union (Union of Soviet Socialist Republics); Wałęsa, Lech

FURTHER READING

Bernhard, Michael. *The Origins of Democratization in Poland*. New York: Columbia University Press, 1993.
Wałęsa, Lech. *The Struggle and the Triumph*. Translated by Franklin Philip. New York: Arcade, 1992.
Wedel, Janine. *The Unplanned Society: Poland during and after Communism*. New York: Columbia University Press, 1992.

Police state

A police state is one that rules its population by force. The term comes from the German word *polizeistaat*, which was used to describe Nazi Germany in the 1930s. A police state employs physical and psychological terror tactics on a mass scale. In communist states terror is directed against ideo-

Nazi officials question new arrivals at one of the many concentration camps established by the regime during World War II.

logical and class enemies. Fascist states typically use terror against religious and racial minorities, particularly the Jews, as well as against their ideological opponents, particularly communists and social democrats. In all authoritarian and totalitarian regimes, terror may be used against anyone, including those in the leadership, who challenge the power of the ruler. Both Stalin in the Soviet Union and Mao Zedong in China used terror randomly and indiscriminately to create an atmosphere of fear and intimidation among the entire citizenry, even members of the ruling party; no one knew who would be arrested and executed next.

Police states gather information about the population (in order to control it) from the secret police (such as the Nazi Gestapo), police informants who conduct surveillance of politically unreliable or disloyal citizens, and party cells (members of the ruling party), which control all social organizations, such as unions, legal and medical professional societies, newspapers and television stations, and universities. These cells insist on political conformity to the "party line." Some police states operate concentration camps (such as the Soviet labor camps,

or gulags) to punish those who refuse to submit to government control and conduct mass executions (used by the Nazis during the Holocaust).

In a police state the courts are also under the direct control of the regime. Judges pass sentences according to government dictates after "show trials" in which guilt is assumed and the trial is merely for propaganda purposes.

SEE ALSO

Concentration camp; Fascism; Holocaust; Nazi Party; Soviet Union (Union of Soviet Socialist Republics); Totalitarianism

FURTHER READING

Browder, George. *Foundation of the Nazi Police State*. Lexington: University of Kentucky Press, 1990.
Chapman, Brian. *Police State*. London: Pall Mall, 1981.
Conquest, Robert. *The Soviet Police System*. London: Bodley Head, 1968.
Wise, David. *The American Police State*. New York: Vintage, 1978.

Pol Pot

• *Born: May 19, 1928, Memot, French Indochina*

Pol Pot has been the leader of the Khmer Rouge revolutionary movement in Cambodia since the early 1950s. He and his colleagues are utterly ruthless leaders who have practiced autogenocide, and he has become a symbol of the exceptional cruelty associated with the Cambodian revolution and its "killing fields."

Pol Pot's original name was Saloth Sar, but he assumed a *nom de guerre* (name for war), following the precedent of other revolutionaries such as Joseph Stalin and Ho Chi Minh. (The name itself is a common rural name with no independent meaning.) Saloth Sar was born into a branch of the Cambodian royal family. He spent three years as a student in Paris in the early 1950s and became a Marxist-Leninist and an admirer of Stalin. He joined the Cambodian underground movement in 1953, engaging in guerrilla warfare against Prince Norodom Sihanouk and later the U.S.-backed Cambodian government of Lon Nol, because he and his followers wished to end foreign influence in Cambodia and establish a communist regime.

After the Khmer Rouge movement gained power in 1975 by defeating the Lon Nol government by force, Pol Pot (as he named himself in 1976) became prime minister and general secretary of the Communist Party of Kampuchea, the name given to the nation by its new rulers. He and his Central Committee forced the evacuation of all the cities and villages and drove practically the entire population into the countryside because they believed that the cities were overwhelmed by French and American influences. They intended to create a "new people" in Cambodia and referred to 1975 as Year Zero, as an indication that their rule marked the start of a new era.

As many as 2 million Cambodians were slaughtered by Pol Pot's forces after being deemed unfit to be part of the new Kampuchea. Then he turned on those of his comrades who had been trained by the North Vietnamese, killing hundreds of thousands of his own supporters. After the North Vietnamese invasion of Kampuchea in 1978, Pol Pot took his followers into a remote area near Thailand, where they waged guerrilla warfare for 10 years.

In the late 1980s the Khmer Rouge, claiming to have renounced communist ideology, participated in peace conferences designed to reunify the country. But Pol Pot, still at large in the jungles in the mid-1990s, remained a terrifying figure for millions of Cambodians. In 1997 his guerrilla movement fragmented and he killed many of his jungle associates, until he was captured by his former associates in 1997 and put on trial by them for his crimes.

SEE ALSO
Autogenocide; Cambodia; Khmer Rouge; Stalin, Joseph

FURTHER READING
Adler, Jerry, and Ron Moreau. "The Devil's Due." *Newsweek*, June 30, 1997, 40-43.
Chandler, David. *Brother Number One: A Political Biography of Pol Pot.* Boulder, Colo.: Westview, 1992.
Kiernan, Ben. *How Pol Pot Came to Power.* London: Routledge, Chapman & Hall, 1985.

Portugal

REPUBLIC OF PORTUGAL (REPUBLICA PORTUGUESA)

• *Capital: Lisbon*

Political history Located in southwestern Europe on the Iberian Peninsula, Portugal was first settled by the Lusitanians in 500 B.C. It was conquered by the Romans between 200 and 100 B.C. In the 4th century A.D. it became part of the Roman prefecture of Hispaniae, and its population converted to Christianity. In the 5th century, after the fall of the Roman Empire, much of it was controlled by the Kingdom of the Suevi, a western Iberian tribe. It was conquered by the Moors, from northern Africa, in the 8th century, who held it as part of the Emirate of Córdoba and then as part of the Ummayad Emirate. The Christian Kingdom of Castile, which ruled much of central Spain, conquered it in the 11th century. Portugal remained a Castilian province until winning its independence in 1143. By 1267 Portugal had driven the Moors from the Algarve region in the south. Portugal remained an independent kingdom except for a

During his reign, which lasted from 1932 to 1968, Antonio Salazar stabilized Portugal's economy while eliminating most political opposition. The end of his regime was marked by unrest over Portugal's handling of its remaining African colonies.

brief period of Spanish rule under the Habsburg monarchy from 1580 to 1640. A military revolt in Portugal in 1640 restored its independence.

By the middle of the 16th century Portugal was a pioneer in the exploration of Africa and the Americas because of its advanced methods of navigation and shipbuilding. It established an empire consisting of vast territories in Brazil, West Africa, East Africa, Indochina, and Malaya but lost some of its African and Asian territories during the period of Spanish occupation. During the 18th century other nations conquered most of Portugal's colonial possessions, and it lost Brazil in 1822 when Dom Pedro I, the Brazilian governor and a member of the Portuguese royal family, declared its independence.

By the end of the 19th century, civil wars over the succession to the throne had reduced Portugal to a minor power, with Great Britain, as its ally, conducting Portugal's foreign policy.

In 1910 a revolution ended the Portuguese monarchy and established the First Republic. But the new government was weak, and after eight presidents in 16 years, an authoritarian military regime was established in 1926. In 1932 the minister of finance, Antonio Salazar, became prime minister. The following year he organized the Estado Novo (New State), a fascist regime modeled on the government of Benito Mussolini in Italy. It was supported by the Catholic Church, which had opposed the radical regime that had separated church and state in 1911. After Salazar's resignation due to ill health in 1968, a military regime from his party took power, but it was unseated in a military coup in 1974 by officers who had grown disaffected with Portugal's wars to retain the African colonies of Angola and Mozambique. Shortly thereafter, Portugal's new military rulers granted independence to the remaining colonial possessions, including Angola and Mozambique.

The military's Revolutionary Council agreed to a short transition to civilian democratic rule, and a socialist government was established in 1976 under a new constitution, which left the military as guardian of the revolution and committed the nation to socialist development. The military's role, however, was ended by constitutional amendments in 1982. After the victory of the center-right Social Democrats in the late 1980s, further constitutional revisions in 1989 ended the commitment to socialism.

Government institutions Under provisions of the 1976 constitution (revised in 1982), Portugal has a parliamentary system. The president is the head of state but has no governing powers other than to appoint the prime minister and the council of ministers, who are accountable to parliament. The unicameral parliament has 230 members, popularly elected for four-year terms. There is an independent judiciary, headed by the Supreme

Court, whose members are appointed by the president.

Parties and movements Portugal is a multiparty democracy. The largest parties are the Social Democrats (liberal) and the Socialists (social democratic), followed by the People's Party (right-wing nationalist), and the Communists. The Social Democrats governed in the early 1990s and ended the nationalization of industries and banks, including the state-run oil industry, that had been promoted by the Socialists in the 1970s. In 1995 the Socialists won the parliamentary elections and in 1996 they won the presidency, giving the Portuguese single-party control of all institutions of government for the first time since the democracy was established in 1976.

Domestic issues Throughout the 1970s and 1980s Portugal had high inflation and a booming economy. In 1989 it began the privatization of state enterprises as part of its integration into the European Community, and it is making the transition from protectionism to competitiveness in industry and agriculture. In the early 1990s Portugal had the highest economic growth rate in Europe, which translated into strong popular support for its multiparty democratic system, although the problems of unemployment, cuts in welfare-state benefits, and inflation led to the Socialist resurgence in 1995.

International issues Although officially neutral, Portugal was sympathetic to the Axis cause during World War II. After the war, however, it became an ally of the United States. Portugal was a founding member of the European Free Trade Association and in 1986 joined the European Community. It was also a founding member of NATO and has permitted the United States to use a base at Lajes, on the island of Terceira in the Azores, as a refueling station for the U.S. Air Force.

Portugal reached an agreement with China on the reversion of its colony of Macao, which will come under Chinese rule in 1999. Portugal is attempting to gain self-determination for the people of East Timor, a former Portuguese colony that was annexed by Indonesia in 1976, causing the two nations to break diplomatic relations. In addition, Portugal played a role in mediating civil wars in Angola and Mozambique, former Portuguese overseas colonies, in the mid-1990s.

SEE ALSO

Angola; European Free Trade Association (EFTA); European Union (EU); Macao; Mozambique; North Atlantic Treaty Organization (NATO)

FURTHER READING

Maxwell, Kenneth. *The Making of Portuguese Democracy.* New York: Cambridge University Press, 1995.
Nataf, Daniel. *Democratization and Social Settlements: The Politics of Change in Contemporary Portugal.* Albany: State University of New York Press, 1995.
Opello, Walter. *Portugal: From Monarchy to Pluralist Democracy.* Boulder, Colo.: Westview, 1991.
Wiarda, Howard. *Politics in Iberia.* New York: HarperCollins, 1993.

Presidential system

A presidential system is a form of government in which a popularly elected president is the head of state and government. The president appoints a cabinet of ministers (or department secretaries) who supervise the bureaucracy. Legislative power is exercised by a separate body, and neither the president nor the department heads are accountable to the legislature. They serve

The 42nd president of the United States, Bill Clinton, reads a briefing document in the Oval Office of the White House.

whether or not they command a majority of votes in the legislature, which may remove them only by an impeachment trial, not by a vote of no confidence, as in a parliamentary system.

In the United States, it is usually assumed that the president's party will control the Congress (although this is often not the case); in other countries it is also assumed that the parliament and prime minister will come from the president's party. When the president's party dominates, it is known as party government: the president usually proposes a great deal of legislation, and the legislature is likely to pass most of it, making few changes. The president is likely to be able to exercise vast executive powers with little interference from Congress, and his interpretations of the Constitution, particularly the sections

regarding the powers of the presidential office, are not likely to be challenged.

Sometimes a president may be elected from one party and a majority of one or both chambers of the legislature from another party, a situation in the United States known as "split government." In other countries, the president may find that the parliament chooses a prime minister from a different party. In these cases, presidents either modify their programs to obtain some votes from opposition legislators or they fail to pass important parts of their program. The United States has gone through several periods of split government, most notably between 1969 and 1997, when there were only six years (four in Jimmy Carter's administration and two in Bill Clinton's) in which the president and both houses of Congress were controlled by the same party. Although it is often claimed that "gridlock" and paralysis will result from split government, that is not the case; much legislation does get passed, and the executive branch remains fully functional (because it is separate from the legislature). What is lost is political accountability, because each party blames the other for failures to solve national problems and the electorate finds it difficult to hold either party fully responsible.

SEE ALSO

Cabinet government; Parliamentary system; Prime minister; Semi-presidential system

FURTHER READING

Pious, Richard M. *The American Presidency.* New York: Basic Books, 1979.
Pious, Richard M. *The Presidency.* Englewood Cliffs, N.J.: Silver Burdett Press, 1991.
Pious, Richard M. *The Presidency.* Boston: Allyn & Bacon, 1996.
Pious, Richard M. *The Young Oxford Companion to the Presidency of the United States.* New York: Oxford University Press, 1994.

Prime minister

The prime minister is the head of government in a parliamentary system. The prime minister is chosen by the head of state to form a government by virtue of the fact that he is the leader of a party that commands a majority in parliament or is the politician best able to create a multiparty majority coalition. The prime minister is "first among equals" in the cabinet, selects the ministers who form it, presides over its deliberations, directs ministers in their duties, and may dismiss them or reshuffle their duties. The prime minister may bypass the full cabinet and work with an "inner cabinet" of key ministers or with his own political advisers and staff in shaping government policy.

The prime minister presides over the cabinet committees that prepare legislative proposals for parliament. He leads the debate in parliament and defends the record of the government. This office coordinates the work of the bureaucracy and sets foreign policy. The prime minister decides when to call for new elections and leads the party during those elections. In a semipresidential system, a prime minister is responsible for domestic policy and the routine workings of government, while the president handles diplomatic, defense, and national security policy-making.

SEE ALSO

Parliamentary system; Presidential system; Semi-presidential system

FURTHER READING

Elgie, Robert. *The Role of the Prime Minister in France, 1981–91.* New York: St. Martin's, 1993.
King, Anthony, ed. *The British Prime Minister.* 2nd ed. London: Macmillan, 1985.
Punnett, Robert M. *The Prime Minister in Canadian Government and Politics.* Toronto: Macmillan, 1977.
Weller, Patrick. *First Among Equals: Prime Ministers in Westminster Systems.* Boston: Allen & Unwin, 1985.

Protectorate

A protectorate is a state or territory that is under the "protection" of a greater power that has assumed control or has strong influence over its foreign policy. The extent of the powers that are ceded by the protectorate to that power are defined by treaties or other international agreements between the two states. The protected state remains nominally independent and self-governing in its internal affairs, but its external sovereignty (its power in defense and foreign affairs) is limited by the agreement with its "protector."

A protectorate may be contrasted with a puppet state, whose rulers are chosen by the imperial power but which remains nominally sovereign under international law. In many cases in Africa and Asia, protectorate status in the late 19th century was a prelude to a full takeover by a foreign power and the imposition of colonial status.

Protectorates were established by European powers in many areas of Africa and Asia in the late 19th and early 20th century. France, for example, signed a treaty with Morocco in 1912 that permitted it to control that state's foreign relations, station French troops in Morocco, and maintain a resident commissioner. Japan has been the only Asian power to establish protectorates: its protectorate over Korea, established in 1905, was endorsed by the United States as a means of ensuring stability in the region, but it ended in 1945 with Japan's defeat in World War II.

The United States had protectorates (although it did not call them that) in the Caribbean and in Central America, including Cuba, Nicaragua, the Dominican Republic, Haiti, and Panama, all of which had to accept the presence of U.S. military forces in the early part of the 20th century. Under the "international police power" of the United States, promulgated by President Teddy Roosevelt, the United States reserved the right to use force to intervene in the internal affairs of these nations, especially when they defaulted on U.S. loans. The proclamation of the Good Neighbor policy by President Franklin Roosevelt in 1933 ended the U.S. claim that it had a right to interfere in the internal affairs of Latin American states and ended U.S. domination of these states.

After World War I and World War II, the victors upheld the right of self-determination at a time when pro-independence movements in the colonies were also exerting pressure. Many protectorates and colonies were converted into mandates and trusteeships, with the colonial powers pledging to the United Nations to prepare colonial peoples for full independence.

SEE ALSO
Colonialism; Imperialism; Mandate; Nation-state; Puppet state; Sovereignty; Trust territories

Puppet state

A puppet state is a nominally sovereign state whose rulers and government are propped up by the presence of armed forces from another state. A puppet state's status is imposed by an imperial power that does not wish to formally incorporate the area into its own empire or assume the costs of governing it either as an internal province or an external colony. Nevertheless, the puppet government does the bidding of the imperial power, and its natural resources and economic activities benefit the imperial power more than its own citizens. When the outside power withdraws its forces, the puppet state falls.

The puppet state of Manchukuo (formerly known as Manchuria) was established by the Japanese in the part of China they controlled after 1936. The Japanese installed the deposed emperor of China as the emperor of Manchukuo, but the Japanese military authorities controlled the territory and used its resources for the war against China in the late 1930s. Manchukuo was dissolved near the end of World War II with the Japanese defeat by the Allies.

When the Nazis occupied Norway in 1940, they established a puppet state under Vidkun Quisling, whom they named president-prime minister in 1942, and whose name became synonymous with collaboration and treason. After the occupation ended, the Norwegians executed Quisling in 1945.

East Germany became a puppet state of the Soviet Union after occupation by the Red Army at the end of World War II, as did Poland, Czechoslovakia, Bulgaria, and Hungary. Their regimes were propped up by the Soviet Union, which intervened militarily in each state when their communist regimes were threatened by popular revolts. On the other hand, Romania, Yugoslavia, and Albania all established communist regimes that, however totalitarian or authoritarian, did not depend on the Soviet Union to remain in power.

During the cold war the term *puppet government* was also used by the Soviet Union and China to refer to a number of U.S. allies that they claimed were dominated by the United States, including South Korea and South Vietnam.

SEE ALSO
Authoritarianism; Communism; Imperialism; Sovereignty; Totalitarianism

Vidkun Quisling was installed by the Nazis as the puppet ruler of Norway after Germany's invasion in 1940. Today, the word quisling *is a synonym for "traitor."*

Qaddafi, Muammar al-

• *Born: 1942, Sirte, Libya*

Muammar al-Qaddafi, a revolutionary Arab nationalist, has been the leader of Libya since 1969. A fiery orator, he has stirred up Arab masses for decades with strident anti-American, anti-Western, and anti-Israeli speeches. He has pursued an erratic foreign policy, sometimes aligning Libya with the Soviet Union during the cold war, sponsoring terrorist organizations, and pursuing a confrontational policy toward Israel and conservative Arab states in the region. Yet at times he has acted in a conciliatory manner toward the western European nations whose funding he needs to develop the Libyan economy. He has always remained personally incorruptible, leading an austere life and battling the endemic corruption in the Libyan economy.

Born into a Bedouin family near Sirte, Qaddafi spent his early years in his family's tent in the desert. He later graduated from the Benghazi Military Academy. In 1967, soon after entering the army upon graduation, Qaddafi organized a coup by the Free Officers Movement, a group of young officers who wished to end corruption and foreign influence in Libya. The movement overthrew King Idris I in 1969 in a swift coup d'état. Qaddafi headed the Revolutionary Command Council, the junta that ran the country, and was simultaneously prime minister and defense minister.

Qaddafi addresses an audience of Pakistanis at an Islamic conference in Lahore, Pakistan. Despite efforts by the United States and other nations to unseat him, Qaddafi has ruled Libya for almost 30 years.

Qaddafi set forth his "Third Universal Theory" in three volumes of *The Green Book,* published between 1976 and 1979, an approach to governing that he claimed would supersede capitalism and communism. Following its precepts, which combined the tenets of Islam with Arab socialism, he abolished the traditional monarchical governmental structure of Libya and created the General People's Congress, an elected body that, in theory, possessed all governmental powers but, in practice, took direction from Qaddafi. Qaddafi resigned from his official posts in 1979 in order to demonstrate that the people were the supreme ruler but effectually remained Libya's undisputed leader, because of his control of the military and police forces.

Because of his anti-Western orientation, Qaddafi has engaged in state terrorism and has permitted terrorist organizations from several nations to use the Libyan desert for their training bases. A 1986 U.S. bombing raid on Libya, ordered by President Ronald Reagan in retaliation for Libyan-organized attacks on U.S. military personnel in Europe, almost killed Qaddafi and badly injured his infant daughter. The raid induced the Libyan leader to end support for groups attacking Americans. In the early 1990s, however, Qaddafi began construction of one of the largest chemical plants in the world, apparently in an effort to develop chemical weapons.

SEE ALSO
Libya

FURTHER READING

Cooley, John. *Libyan Sandstorm.* New York: Holt, Rinehart & Winston, 1995.
Fallaci, Oriani. "An Encounter with Colonel Qaddafi." *New York Times Magazine,* April 14, 1996, p. 130.
Kyle, Benjamin. *Muammar el-Qaddafi.* New York: Chelsea House, 1987.

Sicker, Martin. *The Making of a Pariah State: The Adventurist Politics of Muammar Qaddafi.* New York: Praeger, 1987.

Qatar

STATE OF QATAR (DAWLAT AL-QATAR)

• *Capital: Doha*

Political history Located on the eastern shores of the Arabian Peninsula, Qatar was part of Bahrain until the late 19th century, when it became an emirate (a monarchy headed by an emir, or native leader) within the Ottoman Empire. In 1916 it was conquered by the British, who were interested in using it as a naval base, and it became a British protectorate. Great Britain granted Qatar independence in 1971 and withdrew its military forces. Qatar attempted to join the United Arab Emirates (UAE) for national security reasons but declared its independence after negotiations with the UAE foundered over the issue of taxation.

Government institutions Qatar has been an independent sovereign emirate since 1971. The emir is always a member of the powerful al-Thani clan, which has traditionally provided government leaders. The emir is both the head of state and commander in chief of the armed forces. The government departments are run by a council of ministers accountable to the emir. There is no parliament, but the emir consults with an appointed 30-member advisory council. There is a judiciary that applies both civil and Islamic law; all judges are appointed by the emir.

Parties and movements No political parties are permitted in Qatar.

Domestic issues Relatives of the emir occupy the most important government positions, including the ministries of justice, foreign affairs, defense, oil, and finance. Other sheikhs are given high government posts to solidify support for the emir among the elite.

Qatar receives large revenues from oil and gas production; its North Field is the world's largest gas field. It uses revenues from these industries to support an extensive welfare state, providing free education, health care, and family allowances to citizens, who constitute only one-third of the country's population (the remaining inhabitants are foreigners, laborers from nearby Arab and Asian states who do most of the work in the country). Qatar also has a thriving pearl-diving industry.

The legitimacy of the absolute rule of the emir has been challenged by Islamic fundamentalists who wish to establish a new state under Islamic law and end the corrupt rule of the emir and the sheikhs.

International issues Qatar has a treaty of friendship with Great Britain. Because of that alliance, the emir permitted U.S. forces and their allies to deploy troops in Qatar during the Persian Gulf War against Iraq in 1991.

A border conflict with Saudi Arabia in the early 1990s led Qatar to establish closer strategic ties with Iran, restore relations with Iraq, and sign a defense cooperation pact with the United States, in an attempt to use these nations as counterweights to Saudi pressure. Qatar has also taken the lead among Persian Gulf states in establishing informal diplomatic and commercial relations with Israel.

Qatar's General Petroleum Corporation is engaged in a $10 billion development of gas production in the 1990s with a consortium of Western nations and Japan, which will rely on production from North Field for energy requirements through the early 21st century.

SEE ALSO

Islamic fundamentalism

FURTHER READING

Crystal, Jill. *Oil and Politics in the Gulf.* New York: Cambridge University Press, 1995.

Quebec

Quebec is a province of Canada—the only one of Canada's 10 provinces and 2 territories with a French-speaking majority. In the early 1990s, more than half of its French-speaking citizens (who constitute four-fifths of Quebec's population) sought either to convert Canada into a bi-national state (in which Quebec would be treated as an equal with the rest of English-speaking Canada rather than as just one of its provinces) or to leave Canada and become an independent sovereign state.

The French colony of New France was founded along the shores of the St. Lawrence River in North America in 1608. In 1759 the colony was conquered by the British, but the French population was allowed to retain its linguistic and religious identity and its legal code under Britain's Quebec Act of 1774. This arrangement was partly the result of the British desire to maintain French loyalty in the event of an American revolution. In 1791 the colony was divided into Upper Canada (what is now Ontario) and Lower Canada (Quebec), so that English- and French-speaking settlers could each have their own government. Rebellions against British rule in Lower Canada were crushed in 1837. Quebec became part of the Dominion of Canada in 1867, by forming a confederation with Upper Canada, Nova Scotia, and New Brunswick. The Quebec economy was soon dominated by Anglophones (English speakers) sitting in its provincial

capital, Montreal. Most of Canada assumed that gradually the Quebecois population would lose its language and culture and assimilate into the broader, Anglophone, Canadian culture.

In 1968 René Lévesque and other nationalists concerned about defending Francophone (French-speaking) culture founded the Parti Québécois. It called for Quebec to leave Canada and become a sovereign state. It would then associate itself with Canada in a common market (an arrangement in which there would be no tariffs between Canada and Quebec and goods could move freely across their borders). The PQ won control of the provincial government in 1976, but it lost a 1980 referendum on its bid to negotiate with Canada for sovereignty; 59 percent of the citizens voted no. (Although a majority of the French-speaking voters approved it, the Anglophone voters and immigrants tipped the balance against it.) The PQ was defeated in the 1985 provincial election by the Liberal Party because of its lackluster economic performance.

Meanwhile, the Quebec governments, whether dominated by the Liberal Party or the PQ, promoted French culture and insisted that the province's business be conducted in French. Many English-speaking citizens and corporations, as a result, left Quebec for other provinces, particularly Ontario.

Because a sufficient number of provinces failed to ratify the 1990 Meech Lake Accords—a proposed revision of the federal constitution that would have given Quebec greater autonomy—calls for independence were given renewed impetus. In the 1993 federal elections, the Bloc Québécois, a separatist movement that evolved from the PQ to compete in national elections, won overwhelmingly in Quebec Province.

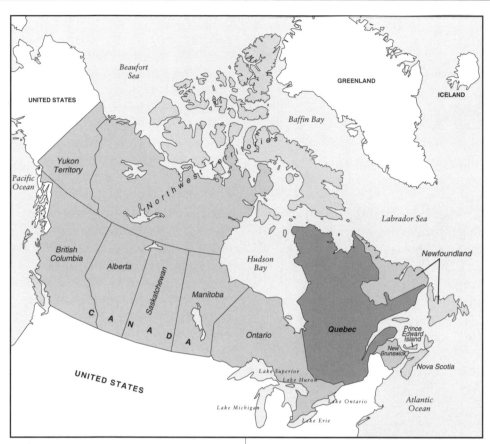

In the early 1990s Quebec's provincial government was controlled by the Liberal Party, which opposed independence. The PQ, the main opposition party, continued to favor independence and held a new referendum after winning the provincial elections in 1994. The Liberal and Conservative parties in the province strongly opposed the independence initiative. The voters defeated the initiative by the narrow margin of 50.6 to 49.4 percent, but 60 percent of the 82 percent of the population that is Francophone supported the referendum. The 18 percent of the population that is English-speaking largely voted against it, thus further polarizing Quebec society. Overall, 80 of the 125 electoral districts in the province favored secession in 1995.

Following the vote, the premier of Quebec, Jacques Parizeau, resigned, blaming "money and the ethnic vote" (non-French-speaking voters) for the defeat. He was succeeded by another separatist leader, Lucien Bouchard, who insisted that "Canada is not a real country" and who promised that there would be more secession referenda until Quebec voted to secede, but only after economic issues, such as high rates of unemployment and a large budget deficit, had been dealt with.

SEE ALSO

Canada; Trudeau, Pierre Elliott

FURTHER READING

Keatin, Michael. *Nations against the State*. New York: St. Martin's, 1996.
Lamont, Lansing. *Breakup: The Coming End of Canada and the Stakes for America*. New York: Norton, 1994.
Resnick, Philip. *Toward a Canada-Quebec Union*. Montreal: McGill-Queen's University Press, 1991.
Young, Robert. *The Secession of Quebec and the Future of Canada*. Montreal: McGill-Queen's University Press, 1995.

Rabin, Yitzhak

- *Born: Mar. 1, 1922, Jerusalem, British Mandate of Palestine*
- *Died: Nov. 4, 1995, Jerusalem, Israel*

Yitzhak Rabin served as prime minister of Israel from 1974 to 1977 and again from 1992 to 1995. He was the first Israeli prime minister to be born in the land of Palestine rather than in Europe. He ended the siege mentality of his nation (the result of wars with Arab states since the establishment of the state of Israel in 1948) and embraced a peace process with his longtime enemy Yasir Arafat, leader of the Palestine Liberation Organization (PLO). After his assassination at the hands of a right-wing Israeli, Yitzhak Rabin became a symbol of the sacrifices Israelis made in the 1990s during the Middle East peace process.

A graduate of the Kadoorie Agricultural School in Galilee, Rabin gave up his dreams of becoming a farmer to fight for the survival of the Jewish people, which was threatened by the Holocaust. He commanded a unit of the Palmach (Jewish fighters) during World War II. The Palmach fought with the Allies against the Germans in the Middle East, in hopes that the British would turn over part of Palestine (a mandate of Great Britain since 1923) to the Jews if the Allies were victorious. With no change forthcoming after the war, Rabin fought in the 1948 Israeli War of Independence against several Arab nations that had invaded Israel and opposed the establishment of a Jewish state. He served as a brigade commander in the Jerusalem front and against Egyptian forces on the Sinai Peninsula. He participated in the armistice talks that ended the fighting in 1949. Later, Rabin participated in the 1956 Israeli invasion of the Sinai Peninsula, territory that belonged to Egypt.

Between 1956 and 1959 Rabin headed the military's Northern Command. He was chief of staff of the Israeli army when it defeated Egypt, Jordan, and Syria in the 1967 Six-Day War.

Rabin left the military to become ambassador to the United States from 1968 to 1973, establishing close relations with the administration of Richard Nixon. As a result, U.S. financial aid and arms sales to Israel increased greatly during Nixon's presidency. Rabin became leader of the Labor Party in 1974 and assumed the post of prime minister after Golda Meir's resignation that year. In 1975 he signed a "disengagement plan" sponsored by the Americans that led to Israeli withdrawal from much of the Sinai Peninsula. In 1976 he ordered a daring and successful raid on the Entebbe airport in Uganda to free Israeli airline passengers held hostage by Palestinian terrorists.

Rabin resigned in 1977 when it was disclosed that he and his wife, Leah, had violated foreign currency restrictions. The scandal contributed to the opposition Likud coalition's assumption of power for the first time since Israel was founded in 1948.

In 1984 Rabin re-entered public life and served as defense minister in a Labor–Likud coalition government. He sent in more troops and ordered them to use force against the Palestinian Intifada, the uprising against Israeli rule in the Gaza Strip and on the West Bank. Rabin once again was elected Labor leader, and he became prime minister again in 1992. He strongly supported the Middle East peace talks that began in 1992 under U.S. auspices, telling his countrymen that "no longer is the whole world against us," but he took a very hard line against Palestinian terrorist attacks on civilians and other resistance to the military in the occupied territories. He was, however, the first leader of an Israeli government to allow direct negotiations between his nation and officials of the PLO, and early in 1994 he concluded an agreement with PLO chairman Yasir Arafat that allowed for Palestinian autonomy in the Gaza Strip and Jericho District. His ultimate goal, as he told his fellow Israelis, was to end the cycle of war and occupation so that Israelis and Palestinians "could live together on the same soil in the same land." Rabin's assassination, by an Israeli opposed to the peace process, indicated just how difficult that goal would be to achieve.

SEE ALSO
Arafat, Yasir; Intifada; Israel; Palestine; Palestine Liberation Organization (PLO)

FURTHER READING
Fedarko, Kevin. "Man of Israel." *Time,* November 13, 1995, 68–72.
Jerusalem Report staff. *Shalom, Friend: The Life and Legacy of Yitzhak Rabin.* New York: Newmarket, 1996.
Rabin, Yitzhak. *The Rabin Memoirs.* Boston: Little, Brown, 1979.
Slater, Robert. *Rabin of Israel.* New York: St. Martin's, 1993.

Radicalism

Radicalism was an 18th- and 19th-century political movement in Europe and the Americas whose members questioned existing political institutions and called for the separation of the state from an established church, along with an end to all church privileges and power in civil society. It was particularly strong in France, Italy, the United States, and Mexico.

Radical thinkers drew their inspiration from the 18th-century French Enlightenment, a philosophical movement that stressed rational and scientific thought. They viewed religious beliefs as superstitions and church leaders as reactionaries more interested in retaining their privileges than in contributing to the progress of humankind. Radicals were strongly opposed to monarchical government, because it was based on inheritance rather than merit, and believed in new forms of government that would promote democracy.

Radical regimes promoted public secular education in the place of church schools as well as land reform (the redistribution of land from the rich to the poor) to eliminate extensive church holdings. They also called for the elimination of tax exemptions for churches, an end to the formal representation of established churches in the national legislature, and elimination of church courts and their jurisdiction over family matters such as marriage and divorce.

Because European monarchs, ever since the Middle Ages, had been crowned by established churches, which recognized the divine right of kings to rule over the state, radicals were opposed to monarchy as well as to church privileges. They incurred the opposition of conservatives not only for their antimonarchical position but also for their opposition to privileges of the aristocracy, such as noble titles and land grants. Radicals were close to liberals in their emphasis on private property and free markets and therefore were opposed by socialists, social democrats, and communists, who preferred state ownership of enterprises.

Radical parties often held the balance of power in multiparty parliamentary democracies between conservatives and socialists. They were usually included in center-left or center-right coalition governments, often achieving influence in the government beyond their proportional representation. They strongly influenced the anticlerical policies (such as ending government support for church schools) of France in the 19th century and Mexico in the 20th century.

After the settlement of most church–state disputes by the 1960s, radical parties lost ground to liberal and Christian Democratic parties in Western Europe and Latin America.

In the United States, radicals achieved their greatest influence at the time of the American Revolution, when leaders such as Thomas Paine in Virginia and Samuel Adams in Massachusetts attacked the authority of King George III and denied that any monarch had the right to rule over a free people. Radicals influenced the development of the 1st Amendment to the Bill of Rights, which guaranteed freedom of religion and prohibited Congress from "establishing" any religion, both provisions designed to ensure the separation of church and state.

Drawing their inspiration from earlier radical movements, in the 1960s students such as Tom Hayden (head of Students for a Democratic Society), Mario Savio (leader of a free-speech movement at the University of California at Berkeley), and Mark Rudd (a leader of Students for a Democratic Society at Columbia University) questioned authority in virtually every American institution, including the national government (which they viewed as undemocratic), the labor movement (corrupt and unrepresentative of working people), and universities (too closely allied with corporations and the military). The student radicals of the 1960s were a major force behind the antiwar movement that caused an end to the escalation of the war in Vietnam, and

they participated in the civil rights demonstrations that eventually led the national and state governments to end racial segregation.

SEE ALSO
Christian Democracy; Communism; Conservatism; Liberalism; Monarchy; Multiparty system; Social democracy; Socialism

Rafsanjani, Ali Akbar Hashemi

• *Born: 1934, Rafsanjān, Iran*

As president of Iran from 1989 to 1997, Ali Rafsanjani guided his country's revolutionary regime after the death of the Ayatollah Khomeini, who had assumed control of Iran in 1979. A fiery orator, known for his sarcasm and wit in addressing hundreds of thousands of people in the capital city of Tehran, Rafsanjani is an accomplished politician who succeeded in ending Iran's isolation from the West while maintaining its focus on Islamic fundamentalism.

Rafsanjani grew up on his parents' pistachio farm in southwest Iran, then became a wealthy landowner himself. He attended the theological seminary at Qom, studying with Khomeini in the late 1950s. He graduated as a *hojatolislam,* one of the highest priestly ranks.

Rafsanjani became the chief organizer in Iran of political and religious opposition to the shah of Iran, after Khomeini was exiled in 1964. He was imprisoned several times by the shah for supporting Muslim fundamentalists in their efforts to establish a theocracy. In 1979 Rafsanjani helped establish the Islamic Republican Party after Khomeini and his supporters overthrew the shah, and he was elected speaker of the Majlis (parliament) in 1980. Rafsanjani was instrumental in ousting moderate president Abol Hassan Bani-Sadr in 1981, which led to more influence for the clerics at the expense of the business leaders in Iran. He also negotiated an end to the war with Iraq in 1988.

After the death of the Ayatollah Khomeini in 1989, Rafsanjani was elected president of Iran. He opened Iran up to western European investments but maintained a harsh anti-American stance. To improve government efficiency, he reduced the influence of Islamic clerics in the government, eliminating most clergy from the cabinet of ministers that ran the day-to-day affairs. Still, the clergy remained the ultimate policymakers for the regime. His efforts to privatize many state enterprises and reduce government regulation of the economy were blocked by a conservative majority in the Majlis.

Rafsanjani's term ended in 1997, and as he left office, the trend in Iran was toward a more progressive and less religious regime. Through Rafsanjani's efforts, the Islamic revolution in Iran had become a fact of life, but its fervor had decreased.

SEE ALSO

Iran; Islamic fundamentalism; Khomeini, Ayatollah Ruhollah Mussavi

Reagan, Ronald

• *Born: Feb. 6, 1911, Tampico, Ill.*

The 40th president of the United States (1981–89), Ronald Reagan was the first actor and the oldest man ever to be elected to that office. Reagan brought conservatives to power in the Republi-can Party and in the nation. He was the first U.S. president since Franklin Roosevelt to serve two full terms and hand over the office to a member of his own party. Known as the Great Communicator, he was a consummate speaker whose use of bold language and vivid metaphors enabled him to capture public opinion and move it toward his conservative ideas. A self-described genial and bluff Irishman, Reagan loved to tell or to hear jokes and had a common touch that made him popular with many people who did not agree with his political philosophy.

After graduating in 1932 with a major in economics from Eureka College, a small Protestant school in northern Illinois, Reagan became a sports announcer on radio programs. In 1937 he became a contract movie actor, and during World War II he made training films for the military. After the war he made B movies—low-budget dramas and comedies—for Hollywood studios. He also served as president of the Screen Actors Guild and was instrumental in ending communist influence in that union. In the 1950s he became a host of a television drama series. After the series ended, he became a spokesman for the General Electric Company and also became active in championing conservative causes.

Reagan was elected governor of California twice, in 1966 and 1970. He tried to cut government spending, particularly for welfare, and reduced property taxes. He also took a strong stand opposing students demonstrating against the Vietnam War.

Reagan defeated President Jimmy Carter in the presidential election of 1980, in large part because voters were upset with high interest, inflation, and unemployment rates and because Reagan promised to restore U.S. military strength. In domestic affairs

Reagan was a staunch conservative. He embraced a supply-side economic theory, which held that by reducing taxes the economy would boom and overall tax revenues would therefore increase, thus enabling the government to reduce the deficit. In 1981 Congress adopted his economic program after Reagan masterfully won over public opinion and lobbied some conservative Democrats to support him. Government revenues fell, however, when the economy went into a recession, and because of this Reagan asked Congress for deep cuts in social welfare programs; for the most part, the Democrat-led Congress rejected his suggestions. With domestic expenditures remaining high and outlays for defense soaring under Reagan, the overall national debt increased from $1 trillion to $3 trillion between 1981 and 1989.

In foreign affairs, Reagan initially took a confrontational line with the Soviet Union, denouncing it as an "evil empire." He announced plans to equip NATO forces in Europe with new medium-range Pershing nuclear-tipped missiles. He asked for funds to deploy a new generation of intercontinental MX missiles. He reversed Carter's decision to cancel the B-1 bomber and ordered development of radar-evading Stealth bombers and fighters. He doubled the size of the navy to 600 surface ships and ordered new submarines and aircraft carriers. He announced a Strategic Defense Initiative program of antimissile weapons to defend against Soviet attack, which his critics promptly dubbed "Star Wars." Under Reagan, the Pentagon increased the annual level of defense spending from $200 billion to $300 billion in five years.

Reagan also equipped the government of El Salvador in its fight against leftist guerrillas, and he funded and equipped the contra rebels in their struggle against the leftist Sandinista government of Nicaragua. He provided covert funding for anticommunist rebels in Afghanistan. And in October 1983, Reagan ordered the invasion of Grenada, ostensibly to protect U.S. medical students during disorders between two factions of the Marxist government, but this action ultimately led to the replacement of the leftist government with leaders backed by the United States. Reagan also used U.S. Marines as part of an international peacekeeping force in Lebanon but withdrew the forces several months later, after guerrillas blew up the marine barracks, killing 241 of the peacekeepers in October 1983.

Reagan handily won reelection in 1984. During his second term, the defense buildup brought the Soviets to the negotiating table. By 1985 the United States and the Soviet Union were negotiating deep cuts in strategic nuclear forces, and in 1987 they agreed on significant cuts in medium- and short-range nuclear missiles in Europe.

In 1986 Reagan committed a major foreign policy blunder that nearly destroyed his presidency. He agreed to sell arms to Iran in a secret attempt to bolster moderates in that nation's government who would, in turn, free Western hostages who had been taken prisoner by pro-Iranian Islamic groups in Lebanon. Some of the profits from the sales were then transferred by Oliver North of the National Security Council to the contra rebels to help fund their battle against the Nicaraguan government. The funding, however, violated the Boland Amendment, which Congress had passed in 1984 to cut off funds to the contras. When the sale was disclosed by a Lebanese newspaper, Democrats in Congress organized a full-scale investigation of the "Iran-Contra" affair. Throughout 1987 Reagan seemed preoccupied with the crisis, and his government was paralyzed. His national security adviser and others on the National Security Council staff resigned. Several top White House aides and his chief of staff also resigned. There was no evidence linking Reagan directly to the transfer of funds to the contras, but the Tower Commission, headed by Senator John Tower and appointed by the president to study the incident, determined that national security affairs in the White House had been mismanaged. President Reagan implemented most of the reforms in procedures that were suggested by the commission.

In retirement, Reagan and his wife, Nancy, lived in California, where he published his presidential memoir and raised funds for the Reagan presidential library. In the early 1990s he was diagnosed with Alzheimer's disease, and by 1994 he no longer made public appearances.

SEE ALSO

Carter, Jimmy (James Earl, Jr.); Iran; Nicaragua

FURTHER READING

Cannon, Lou. *President Reagan: The Role of a Lifetime.* New York: Simon & Schuster, 1991.
Johnson, Haynes. *Sleepwalking Through History: America in the Reagan Years.* New York: Norton, 1991.
Pemberton, William E. *Exit with Honor: The Life and Presidency of Ronald Reagan.* Armonk, N.Y.: M. E. Sharpe, 1997.
Schaller, Michael. *Reckoning with Reagan: America and Its President in the 1980s.* New York: Oxford University Press, 1992.
Schwartzberg, Renee. *Ronald Reagan.* New York: Chelsea House, 1991.

Republic of China

SEE Taiwan

Revolution

A revolution is a fundamental and rapid change in the political, economic, and social systems of a nation, empire, or territory that occurs outside of the law and the constitution. Revolutions may occur under any of the following conditions: when people fight against imperial rule and throw off their colonial rulers (as in Latin America in the 1820s or in Africa and Asia after World War II); when they get rid of authoritarian military regimes or dictators and establish democratic systems (which happened in Spain and Portugal in the 1970s); when weak multiparty democracies are overthrown by fascist or communist movements (Russia in 1917, Italy in 1922, and Germany in 1933); when poor peasants and urban workers overthrow an oligarchy and the government that protects it (this happened in Cuba in 1958 and in Nicaragua in 1979); when secular regimes are removed by religious fundamentalists (for example, when the Ayatollah Khomeini took control of Iran in 1979); or when communist regimes are overthrown by religious fundamentalists (as in Afghanistan in 1989) or by secular democrats and nationalists (which was

A freedom fighter in the African nation of Mozambique waves the flag of the Mozambique Liberation Front (known as FRELIMO) in 1971. At the time, FRELIMO was spearheading the struggle to free Mozambique from Portuguese colonial rule.

the case throughout Eastern Europe in 1990).

Some revolutions do not involve an overthrow of the government but are fomented by those already in power in order to transform political institutions or consolidate their power. During the Cultural Revolution of the 1960s in China and in Libya in the 1970s, leaders at the top whipped up their supporters in the streets to terrorize recalcitrant government officials who were subverting revolutionary goals.

Revolutions have changed empires into nations (the Ottoman Empire was transformed into the nation of Turkey in 1922, and the Soviet Union into Russia and the other states of the Commonwealth of Independent States in 1991) and nations into empires (the Russian Revolution of 1917 united formerly independent states into the Soviet Union, for example). Finally, colonial war may prove so costly to the colonizing power that the home country faces its own internal revolution when the government expends too many lives of its citizens or if it gives up colonies when the people want to retain them. As France was losing the Algerian war in 1958, right-wing military units threatened to revolt. The Fourth Republic fell, and General Charles de Gaulle assumed power and established the Fifth Republic. Many of his followers assumed, wrongly, that he would continue the war in Algeria, but he soon agreed to its demands for independence.

Revolutions may be violent (the American Revolution of 1776 and the French Revolution of 1789) or peaceful (the transformation of the Soviet Union into the Commonwealth of Independent States in 1991). Some revolutionary movements utilize nonviolent action, such as protests, strikes, and demonstrations, to bring down a regime. In India, for example, Mahatma Gandhi led millions of Indians in nonviolent protest against British rule, and their demands for independence were peacefully negotiated after World War II. Other revolutionary leaders hold violence to a minimum by encouraging defections from within the armed forces, which then overthrow the government in a quick coup d'état. The overthrow of most Eastern European communist regimes in 1989–90 was accomplished with a minimum of violence, because the state military forces refused to fight against the rebels, as was the overthrow in 1986 of the Philippine dictator Ferdinand Marcos by "people power."

Other revolutionary movements, such as the Irish Republican Army or Shining Path in Peru, engage in guerrilla warfare against government troops or other terrorist actions, such as hostage taking, assassinations, and bombings, to demoralize civilians who support the government. Most revolutions around the world that rely on guerrilla wars and terrorist campaigns have failed, after provoking violent reprisals by the government security forces and ending in a stalemate that leaves a country's economy and society in a shambles.

Some revolutions, such as the American Revolution, involve a restructuring of the political system but no fundamental changes in economic systems. However, the economy may subsequently be profoundly affected by political changes; after British rule ended in America, restrictions on the exploitation of western territories were lifted and Americans were also able to trade with other European nations. Other revolutions, such as the Russian Revolution of 1917, the Chinese Revolution of 1949, the Cuban Revolution of 1959, and the Cambodian Revolution of 1975, have as their goal radical changes in the economy, such as government control of industries and banks, the elimination of private farms, and radical redistribution of wealth.

Although many revolutions move into a radical phase before moderating, some political leaders, such as Mao Zedong of China, Pol Pot of Cambodia, and Muammar Qaddafi of Libya, promoted "permanent revolution" so that the state and its ruling party could periodically purge moderates and reintroduce revolutionary fervor into political life.

Revolutions are different from coups d'état, in which one set of leaders in a military junta or dictatorship is simply replaced with another.

SEE ALSO

China; Coup d'état; Cuba; Decolonization; Imperialism; Irish Republican Army (IRA); Junta; Mao Zedong; Mexican Revolution; Military regime; Pol Pot; Qaddafi, Muammar al-; Russian Revolution

FURTHER READING

Brinton, Crane. *The Anatomy of Revolution.* Rev. ed. New York: Vintage, 1965.
Goldstone, Jack, et al. *Revolutions of the Late Twentieth Century.* Boulder, Colo.: Westview, 1991.
Skocpol, Theda. *States and Social Revolutions.* Cambridge, England: Cambridge University Press, 1979.

Rhee, Syngman

- *Born: Apr. 26, 1875, Pyŏngsan, Korea*
- *Died: July 19, 1965, Honolulu, Hawaii*

The first president of the Republic of Korea (1948–60), Syngman Rhee led his nation to independence after World War II and preserved it against aggression from North Korea in the 1950s. Austere, a devout Methodist, and conservative in his personal life, he was a fierce patriot who spent most of his life fighting for Korean independence from the Japanese. Eventually, Rhee was forced from office because his autocratic rule was unsuited to the demands for democracy within Korea.

Rhee was the son of a local village leader in Whanghae, and he graduated from a Methodist mission school in Seoul in 1896. The following year, he was arrested for his democratic opposition to the authoritarian Korean government and his formation of the Independence Club, a group dedicated to ending foreign influence in Korea. He served a prison term until 1904. The next year, Rhee traveled to the United States to present the Korean case for continued independence (which was threatened by Japanese power) to the U.S. State Department. The United States, however, agreed to the Portsmouth Treaty of 1905, signed in New Hampshire, which allowed Japan to establish a protectorate over Korea, a concession that was necessary to end a war between Russia and Japan. Korea then became a source of cheap labor for Japanese industry.

Rhee remained in the United States and received a B.A. degree from George Washington University. He earned an M.A. in international relations from Harvard in 1908 and a doctorate in political science from Princeton in 1910, becoming the first Korean to earn a doctorate at a U.S. university.

Rhee returned to Korea to do missionary work for the Methodist church but could not accept Japanese rule (Japan annexed Korea in 1910), and in 1912 he left to become headmaster of a Korean school in Hawaii, where he became the leader of Koreans in exile who opposed Japanese rule. In 1919 he was elected president of the Provisional Government in exile, located in Shanghai, and served in that post through 1939. During World War II Rhee became the emissary of that government in Washington, D.C., but was unable to gain U.S. recognition or a promise of support for Korean independence.

After World War II, the United States occupied South Korea, and with American backing Rhee returned to form the conservative Association for the Rapid Realization of Independence, which won the 1948 elections for the National Assembly. In May of that year Rhee was named chairman of the Assembly for a four-year term, the equivalent of becoming Korea's president.

During the Korean War (1950–53) Rhee rallied his nation to repel communist aggression from North Korea. He consolidated his power by gaining constitutional amendments that provided for direct popular election of the president. Rhee then won a large victory in the presidential election of 1952. After the armistice in 1953, he presided over the reconstruction of Korea's economy.

In 1954 Rhee abolished the post of prime minister and consolidated all executive power in his own office. He also won a constitutional amendment that ended the two-term limit for president so that he could run again in 1956. He won by a narrow margin. In 1960 he won a fourth term, claiming more than 90 percent of the vote, but the election was rigged. Students demonstrated in protest and at first the army and police cracked down on them. After worldwide condemnation and U.S. pressure, however, the army refused to disperse students and Rhee went into exile in Hawaii in May 1960. He died of natural causes there in 1965.

SEE ALSO

Korea, North; Korea, South

FURTHER READING

Allen, Richard C. *Korea's Syngman Rhee: An Unauthorized Portrait*. Rutland, Vt.: Tuttle, 1960.

Romania

ROMÂNIA

• *Capital: Bucharest*

Political history The area in southeastern Europe that is today Romania, located just north of the Balkan Peninsula, was settled by Protothracian tribes from the Balkans by 500 B.C. A later kingdom of the Dacians (from the Carpathian Mountains) was conquered by Rome in A.D. 106, but the Roman emperor Aurelian withdrew his legions in 271 to defend against Goth invasions. Thereafter, independent Romanian kingdoms were conquered by successive waves of tribes coming from the north and east, including the Goths, Slavs, and Bulgars, who ruled after the 7th century and converted the population to Christianity. After 900 the area was conquered by Magyars from Hungary and later by Mongols in the 1200s and Hungarians in the 1300s.

The two principalities of Wallachia and Moldavia, established in the early 14th century, were politically separate at the end of the 1300s, but both became vassal states paying tribute to the Ottomans in 1452 and then became part of the Ottoman Empire in the 1700s. They were then briefly controlled by Russia between 1828 and 1834. They joined together as the Union of Wallachia and Moldavia in 1859, and in 1877 they declared their independence from the Ottomans. In 1881 Romania was formed from the union and became a kingdom and in 1886 a constitutional monarchy.

At first during World War I, Romania remained neutral, but popular sentiment favored the Allies, and in 1916 Romania joined the war. During the

Election posters in the Romanian capital of Bucharest in May 1990 herald the nation's first free, multiparty elections since World War II. Romania's transition to democracy has been a difficult one.

next two years, it was defeated and occupied by the Germans and Austrians. But with the Allied victory in 1918, Romania attacked territory containing Hungarians and defeated the Hungarian army in spite of the opposition of Romania's former allies. Romania gained significant territory containing Hungarians (Transylvania, as well as Bessarabia and Bukovina) in the final peace settlement.

The postwar government was a dictatorship run by King Carol II. In the late 1930s the Iron Guard fascist movement gained influence over the government, converting King Carol into a figurehead, and acted as a death squad, assassinating political opponents. Romania's military dictatorship, led by General Ion Antonescu, supported the Axis powers during World War II but was overrun by the Soviet Red Army. In 1945 the Soviet Union established a communist one-party puppet state in Romania and ended the monarchy. The dictator Nicolae Ceauşescu assumed power and promoted his own brand of Marxist-Leninist thought, and as an ardent nationalist kept Romania from being dominated by the Soviet Union. But in 1989 a violent revolution was started by members of the Hungarian minority in Timişoara and was joined by students and workers, against Ceauşescu's corrupt dictatorship and mismanagement of the economy, which had resulted in a very low standard of living; therafter Romania began the transition to multiparty democracy. Most of the country's new leaders, however, were former communists who had been part of Ceauşescu's government.

Government institutions The 1991 constitution, adopted after the end of Ceauşescu's rule, provides for a semi-presidential system. The president is the head of state, directly elected by popular vote, and serves a maximum of two five-year terms. The prime minister, chosen by a majority of the legislature, is accountable to that body and runs the government. The bicameral legislature consists of a 387-member Assembly of Deputies and a 119-member Senate, both elected by proportional representation, in which parties receive seats in proportion to the percentage of votes they win nationwide. Members serve for four years. There are 40 county courts and an independent supreme court. Appeals are heard by 15 circuit of appeals courts.

Parties and movements Under the 1976 constitution, Romania was a one-party authoritarian state, with all power held by the Communist Party. The 1991 constitution converted Romania into a multiparty democracy. Still, former communists dominate the government through the two main parties that have emerged: the Party of Social Democracy of Romania, whose membership includes socialists as well as ex-communists, and the Democratic National Salvation Front, a breakaway faction. Other parties include the National Liberal Party, which favors free-market reforms, the centrist Civic Alliance Party, the National Peasants Christian Democratic Party (a conservative party), and the Hungarian Democratic Union of Romania, which represents the interests of ethnic Hungarians. No party obtained a legislative majority in the 1992 elections.

Domestic issues Industrial workers mounted protests in 1994–95 against the government because of a steep decline in wages, and the government has responded to protests by using the *securitate,* the former secret police, which exists under a new name, to round up dissidents.

Clashes between ethnic Hungarians and Romanians have occurred in the province of Transylvania (which used to be Hungarian territory) since 1992, leading to a mass exodus of Hungarians and Gypsies in the mid-1990s. Ethnic Germans have also left.

Romania is attempting to privatize some state industries, control inflation, and build up its foreign currency reserves in order to raise the standard of living, without which no regime can hope for popular support. As of 1996, the country has experienced less inflation, an increase in exports, and a stronger currency, due to greater foreign revenues.

International issues Relations between Romania and Hungary, which fought against each other in both world wars, continue to be strained because of ethnic conflicts in Transylvania, home to 1.6 million Hungarians. A 1996 treaty between the two nations was designed to provide for the cultural development and protection of these Hungarians.

Romania has close relations with Moldova, a former Soviet republic with an ethnic Romanian majority, although plans for a merger have been shelved. France has provided foreign aid and cultural exchanges. Romania has protested the resolution of the Russian parliament calling for a peaceful union of former territories of the Soviet Union, fearing that the neighboring Trans-Dniester Republic and Moldova will be under pressure to rejoin Russia instead of forging closer ties with Romania.

Human rights During World War II the fascist dictator Ion Antonescu presided over the murders of at least 250,000 Romanian Jews and 20,000 Gypsies. After the war, the communist Ceauşescu dictatorship tolerated no dissent and used the military and secret police to arrest or murder those who opposed government policies. Military courts in the post-communist era have tried cases involving members of the armed forces who were implicated in a massacre of anticommunist protestors at the city of Timişoara in 1989. Nicolae Ceauşescu and his wife, Elena, were executed in 1991 by the provisional government for the crime of autogenocide—the murder of thousands of innocent Romanians by the security forces of their regime.

SEE ALSO
Moldova; Russia; Soviet Union (Union of Soviet Socialist Republics)

FURTHER READING
Gallagher, Tom. *Romania after Ceauşescu.* Edinburgh: Edinburgh University Press, 1995.
Gilberg, Trond. *Nationalism and Communism in Romania: The Rise and Fall of Ceauşescu's Personal Dictatorship.* Boulder, Colo.: Westview, 1990.

Roosevelt, Eleanor

• *Born: Oct. 11, 1884, New York, N.Y.*
• *Died: Nov. 7, 1962, New York, N.Y.*

Eleanor Roosevelt served on the U.S. mission to the United Nations in the organization's formative years and was a tireless advocate for human rights. The niece of U.S. president Theodore Roosevelt, she married her fifth cousin (once removed) Franklin Delano Roosevelt in 1905 and helped set his domestic agenda as the First Lady during her husband's presidency (1933–45). She became an activist for liberal causes and lobbied strenuously with her husband in support of them. She traveled to inner-city slums and to rural shantytowns, comforting everyone who was out of work, hungry, or homeless. She constantly reassured people that the government cared about them and that Franklin Roosevelt's New Deal would help them find a job.

During World War II, Eleanor Roosevelt traveled abroad as her husband's emissary to raise troop morale on three fronts.

In 1945 President Harry Truman named Eleanor Roosevelt a delegate to the United Nations. She played a major role in securing UN adoption of the Universal Declaration of Human Rights in 1948, although the U.S. Senate refused to ratify it. Roosevelt left her post in 1952 after Republican Dwight D. Eisenhower won the presidential election. She then became a newspaper columnist, lecturer, and leader of the liberal Democrats in New York State. In recognition of her role as a humanitarian leader, in 1961 President John F. Kennedy reappointed Roosevelt to the U.S. delegation to the United Nations, where she served briefly until her death.

SEE ALSO

Human rights; Roosevelt, Franklin D.; United Nations

FURTHER READING

Cook, Blanche Wiesen. *Eleanor Roosevelt.* Vol. 1. New York: Viking, 1992.
Freedman, Russell. *Eleanor Roosevelt: A Life of Discovery.* New York: Clarion, 1993.
Goodwin, Doris Kearns. *No Ordinary Time: Franklin and Eleanor Roosevelt: The Home Front in World War II.* New York: Simon & Schuster, 1994.
Lash, Joseph P. *Eleanor: The Years Alone.* New York: Norton, 1972.
Roosevelt, Eleanor. *The Autobiography of Eleanor Roosevelt.* New York: Harper, 1961.

Eleanor Roosevelt presides over a meeting of the UN Commission on Human Rights. As First Lady and afterward, Roosevelt was perhaps the world's foremost ambassador for human rights.

Roosevelt, Franklin D.

• *Born: Jan. 10, 1882, Hyde Park, N.Y.*
• *Died: Apr. 12, 1945, Warm Springs, Ga.*

As the 32nd president of the United States (1933–45), Franklin Roosevelt served longer than any other U.S. president, guiding the nation through the Great Depression of the 1930s and World War II. His diplomatic and military decisions were instrumental in the triumph of democracy over fascism.

Roosevelt gives his first inaugural address, in which he assured a nation ravaged by the Great Depression that "the only thing we have to fear is fear itself." In his first 100 days in office, Roosevelt proposed numerous measures to restore the nation's economy and confidence.

Even before the United States entered the war, Roosevelt provided aid to Great Britain and the Soviet Union that prevented their defeat at the hands of Adolf Hitler's Nazi Germany, and after the U.S. entry into the war Roosevelt led the Allied coalition to victory over the Axis powers.

Roosevelt was a great speaker who radiated confidence in his own ideas and reassured millions of Americans who listened to his "fireside chats" on the radio. At his first inaugural address, when he said "The only thing we have to fear is fear itself," the nation agreed, and within days people stopped panicking and began the hard work of recovering from the Great Depression. His colleagues said that Roosevelt had no exemplars that he looked to for guidance on how to behave in the White House; his model of what a president should be was himself in the Oval Office. For those who succeeded Roosevelt, however, he became the exemplar of the modern president. Occupants of the White House as different as the liberals Lyndon Johnson and Bill Clinton and the conservative Ronald Reagan modeled their presidencies on Roosevelt's.

Roosevelt was descended from a wealthy family of Dutch settlers, and he was a fifth cousin of President Theodore Roosevelt. He graduated from Harvard College and studied at the Columbia University School of Law. He left law school, however, for a political career and soon won election to the New York state legislature as a Democrat from a heavily Republican district. He was appointed assistant secretary of the navy in 1913 by Woodrow Wilson and served until 1920. That year he won the Democratic vice presidential nomination and campaigned strenuously as a staunch supporter of the League of Nations and Treaty of Versailles, but he was defeated in the election. In 1928 he became governor of New York State.

In 1932 Roosevelt won the presidency by promising economic recovery and in 1936 was reelected by a landslide. In domestic affairs he first had to restore confidence in the financial system that had collapsed after the stock market crash of 1929 and end a panic that had caused people to rush to withdraw their cash from banks, which in turn caused many banks to close. He got Congress to pass an emergency banking bill that restored confidence in the banking system by putting government funds behind banks and ensuring that depositors could withdraw funds. He took the nation off the gold standard to protect dwindling Treasury gold reserves, and he established the Federal Deposit Insurance Corporation to guarantee bank deposits. Congress passed legislation to establish government agencies or implement changes that Roosevelt had proposed as part of his New Deal: The Home Owners Loan Corporation enabled home owners to avoid foreclosures, the Farm Credit Administration provided funds for farmers during growing season, and the Farm Mortgage Refinancing Act helped farmers make mortgage payments.

Congress also passed legislation, at Roosevelt's urging, to create public-sector jobs to decrease the unemployment rate. The Federal Emergency Relief administration gave states funds to provide public-service jobs. The Civilian Conservation Corps put young people to work on environmental projects. The Public Works Administration employed workers to build highways and other facilities, while the Works Progress Administration funded artists, photographers, and writers.

In an attempt to help farmers who had suffered from droughts, low prices, and overproduction for years, Roosevelt got Congress to pass laws regulating markets so that higher prices would encourage less production. The Agricultural Adjustment Administration limited production on farms and estab-

lished marketing quotas; the National Industrial Recovery Act allowed corporations to stabilize prices throughout an industry. Roosevelt also created agencies to regulate the economy, such as the Securities and Exchange Commission to regulate financial markets, the Federal Communications Commission to regulate telephone and radio (and later television), and the National Labor Relations Board to regulate labor-management relations. Roosevelt involved the national government in funding public housing, rural electrification projects, unemployment insurance, welfare, and old-age pensions (Social Security).

In foreign affairs, Roosevelt maintained strict neutrality in European affairs until the summer of 1939. But after the British king and queen made a trip to the United States, he recommended that Congress amend the neutrality laws to allow nations that might go to war with the Axis powers to buy supplies from the United States. After Germany invaded Poland on September 1, 1939, Roosevelt initiated a "cash and carry" policy to arm the British—the United States would sell arms, but would not extend credit, and the weapons could not be transported on U.S. ships.

In the summer of 1940 Roosevelt began a national war-preparedness program, obtained authority from Congress to draft troops, and raised the ceiling on the national debt. In September, Roosevelt concluded a "destroyer deal" with Great Britain: in return for providing the British with 50 overage destroyers that were still useful for submarine warfare, the United States received the use of British military bases in the Caribbean.

Because of the ominous international situation, Roosevelt broke with tradition and accepted a unanimous third nomination for president. He promised the American people, "Your sons will not fight in a foreign war." In his 1941 State of the Union address, he put forth his vision of a postwar world when he enunciated the Four Freedoms: freedom of speech and expression; freedom of every person to worship God in his own way; freedom from want; and freedom from fear.

In 1941 Congress passed the Lend-Lease Act, which provided military assistance to Great Britain and the Soviet Union. The United States, in the president's words, became the "arsenal of democracy" against the Axis dictatorships. Roosevelt gave the navy orders to "shoot on sight" at German submarines in the North Atlantic, landed U.S. troops in Iceland, closed Italian and German consulates in the United States, and froze Japanese assets in the United States. But he did not ask Congress for a declaration of war, because most Americans opposed such a move. In August 1941, he met with British prime minister Winston Churchill to draft the Atlantic Charter, an eight-point plan of common principles for a postwar world. The following month the U.S. Navy began to convoy British merchant ships carrying lend-lease supplies.

After the Japanese attacks on the U.S. possessions of Pearl Harbor, Hawaii, and the Philippines, Guam, and Midway, which took place on December 7, 1941, Roosevelt asked Congress to declare war not only on Japan but also on Germany and Italy. Early in 1942 a coalition of 26 nations subscribed to the Atlantic Charter and, following Roosevelt's suggestions, called themselves the United Nations. That year Roosevelt ordered work to proceed on the Manhattan Project, a secret U.S. research effort to produce an atomic bomb. In 1943, at the Casablanca Conference, Roosevelt and Churchill called for unconditional Axis surrender, and at the Cairo Conference that year Roosevelt, Churchill, and the Chinese leader Chiang Kai-shek coordinated war plans against Japan. In June 1944 Allied troops under the command of General Dwight D. Eisenhower launched the Normandy invasion in France. With the war going successfully, Roosevelt won a fourth term.

In February 1945 Roosevelt traveled to Yalta in the Soviet Union and discussed the plans for peace with Churchill and Soviet dictator Joseph Stalin. They made plans for a United Nations organization. Stalin and Churchill discussed spheres of influence for their nations; Roosevelt, in poor health, was not in a position to argue forcefully against them, leading some critics to claim that Roosevelt had "sold out" the nations of Eastern Europe to Stalin. While resting at Warm Springs, Georgia, in preparation for the San Francisco conference that was to create the United Nations, Roosevelt died of a cerebral hemorrhage. His widow, Eleanor, became a member of the U.S. mission to the United Nations.

SEE ALSO

Atlantic Charter; Churchill, Winston; Roosevelt, Eleanor; Stalin, Joseph; United Nations (UN)

FURTHER READING

Burns, James MacGregor. *The Lion and the Fox*. New York: Harcourt Brace, 1956.

Dallek, Robert. *Franklin Roosevelt and American Foreign Policy, 1932–1945*. New York: Oxford University Press, 1979.

Freedman, Russell. *Franklin Delano Roosevelt*. New York: Clarion, 1990.

Goodwin, Doris Kearns. *No Ordinary Time: Franklin and Eleanor Roosevelt: The Home Front in World War II*. New York: Simon & Schuster, 1994.

Lash, Joseph P. *Dealers and Dreamers: A New Look at the New Deal*. New York: Doubleday, 1988.

Leuchtenburg, William E. *Franklin D. Roosevelt and the New Deal*. New York: Harper & Row, 1963.

Roosevelt, Theodore

- *Born: Oct. 27, 1858, New York, N.Y.*
- *Died: Jan. 6, 1919, Oyster Bay, N.Y.*

The 26th president of the United States (1901–9), Theodore ("Teddy") Roosevelt was the youngest man ever to serve as president of the United States and the first vice president to win election in his own right after succeeding to the presidency. He used his diplomatic powers to gain Great Power status for the United States. His motto was "Speak softly and carry a big stick," yet in spite of his militaristic attitudes, the nation remained at peace during his term. Not a single member of the armed forces died in combat during Roosevelt's presidency, an accomplishment almost unique among U.S. presidents.

Roosevelt was an ebullient man who loved life and lived it to the hilt. He was always in a hurry, always impatient, always ready to do big things. He was an impressive public speaker, whose wit and laughter could always impress crowds. He called the presidency "a bully good pulpit" for his ideas. After leaving office, he wrote, "No President has ever enjoyed himself as much as I have enjoyed myself."

Roosevelt graduated from Harvard College and attended Columbia University School of Law. He was elected to the New York State Assembly as a Republican but took an independent position on many issues. When his wife Alice Lee died in childbirth in 1884 (on the same day he learned of the death of his mother), Roosevelt went out west to a ranch in the Dakota Territory to recover from his grief. He returned to New York City to run for mayor in 1886 but finished third and went back to the ranch with his new wife, his

Roosevelt (center) aboard the presidential yacht Mayflower with the other delegates to the Portsmouth Conference of 1905, where he negotiated an end to the Russo-Japanese War.

childhood friend Edith Carow. There he wrote a history, *The Winning of the West.* In 1889 Roosevelt returned to the East again and was named to the U.S. Civil Service Commission by President Benjamin Harrison. In 1895 he became president of the New York City Board of Police Commissioners.

When President William McKinley took office in 1897, he named Roosevelt assistant secretary of the U.S. Navy. Roosevelt promoted ship construction and deployed much of the fleet in the Far East, where Admiral George Dewey was able to secure Manila Bay and win control of the Philippines at the beginning of the Spanish-American War. Roosevelt himself organized the First U.S. Volunteer Cavalry, known as the Rough Riders, and as their commander in Cuba he led them into battle at Kettle Hill near Santiago de Cuba, which newspaper accounts referred to as the "charge up San Juan Hill."

In 1898 Roosevelt was elected governor of New York State. His reform program designed to end corruption so upset Republican Party leaders that they arranged for him to receive the vice presidential nomination in 1900—just to get him out of the state. On September 14, 1901, just six months after his inauguration, President William McKinley died of a bullet wound and Roosevelt took the presidential oath.

In foreign affairs Roosevelt presided over the expansion of U.S. naval power, and he sent the "Great White Fleet" on a tour around the world between 1907 and 1909 to demonstrate America's power to other nations. He insisted that the United States be the dominant naval power in the Pacific. When the government of Colombia refused to ratify an agreement that would allow the United States to begin construction of a canal through Panama (a Colombian province) that would connect the Atlantic and Pacific oceans, Roosevelt encouraged revolutionists to declare Panama independent. He then used the U.S. Navy to prevent Colombian warships from quelling the revolt. Soon, Roosevelt concluded an agreement with the new nation that leased to the United States a zone in which to construct a canal.

In 1904 the president announced that the United States would act as "policeman" in the Western Hemisphere by intervening with troops to enforce claims by European creditors against Latin American debtor nations.

Later in 1904 Roosevelt was unanimously renominated by the Republican Party and won election in his own right. He continued his activist foreign policies and took full control of the finances of the Dominican Republic in 1905 after that nation defaulted on its debts to foreign banks. When the Senate balked at consenting to a treaty between the United States and that nation to provide for the importing of agricultural crops, Roosevelt put the treaty into effect anyway by calling it an "executive agreement" not requiring Senate consent.

That same year, at the Portsmouth Conference held in New Hampshire, Roosevelt mediated an end to the Russo-Japanese War, and he received the Nobel Peace Prize for his efforts in 1906. He donated his $40,000 prize to a foundation for promoting better labor-management relations. He used his influence with the Russian czar to improve conditions for Jews in the Russian empire.

Toward the end of his life, Roosevelt asked President Woodrow Wilson for a military commission so that he could lead a new group of volunteers to fight in World War I, but Wilson turned him down. Roosevelt died in 1919, shortly after the war's end.

SEE ALSO
Wilson, Woodrow

FURTHER READING
Gould, Lewis L. *The Presidency of Theodore Roosevelt.* Lawrence: University Press of Kansas, 1991.
Harbaugh, William H. *Power and Responsibility: The Life and Times of Theodore Roosevelt.* New York: Oxford University Press, 1975.
Meltzer, Milton. *Theodore Roosevelt and His America.* New York: Franklin Watts, 1994.
Morris, Edmund. *The Rise of Theodore Roosevelt.* New York: Coward, McCann & Geoghegan, 1979.

Rule of law

The rule of law is the principle that the rulers and other officials of a nation-state must follow the constitution and laws of the land and apply them fairly and impartially to all individuals. A government that operates under the rule of law provides for judicial review of official actions, so that a citizen has redress against arbitrary governmental action. Although judges may be appointed on political grounds, once in

Demonstrators make clear their opinion regarding President Nixon's role in the Watergate scandal. The Watergate affair posed one of the greatest challenges to the rule of constitutional law in the United States that the country has ever faced.

office they are expected to act impartially and are not supposed to be subject to political direction by a party or by the government.

A corollary notion is that under the rule of law the state does not possess absolute power over its citizens. Instead, the constitution and laws are the expression of principles in which the people believe. Such principles may include natural law, which is based on religious beliefs that God requires people to adopt certain moral behaviors. They may include the common law, which is based on the customs and traditions of the people. They may involve the law of the market: the set of principles involving supply and demand that determines prices. They may include norms of international law, including the emerging law of human rights as embodied in the United Nations Universal Declaration of Human Rights.

The rule of law also insists that the will of the majority, acting through the legislature or popular referenda, cannot trample upon the minority's property rights, civil rights, and civil liberties and that everyone must receive the equal protection of the law.

In many European nations in the 19th and early 20th centuries, the application of the rule of law led to the cre-

ation by legislatures (or parliaments) of administrative law and administrative courts. These courts (or councils) require that any bureaucratic decision or regulation that imposes costs or burdens on individuals or organizations be justified by reference to a statute passed by the legislature (or parliament). Administrative law reduced the discretionary powers of bureaucrats, especially in economic regulation.

As used in post-communist nations in the 1990s, the phrases "establishing the rule of law" or "creation of a state under law" signified a recognition that no party or movement should claim a "leading role"—as the Communist Party had previously done—enabling it to act outside the law of the state.

SEE ALSO

Constitution; Human rights; Nation-state

FURTHER READING

International Commission of Jurists. *The Rule of Law in a Free Society*. Geneva: International Commission of Jurists, 1960.
Lyons, David. *Ethics and the Rule of Law*. Cambridge, England: Cambridge University Press, 1984.

Russia

THE RUSSIAN FEDERATION (ROSSIYSKAYA FEDERATSIYA)

• *Capital: Moscow*

Political history Russia consists of most of the northern Eurasian landmass and much of eastern Europe. The European forests of Russia were settled by Slavic tribes from northern forests in the 5th century A.D. Known as the Antae, they formed a confederation of tribes that controlled the area between the Dnieper and Dniester rivers. The Khazars, tribes

Nicholas II was destined to be the last czar of Russia. He is shown here in an etching made during his lifetime.

from central Asia, conquered the southern Russian plains, called the steppes, in the 7th century. By the 9th century, principalities were formed by Slavs around Novgorod and Kiev to defend against Turkic tribes invading from the southern steppes. The Mongols conquered the entire territory in the 13th century.

By the 15th century, the Russian Slavic nobility had gained autonomy from the Mongols but had to pledge allegiance and pay taxes to them in the southern town of Sarai. Russia at this time consisted of three large cities—Muscovy (Moscow), Kiev, and Novgorod, where merchants competed with the nobility for power—and a large number of villages and agricultural settlements, where the word of the local nobility was law.

The grand duke of Muscovy threw off the Mongol yoke in 1480. Ivan III, a Muscovite prince, united the nobility in the area around Moscow and proclaimed himself czar of all Russia. A century later, Prince Ivan IV (Ivan the Terrible) crushed the nobility by seizing its vast lands and forcing nobles to serve in the military. He fought against Poland, Lithuania, and Sweden to obtain lands bordering the Baltic Sea. Later, Peter the

Great extended Russia's domains to the east and south and opened Russia to Western influence. Russian influence then extended into central Asia, with the Russians winning some territories from the Ottoman Empire.

During her reign in the latter part of the 18th century, Catherine the Great introduced even more European influences into Russia. She supported Western scientific thinking and corresponded with French thinkers such as Voltaire and Diderot. She developed a modern legal code. To retain the support of the nobles, she acquiesced to their demands for new land provisions that turned peasants (who owned and worked small plots of land) into landless serfs (who were forced to work for large landowners).

Catherine's foreign policy was successful; she gained land at the expense of the Ottoman Empire and Poland. Her administrative reforms created a system of local self-government and a judicial system, both free of control by the landholding aristocracy. But Catherine refused to embrace the radical reforms sweeping Europe as a result of the French Revolution, and the new subjugation of the serfs would eventually lead to social unrest until serfdom was abolished in the 1850s.

The czarist regime lasted more than another century under the Romanov dynasty, but it was overthrown in 1917 by a coalition of movements representing workers, peasants, middle-class reformers, and disaffected nobles. Czar Nicholas II, his wife, Czarina Alexandra, and their five children were held prisoner and eventually executed in 1918 on the direct order of communist leader Vladimir Lenin. They were secretly buried 20 miles outside the city of Yekaterinburg, where their graves were discovered in 1991.

After a brief attempt to establish a multiparty parliamentary system, the

Bolsheviks, under Lenin, seized power and established a communist totalitarian state called the Union of Soviet Socialist Republics (the Soviet Union). By the end of World War II, the Soviet Union ruled over Russians, other Slavs (Belarusians and Ukrainians), Balts (Lithuanians, Latvians, and Estonians), peoples of the Caucasus Mountains (including Armenians, Georgians, and Azerbaijanis), and Muslims of central Asia, as well as the inhabitants of the vast and underpopulated territory of Siberia.

In 1991 the Soviet Union was disbanded by the leaders of its constituent republics so that each could exercise complete power rather than submit further to the Communist Party leadership under Soviet president Mikhail Gorbachev. Russia (formally known as the Russian Federation) joined with 11 other former Soviet republics to form the Commonwealth of Independent States. In 1996 Russia and Belarus announced the formation of a union to bring their states into closer political and economic coordination without renouncing individual sovereignty.

Government institutions In 1991 the Russian Federation established a semi-presidential system similar to that adopted by other Commonwealth states. The president was head of state, held the executive power, and issued decrees with the force of law. He appointed the council of ministers and prime minister to administer the departments of government. Ministers, however, were subject to confirmation by the elected legislature.

The system worked poorly. President Boris Yeltsin and his reformist prime minister and cabinet were opposed by a legislature dominated by old-line communists and their allies, along with a variety of other groups suspicious of Yeltsin's arbitrary exercise of executive power and willingness to tolerate corruption in government ministries.

In 1993 Yeltsin proposed a new constitution, which was adopted in a nationwide referendum and went into effect on December 12, 1993. Under the new system, Russia is considered "a democratic, federative, law-governed state with a republican form of government." It has a presidential system, in which the powers of the presidency vastly outweigh those of the legislature, enabling the president to implement policies even if he lacks a majority in the legislature. The president is directly elected and serves for four years (with a maximum of two terms). Legislative power is vested in the Federal Assembly, consisting of two houses, each popularly elected for four-year terms. The lower house, or State Duma (literally, the "people's legislature"), consists of 450 delegates directly elected by the people. Half of its members are elected in districts and half by proportional representation, with each party receiving representation according to the percentage of the vote it receives nationwide. The upper house, known as the Federation Council, is elected on a regional basis (each province is guaranteed a certain number of representatives).

The president has the right to dissolve the Duma and call for new elections if it fails to pass laws he recommends or fails to approve his cabinet nominations. The president appoints judges and prosecutors, subject to the approval of the legislature. The president can order referenda on issues that he does not want to take to the legislature, and the president can issue decrees (*ukazi*) with the force of law. As head of state, head of government, and head of the armed forces, the president "determines the basic guidelines of domestic and foreign policy."

The constitutional court of the Russian Federation reviews the laws passed by the Duma. The Supreme Court reviews cases on appeal from the lower district civil and criminal courts.

Parties and movements The Russian Communist Party, established in 1990 by members of the former Communist Party of the Soviet Union (CPSU), was banned in August 1991 after some of the leaders of the Russian Party attempted a coup against Mikhail Gorbachev, then president of the Soviet Union, to overturn his reforms. The ban by presidential decree was later overturned by the constitutional court. Eight new communist parties then formed. Early in 1991 the Soviet Union had revised its constitution to permit non-communist parties to form. When Russia left the Soviet Union at the end of 1991, it maintained this provision and began to transform itself into a multiparty democracy. The largest political parties to emerge after the 1993 elections, and their representation in the Duma, were as follows: Russia's Choice (free-market liberals associated with Boris Yeltsin), 76; Liberal Democrats (extreme right-wing nationalists led by the neo-fascist Vladimir Zhirinovsky), 63; Agrarians (communist), 55; Russian Communist Party (old-guard communists led by Gennadi Zyuganov), 45; Russian Party of Unity and Accord (reformist, led by a member of Yeltsin's government, Sergei Shakry), 30; Democratic Opposition, also known as Yabloko (free-market reformist, led by economist Grigory Yavlinsky), 25; Women of Russia (reformist), 23; Democratic Party of Russia (conservative-nationalist, led by former construction boss Nikolai Travkin), 15; and independents, 112. The Duma elected a former communist, Ivan Rybkin, as its Speaker early in 1994.

In the 1995 parliamentary elections, the Communist Party of the Russian Federation doubled its share of the vote, up to 22.3 percent, to become the largest bloc in parliament, with 158 seats. It was

followed by the pro-government party Our House Is Russia, with 54 seats and 10.13 percent of the vote, the neo-fascist Liberal Democratic Party, with 51 seats and 11.1 percent of the vote, and the liberal Yabloko Party, with 4 seats and 6.9 percent of the vote. The Agrarian Party had 20 seats and the independent parties had 77, with minor parties making up the remainder. Communists and their allies had twice as many seats as the liberal reformist parties.

The most worrisome aspect of the multiparty system in the early 1990s was the rise of the neo-fascists, led by Zhirinovsky, who had called for the reconstitution of the Soviet Union by force and the institution of anti-Semitic policies. Zhirinovsky's party won 23 percent of the vote in 1993, but in the 1995 elections it won only 11 percent of the popular vote, as Zhirinovsky's supporters shifted to the Communist Party to register their protest against the Yeltsin government's poor economic performance.

Domestic issues In the mid 1990s the government of Boris Yeltsin was locked in a dispute with the Russian legislature, which was dominated by Communists and their allies, over the pace of economic reforms. Yeltsin dismissed his first prime minister for pushing free-market reforms and making too fast a transition to capitalism. The result of that liberalization, implemented between 1991 and 1993, was a sharp decline in Russian living standards, the rise of a "new rich" class of speculators and organized crime figures, and the privatization of state enterprises and the conversion of some of them into organized crime fronts.

In early 1993 a group of legislators led by Rhuslan Khasbulatov, the Speaker of the Duma, tried to impeach and remove Yeltsin from office, but the Congress of People's Deputies could not muster the two-thirds vote needed for impeachment. To break the deadlock, in the spring of 1993 Yeltsin held a referendum, which resulted in a vote of confidence in his leadership and his proposed reforms. Although he won a majority of the vote, his relations with the Congress remained difficult. The president and the legislature proposed separate budgets for the government, and the legislature suspended the government's privatization program; the president responded by enacting it by decree.

In September 1993 Yeltsin broke the deadlock. First, he suspended Vice President Alexander Rutskoi, a persistent opponent of his regime. Then he announced that he was dissolving parliament and would rule by decree until new parliamentary elections could be held in December. Many delegates, however, refused to leave the building and began a sit-in. They were soon surrounded by police. In the first days of October 1993, anti-Yeltsin delegates of the Congress of People's Deputies locked themselves in the parliament building while anti-Yeltsin crowds roamed the Moscow streets, but their attempts to take control of the television stations failed. Yeltsin sent troops to disperse the crowds and attack the parliament building.

When the fighting was over, 144 people, most of them inside the building, were dead and another 878 were wounded, according to official figures. The leaders of the parliamentary revolt were arrested, including Speaker Khasbulatov and Vice President Rutskoi.

Yeltsin organized a constitutional convention in 1993 that proposed changes in the government structure, including a stronger presidency, a revised bicameral legislature, and a bill of rights that would guarantee private property rights. After the new constitution went into effect, Yeltsin ousted many of the reformers from the government and switched to a more moderate cabinet and a centrist economic policy, in large measure to blunt the discontent that had led to a large fascist vote in the 1993 elections.

After the 1993 and 1995 elections, Yeltsin faced parliaments dominated by Communists and their allies, and he had to rely on issuing decrees to implement his own policies.

Russia faced threats of secession in the 1990s by some of its 88 regions and republics, especially those composed of a major-

Supporters of Boris Yeltsin carry the Russian flag across Red Square in Moscow after the coup to unseat Mikhail Gorbachev failed in 1991. Yeltsin had organized the resistance to the coup.

ity of non-Russians. A 1995 treaty guaranteeing autonomy for Tatarstan ended one crisis. The Sverdlovsk region refers to itself as the Urals Republic, even though it is officially still part of Russia, and separatists in Vladivostok want to proclaim a Maritime Republic in eastern Siberia.

The republic of Chechnya, an oil-producing region of 1.3 million people located in the Caucacus Mountains between the Black and Caspian seas, declared itself sovereign in 1991, but its declaration was not accepted by the Russian government. The Russians backed a rebel group that tried to overthrow the secessionist government, but its indirect efforts failed. On December 11, 1994, Russian troops and bombers attacked the Chechen capital of Grozny, with Yeltsin claiming that the government had to intervene to restore order in the republic. The Chechens, led by their president, Dzhokar Dudayev, mounted a fierce resistance, leaving their capital in ruins and inflicting large casualties on Russian forces, before withdrawing to the mountains to conduct guerrilla warfare.

The Chechens controlled much of the countryside and kept a Russian army of 50,000 on the defensive throughout the mid-1990s. The Russians installed a puppet government led by Doku Zavgayev, but he had no popular support. A partial peace agreement signed in July 1995 broke down several months later as Chechens refused to disarm after negotiations on independence bogged down. The war in Chechnya weakened the Yeltsin government at home and abroad, as casualties mounted and Russian troops were accused of committing atrocities against the civilian population.

The Russian economy in the early 1990s was a disaster, with incomes cut in half compared to 1989, factories closed, foreign investment squandered, and organized crime increasing its hold on small businesses and banking. Industrial output had also decreased by half between 1991 and 1995. Inflation reached crisis levels (more than 250 percent annually in the mid-1990s), with the value of the ruble shrinking against foreign currencies. By 1995 inflation had been brought under control, the privatization of 14,000 firms had begun to increase productivity, and new laws providing for the sale of lands to farmers had been implemented. Nevertheless, Russia's poor economic performance had left Yeltsin's regime severely weakened and allowed the extremist Communists and rightist parties to dominate the parliament.

In 1993 Western nations promised Russia substantial aid if economic reforms were implemented. In the next three years, however, both the reforms and the aid were less than promised. The International Monetary Fund (IMF) pledged $4.1 billion in short-term currency stabilization, but little of the money was distributed, because Russia did not lower its inflation rate. The IMF created a special fund with up to $9 billion in loans and an additional fund of $10.1 billion to stabilize the ruble but refused to disburse the money, because Russia did not negotiate an acceptable currency reform program with it.

The World Bank offered up to $2 billion in development loans, and the Group of Seven promised more than $14.2 billion in export credits during the early 1990s, but they disbursed less than half for the purchase of advanced industrial goods. The government was supposed to cut back on government spending, especially on state enterprises, and end its printing of money, which fuels inflation, but did not follow through on its program. The Paris Club in 1993 and 1994 did reschedule Russia's massive foreign debt (more than $80 billion), which saved the government more than $4 billion annually in interest payments.

International issues A moderate group of foreign service officers favoring closer economic ties with the West and a policy of détente (easing of tensions with the West) was opposed in the 1990s by a group centered in the defense ministry that proposed to regain domination over the "near abroad"—meaning former Soviet republics of the Commonwealth of Independent States. Russian military doctrines announced in 1994 justified the permanent presence of Russian troops in neighboring countries and declared the territory of the former Soviet Union to be its security zone. It has sent troops into some of the central Asian republics to side with pro-Russian leaders in civil wars. It has pressured the members of the Commonwealth of Independent States to submit to Russian security and economic interests. In 1996 the Russian parliament passed a resolution condemning the breakup of the Soviet Union and calling for a new union that would include the members of the Commonwealth of Independent States. The idea was roundly condemned by the Baltic states and by Ukraine.

Russia and Ukraine disputed the ownership of the naval fleet based in the Black Sea but came to an agreement on dividing it between them in 1995. The Russian parliament has made a territorial claim on the Crimea, which was a part of Russia until 1954, when it was transferred to Ukraine. Negotiations with Japan over the fate of the Kuril Islands have deadlocked, which has reduced prospects for Japanese foreign aid and investment.

Russia and the United States have cooperated on the reduction of nuclear weapons and missiles and their disposal, though the Russian parliament has not yet ratified various arms control agreements. The two countries have worked together in other ways as well. At the 1993 Vancouver summit, Russian president Boris Yeltsin agreed to accept from U.S. president Bill Clinton a package of $1.6 billion in food and agricultural aid. The United States supported Yeltsin when he disbanded the parliament and reorganized the Russian government in 1993. The Russians, in turn, have supported U.S. diplomatic initiatives in the Middle East, including the peace process between Israel and the Palestinians, and efforts to halt terrorism in the region. At the request of the United States, Russia contributed peacekeeping troops that worked closely with U.S. armed forces in Bosnia in 1996.

In the mid-1990s Russia used troops to prevent a civil war in Moldova between ethnic Romanians and Russians, protecting the Trans-Dniester Republic established by the Russian minority who seceded from Moldova. Yeltsin also sent troops to the Caucasus Mountains to end conflict between North Ossetia and Ingushetia. Russian troops patrolled the borders of Abkhazia, preventing Georgia from sending in troops to restore its authority to that breakaway province.

Russia has refused to consider returning the Japanese islands of Kunashir, Hurup, and Shikotan, and the Habomai islets, which it seized from Japan after World War II. In response, Japan has refused to invest in the Russian economy or provide significant foreign aid.

Human rights Russia has had a long history of anti-Semitism, which led to pogroms (organized massacres) against Jewish peasants, which in turn resulted in mass emigration in the late 19th and early 20th century. A resurgence of Russian anti-Semitism, led by several nationalist parties, has been condemned by the Yeltsin government.

Throughout the period of communist rule in the Soviet Union, there were no guarantees of basic human rights such as freedom of speech, religion, assembly, association, or petition. The Communist Party was the only political party permitted, and all political expression was controlled by party members. The Soviet Union was officially an atheistic state, and all religious practices were discouraged. The Russian Orthodox Church lost much of its property to the state. In the 1980s President Mikhail Gorbachev eliminated most restrictions on speech and the press with his policy of *glasnost* ("openness"). By the mid-1990s, under the Yeltsin regime, Russians enjoyed complete political, religious, and cultural freedoms.

The Yeltsin regime, however, was criticized throughout the world for its conduct of the war in Chechnya. Its destruction of the capital, Grozny, and surrounding Chechen villages has resulted in hundreds of thousands of civilian deaths.

SEE ALSO

Belarus; Commonwealth of Independent States (CIS); Gorbachev, Mikhail; Moldova; Russian Revolution; Soviet Union (Union of Soviet Socialist Republics); Ukraine; Yeltsin, Boris

FURTHER READING

Belyakov, Vladimir, and Walter Raymond, eds. *The New Constitution of the Russian Federation*. Lawrenceville, Va.: Brunswick, 1994.
Dunlop, John. *The Rise of Russia and the Fall of the Soviet Empire*. Princeton, N.J.: Princeton University Press, 1993.
Hosking, Geoffrey. *Russia: People and Empire, 1552–1917*. Cambridge: Harvard University Press, 1997.
Lapidus, Gail W., ed. *Russia: Troubled Transformation*. Boulder, Colo.: Westview, 1995.
Remnick, David. *Lenin's Tomb*. New York: Random House, 1993.
Remnick, David. *Resurrection: The Struggle for a New Russia*. New York: Random House, 1997.
Riasanovsky, Nicholas V. *A History of Russia*. 5th ed. New York: Oxford University Press, 1993.

Russian Revolution

The Russian Revolution was a series of events involving the overthrow of the Russian czar, or monarch, in February 1917 by a coalition of liberals and social democrats, primarily members of the middle classes and intelligentsia who wanted to establish a parliamentary democracy, followed in October by a Bolshevik revolution, involving primarily workers and soldiers, that established a communist one-party totalitarian state.

In 1914 Russia, Great Britain, and France joined together against Germany, Austria, and Italy in World War I. The defeats of the Russian army in 1916 at the hands of the Germans, along with worsening economic conditions in Russia, created a rebellious mood among workers. On February 23, 1917, women workers at textile and garment factories in Petrograd, the Russian capital, went on strike, and they were joined the following day by hundreds of thousands of male and female factory workers in a general strike. By February 27 the army garrisons were refusing to obey the czar's orders to crush the strike. To consolidate power, Czar Nicholas II, haughty and imperious, dismissed the Duma (parliament), which refused to disband and instead formed a Provisional Government consisting of the Kadets (liberals who supported a parliamentary democracy that would promote industry and commerce) and Octobrists (social democrats who favored a democracy that would provide social welfare benefits to workers and peasants). Meanwhile, members of the revolutionary parties active in organizing the strikes formed a Temporary Executive Committee (or Soviet) of the Workers' Deputies to try to take control of Russia through revolution.

The liberal Provisional Government

Дни революціи. Знаменская пл. 1917г.

A crowd fills the central square of St. Petersburg to celebrate May Day during the early days of the Russian Revolution. In theory, the revolution represented the triumph of the working class over the wealthy and ruling classes. In practice, it resulted in a dictatorial regime.

wanted to continue the war against the Germans in order to gain territorial concessions in Europe secretly promised to it by the Allies. It offered the workers an amnesty if they would end the strike (production had to resume if the government wanted to keep fighting), a constitution guaranteeing civil liberties, and a people's militia to replace the police. Czar Nicholas was forced to abdicate by the Provisional Government in March 1917, but it intended to keep the monarchy, although much weakened, by crowning Nicholas's son and establishing a regency (a system in which the powers of the Crown are exercised by an adult of the nobility until the monarch comes of age). Nothing came of these plans, however, because of popular opposition to a new czar.

The policies of the Provisional Government were opposed by the Executive Committee of the Workers' Deputies (Soviets). The locally based Soviets held their own elections, and representatives from factories and military units formed the Petrograd Soviet. Most of its members were Mensheviks (social democrats who believed in parliamentary government and a peaceful transition from czarist rule to socialism), and only a few were Bolshe-

viks (revolutionaries who believed that a small party should rule dictatorially and oversee the transition to communism). The Menshevik majority agreed to support the Provisional Government, provided it called for elections to a Constituent Assembly and gave up its plans to restore the czardom. But tensions remained because the Provisional Government continued the war despite protests from the Petrograd Soviet.

The Germans, eager to get Russia out of the war, allowed Vladimir Lenin and other Bolshevik revolutionaries in Switzerland (they had been exiled by the czar) to cross Germany by railway and travel to Petrograd in March 1917. Lenin, an uncompromising and radical revolutionary, had no use for the moderate reformers who had taken power. He assumed control of the Bolshevik movement upon his arrival in Petrograd and began to organize the overthrow of the Provisional Government. His tactic was first to seize control of the Petrograd Soviet. Lenin and his colleague Leon Trotsky organized followers in factories and military units, and in a second set of elections the Bolsheviks won significant representation on the Executive Committee, though they remained a minority. Meanwhile, the first Provisional Government fell because of its unpopular war policies, and in July a new government was formed by a coalition of liberals and social democrats led by Aleksandr Kerensky. The Bolsheviks, now dominating the local Soviets, remained in opposition.

In July some Bolshevik workers and soldiers attempted a coup d'état, but the Provisional Government struck back. It banned revolutionary publications, cracked down on street demonstrations, and arrested Trotsky and other Bolsheviks. But more and more Soviets, dominated by factory workers and soldiers, turned to the Bolsheviks.

When General L. G. Kornilov tried to seize power from the Provisional Government in August and establish a military government to restore order, Prime Minister Kerensky, desperate because the army was on the front lines, turned to the Soviets (whose members were armed) to disperse Kornilov's forces and arrest him, an admission of the Soviets' growing strength and the government's continued weakness. Kerensky, more of an intellectual than a politician, was an uninspiring man who could not rally popular support for himself or his party. As a result, in September the Bolsheviks won local elections for positions in the Provisional Government in Petrograd, Moscow, and other cities. By early October, Lenin had won the endorsement of the other Bolshevik leaders for a revolution against the Provisional Government.

Trotsky, an energetic and indefatigable organizer for the revolution, now put together a Military Revolutionary Committee to prepare for a coup. Due to his efforts, much of the Petrograd army garrison and Kronstadt fleet supported the Bolsheviks instead of helping to maintain the Provisional Government. On October 24, Kerensky summoned troops to defend the Provisional Government at the Winter Palace, and the following day the Provisional Government called for an armistice with Germany (in order to win popular support), but it was too late. On October 25, Bolsheviks and their army allies seized control of the city. That evening the Mensheviks walked out of the Petrograd Soviet, declaring the revolution undemocratic. The following morning the Petrograd Soviet elected the All-Russian Central Executive Committee, controlled by Lenin and the Bolsheviks, who formed a majority and ran the Bolshevik movement. In turn, the committee created a government consisting of the Council of People's Commissars, with Lenin as chairman, Trotsky as commissar of foreign affairs, and Bolsheviks in control of all the ministries.

Parliamentary elections in Russia were held in November 1917. The Bolsheviks won only 168 out of 620 seats, but because they controlled the ministries and the Soviets, they dispersed the newly elected Assembly after it met for a single day in January 1918. Lenin's revolutionary demand for "all power to the Soviets" seemed to have come to pass.

In reality, power passed from the disbanded legislature to the Politburo, the top leaders of the Bolshevik (later Communist) Party, which under Lenin's control dominated the government. All other parties were banned and the Communists established a one-party state. Private enterprises were seized by the state and land owned by the upper classes and wealthy peasants was expropriated by the government in 1918. Party ideologists and government bureaucrats replaced the nobility and private financiers and merchants as the ruling oligarchy in the Soviet Union.

After they had established a new government in Russia, the Bolsheviks ended the war with Germany, then organized the Red Army to fight a civil war against the counterrevolutionary White Army, organized by supporters of the czar's regime. After their success in defending the revolution, the Bolsheviks defeated attempts by non-Russian nationalities in the Ukraine, central Asia, the Volga area of Russia, and the Caucasus Mountains to break away from the Russian Empire. With their hold on this vast new territory now secure, the Bolsheviks established the Soviet Union on Marxist-Leninist principles.

SEE ALSO

Bolsheviks; Communism; Kerensky, Aleksandr; Lenin, Vladimir Ilich; Liberals; Marxism-Leninism; Mensheviks; Monarchy; One-party system; Revolution; Russia; Social democracy; Soviet Union (Union of Soviet Socialist Republics); Totalitarianism; Trotsky, Leon

FURTHER READING

Carr, Edward Hallett. *The Russian Revolution: From Lenin to Stalin.* New York: Free Press, 1979.
Fitzpatrick, Sheila. *The Russian Revolution.* 2nd ed. New York: Oxford University Press, 1994.
Massie, Robert K. *The Romanovs: The Final Chapter.* New York: Random House, 1996.
Rabinowitch, Alexander. *The Bolsheviks Come to Power: The Revolution of 1917 in Petrograd.* New York: Norton, 1976.

Rwanda

REPUBLIC OF RWANDA (REPUBLIKA Y'U RWANDA)

• *Capital: Kigali*

Political history A kingdom dominated by the Tutsi ethnic group ruled over Rwanda and Burundi, located to the west of Lake Victoria in East Africa, beginning in the 16th century. Europeans explored the area in 1854 and it became a German colony in 1890. In 1916, during World War I, Belgium occupied the colony and administered it as a League of Nations mandate. The trust territory, called Ruanda-Urundi, was composed of two districts that eventually became Rwanda and Burundi. The mandate was made a United Nations Trust Territory in 1946 and remained under Belgian administration. In 1959 the Hutu ethnic group, constituting a majority of the population, revolted and destroyed the Tutsi *mwami,* or monarchy, through which the Germans and Belgians had ruled over the majority Hutu.

Belgium granted Rwanda independence in 1961, a decision recognized by the United Nations the following year. During the 1960s, Tutsi exiles mounted six invasions, but the Hutu government repelled all of them and slaughtered thousands of Tutsi. Civilian government gave way to a military regime after a coup d'état in 1973, and for the next 20 years the nation was governed by a military junta headed by General Juvénal Habyarimana. He refused to permit Tutsi exiles to return to Rwanda, claiming the nation was overcrowded. In 1990 Habyarimana agreed, under pressure from Western donor nations and international organizations, to begin a transformation from a military regime to a multiparty democracy, and in 1994 he began planning to share power with the Tutsi minority, a policy that lost him support from Hutu hard-liners within his own government.

On April 6, 1994, President Habyarimana died in a crash when his plane was shot down by a ground-to-air missile probably fired by Hutu radicals. In the ensuing chaos, the Hutu hard-liners in the government decided to eliminate the remaining Tutsi minority. They began by killing Hutu opponents of the regime to consolidate their own power, as well as the Hutu prime minister, Agathe Uwilingiyimana, and then they began a campaign of genocide against the Tutsi. They encouraged local Hutu militias and youth organizations from the dominant political parties (the National Republican Movement for Democracy and Development and the Coalition for the Defense of the Republic) to kill 1 million or more of the local Tutsi population.

Most of the remaining Tutsi fled the country.

Exiled Tutsi military forces, many of them veterans of warfare in Uganda, invaded Rwanda to save their countrymen from further massacres. Some 14,000 troops organized by the Rwandan Patriotic Front attacked the Hutu government and defeated it in early July 1994. Tutsi generals installed a new government but allowed moderate Hutu to serve as president and prime minister, in order to reassure the Hutu majority. The power behind them, however, was a Tutsi general, Paul Kagame, who assumed the positions of vice president and defense minister.

Hundreds of thousands of Hutu fled into Zaire and Uganda, and their army reorganized to continue the civil war against the Tutsi. By 1995, out of a pre-war population of 8.2 million, approximately 1 million Hutu and Tutsi had been killed in genocidal slaughter, and some 200,000 had been killed in military confrontations. More than 1 million Hutu and 1 million Tutsi were refugees in Zaire, Burundi, Tanzania, and Uganda.

Government institutions Rwanda has a presidential system, in which the president, elected for a five-year term, is head of state. He exercises executive power with a council of ministers that he appoints. Legislative power is held jointly by the president and the National Development Council, which has 70 members popularly elected for five-year terms. The governors of the ten prefectures (districts) are appointed by the president. Actual power in Rwanda since mid-1994 has been exercised by military officers headed by Defense Minister Paul Kagame.

Lower provincial courts and courts of first instance handle civil and criminal cases. A court of appeal handles appeals from lower courts. A constitutional court reviews legislation, and a court of accounts reviews challenges to government expenditures. The judiciary was almost wiped out in the 1994–95 civil war, when three-fourths of the judges were killed by rebel or government forces.

Parties and movements Under the 1978 constitution, Rwanda became a one-party state, but amendments made in 1991 converted Rwanda into a multiparty democracy. The National Republican Movement for Democracy and Development was formed in 1993 from the Revolutionary Movement for Development, which had been the sole party before that. It was opposed by the Democratic Republican Movement, the Liberal Party, and the Christian Democratic Party.

A guerrilla movement, the Rwandese Patriotic Front, was the major opposition to the Hutu regime and assumed power in July 1994 after the Tutsi army defeated the Hutu. The new government pledged to include members of all political parties, as well as Hutu, in what it described as a future multiparty democracy. It announced that elections would be held in 1999 after the nation returned to normal. The largest party is the Rwandese Patriotic Front, dominated by Tutsi who had been exiled into Uganda in the 1960s, followed by the Movement for a Democratic Republic Party, which has considerable Hutu membership.

Domestic issues The economy is in shambles, and millions live on humanitarian relief supplies sent in by the United Nations and Western donor agencies. Large numbers of Hutu remain in exile, fearful of Tutsi reprisals, and until they return, the nation cannot have a functioning society or economy. As a step toward a multiethnic society, the government in 1995 announced that it would no longer list tribal affiliations on identity cards carried by citizens.

International issues Relations with Uganda, Rwanda's neighbor to the north, are strained because of the presence of 250,000 Tutsi refugees in Uganda. In the early 1990s, guerrilla attacks mounted by the Rwandese Patriotic Front from camps in Uganda led Rwanda to take the battle to Uganda, creating more than 64,000 Ugandan refugees from the battle zone.

In the 1994 civil war, French forces intervened on behalf of the Hutu government but withdrew after the Tutsi victory. In the aftermath of the fighting, the United Nations sent in a force of 5,600 peacekeeping troops to Rwanda at the request of the new Tutsi government. That figure was cut in half by June 1995, after the Rwandan government asked that all UN peacekeepers be removed, claiming that they were undisciplined and not needed by the local population.

Forty-three of the 102 foreign aid agencies in Rwanda were expelled in 1995 by military strongman Paul Kagame to show his irritation with the failure of Western aid agencies to deliver more than a fraction of the $1.2 billion in reconstruction aid promised in 1994.

In 1997 Rwanda provided troops, supplies, and transport for a rebel army led by Laurent Kabila, who assumed power in Zaire (now the Democratic Republic of Congo). Rwandan military and civilian advisers are influential in the new Congolese regime.

Human rights A United Nations Investigating Commission has estimated that the Hutu slaughtered between 500,000 and 1 million Tutsi civilians in 1994. When a Tutsi army reclaimed the country, Hutu refugees fled into Zaire, where many civilians were terrorized by their own military leaders in the refugee camps. Many Hutu prisoners in Rwanda are held in overcrowded prisons, where conditions have led to many deaths and injuries. In 1995 the United Nations Security Council created a war crimes and human rights panel, based in Tanzania, to try cases of war crimes and genocide in Rwanda, but as of 1997, it had moved slowly in bringing war criminals to justice.

SEE ALSO
Belgium; Burundi

FURTHER READING
Destexhe, Alain. *Rwanda and Genocide in the Twentieth Century.* New York: New York University Press, 1995.
Newbury, Catherine. *The Cohesion of Oppression: Clientship and Ethnicity in Rwanda, 1860–1960.* New York: Columbia University Press, 1988.
Prunier, Gerard. *The Rwanda Crisis: History of a Genocide.* New York: Columbia University Press, 1995.

Sadat, Anwar

- *Born: Dec. 25, 1918, Mit Abu el-Kom, Egypt*
- *Died: Oct. 6, 1981, Cairo, Egypt*

As president of Egypt (1970–81), Anwar Sadat was the first Arab leader to make peace with Israel, a policy that changed the history of the Middle East.

Sadat's father was a hospital worker who married a Sudanese woman. Sadat graduated from secondary school in Cairo, attended the Abbassia Military Academy, and joined with Gamal Abdel Nasser (later the president of Egypt) in the Movement of Free Officers, a secret clique that was formed in 1938 with the purpose of eventually overthrowing the corrupt Egyptian monarchy. Because of his opposition to the British occupation of Egypt, Sadat worked with the Nazis during World War II, but his efforts were discovered and he was court-martialed from the army and put in a detention camp in 1942. He escaped in 1944, was recaptured in 1946, and served another three years in prison. In 1949 he was released and began working as a journalist. He reentered the army in 1950.

The Movement of Free Officers overthrew King Farouk in 1952 and ended the monarchy in 1953. Sadat served as a member of the Revolutionary Command Council, which ruled the country under the chairmanship of Gamal Abdel Nasser. Nasser was elected president in 1956, and Sadat served as one of his four vice presidents from 1964 to 1967. He was the single vice president after 1969. After Nasser's death in 1970, Sadat assumed the leadership of Egypt as president.

In 1973, after failing to negotiate with Israel to end the occupation of Egypt's Sinai Peninsula, Sadat ordered a surprise attack on Israel. Egyptian forces crossed the Suez Canal and overwhelmed the small Israeli force on the peninsula. The Egyptians then dug into defensive positions and for some time held off Israeli reinforcements, until the Egyptian Third Army was surrounded by a daring Israeli recrossing of the canal. Sadat then agreed to a cease-fire, which saved his forces from defeat. In lengthy negotiations mediated by U.S. secretary of state Henry Kissinger, Sadat then accepted a mutual withdrawal of Egyptian and Israeli forces in Sinai.

In 1977 Sadat shocked the world by agreeing to meet with Israeli prime minister Menachem Begin in Jerusalem in order to seek a peace agreement. After two years of negotiations mediated by the United States, Sadat and Begin reached an agreement at President Jimmy Carter's Maryland retreat, Camp David, for which the peace accords were named.

Begin agreed to give up occupation of the Sinai Peninsula in return for Sadat's agreement to establish diplomatic relations with Israel and end its state of war. The two men shared the 1978 Nobel Peace Prize for their efforts.

The agreement was denounced by most Arab governments, however, who believed that Egypt had made a peace to regain its own territory while ignoring the claims of Syrians and Palestinians to occupied territory, and Egypt was expelled from the Arab League. Nevertheless, Sadat held firm. Moreover, his diplomacy gained him the support of Western nations, and his relationship with the United States became quite close. The United States replaced the Soviet Union as Egypt's principal military supplier and donor of foreign aid.

Anwar Sadat was assassinated during a military parade in October 1981 by a group of Islamic fundamentalist soldiers opposed to his peacemaking efforts. He was succeeded by his vice president, Hosni Mubarak, who continued his pro-Western diplomatic policies and kept Egypt at peace with Israel.

SEE ALSO

Arab League (League of Arab States); Carter, Jimmy (James Earl, Jr.); Egypt; Islamic fundamentalism; Israel; Mubarak, Muhammad Hosni; Nasser, Gamal Abdel

FURTHER READING

Aufderheide, Patricia. *Anwar Sadat.* New York: Chelsea House, 1985.
Baker, Raymond. *Sadat and After: Struggles for Egypt's Political Soul.* Cambridge: Harvard University Press, 1990.
Carroll, Raymond. *Anwar Sadat.* New York: Franklin Watts, 1982.
Friedlander, Melvin A. *Sadat and Begin: The Domestic Politics of Peacemaking.* Boulder, Colo.: Westview, 1983.
Hirst, David, and Irene Beeson. *Sadat.* London: Faber & Faber, 1981.
Lippman, Thomas W. *Egypt after Nasser: Sadat, Peace, and the Mirage of Prosperity.* New York: Paragon House, 1989.
Sadat, Anwar. *In Search of Identity: An Autobiography.* New York: Harper & Row, 1978.

Saddam Hussein

SEE Hussein, Saddam

Saint Christopher–Nevis

FEDERATION OF SAINT KITTS AND NEVIS

• *Capital: Basseterre*

Political history Saint Kitts (formally known as Saint Christopher) and Nevis, two islands in the Caribbean Sea, were originally settled by Arawak Indians, who were driven out by the Carib Indians before European settlement. The islands were discovered and named by Christopher Columbus in 1493. They were settled by the British in 1623 and 1628, respectively, though France also claimed them, based on its exploration and settlements. In 1713 France relinquished its claim to the British. The Indian population died out (primarily due to disease) and was replaced by black slaves from Africa. The islands formed part of the British colonial Leeward Islands Federation from 1871 until 1958, then were part of the British Federation of the West Indies until 1962, when they decided to remain a British colony while the West Indies became independent. In 1976 colonial status was replaced by an "association" with Britain, an arrangement providing for internal self-government. The nation gained its full independence in 1983.

Government institutions The nation has a constitutional monarchy and is governed by a parliamentary system. The head of state is the monarch of the Commonwealth of Nations, whose power is exercised locally by the governor-general. Executive power is vested in the cabinet and prime minister, who are elected by and accountable to the local parliament. Legislative power is vested in the 15-member National Assembly, which has a Speaker, 2 members appointed by the prime minister and 1 by the leader of the opposition, and 11 other representatives directly elected by the people for five-year terms. Appeals from the local judicial system are heard by the Eastern Caribbean Supreme Court of Appeals in Saint Lucia, whose jurisdiction includes a number of small Caribbean island nations.

Parties and movements The islands are a multiparty democracy. The strongest party is the People's Action Movement (social democratic) followed by the Labour Party (socialist) and the Nevis Reformation Party, which advocates independence for Nevis.

Domestic issues There is a secessionist movement on Nevis, whose inhabitants resent that political power is exercised almost exclusively by the larger Saint Kitts. There is labor unrest on both islands when workers from Saint Vincent and the Grenadines are brought in by farm owners to replace local harvesters for the sugar crop at lower wages than those paid to local workers.

International issues Saint Kitts and Nevis are opposed to a union of Caribbean states, which some of the nearby islands have suggested. The islands have formed an accord with Venezuela that allows both nations to import and export goods without paying tariffs.

FURTHER READING
Dyde, Brian. *St. Kitts: Cradle of the Caribbean*. London: Macmillan, 1989.

Saint Kitts–Nevis

SEE Saint Christopher–Nevis

Saint Lucia

• *Capital: Castries*

Political history Saint Lucia is an island in the Caribbean Sea that was originally inhabited by Arawak Indians, who were driven out by the Carib Indians prior to European discovery in 1550. It was briefly colonized by the British in 1638. The French conquered it in 1650 but ceded it to Britain in 1814 as a result of defeats in the Napoleonic Wars.

In 1967 Saint Lucia's colonial status was replaced by "association" with Britain, providing for full internal self-government but continued British sovereignty. The nation gained its full independence in 1979.

Government institutions Saint Lucia is a constitutional monarchy and is governed by a parliamentary system. The head of state is the monarch of the Commonwealth of Nations, represented locally by the governor-general. Executive power is vested in the cabinet and prime minister, elected by and accountable to a bicameral parliament. Legislative power is vested in the 17-member House of Assembly, all members of which are directly elected by the people, and the 11-member Senate; 5 of the Senate members are elected by the people and 6 are appointed by the governor-general (3 on the advice of the prime minister and 3 on the advice of the opposition leader).

The judiciary is independent and consists of local civil and criminal courts. Appeals are heard by the 10-member High Court of Justice. Final appeals rest with the Eastern Caribbean Supreme Court, based in Saint Lucia.

Parties and movements The island is a multiparty democracy. The strongest party is the United Workers Party (right wing), followed by the socialist Saint Lucia Labour Party and the Progressive Labour Party, which is also a socialist party.

Domestic issues The country's economy is highly dependent on bananas and tourism. Government efforts to control the banana industry have met with resistance from the banana growers, organized into the Banana Salvation Committee, because this would cut their profits and force them to pay higher wages for workers.

The government's efforts to combat drug trafficking and smuggling have been thwarted by police corruption.

International issues Saint Lucia has strongly supported the formation of a unified East Caribbean state consisting of all the island states or, barring that, a Windward Island union for the English-speaking countries of the region. The proposal has met with strong opposition from many of the smaller islands.

FURTHER READING
Saint Lucia. Washington, D.C.: The World Bank, 1985.

Saint Vincent and the Grenadines

• *Capital: Kingstown*

Political history Saint Vincent, an island in the eastern Caribbean Sea, was inhabited by Carib Indians when it was discovered by Spain in 1498. Britain and France fought over it in the 17th and 18th centuries during their naval wars, and France eventually ceded it to Britain in 1783 after the British had conquered it in naval struggles associated with the American Revolution. It attained internal self-governing autonomy under the terms of an agreement of association with the United Kingdom in 1969. Ten years later, it formed a union with the group of eight small islands known as the Grenadines (consisting of Bequia, Balliceau, Canouan, Mayreau, Mustique, Isle d'Quatre, Petit Saint Vincent, and Union Island) and together they gained complete independence in 1979.

Government institutions The nation is a constitutional monarchy and is governed by a parliamentary system. The head of state is the monarch of the Commonwealth of Nations, repre-

sented locally by a governor-general. Executive power is vested in the cabinet and prime minister, who are elected by and accountable to the local parliament. Legislative power is vested in the 21-member House of Assembly, 15 of whose members are directly elected and 6 of whom (4 appointed on the advice of the prime minister and 2 on the advice of the opposition leader) constitute the Senate (although they serve in the Assembly as well).

The judiciary consists of local civil and criminal courts. Appeals are heard by the Eastern Caribbean Supreme Court, which maintains a resident judge on Saint Vincent.

Parties and movements The islands are a multiparty democracy. The strongest party is the centrist New Democratic Party, followed by the United Labour Party (social democratic) and the United People's Movement (socialist).

Domestic issues Agriculture (primarily the banana industry) and tourism sustain the economy. Governments are often unstable, because they lose popular support amid charges of corruption in the provision of government services (particularly health care) and cover-ups involving smuggling and drug trafficking.

International issues The islands advocate eastern Caribbean unity and are part of the Windward Islands group that is seeking to create a Regional Constituent Assembly that would bring together representatives of all the eastern Caribbean islands.

There was a dispute in the 1990s with the Dominican Republic over Saint Vincent's banana exports to the European Union, in which Dominicans charged that such exports infringed on their preexisting markets. The islands agreed to stop further sales of bananas to the United Kingdom to end the dispute.

Sakharov, Andrei Dimitriyevich

- *Born: May 21, 1921, Moscow, Russia*
- *Died: Dec. 14, 1989, Moscow, Soviet Union*

Andrei Sakharov was the father of the Soviet hydrogen bomb and the leading voice for reform in the Soviet Union in the 1970s and 1980s.

Sakharov graduated with honors in physics from Moscow State University in 1942. He became a member of the Lebedev Physics Institute of the Academy of Sciences of the USSR in Moscow in 1945 and earned his doctorate in physics and mathematics in 1947. Between 1948 and 1956 he worked on the development of thermonuclear weapons for the Soviet military. In 1953 he was rewarded with membership in the Soviet Academy of Sciences, the youngest person so honored. He received the Order of Lenin and the Stalin Prize.

Andrei Sakharov (here with his granddaughter Anya) was one of the most prominent dissidents under the communist regime that ruled the Soviet Union. He was awarded a Nobel Peace Prize for his human rights activities.

In his later scientific career, Sakharov worked on efforts to harness thermonuclear energy for electrical power. Gradually, he became convinced that scientists, particularly those who had created nuclear weapons, had a special responsibility to work for peace and end the cold war, a position that led him to study political developments and become active in Soviet politics.

In 1966 Sakharov warned Communist Party leader Leonid Brezhnev against attempting to return to Stalinist dictatorship. Two years later he circulated a manuscript entitled "Progress, Coexistence and Intellectual Freedom," which warned against excessive nationalism, theories of racial superiority, and Stalinism. He called for détente with the West. Sakharov's call for the gradual evolution of the Soviet Union into a multiparty democracy was a direct challenge to the primacy of the Communist Party.

In 1970 Sakharov and two other physicists created the Committee for Human Rights. In 1975 he was awarded the Nobel Peace Prize for his "fearless personal commitment in upholding the fundamental principles for peace between men," according to the Nobel committee. But the Soviet government forbade him to travel to Oslo to receive the award.

Sakharov was expelled from the Academy of Sciences and lost his scientific positions in a government attempt to silence him. He and his wife, Yelena Bonner, also a leader of the dissident forces, were sent into exile from Moscow to Gorki, and for a while he was unable to communicate with colleagues or Westerners. Finally, in 1989, he was released from house arrest by Soviet president Mikhail Gorbachev. Sakharov returned to Moscow, where he assumed the leadership of the organization Pamyat (Memory), devoted to unearthing the truth about Soviet leader Joseph Stalin's purges and murders of millions of people in the 1930s and to honoring his victims. He was elected a deputy of the Congress of People's Deputies, where he remained one of Gorbachev's severest critics, continually calling for an end to the communist monopoly of power and the institution of a multiparty democracy.

Sakharov died in the midst of his struggle for democracy in the Soviet Union, receiving a hero's funeral attended by hundreds of thousands of mourners. Just two years later, the Soviet Union disintegrated, and the new Russian leader, Boris Yeltsin, presided over an emerging multiparty system in Russia.

SEE ALSO

Gorbachev, Mikhail; Soviet Union (Union of Soviet Socialist Republics); Stalin, Joseph; Yeltsin, Boris

FURTHER READING

Bonner, Yelena. *Mothers and Daughters.* New York: Knopf, 1992.

Bonner, Yelena. *Alone Together.* Translated by Alexander Cook. New York: Knopf, 1986.

Lozansky, Edward D., ed. *Andrei Sakharov and Peace.* New York: Avon, 1985.

Sakharov, Andrei. *Memoirs.* Translated by Richard Lourie. New York: Knopf, 1990.

Sakharov, Andrei. *Progress, Coexistence and Intellectual Freedom.* New York: Norton, 1968.

San Marino

MOST SERENE REPUBLIC OF SAN MARINO (SERENISSIMA REPUBBLICA DI SAN MARINO)

• *Capital: San Marino*

Political history Located on the Italian peninsula, the tiny principality of San Marino was founded in the 4th century A.D. as an independent Italian city-state. It did not become part of Italy when the other principalities on the peninsula were united under the king of Sardinia in the mid-19th century. It signed a treaty of friendship with Italy in 1862, making it, in effect, an Italian protectorate.

Government institutions San Marino is divided into nine *castles* (districts), each of which is governed by a castle-captain, who holds office for two years, and an Auxiliary Council, whose members hold office for five years. Legislative power is vested in the unicam-

eral 60-member Great and General Council, whose members are directly elected for five years. Every six months, the Council elects two of its members to act as regents-captain, who function jointly as heads of state and government. The 10-member Council of State, elected by the Great and General Council every six months, runs the government departments.

There is an independent judiciary. Minor cases are heard by justices of the peace. Law commissioners deal with civil and criminal cases, and major offenses are decided by the criminal judges of the Primary Court of Claims. There is a court of appeals for criminal and civil cases. The Council of Twelve serves as a final appeals court for civil cases. With the exception of justices of the peace, the judges in San Marino are foreigners, mostly Italian jurists.

Parties and movements San Marino is a multiparty democracy. The main parties are the Partito Democratico Cristiano Sammarinese (Christian Democrat), the Partito Democratico Progressista (communist), the Partito di Democrazia Socialista (social democrat), and the Partito Socialista Sammarinese (socialist).

Domestic issues San Marino is the only western European state ever to elect a communist coalition government, which ruled between 1945 and 1957 and from 1978 to 1986. Since 1986, various coalitions have ruled, including a communist–Christian Democratic coalition from 1986 to 1992 and a socialist–Christian Democratic coalition beginning in 1992.

San Marino's economy is based on agriculture. From its mountainsides come wheat, barley, and dairy products, as well as olive oil and wine. It exports building stones from its quarries. San Marino is a major tourist attraction, and, as with Monaco, sales of its postage stamps to collectors provides much of its revenue.

International issues San Marino has a customs union with Italy and functions as a part of the European Union, upholding the union's economic regulations and standards, though it is not a formal member. In 1992 it joined the Council of Europe and became a member of the United Nations and the International Monetary Fund.

SEE ALSO
Italy

São Tomé and Príncipe

DEMOCRATIC REPUBLIC OF SÃO TOMÉ AND PRÍNCIPE (REPÚBLICA DEMOCRÁTICA DE SÃO TOMÉ E PRÍNCIPE)

• *Capital: São Tomé*

Political history The unpopulated islands of São Tomé and Príncipe, located off the western coast of Africa, were discovered in 1471 by Pedro Escobar and João Gomes, and they became a Portuguese colony in 1522, servicing ships involved in the African slave trade. In the late 17th and 18th century, Portuguese settlers introduced plantation agriculture, and the islands became a major source of cocoa. In 1951 São Tomé and Príncipe became an overseas province of Portugal, and in 1975 it gained independence. In 1996 the elected civilian government was overthrown in a military coup led by Lieutenant Orlando das Neves, leading to a period of political instability.

Government institutions Under the 1990 constitution, the people estab-

lished a semi-presidential system. The president is the head of state and governs with an appointed council of ministers, led by the prime minister. The president is elected by universal suffrage for no more than two five-year terms. The prime minister is nominated by the deputies of the parliament and is accountable to them. Legislative power is exercised by a 55-member National Assembly whose members are elected for four-year terms. The Supreme Court is appointed by the National Assembly and supervises district courts.

Parties and movements The country shifted from a one-party state to a multiparty democracy in 1990. The largest parties are the Movimento de Libertação de São Tomé e Príncipe–Partido Social Democrático (Liberation Movement of São Tomé and Príncipe–Social Democratic Party), formed out of the independence movement and formerly the sole legal party; the Partido da Convergência Democrática–Grupo de Reflexão (Party of Democratic Convergence), which is a breakaway faction of the dominant party; and the social democratic Coligação Democrática de Oposição (Opposition Democrats).

Domestic issues The nation's debts to Western lenders total three times its yearly domestic national product, a figure that is extraordinarily high by world standards. The government instituted an austerity program in 1991 in order to gain assistance from the International Monetary Fund and World Bank in reducing this debt and stabilizing the value of the currency. Cuts in social welfare and health programs required by these agencies have put islanders' health at risk, especially the many children suffering from malnutrition, resulting in decreased support for the government.

The island of Príncipe has complained about the central government, and in 1994 it received autonomy with its own regional assembly.

International issues The country has trade links with nearby African nations such as Gabon, Cameroon, and Equatorial Guinea. It has cultural and economic links with Portugal and its former African colonies. São Tomé and Príncipe was active in the peace negotiations to end the Angolan civil war in the early 1990s because its diplomats, steeped in Portuguese language and culture, were trusted by both sides in that former Portuguese colony.

SEE ALSO
Portugal

FURTHER READING
Hedges, Tony, and Malyn Newitt. *São Tomé and Príncipe*. Boulder, Colo.: Westview, 1988.

Saudi Arabia

KINGDOM OF SAUDI ARABIA (AL-MAMLAKAH AL-'ARABĪYAH AS-SA'ŪDĪYAH)

- *Capital: Riyadh*

Political history The Arabian peninsula was settled in ancient times by nomadic Bedouin tribes. The various tribes were united for the first time in the 7th century under Muhammad, the founder of Islam. The Arabian peninsula became part of the Ottoman Empire in the 16th century. In the 1800s the Wahhabi kingdom under the House of Sa'ud ruled the region until the dynasty was overthrown in 1890.

In 1902 a Saudi prince, 'Abd al-'Azīzibn 'Abd ar-Rahmān, came out of the desert to capture Riyadh. He gradually extended his domain and proclaimed the Kingdom of Saudi Arabia in 1932.

Government institutions Saudi Arabia is an absolute monarchy. The king and the royal family are sovereign and exercise all governmental powers through their appointed officials. A consultative assembly, the Majlis ash-Shoura (Shoura Council), was created late in 1993, consisting of 60 members appointed by the royal family. They serve four-year terms and meet in private session to advise the king. The members consist of five religious leaders, as well as Islamic scholars, tribal leaders, military officers, and senior government officials.

The king appoints a council of ministers, which makes legislative decisions by majority vote but then requires royal approval. The Supreme Ulma Council is a governmental body of Islamic clergy that interprets religious law, the supreme law in the kingdom. The state courts decide cases based on the council's rulings.

Parties and movements There are no legal political parties. The Islamic Movement, a fundamentalist Sunni Muslim group, was banned in 1990 after it was linked to disturbances at Islamic holy sites because the conservative, pro-Western government believed that it was antimonarchical and would establish a radical Islamic state.

Domestic issues Saudi Arabia has one-third of the world's proven oil reserves. It is the largest petroleum exporter in the world, selling 7 million barrels of oil abroad daily. The United States buys 10 percent of its petroleum from the Saudis. Saudi Arabia has used its oil revenues to build its industrial infrastructure, concentrating on oil refining and petroleum products. It has diversified into agriculture as a wheat exporter and into aquaculture. However, after the boom years of the 1970s and 1980s, when the kingdom spent more than $400 billion of public funds on modernization, the economy went into decline. In the 1990s, oil prices have

Ancient and modern ways intersect in Saudi Arabia, where nomads on camels traverse the same desert route as the Trans-Arabian oil pipeline.

plummeted, export earnings have dropped, and the Saudis now import goods whose total value is more than what they export, creating a trade deficit. Per capita income declined from $21,000 in 1981 to $6,800 in the mid-1990s.

Mismanagement of state enterprises has wasted billions, and fraud and corruption involving many of the 4,000 members of the royal family is rampant. The immediate royal family has a personal fortune estimated at more than $10 billion, much of it derived from commissions on contracts for public works and defense expenditures, as well as the sale of royal lands (*emiri*) to the government at inflated prices. The government budget has been run at a deficit since 1983. As a result, the government has been forced to reduce its previously extensive welfare-state benefits. Saudi Arabia has a rapidly growing young population, and unemployment is predicted to be the major issue after the year 2000.

Saudi rulers are resisting pressure from Islamic fundamentalists and from secular democrats, both of whom want to end the dominant role of the royal house. More than 100 Islamic scholars, in a Memorandum of Advice to the government issued in 1993, demanded more rigorous application of Islamic law and an end to the pro-Western policies of the monarchy. In response, the government has arrested a number of leading Sunni Muslim fundamentalist clerics who favor an Islamic state, including the clerical leaders Salman bin Fahd al-Audeh and Safar bin Abdel Rahman al-Hawali. It has also dismissed antigovernment clerics from the Supreme Authority of Senior Scholars, the highest religious body of Sunni Islam in Saudi Arabia. To shore up its position, the government in 1993 reached an agreement with the Shiites, a branch of Islam in a minority in Saudi Arabia, to guarantee their freedom of religion.

International issues Saudi Arabia is closely allied with Great Britain and the United States, because of oil consumption in the West, and both of these nations sell Saudi Arabia arms and provide military training. The Saudis bought more than $62 billion in U.S. weapons between 1990 and 1995. More than 5,000 U.S. military personnel and 4,400 contract personnel are located in the kingdom to help the army with servicing and training. China has sold long-range ballistic missiles to Saudi Arabia despite the objections of the United States, which believes that they are offensive weapons not needed to protect the kingdom.

Saudi Arabia is one of the largest suppliers of oil to the United States and is one of its major trading partners.

Saudi Arabia is the dominant member of the Organization of Petroleum Exporting Countries (OPEC), established in 1960 to coordinate export and production policies among petroleum-exporting nations. It is a founding member of the Gulf Cooperation Council, a group of six oil-producing monarchies that joined together to ensure stability in the region and provide for their military defense. Saudi Arabia, however, was defended by the United States after the Iraqi invasion of Kuwait and served as a staging area for U.S. forces and their allies in the Persian Gulf War of 1991.

Saudi Arabia is a major financial backer of the Palestinian Authority. Although it opposed the creation of the State of Israel in 1948, it has refrained from military activities against Israel and has not actively opposed Egyptian and Jordanian decisions to end hostilities with Israel.

Human rights Islamic fundamentalists of the Muslim Brotherhood have been arrested for criticizing the government and calling for wider application of religious law. Press censorship has been increased, and there are no rights to freedom of speech, press, or association. In the early 1990s the government banned charitable contributions to Muslim organizations without govern-

mental approval. The religious police—the Committee for the Promotion of Virtue and the Prevention of Vice—enforce censorship of Western culture and media and have harassed foreign workers into obeying Islamic law, especially provisions calling for modest dress and no alcohol.

SEE ALSO

Gulf Cooperation Council (GCC); Islamic fundamentalism; Organization of Petroleum Exporting Countries (OPEC)

FURTHER READING

Aburish, Said K. *The Rise, Corruption, and Coming Fall of the House of Saud.* New York: St. Martin's, 1995.
Cordesman, Anthony H. *Saudi Arabia : Guarding the Desert Kingdom.* Boulder, Colo.: Westview, 1997.
Cordesman, Anthony H. *Western Strategic Interests in Saudi Arabia.* London: Croom Helm, 1987.
Safran, Nadav. *Saudi Arabia: The Ceaseless Quest for Security.* Ithaca, N.Y.: Cornell University Press, 1988.

Scotland

SEE United Kingdom

Second International

The Second International (formally the Second International Working Men's Association) was an organization founded in 1889 by French and German social democratic intellectuals in Paris. Its goal was to develop social democratic thought and plan for the transformation from a capitalist to a socialist society. After 1896 it voted to exclude anarchists and became a loose coalition of leftist political parties and trade unions. By 1904 it had chapters in 21 countries, a membership of 4 million, and an electoral base in Europe of more than 12 million voters.

The Second International, however, was beset by differences between orthodox followers of the late Karl Marx—such as Georgy Plekhanov, a Russian revolutionary who was one of the dominant Marxist political theorists, who believed that industrial workers would eventually overthrow capitalist governments by revolutionary action—and followers of the Marxist revisionist Karl Kautsky and the social democrat Eduard Bernstein, both of whom believed that liberal democratic methods could be used for a peaceful transformation of European societies to socialism.

In 1905 the Second International resolved that social democratic parties should not join in coalition governments with liberal, radical, or centrist parties but should attempt to win absolute control of governments through regular elections.

Given the strength of centrist parties in most European nations at the time, this was an unworkable strategy. In 1910 the Copenhagen Congress, a meeting of socialist parties, passed a resolution that called on workers in different countries not to fight against each other if their governments went to war. However, in 1914, at the outset of World War I, members of the German Social-Democrat Party repudiated this agreement in order to support the German government, followed by the members of practically all other social democratic parties. Soon the organization collapsed as workers of the world took up arms against each other. Contrary to the hopes of the Marxists, the nationalist feelings of workers proved to be stronger than their class solidarity.

SEE ALSO
Communism; Marxism-Leninism; Nationalism; Social democracy; Socialism

FURTHER READING
Joll, James. *The Second International, 1889–1914.* Rev. and extended ed. Boston: Routledge & Kegan Paul, 1974.

Second World

The *Second World* is a term used to describe the economies of the Soviet Union and its Eastern European puppet states during the cold war. Unlike the highly developed industrial nations of the capitalist First World, or the newly industrializing or underdeveloped nations of the Third World, the Second World nations relied on socialist models of economic organization: central planning to set goals, state enterprises to produce goods, state control of investment decisions to modernize the economy, and barter agreements in international trade. Their economies were coordinated by the Council for Mutual Economic Assistance, dominated by the Soviet Union.

Although the nations of the Second World had highly educated populations, the inefficiencies of the socialist model, combined with rampant corruption at all levels of the government and economy, produced poor results: shoddy goods, low output, and environmental damage on a massive scale. The workers were quickly disillusioned in these "workers' states" because of the scarcity of housing, consumer goods, and good food. The Communist Party apparatus prevented workers from organizing free trade unions to improve their situation, and dissident activities of any kind were suppressed, with those involved being sentenced to lengthy jail terms. "They pretend to pay us, and we pretend to work" was one popular joke among workers in many industries, and production goals in these states' five-year plans, in spite of Communist Party propaganda, were rarely achieved.

Because of the poor quality of agricultural and industrial goods produced in the Second World, its products were not in demand either in the industrialized First World or in the developing Third World. For the most part (with the exception of a few states, such as Hungary, Czechoslovakia, East Germany, and Poland), the Second World nations exported primary products (oil, diamonds, industrial or precious metals) to the West for hard currency, which they used to buy technology, heavy industrial equipment, or consumer goods (for their party members). The currency of these nations was considered worthless in the West, so these nations bartered raw materials to obtain the Western currency that financed their trade. Alternatively, they bartered with one another, usually on terms set by the Soviet Union.

As Second World nations left the Soviet Union's sphere of influence after 1989, they converted their socialist economies into mixed economies, welcoming capitalist entrepreneurs from the West, privatizing their state enterprises, and doing away with central planning. They transformed their patterns of trade and commerce, seeking Western markets, and replaced many of their barter relationships with deals based on hard currency.

SEE ALSO

Cold war; Council for Mutual Economic Assistance (COMECON); First World; Soviet Union (Union of Soviet Socialist Republics); Third World

Selassie, Haile

SEE Haile Selassie

Self-determination

Self-determination is the principle that people who claim a common nationality by virtue of common ancestry, religion, culture, or language should be able to organize themselves as sovereign, or self-ruling, nation-states.

Napoléon Bonaparte, emperor of France from 1804 to 1815, proclaimed the right of people to self-determination in order to detach them from their allegiance to European monarchs, such as the Austrian Habsburgs in central Europe, who had created vast multinational empires. Napoléon's armies then trampled on the aspirations of many peoples as he created his own empire. Nevertheless, after Napoléon's defeat by the imperial allies and his abdication in 1815, the principle of self-determination led peoples in the Balkans, such as the Greeks, to win independence from

The East African nation of Somalia achieved its independence on July 1, 1960. Formerly, Somalia had been ruled as two separate colonies by Great Britain and Italy.

the Ottoman Empire, and in the late 19th century self-determination weakened the Habsburgs.

In the 20th century, U.S. president Woodrow Wilson embodied the principle of self-determination in his Fourteen Points, which he proposed as the guidelines for the World War I victors in a speech to Congress on January 8, 1918. That speech created a framework for the territorial settlements made at the Versailles peace conference at the end of the war. In eastern Europe, Hungary and Czechoslovakia were created out of the former Austro-Hungarian Habsburg empire. In the Middle East, the Ottoman Empire was dissolved and Turkey took its place as a nation-state.

After World War II the principle of self-determination was embodied in the charter of the United Nations and led to decolonization in Africa and Asia by the Belgians, British, French, Spanish, and Americans between 1945 and 1960 and by the Portuguese in the 1970s. The Zionist movement was able to organize the State of Israel (out of a part of the British mandate of Palestine) under the auspices of the United Nations in 1948.

In the 1990s self-determination was the principle used by Latvia, Lithuania, and Estonia—which had been incorporated by force into the Soviet Union in 1940—in reasserting their sovereignty, and by the 11 other Soviet republics that formed into the Commonwealth of Independent States after the dissolution of the Soviet Union in 1991. In Russia itself, nationalities such as the Tatars and Chechens proclaimed their own sovereign republics in 1992–93, though these were not recognized by the international community.

Although international law does not recognize the right of minorities in existing nation-states to secede and form new states, the principle of self-determination has been asserted by minority groups, such as the Palestinians, seeking autonomous governing status or full sovereignty in many nations of the world. Many nation-states around the world, such as Russia and China, remain threatened by minority nationalities calling for sovereignty or autonomy.

SEE ALSO

Austro-Hungarian Empire; Autonomy; Colonialism; Commonwealth of Independent States (CIS); Decolonization; Imperialism; Ottoman Empire; Russia; Sovereignty; Soviet Union (Union of Soviet Socialist Republics); State; United Nations (UN); Wilson, Woodrow; Zionism

FURTHER READING

Alexander, Honah, and Robert Friedlander, eds. *Self-Determination: National, Regional, and Global Dimensions*. Boulder, Colo.: Westview, 1980.
Hannum, Hurst. *Autonomy, Sovereignty, and Self-Determination*. Philadelphia: University of Pennsylvania Press, 1990.

Semi-presidential system

A semi-presidential system is a system of government in which a president elected by the people shares the executive power with a prime minister and cabinet accountable to the parliament. Semi-presidential states include the Weimar Republic in Germany (1919–33) and, in more recent times, Austria, Finland, France, Iceland, Ireland, Portugal, and Sri Lanka. A number of African states adopted the system in the 1990s as part of a shift from authoritarian regimes to parliamentary democracy.

The president is responsible for conducting diplomacy, commanding the armed forces, and making national security policy. The president also issues decrees and regulations that have the force of law. The prime minister and cabinet are responsible for formulating domestic policies and obtaining parliamentary approval of proposed laws.

At times during a president's term, his or her party may be defeated in midterm parliamentary elections by a coalition of opposition parties. In that case, a president of one party and a prime minister of another engage in what the French refer to as "cohabitation," an unstable political system likely to lead to stalemate and confrontation. The French Socialist president François Mitterrand, for instance, went through two episodes of cohabitation in the 1980s and 1990s: after the first period his own party regained a dominant position in the French legislature; after the second he himself was defeated and gave up the governing power to another party.

SEE ALSO
Cabinet government; France; Parliamentary system; President; Prime minister; Separation of powers

FURTHER READING
Duverger, Maurice. "A New Political System Model: Semi-presidential Government." *European Journal of Political Research* 8 (June 1980): 168–83.

Senegal

REPUBLIC OF SENEGAL (RÉPUBLIQUE DE SÉNÉGAL)

• *Capital: Dakar*

Political history The area in western Africa that is today Senegal was originally inhabited by nomadic tribes, many of whom converted to Islam through Arab influence in the 11th century. The Portuguese explored the Senegalese coast in the late 15th century and established trading posts. Although forbidden to do so by Prince Henry the Navigator, some Portuguese captains traded goods for African slaves, thus beginning the European slave trade. The French established a fort at Saint-Louis in 1659 and conquered other coastal trading posts from the Dutch, who had also begun to explore the area in the early 1600s.

Senegal became a French colony within French West Africa in 1902 and an autonomous state within the French Community in 1958. It joined with French Sudan to form the Federation of Mali in June 1960 but withdrew in August of that year and declared itself sovereign and independent. Senegal joined in a confederation with Gambia (Senegambia) in 1982 to coordinate defense, foreign, and monetary policies, but that dissolved in 1989, when it resumed its complete independence.

After a period of one-party rule in the 1970s and 1980s, pro-democracy groups in Senegal forced constitutional changes in 1992, including a limit on presidential terms, reestablishment of the position of prime minister (which had been eliminated in 1983) and restoration of a multiparty electoral system .

Government institutions Since 1989 Senegal has been making the transition from an authoritarian state to a republic with a semi-presidential system. The president is head of state and commander in chief of the armed forces. He is directly elected by the people and may serve a maximum of two seven-year terms. The president appoints a prime minister and cabinet who are responsible to parliament for domestic programs. Legislative power rests with the unicameral 120-member National Assembly, whose members are directly elected for five-year terms.

The newly elected president of Senegal, Léopold Senghor (left), and premier Mamadou Dia are greeted by supporters as they parade through the capital city of Dakar in September 1960. Besides being independent Senegal's most important political figure, Songhor is also a world-renowned poet.

There is a High Court of Appeals and lower district courts, whose judges are appointed by the president.

Parties and movements Senegal is a multiparty democracy. The dominant party is the Senegalese Socialist Party. Smaller parties include the Democratic Senegalese Party (social democratic) and the Party for the Liberation of the People, which calls for a neutral and anti-imperialist program that would reduce French influence in its former colony.

Domestic issues In the early 1990s the government adopted an austerity program with the assistance of the International Monetary Fund to adjust to a drop in peanut, phosphate, and oil prices that reduced government revenues and resulted in a large external debt. Senegal faces an insurrection from the Movement of the Democratic Forces of the Casamance in the south, a tribal group seeking independence or autonomy.

International issues Senegal has had border disputes with Mauritania and has charged Mauritania and

Gambia with aiding Casamance rebels. In 1992 the International Court of Justice confirmed Senegal's claim to a maritime zone (territorial waters) contested by Guinea-Bissau, which had also wanted access to the zone's valuable mineral and fishing resources.

SEE ALSO

French Community; Gambia; Guinea-Bissau; Mali; Mauritania

FURTHER READING

Fatton, Robert. The Making of a Liberal Democracy: Senegal's Passive Revolution, 1975–1985. Boulder, Colo.: Westview, 1987.

Separation of powers

Separation of powers is a constitutional principle that requires the partial or complete assignment of executive, legislative, and judicial powers to separate institutions of a government. It is generally credited to the French philosopher the Baron de Montesquieu, author of *The Spirit of the Laws* (1748), although a three-way division (executive, legislative, and diplomatic) had earlier been suggested by the English political theorist John Locke in his *Second Treatise of Government* (1690).

Montesquieu argued that if those who made the laws also executed them, or if those who executed the laws also decided judicial controversies about how they were administered, tyranny would result. Only states that separated the powers and placed them in different hands would remain free.

Constitutions that embody the principle of the separation of powers provide for a president to exercise executive power, a congress (or parliament) to exercise legislative power, and a supreme court and other national courts to exercise judicial powers. The constitution puts each branch on an equal level with the others, making each coordinate with—but independent of—the others. Each branch exercises only the powers assigned to it by the constitution, and it may not delegate its powers to another branch.

Separation of powers is combined with checks and balances in countries with presidential systems such as the United States, so that institutions can check, or limit, actions by other branches of government that might "unbalance" the constitution. "Ambition must be made to counteract ambition," James Madison argued in *The Federalist Papers* (1788), regarding the separation of powers and the

Montesquieu's The Spirit of the Laws *is generally credited with establishing the principle of separation of powers among the different branches of government.*

checks and balances embodied in the U.S. Constitution.

Countries with parliamentary systems, such as the United Kingdom, have neither separation of powers nor checks and balances. Instead, they fuse the legislative and executive powers into a cabinet of ministers that sits in parliament and remains accountable to its majority, which can force a cabinet to resign after a vote of "no confidence" and can replace it with a different cabinet more to its liking.

The courts in countries with parliamentary systems, though independent, rarely have the power to overturn acts of parliament or cabinet decrees. Instead of relying on the mechanisms of government to preserve their liberties, citizens in a parliamentary system depend primarily on elections to make politicians responsive to their wishes.

SEE ALSO

Cabinet government; Checks and balances; Parliamentary system; Presidential system; Semi-presidential system

FURTHER READING

Gwyn, W. B. *The Meaning of the Separation of Powers.* New Orleans: Tulane University Press, 1965.

Madison, James, et al. *The Federalist Papers.* New York: New American Library, 1961. (See especially numbers 47–51.)

Vile, M. J. C. *Constitutionalism and the Separation of Powers.* Oxford: Clarendon Press, 1967.

Serbia

Serbia is one of the two provinces of Yugoslavia (the other is Montenegro) that remained after the 1991 secession of the

other Yugoslav provinces of Croatia, Slovenia, Bosnia and Herzegovina, and Macedonia. For all intents and purposes, it is an independent country, since tiny Montenegro shares no real power in the Yugoslav federation.

The area of what is now Serbia was settled by the "Sorbs" from Hungary in the 7th century A.D. They converted to Eastern Orthodox Christianity in 879 A.D. under their leader Mutimer. They established an empire that reached its greatest influence between 1331 and 1355, when they controlled what is now Albania and Greece.

The Serbs lost their independence to the Turks at the Battle of Blackbird Fields, at Kosovo, on June 28, 1389, when their leader, Prince Lazar Hrebeljanovic, was captured and beheaded. Serbia was annexed by the Ottoman Empire in 1459, and the Serbs became enslaved serfs of the Turkish landowners. Their church was reestablished in the late 16th century, and they were

recognized as a nationality under Turkish rule. They received autonomy in 1804. After the 1828–29 wars between Turkey and Russia, Serbia was made a Russian protectorate with nominal Turkish control of Serbia's foreign affairs. It gained complete independence in 1878. A Serbian monarchy was established on March 6, 1882.

In 1914, when Archduke Francis Ferdinand of Austria was killed in Sarajevo by a Serbian nationalist, Austria used the incident as an excuse to declare war on Serbia, leading immediately to World War I.

Serbia was incorporated into Yugoslavia after World War I. The Serbian resistance fighters, known as Chetniks, were instrumental in liberating the country from Nazi Germany after it was conquered in 1940. During World War II, Serbs were killed by the tens of thousands in the Jasenovac concentration camp run by the Croatian fascists (Ustashe).

After World War II, Serbia remained part of Yugoslavia, governed by communist rulers until a nationalist regime led by Slobodan Milošević took power in 1991. After the dissolution of Yugoslavia in December of that year, with the secession of almost all its constituent republics, the Serbs and the republic of Montenegro reconstituted a Yugoslav federal government, with the capital in Belgrade, in 1992.

Serbian leaders have transformed themselves from communists focusing on economic issues to nationalists who emphasize recovery of Serbian culture, religion, and language. Their goal is a "Greater Serbia" uniting Serbs in Serbia and Bosnia. The Serbian Socialist Party, consisting of ex-communists, won the first free election of the post-communist era. Despite securing the support of the majority, the party rules with the aid of its 46,000-member internal security police, which uses force against political opponents.

Milošević gave substantial assistance to Serbian separatists in Bosnia and Herzegovina during the Bosnian civil war in the early 1990s, providing supplies across the border. He coordinated policy with the Serbian leader in Bosnia, Radovan Karadzic, and was implicated by Western observers (as well as by the Serbian Radical Party, an opposition force), in "ethnic cleansing" and other war crimes in Bosnia between 1992 and 1995, although the top Serbian leadership denies any complicity in crimes committed by the Bosnian Serbs.

Milošević won the 1992 presidential election, which was essentially a referendum on his war policies. In the 1993 parliamentary elections, his Socialist Party greatly increased its number of seats, though it fell short of an absolute majority.

Because of the aid it gave to Serbs in the Bosnian war, Serbia suffered from a UN economic embargo imposed in 1992, which permitted only food and medicine into the country. The embargo was lifted in 1995 when Serbia accepted the Dayton Peace Accords that provided for a settlement of the war in Bosnia. Inflation in 1993 approached 10,000 percent annually, more than half of the work force was unemployed, and industrial and agricultural production plummeted as a result of the war. There was rampant corruption at the highest levels of the government, including the security forces, much of it involving disposal of war booty looted from Bosnia.

Muslims predominate in regions of Kosovo and Vojvodina, and Hungarians in Sandzak, and these groups fan separatist movements that threaten Serbia's internal cohesion, even as it attempts to become "Greater Serbia" by waging wars of aggression against its neighbors.

Serbia has not cooperated with the international war crimes tribunal in The Hague, and has made no effort to turn over suspected war criminals involved in the Bosnian war. By 1996 the Milošević regime was intensifying its repressive measures. Opposition politicians and newspapers were harassed, and some opposition politicians were drafted into the army. The government has outlawed demonstrations by the opposition in Belgrade's Freedom Square, and the main private television station, Studio B, was nationalized.

SEE ALSO
Bosnia and Herzegovina; Croatia; Macedonia; Montenegro; Ottoman Empire; Slovenia; Yugoslavia

FURTHER READING
Dragnich, Alex, ed. *Serbia's Historical Heritage.* New York: Columbia University Press, 1974.
Judah, Tim. *The Serbs: History, Myth, and the Destruction of Yugoslavia.* New Haven: Yale University Press, 1997.

Ramet, Sabrina. *Nationalism and Federalism in Yugoslavia*. Bloomington: Indiana University Press, 1992.

Tanner, Marcus. *Croatia: A Nation Forged in War*. New Haven: Yale University Press, 1997.

Seychelles

REPUBLIC OF SEYCHELLES

• *Capital: Victoria*

Political history Located in the western Indian Ocean, the islands of the Seychelles were uninhabited until the French established spice plantations there after 1756 to break a Dutch monopoly on the spice trade in the Far East. The English captured the islands in 1794 and administered them as a dependency of Mauritius after 1814. In 1903 the Seychelles became a British Crown Colony. Internal self-government was granted in 1975 and independence in 1976. A military coup d'état overthrew the elected government in 1977. The Seychelles was an authoritarian state, dominated by military leaders, with a facade of civilian institutions, until it began the transition to democracy in the 1990s. In 1992 it instituted a multiparty system, and in 1993 a new constitution was approved by 74 percent of the voters in a referendum, establishing a democracy.

Government institutions The president is head of state and government. He is elected for a five-year term by direct popular vote and may serve a maximum of three terms. The president appoints and chairs the council of ministers, which runs the departments of government, and appoints all judges. Legislative power is exercised by a 33-member popularly elected unicameral National Assembly. There is an independent judiciary, headed by a Court of Appeals, which hears appeals from the intermediate Supreme Court as well as from the lower magistrate's courts.

Parties and movements In 1978 all parties were banned except the People's Progressive Front, and Seychelles became a one-party state. The ban was ended in 1992 when a multiparty democracy was implemented. The Front remains the largest party. Other parties include the Christian Democrat Party, the Seychelles Movement for Democracy (liberal), and the New Democratic Party (centrist).

Domestic issues The Seychelles has a centralized planned economy. The five-year plan of the mid-1990s emphasized foreign investment and assistance for environmental protection from the World Bank. Seychelles has a high foreign debt and is currently operating under an austerity plan imposed by the International Monetary Fund and the World Bank. Its leading political party, however, does promise that social welfare expenditures will be increased, which is a popular position enabling it to retain political power.

International issues Seychelles has a nonalignment policy and supports the idea of an Indian Ocean Zone of Peace that would ban foreign military bases and warships. It is a member of the Indian Ocean Commission, which deals with fishing, ecological, and other maritime issues. In the late 1980s the Seychelles began cooperation with the Comoro Islands and Mauritius on the control of infectious diseases. The United States maintains a large space satellite-tracking installation in the Seychelles, which is also used to track the space shuttles.

SEE ALSO

Comoro Islands; Mauritius

FURTHER READING

Benedict, Marion, and Burton Benedict. *Men, Women and Money in Seychelles*. Berkeley: University of California Press, 1983.

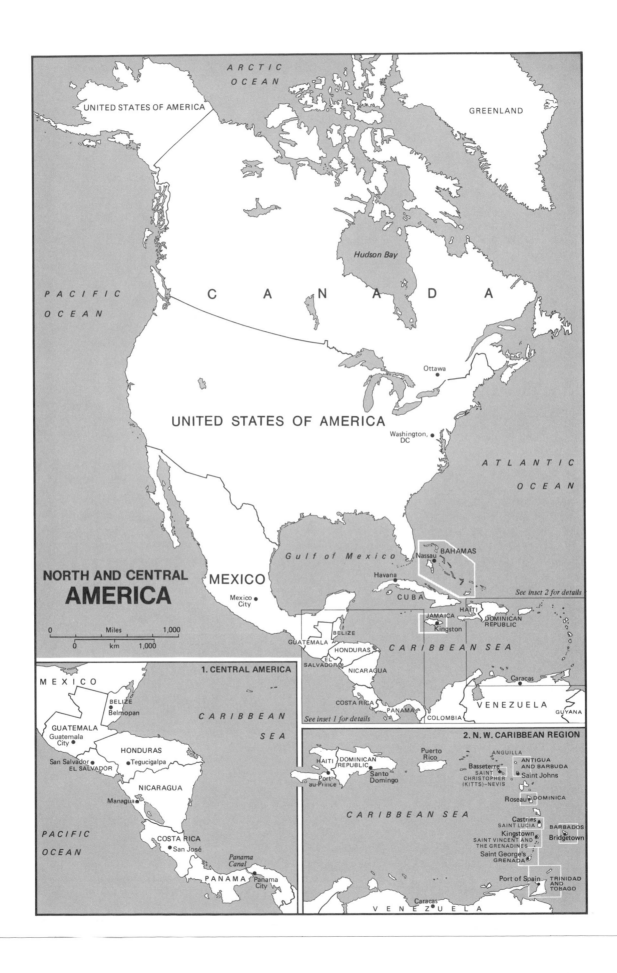

ARCTIC OCEAN

UNITED STATES OF AMERICA

GREENLAND

Hudson Bay

PACIFIC OCEAN

C A N A D A

Ottawa

UNITED STATES OF AMERICA

Washington, DC

ATLANTIC OCEAN

Gulf of Mexico

BAHAMAS
Nassau

See inset 2 for details

Havana

CUBA

HAITI
DOMINICAN REPUBLIC

NORTH AND CENTRAL
AMERICA

MEXICO

Mexico City

JAMAICA
Kingston

CARIBBEAN SEA

0   Miles   1,000
0   km   1,000

BELIZE

GUATEMALA

HONDURAS

EL SALVADOR

NICARAGUA

COSTA RICA

See inset 1 for details

PANAMA

Caracas

VENEZUELA

GUYANA

COLOMBIA

1. CENTRAL AMERICA

MEXICO

BELIZE
Belmopan

GUATEMALA
Guatemala City

CARIBBEAN SEA

San Salvador
EL SALVADOR

HONDURAS
Tegucigalpa

NICARAGUA
Managua

PACIFIC OCEAN

COSTA RICA
San José

Panama Canal

PANAMA
Panama City

2. N.W. CARIBBEAN REGION

HAITI
DOMINICAN REPUBLIC

Puerto Rico

ANGUILLA

ANTIGUA AND BARBUDA
Saint Johns

Port-au-Prince

Santo Domingo

Basseterre
SAINT CHRISTOPHER (KITTS)-NEVIS

Roseau
DOMINICA

CARIBBEAN SEA

Castries
SAINT LUCIA

BARBADOS
Bridgetown

Kingstown
SAINT VINCENT AND THE GRENADINES

Saint George's
GRENADA

Port of Spain
TRINIDAD AND TOBAGO

Caracas

VENEZUELA

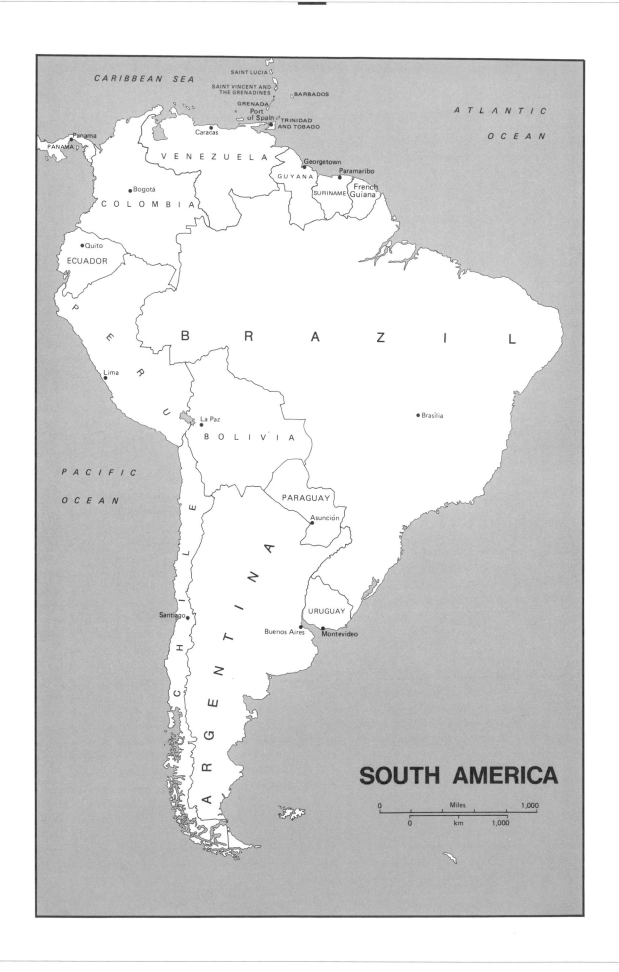

CARIBBEAN SEA

SAINT LUCIA

SAINT VINCENT AND
THE GRENADINES

BARBADOS

ATLANTIC

GRENADA
Port
of Spain

OCEAN

TRINIDAD
AND TOBAGO

Panama

•Caracas

PANAMA

V E N E Z U E L A

Georgetown

•Paramaribo

G U Y A N A

•Bogotá

SURINAME

French
Guiana

C O L O M B I A

•Quito

ECUADOR

P

E

R

U

B   R   A   Z   I   L

•Lima

•La Paz

•Brasília

B O L I V I A

PACIFIC

OCEAN

PARAGUAY

•Asunción

A

R

G

E

N

T

I

N

A

C
H
I
L
E

URUGUAY

Santiago•

Buenos Aires•

•Montevideo

SOUTH AMERICA

| 0 | Miles | 1,000 |
| 0 | km | 1,000 |

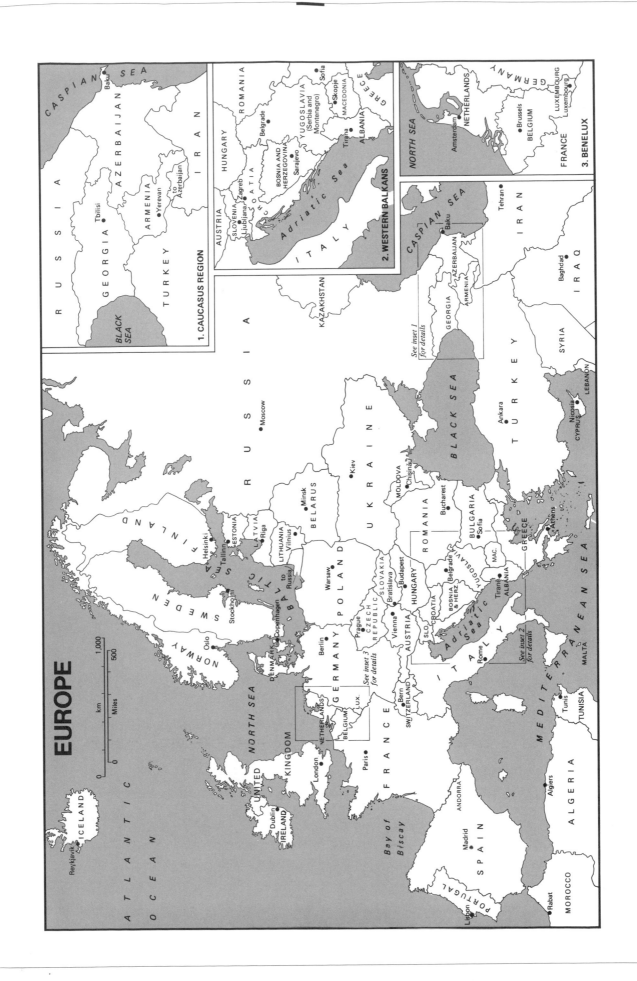

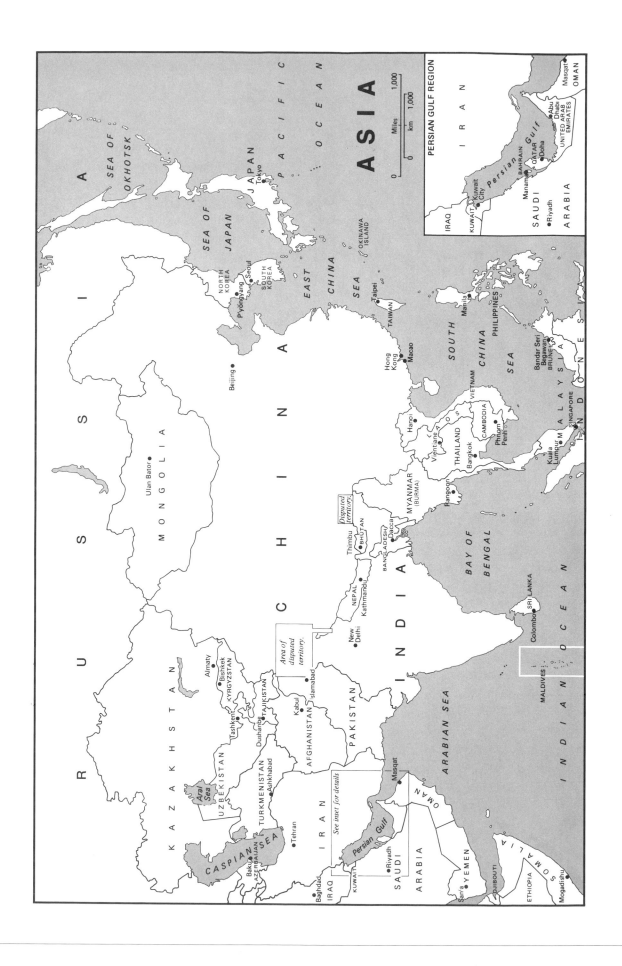

ASIA

PERSIAN GULF REGION

Miles 1,000
km 1,000

IRAN

Masqat OMAN

Abu Dhabi
UNITED ARAB EMIRATES

Persian Gulf

BAHRAIN QATAR
Manama Doha

KUWAIT
Kuwait City

IRAQ

SAUDI
Riyadh ARABIA

RUSSIA

SEA OF OKHOTSK

SEA OF JAPAN

JAPAN
Tokyo

PACIFIC OCEAN

NORTH KOREA
Pyŏngyang
Seoul
SOUTH KOREA

EAST CHINA SEA

OKINAWA ISLAND

Beijing

Taipei
TAIWAN

Hong Kong
Macao

Manila

PHILIPPINES

SOUTH CHINA SEA

MONGOLIA
Ulan Bator

CHINA

VIETNAM

Bandar Seri Begawan
BRUNEI

Hanoi

LAOS
Vientiane

THAILAND

CAMBODIA
Phnom Penh

MALAYSIA

Singapore

INDONESIA

Kuala Lumpur

Bangkok

MYANMAR (BURMA)

Rangoon

Disputed territory

Thimbu
BHUTAN

BANGLADESH
Dacca

BAY OF BENGAL

NEPAL
Kathmandu

Area of disputed territory.

New Delhi

INDIA

SRI LANKA
Colombo

INDIAN OCEAN

KAZAKHSTAN

Almaty
Bishkek
KYRGYZSTAN

Tashkent
UZBEKISTAN
Dushanbe
TAJIKISTAN

Kabul
AFGHANISTAN
Islamabad

PAKISTAN

Aral Sea

TURKMENISTAN
Ashkhabad

MALDIVES

CASPIAN SEA

Baku
AZERBAIJAN

Tehran

IRAN

See inset for details

Persian Gulf

ARABIAN SEA

Masqat

OMAN

Baghdad
IRAQ

KUWAIT

Riyadh

SAUDI ARABIA

YEMEN
San'a

ETHIOPIA

DJIBOUTI

SOMALIA
Mogadishu

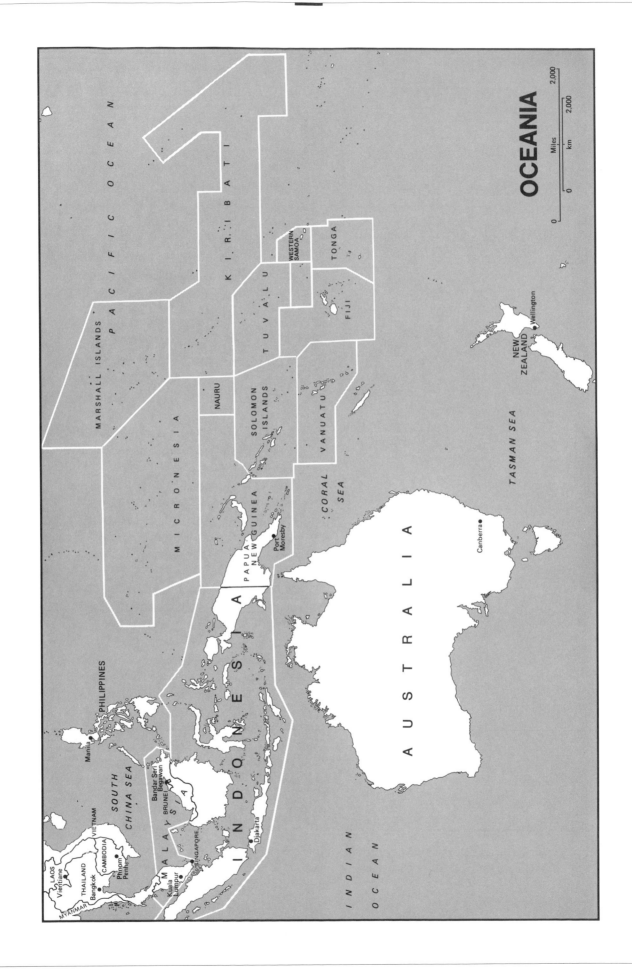

OCEANIA

Miles
km
0
2,000
2,000

PACIFIC OCEAN

K I R I B A T I

MARSHALL ISLANDS

M I C R O N E S I A

NAURU

T U V A L U

WESTERN SAMOA

TONGA

FIJI

SOLOMON ISLANDS

VANUATU

CORAL SEA

PAPUA NEW GUINEA

Port Moresby

I N D O N E S I A

PHILIPPINES

Manila

SOUTH CHINA SEA

VIETNAM

LAOS

Vientiane

THAILAND

Bangkok

CAMBODIA

Phnom Penh

MYANMAR

Kuala Lumpur

Singapore

M A L A Y S I A

BRUNEI

Bandar Seri Begawan

Djakarta

INDIAN OCEAN

A U S T R A L I A

Canberra

TASMAN SEA

NEW ZEALAND

Wellington

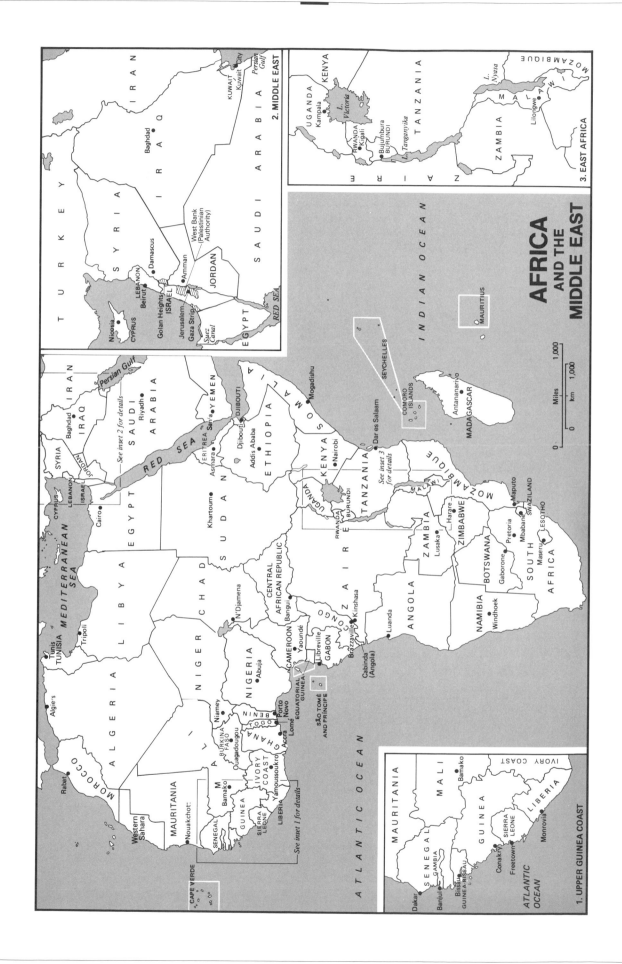

AFRICA AND THE MIDDLE EAST

2. MIDDLE EAST

3. EAST AFRICA

1. UPPER GUINEA COAST